The Serampore
Form of Agreement

A Commentary

The Serampore Form of Agreement

A Commentary

Edited by
Samuel E. Masters and Peter de Vries

The Serampore Form of Agreement: A Commentary

Copyright © 2025 Samuel E. Masters, Peter de Vries, All rights reserved.

This book may not be reproduced, in whole or in part, without written permission from the publishers.

H&E Academic, West Lorne, Ontario
www.hesedandemet.com

Cover Image: A view of Serampore, from the Park at Barrackpore by James Baillie Fraser 1826. From the British Library Collection. Used with permission.

Paperback ISBN: 978-1-77484-165-5
eBook ISBN: 978-1-77484-166-2

CONTENTS

ACKNOWLEDGEMENTS ix

GLOSSARY xi

PROLOGUE 15
The Provenance of the Serampore Form of Agreement
Michael A.G. Haykin

INTRODUCTION 19
The Origins of the Serampore Form of Agreement
Samuel E. Masters

STATEMENT ONE 41
The Rationale for Missionary Identity at Serampore
Bennie R. Crockett, Jr.

STATEMENT TWO 63
To Acquaint ourselves with the Snares which hold
the Minds of the People
Joshua Bowman

STATEMENT THREE 81
Abstaining from Whatever Deepens Prejudice Against the Gospel
Johnson Thomaskutty

STATEMENT FOUR 101
Dinner, Disease, and Duty
Myron Noonkester

STATEMENT FIVE 127

"Christ the Crucified, the Great Subject of our Preaching"
Peter de Vries

STATEMENT SIX 151

Hospitality, Counsel, Equality, and Respect
G. Landon Adams

STATEMENT SEVEN 173

"Caring for the Gathered Souls"
Peter de Vries, Samuel Masters, and Matthew M. Reynolds

STATEMENT EIGHT 199

The Serampore Mission's Principle of Indigeneity
Michael Chatterjee

STATEMENT NINE 219

Scripture Translation: A Road to Cross-cultural Relationships
Pratap Chandra Gine

STATEMENT TEN 235

Prayer and the Cultivation of Personal Religion
Peter J. Morden

STATEMENT ELEVEN 257

Lives on the Altar
Johan Kommers

APPENDIX 275

Form of Agreement

CONTRIBUTORS 287

BIBLIOGRAPHY 289

SUBJECT INDEX 325

ACKNOWLEDGEMENTS

The Serampore Form of Agreement (SFA) stands at the fountainhead of the modern missionary movement. More than two hundred years after its publication, it remains unrivaled as a succinct summary of missionary principles. It might be said that the purpose of this present volume, a commentary on the SFA, is to say in many words what William Ward said in few. Hopefully, this will lead to a deeper understanding of the SFA's principles and a renewed commitment to their practice.

In one sense, this volume is a testament to the fruitfulness of the SFA and the modern missionary movement. The contributors hail from four or five continents, depending on how you count. They include missionaries and professors, all of whom can trace their influences in some way back to Serampore.

The modern missionary movement experienced its first growth among Particular Baptists. Of course, its precursors can be found among the Puritans and the Moravians. And it soon spread beyond the Baptists. So, it should not surprise us to see the Serampore Mission's influence still affecting a broad diversity of Christian communities today. The contributors to this volume represent some of those traditions in India and beyond. Each author has approached the subject from their unique vantage point. Nonetheless, they share a commitment to historical accuracy and a desire to see the principles of the SFA translated for a new generation. Each author has taught me something new or challenged my perspective. And each has encouraged me in the practice of missions. This volume owes a great deal to the efforts of Peter de Vries. There is no page he has not improved in some way.

This commentary is part of a series published in 2023 to mark the bicentennial of Ward's death. The idea grew from a conversation with Michael A.G. Haykin. The series consists of a brief biography, this commentary on the Serampore Form of Agreement, and a sourcebook containing key examples of Ward's writing. These works are offered not as the final word on Ward but as an encouragement to younger scholars to travel further down the path explored by Ward's first biographers, Samuel Stennett and E. Daniel Potts. More importantly, I hope the story of the work at Serampore will provide instruction and inspiration for a new generation of missionaries sent out from countries around the world.

I would like to thank all those who made this series possible. These include the contributors to the volume on the Serampore Form of Agreement, and I am grateful for support from Michael Haykin and Matthew Reynolds whose own volume on William Ward's spirituality was recently published. Again, Peter de Vries merits special mention. He generously gave his time and expertise and offered vital encouragement at critical points. This work would not have been possible without the access he provided to the archives of the Carey Research Library at Serampore College and his encyclopedic knowledge of all things Serampore. And we have the world's longest WhatsApp thread to prove it. I am also grateful to Benjamin Yede for his help producing the index.

Sam Masters
Cordoba, Argentina

GLOSSARY

Term	Meaning
ayah	caregiver of children
banian	intermediary in trade (North India)
bhakti	devotional worship
Brahmin	upper caste Hindu
bungalow	typical *bangla* style thatched hut
Churuk or Charak Puja	Hook swinging festival
debtah	demi god (often in form of idol)
dubashi	intermediary, go-between (South India)
durwan	gatekeeper
Firanghi(s), Firingee(s)	foreign(er), used in disparaging sense
gayatri	mantra given by spiritual teacher (*guru*)
munshi	language interpreter
pandit / pundit	language scholar
Peshwa	Chief, high official in the Maratha Empire
poita	Holy thread of a Brahmin
purdah	Seclusion of women (Persian), a curtain.
Rajah, Raja	Indian prince (title)
ryots	small village based landholders
Sahaib, Sahib	polite form of address, gentleman
sepoy	Indian soldier under European command
shasters	Hindoo religious books
sircar, sarkar	house-steward, writer or accountant.
Sooder, Sudra	lower labourer Hindu caste
suttee / sati	Hindu practice of widow burning
Zamindars	Landholders, landed aristocracy
zamindari	System of landholding
Zenana, zanana	women's quarters in a household

"Redeeming love has been my theme."

PROLOGUE

The Provenance of the Serampore Form of Agreement

Michael A.G. Haykin

It was not uncommon for some seventeenth- and eighteenth-century Puritan and Baptist congregations to promote and safeguard their experience as communities of Christian disciples through the adoption of a written covenant.[1] Champlin Burrage, writing on this subject in 1904, suggested that the idea of a church covenanting together may well have originated among German Anabaptist communities in the 1520s.[2] Be this as it may, by the seventeenth century, written covenants were common to both Scottish Presbyterians—where they eventually took the form of a national covenant rather than one agreed to by an individual local congregation—and those Puritans who had separated from the Church of England.[3] The heart and substance of these church covenants was usually a series of carefully formulated commitments that were biblically based and that church members voluntarily made to God and to one another. Whereas confessions of faith from this era

---

[1] For the views of Baptist leaders who felt that a church need not have a written covenant, see Champlin Burrage, *The Church Covenant Idea: Its Origin and Its Development* (Philadelphia: American Baptist Publication Society, 1904), 113–121, 124–125; Charles W. Deweese, *Baptist Church Covenants* (Nashville: Broadman Press, 1990), 26–27; Gwyn Davies, *Covenanting with God. The story of personal and church covenants and their lessons for today* (Bryntirion, Bridgend, Mid Glamorgan: Evangelical Library of Wales, 1994), 51–52.

[2] Burrage, *Church Covenant Idea*, 13–25. See also Deweese, *Baptist Church Covenants*, 20–21.

[3] Davies, *Covenanting with God*, 39; Deweese, *Baptist Church Covenants*, 22–23.

The Serampore Form of Agreement

were centred mainly on vital doctrinal issues, these covenants deal primarily with Christian conduct.[4] In the words of Charles Deweese, a Southern Baptist historian, they were designed to "deepen the quality of a church's fellowship, sharpen a church's awareness of vital moral and spiritual commitments, clarify biblical standards for Christian growth, and create and maintain a disciplined church membership."[5]

In fact, before setting sail to India in 1793, William Carey (1761–1834) had used a church covenant to restore order and discipline to the local church that he was pastoring in Leicester. Plagued by drunken deacons and bitter strife among a number of unruly members in this pastorate, Carey had proceeded to recommend the dissolution of the church in September, 1790. This was agreed to by a majority of the members. With the support of this majority, the church was then reconstituted on the basis of a covenant, so as "to bind them to a strict and faithful New Testament discipline." The result, according to Carey's great-grandson, was that "they filled the fellowship with faithful love" and the "nettles gave place to the Spirit's flowers and fruits."[6] Of course, the Serampore Form of Agreement is not a church covenant *per se*, but the men who drafted this text were clearly very familiar with covenants and covenant-making from their Particular Baptist world in England.

The Serampore Form of Agreement is a remarkable document, one that bespeaks both cultural sensitivity as well as the deep commitment of the signatories to the mission in India despite the challenges it posed. There was a clear determination to avoid a number of elements that implied Anglo-European superiority:

---

[4] Deweese, *Baptist Church Covenants*, viii–ix; David Fountain, "Can the old Church Covenants help us today?," *Sword & Trowel* (December 4, 1985): 8.

[5] Deweese, *Baptist Church Covenants*, x. For two examples of church covenants, see that of Swansea Baptist Church in Massachusetts (Deweese, *Baptist Church Covenants*, 132–133) as well as that of the Baptist work in Bourton-on-the-Water, Gloucestershire ("The Bourton Church-Covenant," *Transactions of the Congregational Historical Society* 1 [1901–1904]: 270–274 or Deweese, *Baptist Church Covenants*, 122–124).

[6] S. Pearce Carey, *William Carey D.D., Fellow of the Linnaean Society* (London: Hodder and Stoughton, 1923), 57–60.

Provenance

- "Those parts of English manners which are most offensive to them should be kept out of sight as much as possible. We should also avoid every degree of cruelty to animals. Nor is it advisable at once to attack their prejudices by exhibiting with acrimony the sins of their gods; neither should we on any account do violence to their images, nor interrupt their worship. The real conquests of the Gospel are those of love …" (Statement 3).
- "We ought to be easy of access, to condescend to them as much as possible, and on all occasions to treat them as our equals. … All force, and everything haughty, reserved and forbidding, it becomes us ever to shun with the greatest care." (Statement 6).
- "[W]e think it our duty, as soon as possible, to advise the native brethren who may be formed into separate Churches to choose their pastors and deacons from amongst their own countrymen" (Paragraph 8).
- "We have thought it our duty not to change the names of native converts, observing from Scripture that the Apostles did not change those of the first Christians turned from heathenism …" (Statement 8).

Would that this way of dealing with local cultures had been carried forward in all of the missions set afoot by the Anglo-American and European churches in the nineteenth and twentieth centuries! It needs noting, therefore, that the following studies of this document have been undertaken with the clear conviction that interest in this text is not what might be called mere antiquarianism. Rather, informing this entire volume of essays is the belief that this document is yet an enormously helpful guide to modern-day missions, be they in Asia, Africa, or the Americas.

The Serampore Form of Agreement

Finally, this text also drew from a rich reservoir of spirituality that the signatories found in their seventeenth-century and eighteenth-century past, especially, that of the Moravians and their inspirational missions.[7] The emphasis on divine love as it has been preëminently displayed in the crucified Christ (Statement 3 & 5) is particularly noteworthy. Here, we have an insight into the character of not only all of the signatories, but especially the heart of William Ward (1769–1823) who, on behalf of the Serampore community, penned this document. As Ward noted in a sermon on the death of Christ, preached some fifteen years after he had signed the Serampore Form of Agreement: "The death of Christ was in itself the greatest act of disinterested benevolence that could possibly be exhibited; and it contemplated the diffusion of happiness upon a scale the most magnificent and the most extensive imaginable."[8] In early nineteenth-century parlance, the phrase "disinterested benevolence" referred to a determination to do good for the happiness of others rather than for personal gratification. The crucifixion of Christ was *the* supreme example of such love. Ultimately, it was this love and a love for the lost in the Indian sub-continent that drove the men who signed this covenantal text.

---

[7] See Samuel E. Masters, "The Serampore mission and the Moravian connection," *The Journal of Andrew Fuller Studies* 9 (Fall 2024): 56–69.

[8] William Ward, *The Love of Christ Beareth Us Away. The Design of the Death of Christ Explained* (London: Black, Kingsbury, Parbury, and Allen, 1820), 7.

INTRODUCTION

The Origins of the Serampore Form of Agreement

Samuel E. Masters

"The pen is mightier than the sword."[9] This maxim might not hold in every age, but it did in 1839 when Edward Bulwer-Lytton (1803–1873), a Whig politician and literary figure, coined the phrase. In the early nineteenth century, the West still felt the aftershocks from the radical ideas that had produced world-shaking revolutionary movements in the late eighteenth century. The spread of the Enlightenment, the wide dispersion of printing technology, and the growth of a transatlantic intellectual community enabled thinkers of every stripe to publish and expect to be taken seriously. The result was an outpouring of books, tracts, and manifestos dealing with everything from the natural sciences to philosophy and politics. Influential political tracts of the day included Thomas Jefferson's *Declaration of Independence* (1776) and Thomas Paine's defense of the French Revolution, *The Rights of Man* (1791).

While perhaps more influenced by the great evangelical awakenings in the first half of the eighteenth century than the Enlightenment, the fathers of the modern missionary were aware of the cultural currents of their times. Particular Baptist pastors such as Robert Hall (1764–1831) and Andrew Fuller (1754–1815) produced their own seminal works[10] that led to revival among the churches of the Northamptonshire Baptist Association

---

[9] Edward Bulwer-Lytton, *Richelieu, or the Conspiracy, a Play in Five Acts* (London: Saunders and Otley, 1839), 39.

[10] See Robert Hall's *Help to Zion's Travelers* (1781) and Andrew Fuller's *The Gospel Worthy of all Acceptation* (1785).

and laid the groundwork for the great missionary leap that William Carey would advocate in his own manifesto, the *Enquiry*.[11]

The *Enquiry* recovered the Great Commission as a mandate incumbent on the contemporary church. Additionally, it surveyed the world's spiritual needs and argued for the use of means to evangelize the nations. Beyond this, the *Enquiry* proposed the founding of new organizations as specific means to fulfill the task: a missionary society to send workers abroad and a Moravian-style community to maintain them on the field.

In 1793, Carey and Dr. John Thomas (1857–1801) went to India as the first missionaries from the Particular Baptist Missionary Society (BMS). After years of struggle, the mission found its stride when a new group of recruits joined Carey and formed the Serampore Mission in 1800. Five years later, the missionaries produced the *Serampore Form of Agreement* (SFA). This covenant summarized the more mature missiology of Carey and his fellow missionaries, including Joshua Marshman (1768–1837) and William Ward (1769–1823). The principles expressed in this covenant from the dawn of modern missions can scarcely be improved on today as a guide for the work of missions.

A Manifesto and a Covenant

Carey's *Enquiry* is a manifesto. One definition of "manifesto" is "a document publicly declaring the position or program of its issuer. A manifesto advances a set of ideas, opinions, or views but can also lay out a plan of action."[12] This description fits the *Enquiry* nicely. The definition goes on to state that manifestos can address any topic. In this case, it is Christian missions. The definition continues, "Manifestos are generally written in the name of a group sharing a common perspective, ideology, or purpose rather than in the name of a single individual." This also fits. Carey wrote at the urging of the pastors of the Northamptonshire Association. The definition further states, "Manifestos often mark the adoption of a new vision, approach, program, or genre. They criticize a present state of affairs but

---

[11] Full title of Carey's work: *An Enquiry Into the Obligations of Christians, to Use Means for the Conversion of the Heathens: In Which the Religious State of the Different Nations of the World, the Success of Former Undertakings, and the Practicability of Further Undertakings Are Considered* (1792).

[12] https://www.britannica.com/topic/manifesto

Origins

also announce its passing, proclaiming the advent of a new movement or even of a new era." Carey's *Enquiry* was a call to action that marked a new era in church history—the modern missionary movement. While the *Enquiry* grew organically from the ideas advocated in the Northamptonshire revival, it also represents a radical expansion of those ideas. As a key source of the great protestant missionary expansion of the 19th century, the *Enquiry* must be seen as one of the most influential manifestos of all time.

On the other hand, the *Serampore Form of Agreement* is not a manifesto. It is an outgrowth of the *Enquiry*, sets out a group's principles and ideas, and calls for action. Nonetheless, the SFA was less a public declaration of those ideas than an internal document committing the signers to a course of conduct and a pattern of relationships. In other words, a covenant. Of course, this is the title's meaning, the *Serampore Form of Agreement*.

Two Brief Summaries of the *Form of Agreement*

The SFA lays out a series of missiological principles summarized by Samuel Pearce Carey (1862-1953), the great biographer of William Carey:

1. To set an infinite value on men's souls.
2. To acquaint ourselves with the snares which hold the minds of the people.
3. To abstain from whatever deepens India's prejudice against the gospel.
4. To watch for every chance of doing the people good.
5. To preach 'Christ crucified' as the grand means of conversions.
6. To esteem and treat Indians always as our equals.
7. To guard and build up 'the hosts that may be gathered.'
8. To cultivate their spiritual gifts, ever pressing upon them their missionary obligation, since the Indians only can win India for Christ.
9. To labour unceasingly in biblical translation.
10. To be instant in the nurture of personal religion.
11. To give ourselves without reserve to the cause, 'not counting even the clothes we wear our own.'[13]

---

[13] S. Pearce Carey, *William Carey: 'The Father of Modern Missions.'* Edited by Peter Masters (London: Wakeman Trust, 1993), 238. Peter Masters' edition is based on S. P. Carey's revised and expanded 1934 edn. This work quotes from all three 1923, 1934, and 1993 editions.

The Serampore Form of Agreement

A comparison of S.P. Carey's summary with the actual content of the SFA shows that his list is somewhat arbitrary and does not always give an accurate description of the content of every statement. While he admired William Carey and the Serampore missionaries, I suspect that S.P. Carey did not always sympathize with their theology. At the same time, it is also true that the style of the SFA is occasionally convoluted, and not every statement is easily summarized.

Historian Daniel Potts (1930–2019) offers a fuller summary list:

1. To have as a first concern a deeply-felt care for the spiritual welfare of others; and to believe in the ultimate universal triumph of Christianity.
2. To gain systematically all the information possible about Indian philosophy by reading, by conversing with intelligent Indians, and 'by attentively observing their manners and customs.'
3. To keep 'out of sight' anything in their European manners which would be offensive to Indians. Among still other things, missionaries were to avoid being cruel to animals, refrain from criticizing Indians 'by exhibition with acrimony the sins of their gods', and resist any temptation they might have to 'do violence to their images' or interrupt their worship.
4. To do good at every opportunity.
5. To 'make the great subject of our preaching, Christ the crucified.'
6. To make themselves always available to enquirers; to treat all Indians as equals and not to use force under any circumstances other than self-defence; to give any who asked 'the kindest advice', and to decide any disputes 'in the most open, upright, and impartial manner.'
7. To spend as much time as possible in building up and strengthening converts in their faith, to keep in mind the sacrifices they made in becoming Christians, to teach them habits of industry and held them secure employment, urge obedience to the civil authorities, and in general be 'a father to his people.'
8. To form the 'native brethren to usefulness, fostering every kind of genius, and cherishing every gift and grace' in order that they in turn could 'press upon their countrymen the glorious Gospel of the blessed God.'

9. To labour with all their might to forward translations 'of the sacred Scriptures in the languages of Hindoostan', to distribute these translations and other publications, and both to establish and urge other Europeans to establish schools.
10. To pray and cultivate their personal religion.
11. To give themselves up 'unreservedly to this glorious cause', never to engage in private trade, continually to guard against a 'worldly spirit,' and to cultivate a christian indifference towards every indulgence.'
12. To read the agreement publicly at every missionary post three times a year.[14]

A comparison of these two summaries reveals how historians sometimes filter source materials. S.P. Carey's summary of Statement Two reads, "To acquaint ourselves with the snares which hold the minds of the people." Potts writes, "To gain systematically all the information possible about Indian philosophy by reading, by conversing with intelligent Indians, and 'by attentively observing their manners and customs.'" Potts's summary of this point seems to reflect the evolution in social sensibilities in the second half of the twentieth century. Writing at the beginning of the twentieth century, S. P. Carey felt no reluctance to use "snares" though he passes over "delusions." The actual text of the SFA reads: "It is very important that we should gain all the information we can of the snares and delusions in which these heathens are held." Neither author speaks of heathens.

Consistent with the text of the SFA, S. P. Carey enumerates eleven points. Potts takes the final sentence as a twelfth point: "To read the agreement publicly at every missionary post three times a year." Of more significance, both S. P. Carey and Potts pass over the preamble to the SFA with its crucial theological declarations.

A Brief History of the SFA

The *Form of Agreement* was composed in 1805. It grew from an original agreement made by the missionaries on Saturday, January 18, 1800, when

---

[14] E. Daniel Potts, *William Ward: A Biography* (Lismore, NSW, 1994), 105-107, Mss., CLRC, Serampore.

they were first established in the Danish trading post of Serampore. The new team of missionaries sent by the BMS had arrived in India in October 1799. At that time, colonial authorities, dominated by the East India Company, prohibited the arrival of missionaries. Against the advice of Carey, they declared their missionary purpose to the port authorities. Carey and his family were settled at Mudnabati near Malda on an indigo plantation, far from the center of colonial administration at Calcutta. His plan had been a Moravian-style missionary community that would sustain the entire team through the production of indigo. With this project scuttled, he made the trip downriver to join the rest of the team, who had found asylum in the Danish colony of Serampore.

The new missionaries' decision to ignore his advice must have disconcerted Carey. His concern would have only increased when, upon his arrival in Serampore, he discovered serious tensions were brewing among the team members. Four missionaries had arrived: a single man, William Ward, and Daniel Brunsdon, William Grant, and Joshua Marshman, who were married. In his journal, William Ward recorded that these tensions had reached a boiling point at sea. Two of the wives quarreled, and Ward found himself playing a mediating role. On Friday, July 5, 1799, he wrote in his journal, "Something unpleasant amongst our company again occurred. We discussed the business in a Brethren's conference, with the hope of settling it amicably. I dread the consequences. Satan seems to envy our happiness. How dreadful, if our differences should reach the crew. Gracious Father! We are perverse children."[15]

Once established in Serampore, the tensions again reached a boiling pitch. The improvised living quarters were crowded, and the tension was unsurprising under the stresses of adapting to a new culture and climate. Two missionaries, Bro. F. and Bro. B., "quarrelled & fought in the garden before several natives; that is, bro. B. punched his ears, & he did what he

---

[15] Friday, July 5, 1799. William Ward, *William Ward's Missionary Journal, (1799–1811)*. BMS. Mss. 4 Vols. ed. E. Daniel Potts (Typed transcription, n.d.), I, 24. Hereafter, *Ward's Journal*.

could to hurt Bro. B."[16] The fight was particularly egregious since it occurred in the Bengalis' presence.[17]

William Ward wrote:

> I tremble, almost before we begin to live together. So much depends on a man's disinterestedness, forbearance, meekness and self-denial. One man of the wrong temper could make our house a hell. Much wisdom will be necessary. It is but here and there that a man makes conscience of strangling his thoughts, and of esteeming others better than himself. Only a few are fit to live in such a settlement as ours is to be, where selfish passions must be crushed, and the love of Christ swallow up all else.[18]

These brewing tensions led the missionaries to establish house rules on January 18, 1800. They based the Mission's organization on absolute equality. Various responsibilities were assigned on a rotating basis, and each took an equal role in public ministry, such as prayer and preaching. To resolve disputes, they set aside Saturday evening for "the adjusting of differences, and pledging ourselves to love each other."[19] While the Serampore missionaries followed Moravian precedents in many instances, in one crucial exception, Carey rejected the role of housefather and insisted on equality. While this demonstrated noble humility, it left a leadership vacuum that would create problems in the future.

In 1805, the Serampore missionaries updated the original rules. This document, the *Form of Agreement*, was signed on October 6 by nine missionaries, including Felix, Carey's son.[20] Ernest Payne indicates the day

---

[16] Cited from E. Daniel Potts, *William Ward: A Biography,* 59. Potts provides the following sources: Saturday, March 29, 1800. *Ward's Journal*, I, 74-75; Ward to Andrew Fuller, Serampore, September 9, 1800. Strangely, despite Potts' usual punctilious accuracy, these citations seem inaccurate. We have yet to locate this source, though the actual incident is attested in other sources: S. Pearce Carey, *William Carey* (1993), 182. Potts' citation is included here since it highlights the serious nature of the quarrel.

[17] Carey, *William Carey*, 182.

[18] Carey, *William Carey*, 182.

[19] Saturday, January 18, 1800. *Ward's Journal*, I, 66.

[20] The signatories were: William Carey, Joshua Marshman, William Ward, John Chamberlain, Richard Mardon, John Biss, William Moore, Joshua Rowe, and Felix Carey. Secretary Andrew Fuller added these names to his publication of the SFA in the *Periodical*

marked the celebration of the twelfth anniversary of the formation in Kettering of the Baptist Missionary Society:

> There was a prayer-meeting at 6 a.m. at which Marshman gave a short address. At 10.30 a.m. there followed a Church meeting. At this Marshman and Ward were chosen as co-pastors with Carey, and six deacons were appointed—four missionaries, Mardon, Biss, Moore and Rowe, and two Indian converts, Krishna Pal and Krishna Prasad. During the hours that followed, there were three preaching services. Two Indians, a man and a woman, were baptised. At the close of the day the Lord's Supper was observed, Marshman and Ward leading the service, and Carey receiving the new members into the fellowship.[21]

Ward wrote in his diary, "Such a day was never seen at the Mission house before."[22]

From a historical distance, the question arises of how the Serampore Mission was related to the Baptist Church at Serampore. Payne describes a church celebration on October 6, but they did not sign the *Form of Agreement* until the next day, Monday the 7th.[23] This indicates the *Form of Agreement* was not a church covenant but a missionary agreement binding the partners in the Serampore Mission, an organization distinct from the church at Serampore despite the overlap in membership.[24]

The Serampore missionaries were concerned about proper church order. An example from Carey's time at Mudnabati will suffice. In 1795

Accounts relative to the Baptist Missionary Society, Vol. III (1806): 198-211. The original text of the SFA, printed by Ward at The Brethren's Press, Serampore, is reproduced in the Appendix. For the textual variants, refer Chapter 1 of this work.

[21] Ernest A. Payne, "The Serampore Form of Agreement." *Baptist Quarterly* 12, no. 5 (January 1947): 126. Though the authorship of this important article is omitted in the *BQ*, its style and subject matter point towards E. A. Payne, the Baptist historian of the 1930-1960s, as the most likely author.

[22] Lord's Day, October 6, 1806. *Ward's Journal*, II, 441.

[23] See the Title Page of the SFA in the Appendix.

[24] There seems to be some confusion about the origin of the church at Serampore. A natural assumption is that it was founded at Serampore. However, the church at Serampore may be the same church founded at Mudnabati by Carey now transferred to Serampore. See footnote 53, Samuel E. Masters, "'Will Anyone Say the Lord is not Among Us?' The Serampore Mission and its Covenant" (Ph.D. diss., The Southern Baptist Theological Seminary, Louisville, 2020), 139.

Origins

Carey and fellow missionary John Thomas formed a congregation, and following the baptism of Thomas's nephew, Samuel Powell, they constituted the church. The two missionaries had refrained from participating in the Lord's Supper until the church had been formally constituted.[25] In the future, the Serampore missionaries would disagree over the issue of open communion. While they differed regarding who should be admitted to the Lord's table, the debate provides evidence both parties cared about proper church order.

Despite their concern for proper church order, the boundaries between the Mission as a parachurch organization and the church at Serampore may not have always been clear. This ambiguity became evident at times in cases of discipline involving missionary conduct.[26] Nonetheless, it seems clear that the *Serampore Form of Agreement* was not a church covenant but a missionary one. On Saturday, October 19, 1805, Ward wrote in his journal,

> I have suggested an idea to the brethren, which we seem all to think ought to be adopted, viz. that in planting separate churches native pastors shall be chosen, & native deacons, & that the missionaries shall preserve their original character, giving themselves up to the planting of new churches, & superintending those already planted. The benefits of this plan are detailed in the Form of Agreement which we are printing.[27]

The *Serampore Form of Agreement* was a covenant consisting of missiological principles meant to guide the work of the missionaries in planting new churches.

---

[25] Payne, "The Serampore Form of Agreement," 126.

[26] As leaders of the Baptist Church at Serampore, the missionaries practiced church discipline. Nonetheless, from a historical distance, the question arises of how the church interacted with the Mission on this issue. In one case, a missionary wife was called to account for excessive drinking. This seems to have been done by the Serampore community of missionaries and not the church at Serampore. Entry, Friday, June 26, 1807. *Ward's Journal*, III, 555.

[27] Saturday, October 19, 1805. *Ward's Journal*, II, 443/4–445.

The Serampore Form of Agreement

The Author of the Form of Agreement

The SFA expresses the accumulated experience of the Serampore missionaries at the time of its composition. By 1805, Carey had been in India for twelve years. Ward and Marshman had been there five. William Ward was the author, not Carey. In the 1940s, A. H. Oussoren attributed the authorship to Carey,[28] but John Clark Marshman, writing nearly one hundred years earlier, insisted the SFA was composed by Ward.[29] Comparing the styles of the SFA and the *Enquiry* supports this view.

Carey's style is urgent, plain, and straightforward. The SFA is equally urgent but sometimes leans towards a more florid sensationalism. John Clark Marshman described Ward's style as "fervid."[30] In his biography of Carey written later in the 19th century, George Smith echoes Marshman, "No one will understand William Carey, or do justice to the Serampore brotherhood, who does not study [the Form of Agreement]. It is the ripe fruit of the first eleven years of Carey's daily toil and consecrated genius, as written out by the fervent pen of Ward. In the light of it the whole of Carey's life must be read."[31]

The repetition of specific phrases marks Ward's style. He prays God will "famish" the idols of India, and he looks with anticipation to the day when these idols will be thrown to the "bats and moles."[32] Statement Eleven, which deals with the spartan Moravian communalism adopted by the missionaries in financial matters, contains an example of elevated language:

> Let us give ourselves up unreservedly to this glorious cause. Let us never think that our time, our gifts, our strength, our families, or even the clothes we wear, are our own. Let us sanctify them all to God and his cause. Oh! that he may sanctify us for his work. Let us for ever shut out the idea, of laying up a cowry for ourselves or our

---

[28] Payne, "The Serampore Form of Agreement," 129.
[29] John Clark Marshman, *The Life and Times of Carey, Marshman, and Ward. Embracing the History of the Serampore Mission* (London: Longman, Brown, Green, Longmans & Roberts, 1859), I, 229.
[30] Marshman, *Life and Times*, I, 229.
[31] George Smith, *The Life of William Carey, D.D.* (London: John Murray, 1885), 130.
[32] Statements One and Nine. No doubt, a reference to Isaiah 2:20.

children. If we give up the resolution which was formed on the subject of private trade, when we first united at Serampore, the Mission is from that hour a lost cause.[33]

Daniel Potts attributes Ward's style to his lack of formal education. Ward attended school for a few years as a child but was apprenticed as a teenager to a printer.

> This simple schooling was usual for a family of their standing. Ward's informal education, marked by its serious lack of discipline, however, while it may have helped to fit him for the managing of commercial affairs, handicapped him in his formal writing. Undoubtedly the various editions of his *Hindoos* would have been improved had he been given the advantage of a Grammar school and University education.[34]

The "fervid style," while reflecting Ward's ardent nature, may have resulted from his years as a newspaperman in Derby and Hull, where he advocated for radical causes.

We find a possible early example of Ward's style in the *Derby Address*, a defense of the freedom of speech and association published by the Society for Political Information. While this statement is signed by the society's chairman, S. Eyre, Daniel Potts makes the case that it was composed by William Ward. If not Ward, the author shared his "fervid" style: "Are we in England? — Have our forefathers fought, and bled, and conquered for liberty? And did they not think that the fruits of their patriotism would be more abundant in peace, plenty, and happiness? — Are we always to stand still or go backwards? Are our burthens to be as heavy as the most enslaved people? — Is the condition of the poor never to be improved?"[35]

Frankly, while the SFA exhibits a rousing style, it is not as well organized as the *Enquiry*. The *Enquiry* consists of five clearly differentiated sections, and the argument proceeds with simple logical clarity. On the other

---

[33] Statement Eleven.
[34] E. Daniel Potts, "William Ward: the making of a Missionary in the 18th Century," *Bicentenary Volume: William Carey's Arrival in India 1793-1993* (Serampore: Serampore College, 1993), 28.
[35] Potts, *William Ward: A Biography*, 9; Marshman, *Life and Times*, I, 94.

hand, the various statements of the SFA vary widely in length and development, and some enumerated statements combine subjects in ways that make it challenging to identify the central thought. Nonetheless, the effect of the whole is powerful.

The Expiration of the SFA

As a working covenant, the SFA only endured a few years. It soon became a fatality of a brewing conflict between the senior Serampore missionaries and new arrivals from Britain. The younger missionaries resented the ascetic life required and found fault with the administration of the older missionaries, in particular, Joshua Marshman:

> Only two years after agreeing to the SFA, the younger missionaries were released from its strictures. Grumblings had reached such a pitch that Fuller threatened to bring some of them home. The new arrangement placed the junior missionaries under the authority of the BMS, though they were still expected to work with the senior Serampore missionaries. For Ward, this came as a relief, "The burden of four years has been taken off my mind. I have been sighing over the Mission and its fate, when it should fall into the hands of (blank) and (blank); but this regulation prevents all I feared.[36]

Over the years, the differences between the senior and junior missionaries grew into the Serampore Controversy, which divided the BMS missionaries on the field and severed the Serampore Mission from the BMS itself. Sadly, the true focus of the SFA was obscured in the process.

Serampore Mission had always been an independent entity that cooperated with the BMS. This independence was respected and encouraged under Fuller, the first secretary of the BMS. However, upon his death in 1815, the BMS committee sought greater control of the Mission. The members attempted to leverage the sentiments of Statement Eleven to justify their control of the property. However, because of the resistance of the younger missionaries, the SFA had ceased to be a working covenant even earlier, soon after its adoption. Additionally, Carey pointed out that even

---

[36] Masters, "Will Anyone Say the Lord is not Among Us?", 289. quoted from Marshman, *Life and Times*, I, 303.

Origins

if the SFA had remained in full effect, it was an agreement among the missionaries to which the committee itself was not a party:

> Like every other body of men associated in a new undertaking of some difficulty, we have been constrained to follow that judgment which appeared most correct. When the lapse of time, or the course of circumstances, has discovered the error of that judgment, we have not scrupled to adopt a different line of conduct. Thus in 1805 Mr Ward drew up his ideas of missionary economy, in the "agreement" respecting the way in which we thought missionaries ought to act in money matters, and obtained the concurrence and signature of his brethren to it; in less than a year it was found impracticable, and was consigned to oblivion. We were no parties to its publication [in England], from which [the publishing sales only?] we never reaped a farthing of benefit; and if we could have seen the unfair use which was made of it to our disparagement, we should certainly have sent home for publication, a formal abrogation of it in 1806.[37]

While Carey states the agreement had become unworkable, this was not a repudiation of the principles of the SFA. The focus here rests on the controversial Statement Eleven, which the BMS committee attempted to wield as a weapon against the Serampore missionaries. It should be noted that Carey's statement confirms the authorship of Ward. We might wonder if his phrasing reveals some ambivalence about Ward's framing of Statement Eleven.[38] If so, Carey's previous advocacy for a Moravian-style community should clarify that any differences were merely rhetorical and not of substance.

The Moravian communal arrangement of the eleventh statement was not the only point of contention. The younger missionaries objected to being sent to work in the interior and resisted William Carey's insistence that the future of the work in India depended on raising national leaders.

---

[37] Joshua Marshman, *Letters from the Rev. Dr. Carey Relative to Certain Statements Contained in Three Pamphlets lately published by the Rev. John Dyer, Secretary to the BMS, W. Johns, M.D., and the Rev. E. Carey and W. Yates* (London: Parbury, Allen and Co., 1828), 56–57.

[38] "Mr Ward drew up *HIS* ideas of missionary economy, in the "agreement" respecting the way in which we thought missionaries ought to act in money matters, and obtained the concurrence and signature of his brethren to it." Emphasis mine.

The Serampore Form of Agreement

While the SFA only functioned as a binding covenant for a few years, the senior missionaries worked with an unwavering commitment to its principles throughout their ministries. This alone is sufficient to commend it to our attention. Its core principles are still valid today, including the controversial eleventh statement. Its call for a sacrificial lifestyle is still valid, even if the Moravian organization proved unworkable.

The Sources of the SFA

Two apparent sources stand behind the *Form of Agreement*: Baptist church covenants and Moravian community covenants. Though not all Particular Baptists used church covenants, they were common. William Carey employed church covenants in his pastorates at Moulton and Leicester to bring unity and order to the congregations. Carey composed a new covenant at Moulton to reorganize a General Baptist congregation along Particular Baptist lines.

While both covenants contained doctrinal elements, they emphasized the conduct expected of church members. Commitments included "To seek by all proper means the good of the Church with which we stand connected. To esteem our Pastor very highly in Love for his Work's sake. To walk in Love towards them with whom we stand connected in Bands of Christian Fellowship."[39] Clear doctrine stood behind both covenants, but the focus was on practical application in the church's daily life.

The Serampore brethren may have had in mind the Moravians' *Brotherly Agreement* (1727). Moravian influence on the specific content of the SFA seems evident when read in parallel with August Spangenberg's *Instructions for the Members of the Unitas Fratrum, who minister in the Gospel among the Heathen* (1784). Numerous similarities exist between the *Serampore Form of Agreement* and Spangenberg's *Instructions*. Like the SFA, Spangenberg's work consists of numbered statements. While not as

---

[39] William Carey, "Carey's Covenant for the Church at Moulton," October 1, 1786. I was given a copy of the Moulton covenant by a church member, Margaret Williams in 2010. It contains a facsimile of the handwritten covenant and a typewritten transcription. The first sheet explains the provenance: "When William Carey became Minister at Moulton the church was in serious decline. Its building was 'ruinous', its services irregular and its members discouraged. Carey brought order, discipline and unity to the church. His first step was to draw them into a covenant with one another and with God. The original document in his neat handwriting is in our museum, contained in a Church Minute Book."

Calvinistic, the *Instructions* contain an initial statement of theological principles. The *Instructions* also advances a strong argument for the priority of missions. Like the SFA, the *Instructions* emphasizes the role of women and deals with missionary attitudes, character, and spiritual life. One of the most significant differences between the two documents is that the *Instructions* lay down general principles valid for missionaries anywhere in the world, while at times, the SFA applies more specifically to the unique context of India.

Principle Themes
As stated, the SFA extends a chain of publications, including Andrew Fuller's *The Gospel Worthy of all Acceptation* and William Carey's *Enquiry*. The undergirding theology of each is the same. Where Fuller's writings were aimed at deficiencies in the ministry of local Baptist churches and the preaching of the pastors in Britain, the *Enquiry* proposed the extension of these evangelistic endeavors to the nations.

In the *Enquiry*, Carey recommends mechanisms for sending missionaries to the field. In other words, the *Enquiry* bridges the gap between the local church, the church association, and the mission field by proposing an intermediate organization—the missionary society—as sending agency. The SFA recommends principles for the next stage: the actual work of evangelism and church planting on the field. Four primary themes appear in the Serampore Form of Agreement: theological foundations, missiological principles, missionary character, and concrete policy and plans.[40] The last three themes will be developed in the various chapters of this book. However, in the next section of this introduction, we will look at the theological principles expressed in the preamble of the SFA.

The Theological Preamble
The SFA begins with a statement of theological principles. While the SFA shows the practical influence of the Moravians, its true theological roots must be found in the evangelical revivals of the English-speaking world associated with George Whitefield and Jonathan Edwards. These principles

---

[40] For more detailed development see Masters, "Will Anyone Say the Lord is not Among Us?", 148–162.

included the free offer of the gospel, and an understanding of election and salvation filtered down to the pastors of the Northamptonshire Association, especially through the writings of Edwards.

The SFA begins with a theological preamble consistent with the principles of Evangelical Calvinism. The statement lays out three interconnected ideas. First, in the opening sentence of the SFA, Ward alludes to the importance of divine providence: "The Redeemer, in planting us in this heathen nation rather than in any other, has imposed upon us the cultivation of peculiar qualifications." They saw their presence in India as a direct consequence of divine providence. The same sentence goes straight to the missiological application of this theology. It implied that they must cultivate "peculiar qualifications." That is, they had to take steps to become the most effective missionaries possible to the specific culture in which they found themselves. They must learn the language and the culture and adapt their preaching to the realities of India.

The Serampore missionaries were aware of the anti-supernaturalistic tendencies gaining prevalence in their day. Convinced God directly ordered details great and small for the gospel's advance, they stood firmly against deism. Carey had already begun to explore the relation between divine providence and missions in the *Enquiry*:

> It has been said that we ought not to force our way, but to wait for the openings, and leadings of Providence; but it might with equal propriety be answered in this case, neither ought we to neglect embracing those openings in providence which daily present themselves to us. What openings of providence do we wait for? We can neither expect to be transported into the heathen world without ordinary means, nor to be endowed with the gift of tongues, &c. when we arrive there. These would not be providential interpositions, but miraculous ones. Where a command exists nothing can be necessary to render it binding but a removal of those obstacles which render obedience impossible, and these are removed already.[41]

---

[41] William Carey, *An Enquiry into the Obligations of Christians, to Use Means for the Conversion of the Heathens* (Leicester: Ann Ireland, 1792), 11.

Ward carries forward this perspective in the SFA, "In many ways the progress of providential events is preparing the Hindoos for casting their idols to the moles and the bats, and for becoming a part of the chosen generation, the royal priesthood, the holy nation."[42]

The SFA applies the doctrine of divine providence directly in practical issues of missiology. Women's ministry provides an example: "If we consider how much the Asiatic women are shut up from the men, and especially from men of another cast. It behoves us, therefore, to afford to our European sisters all possible assistance in acquiring the language, that they may, in every way which Providence may open to them, become instrumental in promoting the salvation of the millions of native women."[43] And Providence provided the backdrop to discussions about the names of Indian converts, "We think the great object which Divine Providence has in view in causing the gospel to be promulgated in the world, is not the changing of the names, the dress, the food, and the innocent usages of mankind, but to produce a moral and divine change in the hearts and conduct of men."[44]

The second great theological principle stated in the preamble is God's sovereignty in salvation: "We are firmly persuaded that Paul might plant and Apollos water, in vain, in any part of the world, did not God give the increase. We are sure, that only those who are ordained to eternal life will believe, and that God alone can add to the church such as shall be saved." Perhaps this statement is not remarkable coming from Particular Baptist ministers. What does stand out is the way God's sovereignty in salvation is paired with the third great theological idea: a statement of human responsibility in missions:

> Nevertheless we cannot but observe with admiration, that Paul, the great champion for the glorious doctrines of free and sovereign grace, was the most conspicuous for his personal zeal in the work of persuading men to be reconciled to God. In this respect he is a noble example for our imitation. Our Lord intimated to those of his apostles who were fishermen, that he would make them fishers of men,

---

[42] Statement Nine.
[43] Statement Seven.
[44] Statement Eight.

intimating that in all weathers, and amidst every disappointment, they were to aim at drawing men to the shores of eternal life. Solomon says, "He that winneth souls is wise," implying, no doubt, that the work of gaining over men to the side of God, was to be done by winning methods, and that it required the greatest wisdom to do it with success.[45]

Ward concludes the preamble with this statement: "Upon these points we think it right to fix our serious and abiding attention." In other words, the rest of the SFA develops these three theological principles in the context of the work in Bengal.

The SFA's preamble functions much like the declaration of faith Andrew Fuller made when under consideration for the pastorate at Kettering. Fuller wrote:

> I believe it is the duty of every minister of Christ plainly and faithfully to preach the gospel to all who will hear it; and as I believe the inability of men to spiritual things to be wholly of the moral, and therefore of the criminal kind, and that it is their duty to love the Lord Jesus Christ, and trust him for salvation, though they do not; I therefore believe free and solemn addresses, invitations, calls, and warnings to them, to be not only consistent, but directly adapted as means, in the hand of the Spirit of God, to bring them to Christ. I consider it as part of my duty that could not omit without being guilty of the blood of souls.[46]

The SFA's preamble shows the influence of the biblical theology which was a key to the revival among Northamptonshire Baptists. Fuller and others had turned from a more speculative theology influenced by the rationalism of the age to a simpler biblicism that emphasized "the practice of Christ and his apostles."[47] Against the rationalizations of high Calvinism, Fuller simply pointed out that the New Testament example of the apostles was to offer the gospel freely.

---

[45] Preamble.
[46] Peter J. Morden, *Offering Christ to the World* (Milton Keynes: Paternoster, 2003), 106.
[47] Andrew Fuller, *The Complete Works of Rev. Andrew Fuller* (Philadelphia: American Baptist Publication Society, 1845), 2:386.

Origins

This approach was also evident in Carey's *Enquiry*. A simple reading of the Great Commission clarified that it was still the church's responsibility. Like Fuller, Carey moved on to the issue of the means required for simple obedience. The two seemingly contradictory ideas of divine sovereignty in salvation and the human use of means are held together by the doctrine of providence.

The Serampore Model

The SFA outlines the primary missiological principles of the Serampore missionaries but does not provide a full-fledged description of the plans that flowed from these principles. Nonetheless, we see how they moved from principles to plans in Statement Eight. This statement highlights the importance of training Indian leaders and establishing Indian churches.

The Moravian-style community was simply an auxiliary organization formed as part of a plan to reproduce an association of independent local churches like those in Britain. Like the BMS, it was a bridge organization that facilitated the work of evangelization and church planting in India. The Serampore missionaries established additional auxiliary organizations, such as the Serampore Press and Serampore College. These auxiliary organizations answered the question Carey posed in the *Enquiry*: should means be used for the salvation of the heathen?

Serampore College found its counterpart in Britain in such Baptist institutions as Bristol College and Fawcett's Academy. The Serampore press had no immediate Baptist equivalent in Britain, although the British Baptists were active in publishing books, hymns, and circular letters. However, in Britain, there was no need to produce and distribute English translations of the Scriptures. Except for the Serampore Mission itself, all these organizations survived. Again, despite their importance, they must be seen as auxiliary organizations. They were a means to an end. Not the end itself. The goal was a network of gospel churches, pastored by Indians, spread across the subcontinent.

The first ten statements of the SFA deal with various missiological principles for evangelism, church planting, and the training of national leaders. The final statement laid down critical principles for the Moravian-style community. When Carey first went to India, the Moravian model seemed the only viable option. And it appealed to Carey's sacrificial nature. Nonetheless, the Moravian-style community was just one of the auxiliary organizations envisioned. This is clear from a report sent to the BMS, in 1815, just before the death of Andrew Fuller. This report described their strategy and outlined three essential agencies:

> First, the formation of stations, where the "the standard of the Cross shall be erected, and the Gospel preached to the people, and from whence ultimately spring churches." Secondly, the translation of the Scriptures; and, thirdly, the instruction of youth in the knowledge of the Bible and of the literature suited to the state of the country: that thus divine knowledge may be diffused abroad, and teachers and pastors be raised up to make known the Gospel.[48]

These agencies worked in tandem: "If the Scriptures be not translated and published, the most strenuous efforts would abide only for a season. Unless youth be instructed the Scriptures would be little read, and without missionaries to form stations schools could not be established, or the Scriptures circulated to any extent."[49]

The stations were to grow in an expanding network. Carey wrote: "It has long been a favourite object with me to fix European brethren in different parts of the country at about two hundred miles apart, so that each shall be able to visit a circle of a hundred miles' radius, and within each of the circuits to place native brethren at proper distances, who will, till they are more established, be under the superintendence of the European brethren in the centre."[50]

As mentioned, Statement Eight provides a glimpse of the movement from missiological principles to concrete plans. The statement begins, "Another part of our work is the forming our native brethren to usefulness, fostering every kind of genius, and cherishing every gift and grace in them." Behind this statement lies the missionaries' theological commit-

---

[48] Marshman, *Life and Times*, II, 97.
[49] Marshman, *Life and Times*, II, 98.
[50] Smith, *The Life of William Carey*, 164.

ments to the essential equality of all men and a New Testament understanding of the church that excluded distinctions like those of the caste system. These principles were expressed in a plan that expected European leadership to be replaced by Indians in the local churches.

> Still further to strengthen the cause of Christ in this country, and, as far as in our power, to give it a permanent establishment, even when the efforts of Europeans may fail, we think it our duty, as soon as possible, to advise the native brethren who may be formed into separate churches, to choose their pastors and deacons from amongst their own countrymen, that the word may be statedly preached, and the ordinances of Christ administered, in each church, by the native minister, as much as possible, without the interference of the missionary of the district.[51]

While the Serampore missionaries believed in using all legitimate means to expand the gospel, including various auxiliary organizations, the objective was to reproduce the New Testament pattern of local churches led by Indian pastors.

The Enduring Value of the SFA

The SFA offers a model for missionary endeavors. Perhaps its most significant value can be found as a fruitful example of moving from theological principle to practical application on the mission field. It broke important ground in areas such as the role of missionary women, the critical importance of training and empowering national leaders, and its nuanced view of culture. Not every auxiliary agency proposed by the Serampore missionaries succeeded. The Moravian community did not endure. Nonetheless, even here, the example of selflessness still provides a standard for the missionary life. George Smith, writing at the end of the 19th century, opined:

> We know nothing in the history of missions, monastic or evangelical, which at all approaches this in administrative perfectness as well as

---

[51] Statement Eight.

The Serampore Form of Agreement

in Christ-like self-sacrifice. It prevents secularisation of spirit, stimulates activity of all kinds, gives full scope to local ability and experience, calls forth the maximum of local support and propagation, sets the church at home free to enter incessantly on new fields, provides permanence as well as variety of action and adaptation to new circumstances, and binds the whole in a holy bond of prayerful co-operation and loving fellowship.[52]

Smith could produce his own "fervid" prose. Regarding the Moravian community in view in Statement Eleven of the SFA, the evidence shows it was not an exemplar of "administrative perfectness" so much as an example of noble intentions gone awry. Nonetheless, Smith rightly draws attention to the critical element for missionary fruitfulness: the Christ-like self-sacrifice of the Serampore missionaries. This call for radical commitment to the cause of the gospel makes the *Serampore Form of Agreement* more than a time-bound covenant. It is a manifesto for the missionary age.

---

[52] Smith, *The Life of William Carey*, 129–130.

STATEMENT ONE

The Rationale for Missionary Identity at Serampore

Bennie R. Crockett, Jr.

Statement One of the Serampore Form of Agreement (SFA) provided the foundational rationale for the Serampore missionary project. Like a brilliant jewel, it retains its value even today as a definitive statement concerning human identity and Christian missions. The mission project at Serampore grew from the missionaries' view of the infinite value of all immortal souls. Contrasted with the ideology of a controlling and acquisitive British Empire, the missionaries' vision in Statement One offered a Christian understanding of the value and accountability of every individual soul to God in Christ. As God had brought the ancient polytheistic Britons into Christian identity, the missionaries also argued that God could and would do a similar work in polytheistic India.

Unlike the strategic and methodological Statements that follow it, Statement One serves as *the* ideological and theological foundation for the subsequent Statements. This foundational nature can be seen in three distinct contexts. First, the print history of SFA offers interpretive insight into SFA's original rhetoric in contrast to misleading subsequent orthographic changes. Secondly, SFA's original title page provides key insights into the missionaries' communal effort in instructing Indian natives; subsequent editions obscured this focus. Finally, Statement One presents an elegant and compelling foundational argument for Christian missionary practice resting upon the need of all persons' faith in Christ, who holds and offers eternal salvation.

The Serampore Form of Agreement

Print History Affecting Statement One

Copies of the original 1805 SFA are rare. SFA appeared reprinted at least thirteen times in other nineteenth-century forms, and the various reprints reveal changes in the text of SFA, Statement One. Variant readings in the print history of SFA reveal key markers in the original intent of SFA as the rationale for missionary identity at Serampore. By introducing textual changes to the original title, title page, and Statement One, subsequent print editors provoked readers' misunderstanding of SFA. Identifying the subsequent misleading changes in the print history helps remove anachronistic impediments to understanding Statement One.

For clarity, the explanatory title of the 1805 SFA was *Form of Agreement, Respecting the Great Principles upon which the Brethren of the Mission at Serampore Think It Their Duty to Act in the Work of Instructing the Heathen.*[1] In reprints, the title became shortened, reformatted, changed, or deleted, obscuring the intent of 1805 SFA.

In the original 1805 SFA, Statement One received an indented paragraph side heading "FIRST," and the other following statements received like indented side headings of the ordinals in adverb form: "SECONDLY," "THIRDLY," ... "TENTHLY." The last statement received the side heading "FINALLY." The contrast of the ordinal "FIRST" (not "FIRSTLY")[2]

---

[1] *Form of Agreement, Respecting the Great Principles upon which the Brethren of the Mission at Serampore Think It Their Duty to Act in the Work of Instructing the Heathen* (Serampore: Printed at the Brethren's Press, 1805), hereinafter SFA; specific Statements appear as "Statement" followed by Arabic numbers. I acknowledge Emily Burgoyne, Angus Librarian, Regent's Park College, Oxford University, for providing a copy of the 1805 SFA to Peter de Vries, Samuel Masters, and then to me. For the text, see the Appendix.

[2] William Ward, the composer *and* printer of SFA, may have been aware that "firstly" and "eleventhly" did not appear in Samuel Johnson, *A Dictionary of the English Language: In Which the WORDS are deduced from their ORIGINALS, and Illustrated in their Different Significations by EXAMPLES from the best WRITERS*, 2 vols. (London: Printed by W. Strahan, 1755, 1765). Johnson listed "first" as meaning "Earliest in time," "Foremost in place," and "Highest in dignity," but when used as an adverb, "Before anything else." Johnson's *Dictionary*, tenth edition (abstracted), listed Charles Dilly as one seller; Dilly likewise was a London seller for William Carey, *An Enquiry into the Obligations of Christians to Use Means for the Conversion of the Heathens. In which the Religious State of the Different Nations of the World, the Success of Former Undertakings, and the Practicability of Further Undertakings, are Considered* (Leicester: Ann Ireland, 1792).

William Carey to John Ryland, December 10, 1811, in George Smith, *The Life of William Carey, D.D., Shoemaker and Missionary* (London: John Murray, 1885), 248–249, notes that he

Statement One

with the subsequent ordinal adverbs "SECONDLY," etc., supports the view that Statement One may be read as a unique foundational statement. By the ordinal "FIRST," one could interpret the meaning as "FIRST AND FOREMOST" regarding importance and rank since "FIRST" signals a categorical difference from "SECONDLY," "THIRDLY," ... "TENTHLY," "FINALLY." "FIRST"—in the sense of "FIRST AND FOREMOST"—and the content of Statement One[3] conveys the idea of "the singular foundation of the Great Principles." "FIRST" reveals a rank of importance *necessarily before* all others in a series of ideas, and the series of Statements Two to Eleven could have a different order without affecting SFA's foundational content in Statement One.

In ten nineteenth-century reprint editions of the 1805 SFA—William Brown, M.D.[4] (five editions) and William Yates[5] (five editions)—the ordinal and ordinal adverbs appeared as Roman numerals I, II, III, etc. The

---

(Carey) planned to structure *"An Universal Dictionary of the Oriental languages derived from the Sanskrit ... in the manner of Johnson."*

[3] The SFA 1806 London version includes ordinals changed to Roman numerals I-X, and "FINALLY" became "XI." See William Carey, Joshua Marshman, William Ward, John Chamberlain, Richard Mardon, John Biss, William Moore, Joshua Rowe, Felix Carey, "Form of Agreement," *Periodical Accounts Relative to the Baptist Missionary Society*, III, no. XVI (London: Printed by J. W. Morris; Sold by Button and Burditt, 1806), 198-211.

[4] See William Brown, M.D., *The History of the Propagation of Christianity Among the Heathen Since the Reformation*, vol. 2 (London: Printed for Longman, Hurst, Rees, Orme, & Brown, and Edinburgh: David Brown, 1814), 215-230; William Brown, M.D., *The History of the Propagation of Christianity Among The Heathen Since the Reformation*, vol. 2, First American, from the last London Edition (New York: Printed and Published by T. Low, 1816), 178-190; William Brown, M.D., *The History of Missions: or, of The Propagation of Christianity Among the Heathen, Since the Reformation*, vol. 2, First American Edition (Philadelphia: Published by B. Coles, 1816), 203-215; William Brown, M.D., *The History of the Propagation of Christianity Among the Heathen Since the Reformation*, vol. 2, 2nd edn. (Edinburgh: Published by A. Fullarton & Co.; Glasgow: Khull, Blackie, & Co. and Chalmers & Collins; Edinburgh: David Brown and Waugh and Innes; London: W. B. Whittaker; Dublin: R. M. Tims, 1823), 166-174; William Brown, M.D., *History of the Propagation of Christianity Among the Heathen Since the Reformation*, vol. 2, 3rd edn. (Edinburgh and London: William Blackwood and Sons, 1854), 32-38, also has Roman numerals with omissions and rearrangements.

[5] See "Form of Agreement," in William Yates, *Memoirs of Mr. John Chamberlain, Late Missionary in India* (Calcutta: Printed at the Baptist Mission Press, 1824), 216-228; "Form of Agreement," in William Yates, *Memoirs of Mr. John Chamberlain, Late Missionary in India*, Republished under the Direction of the Committee of the Baptist Missionary Society. With a Preface by F. A. Cox (London: Printed for Francis Westley, and Sold by C. J. Westley, and G. Tyrrell, Dublin, 1825); 190-201; "Form of Agreement," in William Yates, *Memoirs of Mr. John Chamberlain, Late Missionary in India* (Calcutta: Printed at the Baptist Mission Press; London: Re-printed for Wightman and Cramp, 1826), 190-201; "Appendix. Principles of Missionary

change obscured the 1805 presentation of "FIRST" (i.e., "FIRST AND FOREMOST") as the intended foundation. Using Roman numerals may give *more* of an impression of a series list in ranked order. In contrast to the reprints in the BMS (1806), the Brown editions, and the Yates editions, including the Calcutta Baptist Mission Press of Yates (1824), only the Calcutta reprint of 1874 and the London reprint of 1885 retained the intent of William Ward's 1805 Serampore copy that included "FIRST," SECONDLY," "THIRDLY,"... "TENTHLY," and "FINALLY."[6] Both reprints (1874 and 1885) substituted lowercase for the words (i.e., "First").

Regarding the composition of SFA, thirteen days short of his thirty-sixth birthday, Ward said,

> At our evening council, I delivered to each Bren. a copy of a 'Form of Agreement respecting the Principles upon which we think it our duty to act in instructing the Heathen.' I wished much that we should leave to our successors something like this, & therefore drew it up, read it to the Brethren, & to-night gave to each a copy for their corrections and additions.[7]

Whether any of the other eight who signed the SFA offered corrections or additions is elusive, but the length of Statements Seven to Nine elicits attention differently than Statements One to Six and Ten to Eleven. Possibly, various statements' or sentences' provenance may have been other documents, for at the time of Ward's drafting SFA, Joshua Marshman

---

Labour. Form of Agreement," in William Yates, *Memoirs of the Early Life of John Chamberlain, Late Missionary in India. With His Diary of Religious Exercises*; Abridged from the Calcutta Edition (Boston: James Loring, Sabbath School Book-Store, 1831), 189-204; "Appendix. Principles of Missionary Labour. Form of Agreement," in William Yates, *Memoirs of the Early Life of John Chamberlain, Late Missionary in India. With His Diary of Religious Exercises* (Boston: New England Sabbath School Union, 1831), 189-204.

[6] See *Form of Agreement Respecting The Great Principles upon which The Brethren of the Mission at Serampore Think It Their Duty to Act in the Work of Instructing the Heathen* (Serampore: Printed at the Brethren's Press, 1805; Calcutta: Reprinted at the Baptist Mission Press, 1874), 1-12; and "Appendix I. The Bond of the Missionary Brotherhood of Serampore," in Smith, *The Life of William Carey, D.D.*, 441-450. Carey, *An Enquiry*, 64-66, used "FIRST," SECONDLY," "THIRDLY," "FOURTHLY," and "FIFTHLY."

[7] Saturday, October 5, 1805. *William Ward's Missionary Journal, 1799-1811*, transcribed by E. Daniel Potts, 4 Vols. Mss. Baptist Missionary Society Archives, Angus Library, Regent's Park College, Oxford. Hereinafter, *Ward's Journal*.

Statement One

wrote a "plan of Union for the family which will accompany the family rules, as this agreement [SFA] will accompany the Station Rules. The station rules are also of my [i.e. Ward's] drawing up."[8] Aside from the possibility of fused documents, Statement One is the logical foundation for SFA, and it should bear no suspicion about its authenticity to Ward's composition.

Twenty-two years later, William Carey and John Clark Marshman wrote the striking statement that Ward "drew up his ideas of missionary economy, in the 'agreement' respecting the way in which we thought missionaries ought to act in money matters, and obtained the concurrence and signature of his brethren to it; in less than a year it was found impracticable, and was consigned to oblivion."[9]

Consignment "to oblivion" in India did *not* render Statement One irrelevant. Instead, Statements One to Ten remained central to the Serampore Mission's Christian identity, moral virtues, and motivation for missionary activity. Possibly, what "was consigned to oblivion" alone was Statement Eleven ("FINALLY" in the 1805 original) due to its communal ownership perspective. Based on the lived practice of the missionaries at Serampore, 1805–1827, Statements One to Ten seem instead to have been *consigned to standard missionary practice,* with Statement One serving as the foundational motivation of missionary purpose and activity. Despite John Clark Marshman's stated "copious analysis"[10] of SFA, he did *not* com-

---

[8] Saturday, October 5, 1805. *Ward's Journal*, II, 440.

[9] William Carey and John Marshman to the Committee of the Baptist Missionary Society, November 15, 1827, in *Letters from The Rev. Dr. Carey, Relative to Certain Statements Contained in Three Pamphlets Lately Published by the Rev. John Dyer, Secretary to the Baptist Missionary Society: W. Johns, M.D. and The Rev. E. Carey and W. Yates*, 3rd edn. (London: Parbury, Allen, and Co., 1828), 56. This statement seems Carey's alone since John Clark Marshman was eleven years old at the time of SFA's composition.

Also, see John Clark Marshman, *The Life and Times of Carey, Marshman, and Ward. Embracing the History of the Serampore Mission* (London: Longman, Brown, Green, Longmans, & Roberts, 1859), I, 229.

[10] Marshman, *Life and Times*, I, 227–230.

ment on or analyze Statement One. He gave the impression that SFA concerned missionary strategies without an ideological foundation that Ward said was "absolutely necessary."[11]

Further, given SFA's nineteenth-century literary history in Britain and the U.S.A., the SFA's consignment to oblivion never occurred in the West. Rather, amidst the *supposed* Serampore "oblivion," the Serampore *mythos* in Britain and the U.S.A., and SFA's frequent reprinting, the "First" statement remained an ideological foundation for many Christians in the missions century.[12] Among thirteen nineteenth-century reprints, all copies include Statement One, in full or *abbreviated*.[13]

The latter ten Statements were the missionaries' desired methodological strategies for their activities in India. However, without the foundational rationale of Statement One, the rest of the "great principles" in Statements Two to Eleven would have been irrelevant for the Baptist missionaries who went to India with the Christian message to "proclaim ... the glad tidings of salvation."[14] Statement One was not only a "great principle," it was *the* foundational principle for all the missionaries' expected

---

[11] Statement One.

[12] For the nineteenth century's importance for Christian mission, see Kenneth Scott Latourette, "The Christian Missionary Movement of the Nineteenth and Twentieth Centuries: Some Peculiar and General Characteristics," *The Catholic Historical Review* 23 no. 2 (July 1937): 153-159, and Paul A. Crow, "19th century efforts," in "Christianity," *Encyclopedia Britannica*, June 1, 2022 <https://www.britannica.com/topic/Christianity/19th-century-efforts>.

[13] See Brown, *The History of the Propagation of Christianity* (1823), 167, and Brown, *History of the Propagation of Christianity* (1854), 32, for the *removal* of the last sentence from Statement One. Of all fourteen SFA editions 1805-1885 identified herein, the 1823 and 1854 editions have the most changes from SFA 1805.

[14] Statement Four. The phrase "proclaim glad tidings of salvation" mixes the glosses of εὐαγγελίζω (proclaim glad tidings/proclaim good news/proclaim the gospel, see Romans 10:15) and σωτηρία (salvation/wholeness). These two Greek words do not appear together in the Bible translated as "proclaim glad tidings of salvation." In the eighteenth century, this English phrase became common in Bible dictionaries, sermons, and in some renditions of lyrics of Handel, *Messiah*. Alone, "glad tidings" appears in the King James Bible (Luke 1:19; 8:1; Acts 13:32; Romans 10:15). Hereinafter, all Bible quotes derive from the KJB. Ward's theological mentor used the phrase before Ward arrived at Ewood Hall; see John Fawcett, *Considerations Relative to the Sending of Missionaries to Propagate the Gospel among the Heathens* (Leeds: Printed by Thomas Wright, 1793), 7. Abraham Booth, *Glad Tidings to Perishing Sinners: Or, The Genuine Gospel a Complete Warrant for the Ungodly to Believe in Jesus* (London: Printed for the Author; and Sold by W. Button, Paternoster Row; and T. Knott, Lombard Street, 1796); 7, 57, 66, 158, 159, popularized and used the exact phrase "glad tidings of salvation" while also using "glad tidings" many times

Statement One

duties in the Christian missionary work of instructing the heathen. Or, as John Brown representatively wrote for late eighteenth-century evangelical ministers and missionaries,

> the gospel strictly taken, is the centre in which the lines of revelation meet, the whole of divine truth, whether law or gospel strictly taken, is called the gospel ... [and] must be preached, to alarm and drive men to hear the glad tidings of salvation to them in particular ... The preaching of these glad tidings of free and full salvation, is called the gospel.[15]

William Ward certainly proclaimed such a "gospel" view in India, for he wrote that "We preach, & the news of Xt's [Christ's] death is, in their own language, a good word, glad tidings. A brahman comes & says it is not good; they [villagers] therefore ... think no more of Xt. and the good news of the Gospel."[16]

Before he arrived in India in late 1799, William Ward had honed his literary abilities through his printing and editing work with three British newspapers—*Derby Mercury*, *Staffordshire Advertiser*, and the *Hull Advertiser and Exchange Gazette*. In these papers, Ward often included some of his own compositions of poetry and essays.[17] With Dr. John Fawcett during 1797–1798, Ward developed theological judgment at Ewood Hall, near Halifax in Yorkshire. This location also provided Ward opportunities for village preaching that served him well in India. In India, Ward wrote of

---

with different nominal modifiers. Of note, T. Knott, Lombard Street, distributed Samuel Johnson's *The Life of the Rev. Isaac Watts, D.D.* (1791), William Carey's *Enquiry* (1792), and Booth's *Glad Tidings*.

[15] John Brown, *A Dictionary of the Holy Bible*, 2nd edn., 2 vols. (Edinburgh: Printed for W. Anderson, 1778), 1:550.

[16] Tuesday, October 11, 1803. *Ward's Journal*, II, 335.

[17] For an example of his poetry, see William Ward, "Addressed to the Dealers in Human Flesh—On the Loss of Mr. Wilberforce's Bill for the Abolition of the Slave-Trade," *Derby Mercury*, May 12, 1791, which also appears much later in another form in Samuel Stennett, *Memoirs of the Life of the Rev. William Ward, Late Baptist Missionary in India; Containing a Few of His Early Poetical Productions, and a Monody to his Memory* (London: Printed by J. Haddon, 1825), 269-271. For a short essay, see William Ward, "Moonlight," *Hull Advertiser and Exchange Gazette*, April 23, 1796, 4. Also, see William Ward, *The Abolition of the Slave Trade, Peace, and a Temperate Reform Essential to the Salvation of England* (London: Printed for Crosby, 1796).

The Serampore Form of Agreement

Bible distribution, "We should endeavour to ascertain where large assemblies of the natives are to be found, that we may attend upon them, and gladden whole villages at once with the tidings of salvation."[18] Though Bible distribution in local languages was a primary focus of the Serampore missionaries, Ward, as noted above, likewise often spoke the "glad tidings" in various villages.[19] In SFA, he wrote that "the real conquests of the gospel are those of love,"[20] with particular reference to Jesus' being lifted up on a cross. Still, the natives' "little knowledge of the scriptures" implies, "They know only the Saviour and his doctrine as they shine forth in us."[21] The "glad tidings of salvation" would be distributed primarily as printed Bibles, Bibles preached or explained in varied social contexts, or Bibles lived with consistent Christian integrity and moral virtue.

The Title Page as a Key to Interpreting Statement One

The functional title of SFA 1805 subsequently became shortened, reformatted, changed, or deleted. In London in 1806, a reprint of SFA appeared in the *Periodical Accounts Relative to the Baptist Missionary Society*. This 1806 edition introduced some orthographic changes within Statement One and other places. It significantly downgraded William Ward's typeset presentation of the title page[22] into three lowercase, single-spaced, italicized lines for the title, two lines for the note of the essay's approval, and complete omission of "Serampore: Printed at the Brethren's Press." Ward intended that "Serampore: Printed at The Brethren's Press" would ensure the identification of the Press as a *joint, Christian, and communal* effort in the publication of the great principles of "the glad tidings of salvation."

---

[18] Statement Ten.

[19] For Bible distribution *and* village preaching, see entries April 30, 1803; September 25, 1803; October 1, 1805; October 4, 1803; November 1, 1803. *Ward's Journal*, II, 297, 323-325, 329, 331, 343.

[20] Statement Three.

[21] Statement Seven.

[22] Attention here points to Ward's *typesetting* of the document and its visual impression. With the exception of SFA 1805 and SFA 1874, subsequent reprints have removed the impressive title page, and thereby removed the meaning of SFA, and the historical reference to "The Brethren's Press."

Statement One

In Statement One, there are seven sentences and 295 words, 71% being monosyllables. Impressively, seventeen words (5.76%) are first-person plural pronouns ("our"—7x; "we"—7x; "us"—3x). These pronouns reveal Ward's communal understanding of missionary outreach as seen in the title page phrase, *The Brethren's Press*. This phrase became lost in subsequent printings except for the 1874 Calcutta Baptist Mission Press copy. The existence of other Serampore publications in English from "The Brethren's Press" seems absent; the 1805 SFA may be the only extant English publication with the beautifully communal name for the Press.[23]

In graphic contrast to the 1806 SFA (London) and other reprints (except for the 1874 Calcutta edition), the original 1805 SFA has a *separate* title page that appears *in all capital letters*. Those capitals focus on key phrases that Ward presumably typeset. With font size alone, the phrase "Form of Agreement" attracts the most attention with the single word "Agreement" being the largest font on the title page. Then, "Instructing the Heathen" is the second largest font, followed by a slightly smaller font for "The Great Principles." Then, in even smaller italicized capitals, Ward set the phrase "Think It Their Duty to Act." Interpreting font size as a visual hermeneutical clue to Ward's intent, one could draw the sequential conclusion that SFA was an: 1) *agreed-upon essay* for the purpose of 2) *instructing the heathen* in 3) the *great principles* of 4) the *brethren's duty to act*.

Assuming Ward acted alone in the typesetting, these four typeset phrases reveal *Ward's* rhetorical emphasis for the document. In the fifth place are the even smaller italicized capitals in the unique phrase at the

---

[23] SFA 1805 stands unique with "Serampore: Printed at the Brethren's Press." However, Serampore College holds *Brief Memoirs of Four Christian Hindoos, lately deceased* (Serampore: Printed in the year 1810), and a similarly titled work appears on WorldCat as originating from "Brethren's Press, 1809-1810," though the WorldCat entry includes no library identification. Early publications' title pages from Ward at Serampore appear listed as "Serampore" with the publication date or "Serampore: [Printed at] The Mission Press" with the date. See H. T. Colebrook, *Hitōpadēśa, or Salutary Instruction. In the original Sanscrit* (Printed at Serampore, 1804); William Carey and Joshua Marshman, *The Ramayuna of Valmeeki, in the Original Sungskrit. With a Prose Translation, And Explanatory Notes*, vol. I (Serampore, 1806); W. Carey, D.D., *A Dictionary of the Mahratta Language* (Serampore, 1810), and W. Carey, *A Grammar of the Bengalee Language* (Serampore: Printed at the Mission Press, 1801).

bottom of the page: "Printed at the Brethren's Press." Given the favorable naming of the Moravians in SFA,[24] there may be an allusive comparison of the Serampore "Brethren's Press" to the Moravian Brethren. Of note, the word "brethren" in SFA *always* refers to native Christian believers, except on the title page, which refers to the missionaries.[25] This biblical word reinforces theologically the missionaries' assertion in Statement One, "that we set an infinite value upon immortal souls."[26] Extending the gospel to Indian immortal souls yielded a context in which Christ "made both one"[27]—British "brethren" and "the native brethren."

Subsequently, all five editions of William Brown's *The History of the Propagation of Christianity among the Heathen since the Reformation* included the text of SFA. In every edition, he removed the key title page information, except for "Form of Agreement." Also, William Yates, a Baptist missionary to India in 1815, reprinted the SFA five times in his *Memoirs of the Early Life of John Chamberlain, Late Missionary in India*.[28] Chamberlain (1777-1821), a missionary in Cutwa (Katwa), signed the SFA likely when he arrived twenty days after the Serampore Brethren agreed on the SFA, October 7, 1805.[29] Yates removed the SFA title page in his various reprints but retained "Form of Agreement." The Boston editions include the SFA as an Appendix. George Smith (London, 1885) also reprinted the SFA as an appendix titled "The Bond of the Missionary Brotherhood of Serampore."[30] Seemingly taken from the Calcutta Baptist Mission Press 1874 edition, Smith introduced two spelling changes to Statement One.

---

[24] Statement Three; Statement Five.

[25] In reference to the missionaries, "brethren" appears twice on the title page of SFA. "Native brethren" appears five times (Statements Seven-Eight), and "brethren" appears for native believers once (Statement Eight).

[26] Statement One. In the King James Bible, "brethren" appears over two hundred times in the New Testament.

[27] Ephesians 2:14.

[28] Copies of SFA 1824, Calcutta, Baptist Mission Press, are rare. One copy exists in the Angus Library, Regent's Park College, and another in Bibliothèque nationale et universitaire de Strasbourg. I acknowledge Emily Burgoyne, Angus Librarian, and Rebecca Shuttleworth, Library Assistant, Angus Library, Regent's Park College, for providing a copy of this source.

[29] Lord's Day, October 27, 1805. *Ward's Journal*, II, 446. The SFA 1805 title page notes the agreement date.

[30] Smith, *The Life of William Carey*, 441.

Statement One

The Calcutta 1874 SFA was the only nineteenth-century reprint with the complete title page and ordinal numbering of the Statements.

Since 1885, some reprint copies of SFA have appeared. *The Baptist Quarterly* 1947 reprint of the London 1806 SFA is possibly the most known.[31] Two years prior, in 1945, A. H. Oussoren had appended the SFA (titled "The Bond of the Missionary Brotherhood of Serampore") into his book on William Carey's missionary principles.[32] In Oussoren's reprint of Statement One, an unfortunate misspelling appeared that caused a significant interpretive conundrum: "Scottish" for the original word "sottish." In 1992, James R. Beck introduced a new title for the SFA as, "Serampore Compact," and repeated Oussoren's error "Scottish."[33] In 2018, Michael Haykin appended the SFA to his book on William Carey.[34]

Exposition of Key Ideas in Statement One

"Infinite Value upon Immortal Souls."—Possibly the most important sentence in the SFA is, "In order to be prepared for our great and solemn work, it is absolutely necessary that we set an infinite value upon immortal souls."[35] In this one sentence, the SFA *necessarily*[36] links the empirical and

---

[31] Ernest A. Payne, ed., "The Serampore Form of Agreement," *The Baptist Quarterly* 12 no. 5 (1947): 125-138. This edition has a very helpful introduction on 125-129 followed by the text of SFA.

[32] A. H. Oussoren, "The Bond of the Missionary Brotherhood of Serampore," in *William Carey, Especially His Missionary Principles* (Leiden: A. W. Sijthoff's Uitgeversmaatschappij N.V., 1945), 274-284.

[33] James R. Beck, "Serampore Compact," in *Dorothy Carey: The Tragic and Untold Story of Mrs. William Carey* (Grand Rapids: Baker Book House, 1992), 199-206.

[34] Michael A. G. Haykin, "The Serampore Form of Agreement (1805)," *The Missionary Fellowship of William Carey* in The Long Line of Godly Men Profiles, ed. Steven J. Lawson (Sanford, Florida: Reformation Trust, 2018), 137-154.

[35] Statement One has the result of opposing the radical Enlightenment rejection of the immaterial, immortal soul, led by David Hume, *Essays and Treatises on Several Subjects*. Vol. II *Containing An Enquiry Concerning Human Understanding; A Dissertation on the Passions; An Enquiry concerning the Principles of Morals; and The Natural History of Religion*, new edn. (London: Printed for T. Cadell, 1772), 149-166, 183; and posthumously, *Essays on Suicide and the Immortality of the Soul*, new edn. (Basil: Printed for the Editor of the Collection of English Classics, 1799), 15-25, 35-45.

[36] SFA contains nine references (Statements One, Three, Six, Seven, Eight, Nine) to the idea of "necessity" with three uses including the intensifying adverb "absolutely." By such logic, Ward removed the logical or empirical possibility for natives not having infinite value as immortal

The Serampore Form of Agreement

very difficult missionary work to a Christian logic that affirms an eternal teleology for "the millions of souls, spread" on the "habitable globe."[37] The first sentence of Statement One asserts the essential equality of *all* humans as immortal souls who need conversion by Christ for eternity. The missionaries' "great and solemn work" was that of "gaining over men to the side of God," analogous to Paul's "persuading men to be reconciled to God."[38]

In the eighteenth and early nineteenth centuries, the phrase "fellow creature" became a common rhetorical phrase for a connection of the "infinite value" of "immortal souls," whether Britons, Europeans, Africans, or Indians. "Fellow creature" received special meaning in the abolition movement among Quakers,[39] and Anthony Benezet (1713-1784) brought focused attention to the term in his abolition arguments:

> To make known the aggravated iniquity attending the practices of the Slave-trade; whereby many thousands of our fellow-creatures, as free as ourselves by nature, and equally with us the subjects of Christ's redeeming Grace, are yearly brought into inextricable and barbarous bondage; and many, very many, to miserable and untimely ends.[40]

> Why are those masters of vessels ... thus suffered to be the sovereign arbiters of the lives of the miserable Negroes; and allowed, with impunity, thus to destroy, may I not say, murder their fellow-creatures, and that by means so cruel, as cannot be even related but with shame and horror?[41]

---

souls. About sixteen years later, Ward wrote "Necessity of Christianity to India. Population, 150,000,000" (Boston: 1821).

[37] Statement Eight.

[38] Statement, Preamble.

[39] The People Called Quakers, *The Case of Our Fellow-Creatures, the Oppressed Africans, Respectfully Recommended to the Serious Consideration of the Legislature of Great-Britain* (London: James Phillips, 1784).

[40] Anthony Benezet, *A Caution to Great Britain and Her Colonies, in a Short Representation of the Calamitous State of the Enslaved Negroes in the British Dominions*, new edn. (Philadelphia Printed: London Reprinted and Sold by James Phillips, 1785), 3-4.

[41] Benezet, *A Caution to Great Britain and Her Colonies*, 27-28.

Statement One

How dreadful then is the Slave-Trade, whereby so many thousands of our fellow-creatures, free by nature, endued with the same rational faculties, and called to be heirs of the same salvation with us, lose their lives, and are truly, and properly speaking, murdered every year![42]

English Baptists likewise used "fellow creature" in the sense of an immortal soul with infinite value for whom Christ died. Possibly most clear was John Fawcett, Ward's mentor at Ewood Hall. Following William Carey's publication of his *Enquiry*, May 12, 1792,[43] Carey's Nottingham sermon, May 30, 1792, and Carey's departure for India with Dr. John Thomas, John Fawcett most eloquently affirmed:

Ought not the love of Christ, and a sincere regard for the welfare of immortal souls, to constrain us chearfully to exert ourselves to the utmost in such a case?

The souls of all men are equally precious. They are endowed with capacities and powers capable of being conformed to the great Creator's image; of being made happy in the enjoyment of his favour, and of partaking of all the felicity of his heavenly kingdom, through eternal ages. The soul of a *Negro*, a *Hindoo*, or even of a *Hottentot*, is of equal value with that of the most enlightened European.

That God who has made of one blood all nations of men on the face of the earth, requires us to look upon the most abject of our fellow-mortals as brethren. One God is our creator, our preserver and upholder; from one flock we originally sprung, and to sovereign judge we are all accountable.[44]

As early as 1788, William Carey used "fellow creature" to affirm his belief that the Gospel should go to the whole world. In a letter to his father, Carey wrote about "a Soul that's Destitute of Christ in all the World" - "The tho't of a Fellow Creature Perishing for Ever should rouse all our

---

[42] Benezet, *A Caution to Great Britain and Her Colonies*, 40.
[43] *Leicester Herald*, May 12, 1792.
[44] John Fawcett, *Considerations Relative to the Sending of Missionaries to Propagate the Gospel among the Heathen* (Leeds: Printed by Thomas Wright, 1793), 4.

The Serampore Form of Agreement

Activity and engage all our Powers."[45] Likely relying on the King James Bible's rendering of Jesus' statement, "preach the gospel to every creature" (Mark 16:15), Carey wrote of "our fellow creatures, whose souls are as immortal as ours."[46] Just nine months after the publication of Carey's *Enquiry*, the Harvey Lane Baptist Church, Leicester, in which Carey served as pastor, included a note in its Minute Book about Carey: "Mr. Carey our Minister left Lster [Leicester] to go on mission to the East Indies in order to take the Gospel amongst the Poore Heathen this is inserted to show the love he had to the Souls of his fellow Creatures."[47]

Fuller also employed "fellow creatures" when he wrote:

The brutality with which millions of our fellow creatures have been torn from their connexions, bound in irons, thrown into a floating dungeon, sold in the public markets, beaten, maimed, and many of them murdered for trivial offences, and all this without any effectual restraint from the laws, must load our national character with everlasting infamy.[48]

Samuel Pearce prayed that he "felt the aggregate value of their immortal souls," that is, "the millions of heathen."[49] In short, "fellow creature" and "infinite value upon immortal souls" seem practically synonymous.

Within six months of his arrival in India, Ward narrated his observation of "the dead body of a fellow-creature lay[ing] for the dogs to devour"[50] while all in the village ignored the corpse. If such a person merited the phrase "fellow creature," then *all* persons—Europeans, Africans, and Indians—actually *were* persons in the image of God who could "experience

---

[45] William Carey, Moulton, to Edmund Carey, January 12, 1788, in Terry G. Carter, ed., *The Journal and Selected Letters of William Carey* (Macon, GA: Smyth & Helwys, 2000), 72.

[46] Carey, *An Enquiry*, 69.

[47] Church Covenant, March 24, 1793. Harvey Lane Baptist Church, Leicester, Mss., The Record Office for Leicestershire, Leicester & Rutland.

[48] Andrew Fuller, *The Gospel Its Own Witness; or, The Holy Nature, and Divine Harmony of the Christian Religion, Contrasted with the Immorality and Absurdity of Deism*, 2nd edn. (Clipstone: Printed at the Office of J. W. Morris, 1800), 109-110.

[49] "Diary of Samuel Pearce," October 10, 1794, in *Memoirs of the Late Rev. Samuel Pearce, A. M. Minister of the Gospel in Birmingham; With Extracts from Some of His Most Interesting Letters. Compiled by Andrew Fuller* (Clipstone: Printed by J. W. Morris, 1800), 120.

[50] Friday, May 2, 1800. *Ward's Journal*, I, 82.

Statement One

the blessedness that is in Christ."[51] However, Ward was realistic and not naïve about the difficulty of missionary work with immortal souls. He admitted, "Every conversation that I have with the natives makes me perceive more & more at what a distance these immense multitudes of immortals are from embracing the truth as it is in Jesus."[52] Nevertheless, the seriousness of the phrase "infinite value" is clear in Ward's use of it regarding Jesus. In conversation with a Hindu man named Arungdhose, Ward said, "I shewed him the infinite value of Xt. & the vanity of all earthly good."[53] If Christ himself had "infinite value," then Ward's important—yet equivocal—usage of that phrase for "immortal souls" *in need of Christ* seems obvious.

"*An Unconverted Soul Launched into Eternal Punishment.*"—Another teleological identification in the "great and solemn work" was the affecting of "our mind with the dreadful loss sustained by an unconverted soul launched into eternity." In conjunction with being an immortal soul, one's relation to Christ determined whether one received eternal life with Christ or eternal punishment apart from Christ. This dualism of accountability was *unlike* either Plato's doctrine of the immortal soul or the Hindu doctrine of the transmigration of the soul leading toward *moksha* (i.e., release from the perpetual reincarnation process).[54] By contrast, the missionaries affirmed the necessity of individuals' exercise of accountability before God in Christ.

The literary parallelism of "to affect our minds with the dreadful loss," "to fix in our minds the awful doctrine of eternal punishment," "to realize frequently the inconceivably awful condition of this vast country," and "mourn over their miserable condition" is repetitive, memorable, and full of sentiment. The three infinitives convey the intentional operations of the

---

[51] Statement Nine.
[52] Wednesday, September 28, 1803. *Ward's Journal*, II, 327.
[53] Monday, November 7, 1803. *Ward's Journal*, II, 345.
[54] Plato, *Phaedo* 69E-84B; *Bhagavad Gita*, 2.22. Cf. William Ward, *A View of the History, Literature, and Religion of the Hindoos: Including a Minute Description of their Manners and Customs, and Translations from their Principal Works*, 2nd edn. (Serampore: Printed at the Mission Press, 1818), 2:347-366.

mind in provoking, establishing, and knowing the eternal result of non-conversion to Christ, which causes the pain of mourning. Among the infinitival phrases, the middle idea "eternal punishment" offers the actual meaning of both "dreadful loss" and "awful condition;" these three infinitives could function as a chiasmus with the first and last infinitives being defined by the central concept of "eternal punishment." The missionaries' awareness of others' "eternal punishment"[55] incentivized them in their missionary work. The reason for such concern concurred with Fuller's comment, "Love to a fellow creature will render every thing we do subservient to the object."[56] If people love *the other*, they will try to relieve the option of a "dreadful loss" and "awful condition" of "eternal punishment" for *the other*. The Serampore missionaries battled the embrace of the "wicked one" while offering Jesus' open arms of blessing.[57] "[I]n spite of ... the Devil our Saviour openeth & no more shutteth."[58]

The "eternal punishment" of sinners is evident from the missionaries' perspective. Early in his journal, Carey wrote, "Lord's day – all the Morning I had a most unpleasant time, but at last found much pleasure in reading Edwards *on the Justice of God in the Damnation of Sinners.*"[59] Carey's "pleasure" with this text certainly did not include rejoicing over anyone's eternal punishment. Instead, his pleasure was with Edwards's exposition of Romans 2–3 with its empirical focus on the universal sinful nature of Jew and Gentile that necessarily identifies *all* people of all times as sinners under judgment by God. Such an identity reveals the need for Christ as the

---

[55] See Matthew 25:41, 46; Hebrews 6:2; Jude 7.

[56] Andrew Fuller, "The Nature and Importance of Love to God," in Andrew Gunton Fuller, *The Complete Works of the Rev. Andrew Fuller with a Memoir of His Life* (London: G. and J. Dyer, 1846), 621.

[57] For "the wicked one," see Matthew 13:19, 38; 1 John 2:13, 14; 3:12; 5:18. The phrase "lying in the arms of the wicked one" appears in some Methodist literature of the eighteenth century, but Ward may have noticed it in John Bunyan, *The Pilgrim's Progress ... Part I, To Which are Added Notes by Mr. William Mason, Recommended by the Rev. Mr. Ryland, of Northampton* (London: Printed for Alex. Hogg, 1784), 10, n. (b).

[58] Tuesday, May 12, 1801. *Ward's Journal*, I, 153. See Revelation 3:7.

[59] William Carey, January 26, 1794, *Journal*, Baptist Missionary Society Archives, 16. Cf. Jonathan Edwards, "The Justice of God in the Damnation of Sinners," in Sermons and Discourses, 1734–1738, in *The Works of Jonathan Edwards*, vol. 19, ed. M. X. Lesser (New Haven: Yale University Press, 2001), 340–377; available online at the Jonathan Edwards Center, http://edwards.yale.edu/.

only "Savior from deserved punishment."[60] "How reasonable are Christ's terms, who offers to save all those that willingly, or with a good will, accept of him for their Savior!"[61]

Such arguments had precedent and cultural influence from confessional sources. The Anglican Thirty-Nine Articles stated that every person born "deserveth God's Wrath and Damnation."[62] The Baptist Second London Confession affirmed that Adam, Eve, and their descendants are "by nature children of wrath, the servants of sin, the subjects of death, and all other miseries, spiritual, temporal, and eternal, unless the Lord Jesus set them free."[63] In 1791, the Harvey Lane Church, Leicester, where William Carey served as pastor, issued its "Covenant," which says "all rational Creatures are under indispensable obligation to obey the law of God ... but ... all men have broke(n) it and are liable to eternal Punishment."[64]

The word "unconverted" appears only once in SFA, but the nominal "convert" and the adjectival "converted" appear eight times in reference to native Indians who became Christians. Possibly informing the common missionary rhetoric was "I teach transgressors thy ways; and sinners shall be converted unto thee."[65] As a result, Statement One focuses on the logical consequence for every individual immortal soul who is *not* a Christian convert. Ward summarized his view in conversation with Boxoo, a native Hindu: "Well, Boxoo; you and all of us are sinners; can you tell me how sin can go away. He answered – "Nay-Sahib." I assured him that the punishment of hell was eternal ... I said, you have heard of the incarnation, sufferings & death of Jesus Xt. – Without him there is no Saviour."[66]

Despite Boxoo's view, Ward encountered other Hindus who denied eternal punishment yet believed that Christ's death resulted in all people

---

[60] Edwards, "The Justice of God in the Damnation of Sinners," 361.
[61] Edwards, "The Justice of God in the Damnation of Sinners," 362.
[62] *Thirty-Nine Articles*, IX.
[63] *The London Baptist Confession of Faith* (1689), 6.3.
[64] Church Covenant, Harvey Lane Baptist Church, Leicester.
[65] Psalm 51:13 (KJB); other similar texts include Psalm 19:7; Isaiah 1:27; 6:10; 60:5; Matthew 13:15; 18:13; Mark 4:12; Luke 22:32; John 12:40; Acts 3:19; 28:27; James 5:19-20.
[66] Friday, June 26, 1801. *Ward's Journal*, I, 161.

being liberated at the day of judgment.[67] Of interest for eternal punishment is the metaphor of "launched into eternity." Ward's mentor John Fawcett had a previous similar point:

> Now that I am upon the verge of eternity, and perhaps just going to launch into the visible world, I can find consolation in nothing short of this precious truth:—complete, entire, everlasting satisfaction made for sin, by the death of Christ.[68]
> His [Christ's] merits are my anchor, when I launch into the boundless ocean of eternity.[69]

"Awful ... awful ... awful."—The enormous number of unconverted people and the pain they endure caused Ward to use the language of sentiment in Statement One: "the awful doctrine of eternal punishment," "the inconceivably awful condition of this vast country,"[70] and "this awful sense of the value of souls." Ward used "awful" in its sense of "full of awe" or "reverential fear"[71] for souls without Christ. The missionaries required effort to "endeavour to affect" their minds with that horror or to allow that "affect" to motivate them "to proclaim the glad tidings of salvation." For the missionaries, *care for the others' eternal destiny* demanded their engagement in proclamation.

Missionary efforts, such as social improvement, nutritional and medical intervention, and education, *resulted from* the value of souls potentially suffering eternal punishment. If the missionaries worked only on these latter activities without the former, then it would be better for them to be "in any other situation" than that of a missionary. Without "the awful sense

---

[67] Thursday, November 15, 1804. *Ward's Journal*, II, 396.

[68] John Fawcett, *The Sick Man's Employ: or, Views of Death and Eternity Realised, Occasioned by a Violent Fit of the Stone*, new edn. (Halifax: Printed by Holden and Dowson, 1800), 27-28. This book originally appeared in 1774.

[69] Fawcett, *The Sick Man's Employ*, 108.

[70] In Brown, *The History of the Propagation of Christianity* (1823), and Brown, *History of the Propagation of Christianity* (1854), "awful condition" became "dreadful condition," and "awful sense" became "deep sense."

[71] Johnson, "awe," "awful," *A Dictionary of the English Language*.

of the value of souls," all other activity related to their missionary work could not "feel aright."[72]

Natives' "recovery" from awful eternal punishment could parallel "the sottish and brutalized Britons ... [who] sit in heavenly places."[73] Here, the argument was that if the "dull, stupid, ... senseless,"[74] and assaulted ancient Britons could respond to the Gospel in the Middle Ages,[75] then native Indians could do so as well. Ward's language of caring sentiment for "the others" and the use of "feel" appears in this *equivalent comparison* of European and sub-continental peoples' needs. William Carey had used the word "feel" *frequently* as an equivalent for thoughts, emotions, or spirituality ("Felt not much spirituality to Day;"[76] "felt some new devotedness of God"[77]). Such emotional language in Carey and SFA compared to the eighteenth and early nineteenth century's broader cultural focus—Christian and non-Christian—on sympathy for others as a moral incentive regarding one's fellow creatures.[78]

The sentimental rhetoric continues with two parallel wishes: "Oh! may our hearts bleed[79] over these poor idolaters ... may their case lie with continued weight on our minds," and the graphic verb "we mourn over their miserable condition." The interjection "Oh!" appears four times in SFA,

---

[72] Capitalized "Missionary" here in SFA, 1805. Nineteenth century SFA editions except for 1831, Boston editions, 1874 Calcutta, and 1885 London removed the capitalization. Separately, SFA, 1823, changed the text to read "would have been better for us to have held any other office."

[73] Statement One. For "to sit heavenly places in Christ Jesus," see Ephesians 2:6. The use of "sottish" may derive from Jeremiah 4:22, "For my people is foolish, they have not known me; they are sottish children." The spelling of "brutalized" changed to "brutalised" in Smith, *The Life of William Carey*, 442.

[74] "Sottish" was "Dull; stupid; senseless; infatuate; doltish," Johnson, *A Dictionary of the English Language*, vol. 2.

[75] See Carey, *An Enquiry*, 33, 69 ("barbarous *Britons*"), 87.

[76] June 28, 1794, *Carey's Journal*, 65.

[77] August 31, 1794, *Carey's Journal*, 79.

[78] See David Hume, *An Enquiry Concerning the Principles of Morals* (London: Printed for A. Millar, 1751), 1-9, 101, 197-199, and Adam Smith, *The Theory of Moral Sentiments*, 2nd edn. (London: Printed for A. Millar, 1761), 1-10, 116, 155.

[79] In Bunyan, *The Pilgrim's Progress*, 215, Christian says, "it makes my heart bleed to think that he [Christ] should bleed for me."

and each occurrence conveys a strong emotional focus of concerned eagerness.[80] Like uses of the interjection appear in Ward's journal, such as "Oh! that they were won for Xt."[81] In addition, the emotional language intensifies with Statement One's triad: "poor idolaters," "miserable condition," and "slaves of superstition." Using such language affected readers' *pathos* for immortal Indian natives.

Though "Paul" does not appear in Statement One, the scripture reference behind the sentence regarding travail and childbirth[82] is Galatians 4:19. Along with Jesus' command and example in preaching the Gospel, the missionary work of Paul became the foundational support for advocacy of missionary work. One purpose of framing the mind toward the other was so the missionaries could resemble "that eminent missionary," the apostle Paul. Paul's name or allusions to him through quoted scripture texts frequently appear in the SFA.[83]

If God could raise "the sottish and brutalized Britons," He likewise could raise Indian "slaves of superstition."[84] The raising of these slaves to Christ would "purify their hearts by faith"[85] to worship "the one God"[86] "in spirit and in truth."[87] Being "worshippers of the one true God" would preclude being "amongst the worshippers of Kallee" who set up "their

---

[80] Statement One; Five [2x]; Eleven. Ward used "Oh!" similarly in his letters; see Stennett, *Memoirs of the Life of the Rev. William Ward*, 58; 122-123. Subsequent to SFA in the span of a letter of 767 words, Ward used the emotional "Oh!" eight times; see "William Ward to [Mr.] Stewart in Calcutta," Serampore, Nov. 28, 1806, Angus Library, Regent's Park College, Oxford University, transcription by Peter de Vries.

[81] Monday, June 24, 1799. *Ward's Journal*, I, 20.

[82] The SFA 1823 edition changed the original word "travail" to "anxiety."

[83] Paul's name appears in the Preamble and Statements One, Three and Five, but his words and phrases appear in various statements (i.e., "instant in season and out of season" in Four, "eternal salvation" in Six, assuming Paul wrote Hebrews, "Epaphroditus, Phebe ..." in Eight, "instant in prayer" and "fervent in spirit" in Ten, "learn to be content" in Eleven). Carey, *An Enquiry*, title page, 10, 20-28, 71, 87, set the standard for appealing to Paul as the exemplary Christian missionary.

[84] "Superstition" features prominently in Ward's Journal, 1800-1805. In his entry for November 1, 1800—within the first year of his life in India—Ward described the people surrounding a Hindu temple as "They all seemed to be drunk with superstition." *Ward's Journal*, I, 110.

[85] Acts 15:9.

[86] Malachi 2:10; Mark 12:32; 1 Corinthians 8:6; 1 Timothy 2:5.

[87] John 4:24.

Statement One

own wives as the representatives of this goddess and worshipping them."[88] Native Hindu polytheism would be put away, and Hindu "gentiles" (Acts 15:6) would "purify their hearts by faith," thereby causing a union of two different societies (i.e., Western British and native Indian) on the analogy of the Jews and Gentiles in Acts 15.

Despite two nineteenth-century reprints of the SFA removing the last sentence from Statement One,[89] the sentence blends several prophetic Scripture texts affirming the hope for the arrival of the kingdom promised by Jesus.[90] Here at the end of Statement One, there is the prophetic fusion of Zephaniah 2:11, "he will famish all the gods,"[91] Isaiah 2:20, "cast ... idols ... to the moles and to the bats,"[92] and Isaiah 2:8 "the work of their own hands."[93] Taking Isaiah's and Zephaniah's texts, God's judgments originally directed at idolaters in Edom, Philistia,[94] Assyria, Moab, and Ammon[95] become focused on India. The missionaries agreed that God would starve, and thereby destroy, the polytheism of India, which, in turn, would cause individual natives to cast away and spiritually renounce the idols made with hands. Despite such stated optimism, Ward, in 1821, published his empirical assessment that upwards of "150,000,000 ... immortal beings have, every thirty years, been passing into eternity, like the worshippers of the goddess Diana, 'without God, without Christ, and without hope in the world."[96] Apart from those losses, the missionaries felt obligated and emotionally moved to proclaim "the glad tidings of salvation" to every immortal soul they could reach.

---

[88] Saturday, March 5, 1803. *Ward's Journal*, II, 285.
[89] See above, footnote 13.
[90] See, Carey, *An Enquiry*, 3, 5, 37, 66, 76, 82, 87.
[91] Cf. Statement Ten.
[92] Despite eighteenth and nineteenth century KJB reprints reading "to the moles and to the bats," SFA, 1806, 1814, 1816 (two eds.), 1826, and 1831 (two eds.) changed the text "to the moles and the bats." SFA 1874 and 1885 followed the 1805. I acknowledge Peter de Vries for locating the phrase's appearance in Samuel Powell, "Account of Mr. F[ernandez]," *Missionary Magazine* VI (1801): 253.
[93] Jeremiah 1:16; 25:14; and Acts 7:41 read "works," not "work" for a like phrase.
[94] Isaiah 2:6.
[95] Zephaniah 2:8-9,12-13.
[96] Ward, "Necessity of Christianity to India," 3. Ward used Ephesians 2:12 to identify the Ephesian worshippers of Diana (Acts 19:24-35) with the recipients of the Ephesian letter.

STATEMENT TWO

To Acquaint ourselves with the Snares which hold the Minds of the People

Joshua Bowman

The Serampore missionaries had strong theological convictions about the nature of God and the fate of those unconverted to the gospel of Jesus Christ. Furthermore, the missionaries were sure that God uses human instruments in his mission of reconciling people to himself. The introduction to the Serampore Form of Agreement (SFA) clarifies the missionaries' beliefs about God's sovereignty and humanity's dependence on his intervening grace.

Statement Two, concerning the understanding of local people and cultures, derives from the belief that humanity's greatest problem is sin that separates them from eternal life with their Creator. The SFA is a document built on a conversionist theology that prioritizes the proclamation of the gospel by the power of God's Spirit to bring those spiritually dead into a right relationship with their Redeemer, Jesus Christ. These deeply rooted Biblical beliefs provided the theological foundation for their commitments regarding missiological principles, initial plans, and missionary character.[1]

As stated in the previous chapter, Statement One shows the missionaries' high value on every human soul. Sympathy and grief over the hopeless spiritual condition of men and women are evident as they mention how their hearts bled over their eternal destiny. The missionaries' anger was toward the "wicked one" who blinded minds and held them in slavery to superstition, idolatry, and false worship. The physical and spiritual plight

---

[1] Samuel E. Masters, "'Will Anyone Say the Lord is not Among Us?' The Serampore Mission and its Covenant" (Ph.D. diss., The Southern Baptist Theological Seminary, Louisville, 2020), 148.

of Indian men and women weighed on the conscience of the Serampore missionaries. They felt a personal responsibility to work towards transforming the terrible conditions they observed. Suffering of all kinds touched their hearts, but Statement One clearly shows their greatest desire was for Indians to renounce their false idol worship and turn to the one true God.

Focus and Purpose

Theologians, mission practitioners, and social scientists may take particular interest in Statement Two because of the implications for anthropology, ethnography, religion, culture, language, and cross-cultural communication. The breadth of these topics may interest researchers, but the Serampore missionaries' theological motivations provide limits for this chapter. In Statement Two, the missionaries committed themselves to learning culture and religion by observation and conversation so they might commend themselves and the gospel message.

Statement Two provides a methodology and rationale for learning culture. The SFA does not provide action steps and detailed plans for daily activities. Instead, the statement gives overarching objectives and goals that provide an umbrella for strategically accomplishing their mission. The first step was to gain information for cultural awareness. Their commitment to learning sprang from the theological presupposition that "snares and delusions" were in the religious and cultural worldview of Indians.

Twice in this second statement, the missionaries articulate a desire to "converse" with the people to obtain knowledge and understanding. The following decades of ministry, research, and writing proved their commitment to listening and learning was not merely lip service. Many foreigners have idle curiosities about surface-level differences between cultures. Statement Two of the SFA shows a deeper resolve to understand how people thought and why they believed and behaved differently.

The authors of the SFA saw the potential danger of being categorized as irrelevant foreigners who did not understand local customs. A lack of understanding and community acceptance would perpetuate their alien status, thus robbing them of the opportunity for gospel impact. Therefore, they committed themselves to building relationships and credibility. They rightly assumed that trust would come by missionary adaptation to the culture, not by Indians conforming to Western expectations.

The SFA proposes a simple yet profound method: read their books and observe their manners and customs. The statement's rudimentary proposal may initially be unimpressive to anthropologists and ethnographic researchers. However, anyone visiting the archives at Serampore College today would be astounded by the depth and breadth of writing these missionaries bequeathed.

Commitment to Cultural Exegesis

The Serampore missionaries committed themselves to understanding a culture and context that was both complex and different from their own. These missionaries lived with the tension of being cultural outsiders who wanted to understand another culture. They compared their observations with Scripture and made moral judgments. These judgments led them to advocate for religious and social transformation. A challenge for foreign observers is the tendency to see differences as automatically wrong. Personal cultural values and preferences may lead to the mischaracterization of the new culture. Attitudes of superiority and control may surface, even if unintentionally.

Carey and his team were trailblazers who committed to cultural exegesis at the beginning of the "Great Century"[2] in global missions. Ed Stetzer describes cultural exegesis as follows:

> To exegete the culture is to study the setting in such a way that one receives guidance for understanding the meanings of cultural patterns, systems, and behaviors ... every culture is unique. And yet every culture has similarities to others. The result of the missional church planter's exegesis will be a cross-cultural understanding

---

[2] Kenneth Scott Latourette, *The Great Century: The Americas, Australia, and Africa A.D. 1800–A.D. 1914*, vol. 5 of *A History of The Expansion of Christianity* (New York: Harper & Brothers, 1943), 465–470.

The Serampore Form of Agreement

because in reality that's what we all are—products of many cultures with defining distinctives.³

The second statement of the SFA states the missionaries' commitment to observe what is happening in a different cultural context. Because of their perspective as cultural outsiders and their goal of gospel transformation, they wisely accepted their initial role as students of the people and their beliefs. Their evaluation of the customs was not always perfect, but their commitment was first to the authority of Scripture.

Their application of Scripture to Indian society would only come through proper understanding and evaluation. The danger for all missionaries, like the Serampore team, is the possibility of misapplying Scripture or importing extra-biblical requirements from another culture. Furthermore, a lack of cultural understanding may lead to an over-sympathetic understanding of another culture, or on the other hand, an uncritical evaluation of what is contrary to Scripture.

The SFA emphasizes that missionaries want to lead unbelievers to respond to divine revelation in God-honoring and culturally appropriate ways. Statement Two outlines an approach to the necessary element of contextualization, which Hesselgrave defines as "the attempt to communicate the message of the person, works, Word, and will of God in a way

---

³ Ed Stetzer, *Planting Missional Churches* (Nashville, TN: Broadman & Holman, 2006), 115-116. Kevin Vanhoozer provides the following summary of the goals of cultural exegesis: "Why should Christians read culture? To get understanding; to grasp the meaning of the complex whole that is our everyday environment, an ecosystem of meaning that inevitably shapes our imaginations and nurtures concrete forms of life. How should Christians read culture? By offering theologically thick (e.g., multiperspectival, multilayered, multidimensional) descriptions of everyday texts and trends, products and practices. Well and good. But the understanding of the world of cultural texts for which faith seeks must not end here. Faith's search for understanding of our everyday world is not merely theoretical. Everyday theologians must demonstrate their understanding in practice by becoming cultural agents. Indeed, if the church is a community of interpreters— of Scripture and of culture— it is for the sake of becoming an effective community of cultural agents. This involves, first, interpreting culture in light of a biblical-theological framework and, second, interpreting Scripture by embodying gospel values and truths in concrete cultural forms. The mission of the church is to witness to the truth of the gospel by participating in God's building project, realizing the well-wrought world redeemed in Christ." Kevin J. Vanhoozer, Charles A. Anderson, and Michael J. Sleasman, *Everyday Theology: How to Read Cultural Texts and Interpret* Trends (Grand Rapids, MI: Baker Academic, 2007), 54-55.

Statement Two

that is faithful to God's revelation, especially as it is put forth in the teachings of Holy Scripture, and that is meaningful to the respondents in their respective cultural and existential contexts."[4]

As the Serampore missionaries entered a Hindu society, they made decisions regarding rejecting, replacing, and modifying cultural traditions and practices. Missiologist Paul Hiebert refers to this process as critical contextualization.[5] Critical contextualization is not the blind acceptance or rejection of old beliefs of the community. Instead, missionary outsiders partner with local believers to continually test actions and beliefs against the norms of Scripture.

Practically, issues such as marriage, music, festivals, idolatry, birth, death, ancestors, medicine, and others confronted missionaries. Of course, the Serampore team had never dealt with many issues in their home country. Therefore, they committed themselves to cultural exegesis by observing and analyzing local customs and beliefs. Simultaneously, the missionaries sought to evaluate and subject their experiences to God's Word.[6] Initially, local believers were unavailable to partner in discerning the value of certain Indian customs and beliefs.

Commitment to Language Learning and Translation

In Statement Two of the SFA, the Serampore missionaries proposed the broad goal of learning the people and their ways by conversing with them regularly and studying their literature. One of the most prominent and effective ways the missionaries realized this goal was by thoroughly acquiring local languages. Bible translation has often been a hallmark of Christian

---

[4] David J. Hesselgrave and Edward Rommen, *Contextualization: Meanings, Methods, and Models* (Grand Rapids, MI: Baker Book House, 1989), 1-2.

[5] Paul G. Hiebert, "Critical Contextualization," *Anthropological Reflections on Missiological Issues* (Grand Rapids, MI: Baker Books, 1994), 75-92.

[6] David K. Clark, *To Know and Love God: Method for Theology* (Wheaton, IL: Crossway Books, 2003), 90. Clark describes evangelical commitments to theological contextualization by stating, "Theological contextualization addresses the concerns that arise in particular cultural contexts. It responds to those issues from Scripture. It demands obedience and spiritual sensitivity to the Holy Spirit's voice. It permits initial answers to emerge and take shape. It seeks dialogue with Christian in other contexts. And then it allows feedback loops to lead back to Scripture for fresh insight and wisdom. This dialogue leads to theological understanding that are both genuinely contemporary and solidly biblical. This is evangelical contextualization."

The Serampore Form of Agreement

missions since Christ commissioned his church (Matt 28:16-20). However, the signatories of the SFA did not merely adhere to a general translation commitment. In fact, for two centuries, the Serampore mission has served as an exemplar of the need to translate Scripture into local languages.

Learning local languages was never seen as an end but rather as a means to communicate a message. Daniel Potts, in his *British Missionaries in India 1793-1837*, emphasizes this fact by stating, "Translations of the Bible and other Christian literature were undertaken by the Baptists, as by other missionaries, for one overall purpose—to aid missionary attempts to spread the knowledge of Christianity throughout India."[7] Understanding the missionaries' motivation for language competence provides the proper perspective on how and why they endured such hardship to realize their ultimate goal. J.C. Marshman summarizes the intention of the Serampore team by saying,

> They regarded it as the duty of a missionary to obtain as complete a knowledge as possible of the language and religious institutions, the literature, and the philosophy of the people among whom he laboured, and to leave a record of his acquisitions, through the medium of the press, for the benefit of his successors. They considered that every contribution to this store of knowledge was an additional facility for the prosecution of missionary labours, and they were anxious that these researches should go hand-in-hand with the communication of secular and divine truth to the people.[8]

William Carey felt the need to learn Sanskrit, which is foundational for many other languages, such as Bengali, Oriya, Hindi, and Assamese. Carey's commitment to language fluency, paired with his natural linguistic abilities and facility with Biblical languages, made him the best available

---

[7] E. Daniel Potts, *British Baptist Missionaries in India, 1793-1837: The History of Serampore and its Missions* (London: Cambridge University Press, 1967), 79.

[8] Potts, *British Baptist Missionaries,* 112. Potts quotes from John Clark Marshman, *The Life and Times of Carey, Marshman, and Ward. Embracing the History of the Serampore Mission* (London: Longman, Brown, Green, Longmans, & Roberts, 1859), I, 465-466.

Statement Two

editor and judge of the quality of translation.[9] Together with the team of indigenous speakers, original drafts were regularly revised for accuracy and precision.

Another aspect of Statement Two that surfaces from translation work is the missionaries' commitment to converse with natives by partnering with Indian nationals. The Serampore missionaries' supporters in England often questioned the employment of Hindus in translation work, but they maintained enough confidence to continue their operations. One of the few images of William Carey shows him seated and pouring over his translation work while seated with a Hindu pandit.[10]

On the occasion of Carey's 250th birthday, several Christian and non-Christian commemorations were held in India. Commendations from Indian Hindus regarding language achievements carry a heavier weight than the expected appreciation by British Christians. The revered Indian Poet, Sir Rabindranath Tagore, said, "Carey was the pioneer of all the revived interest in the vernaculars."[11] In 1866, a Bengali social reformer, Keshub Chunder Sen, noted the gratitude of the country of India for the "various intellectual, social, and moral improvements which they have effected."[12] In Kolkata, a government official of West Bengal gave a speech honoring the achievement of Carey as a social reformer, linguist, educationalist, and botanist.[13] The governor spoke about the renaissance in Bengali literature and art in the early 20th century and linked Carey to this movement. While the speech did not focus on his evangelistic efforts, it did show Carey's broad impact through his commitment to learning and gaining information about the Bengali people.

---

[9] Potts, *British Baptist Missionaries*, 82-83. H. H. Wilson remarked he was "placed high amongst the most distinguished of our Sanskrit scholars." E. Carey, *Memoir of William Carey, D. D., Late missionary to Bengal, Professor of Oriental Languages in the College of Fort William, Calcutta* (London: Jackson & Walford, 1836), 587, 590.

[10] Potts, *British Baptist Missionaries*, 80-85.

[11] Potts, *British Baptist Missionaries*, 94. S. Pearce Carey, "New Light on Dr. Carey," *Baptist Quarterly* 1.7 (1923), 314-321.

[12] Potts, *British Baptist Missionaries*, 62, quoting Keshub Chunder Sen, *Jesus Christ: Europe and Asia* (London: John Snow & Co., 1866), 17.

[13] This lecture was attended by the author, Joshua Bowman. The event was held in August 2011 at the G.D. Birla Sabhagar Auditorium which is located in the basement of the Birla Temple in Kolkata.

The Serampore Form of Agreement

Discernment of Snares and Delusions

The SFA shows a dual commitment to cultural understanding and theological conviction. Statement One clearly states that the unconverted are separate from God and need salvation. Statement Two, the focus of this chapter, displays a desire to learn. The missionaries did not merely come as students of religion. They went with the Biblical presupposition that idolatry is grievously corrupt. Statement Three shows that this is not mere cultural arrogance and bigotry because they committed to abstaining from personal manners and customs that would unnecessarily offend nationals. The missionaries desired to remove cultural offenses while refusing to remove the actual stumbling block, which is the gospel of Jesus Christ.

The information gathering proposed in the first sentence of Statement Two is not merely a commitment to observe and describe what another culture is doing. Collecting field research to build an ethnographic profile was not their goal. Instead, they wanted to understand the "snares and delusions" related to their belief system and worship practices so they could better communicate the message of the cross.

Sixteen years after the SFA, William Ward published *Farewell Letters*, where he attempted "an abstract of the philosophical doctrines most popular among the Hindoos, and a very rapid sketch of the moral state of those who lived and died under the full influence of these theories."[14] Ward describes how Hindu teachers emphasize the deity of every person and that emancipation from suffering comes from endless cycles of birth and rebirth.[15] Ward laments the 100 million Hindus deceived by this teaching and ends by remembering the glorious gospel.

The Hindu practice of sati was the practice that most impacted the Serampore team and caused them to work for social reform and government involvement. Ward describes the fate of many Hindu women of his day by writing, "But the awful state of female society in this miserable country appears in nothing so much as in dooming the female, the widow,

---

[14] William Ward, *Farewell Letters to a Few Friends in Britain and America, on returning to Bengal in 1821* (New York: Bliss & White, 1821), 42.

[15] Ward, *Farewell Letters*, 44.

Statement Two

to be burnt alive with the putrid carcass of her husband. The Hindoo legislators have sanctioned this immolation, showing herein a studied determination to insult and degrade woman."[16]

Ward writes with deep grief about his presence at the burning of three widows.[17] He describes the horrific scenes of a mother forced to participate against her will and how her son lights the funeral pyre. Ward rails against a religion that would approve of this conduct and his own British government that allowed it to continue during these early years.

Ward's descriptions of the horrors of human sacrifices by hooks and the shrieks of widows at sati are agonizing.[18] Modern minds may first judge Statement Two for its seeming intolerance for speaking of "snares and delusions." However, his eyewitness accounts of these atrocities in the name of Hindu deities provide an essential perspective.

Ward's letters show the commitment of the missionaries in the intervening years to study and translate Hindu writings. His disdain for illicit sexual references leads him to conclude, "What must we think then, what must we feel, when reading the history of the Hindoo deities; when the object of worship appears before us as the personification of sin itself."[19] Ward admits the purpose of his strong tone by saying, "I hope I shall be forgiven for venturing thus far to expose their abominations. It is because they are connected with what should be divine worship, that I cannot be wholly silent on this painful subject."[20] Ward's statement reminds us of the purposeful study of culture and the more profound desire to understand the religious beliefs of those they encountered. Ward's vivid descriptions were not a publicity stunt. Instead, it shows his heartfelt concern for the spiritual condition of Indian men and women.

Commitment to Cultural Learning

Before becoming a missionary, Carey wrote in his famous *Enquiry* of his conviction about learning the language and culture of the people. Carey said,

---

[16] Ward, *Farewell Letters*, 68.
[17] Ward, *Farewell Letters*, 69.
[18] Ward, *Farewell Letters*, 78–87.
[19] Ward, *Farewell Letters*, 89–90.
[20] Ward, *Farewell Letters*, 92.

The Serampore Form of Agreement

As to learning their languages, the same means would be found necessary here as in trade between different nations. In some cases interpreters might be obtained, who might be employed for a time; and where these were not to be found, the missionaries must have patience, and mingle with the people, till they have learned so much of their language as to be able to communicate their ideas to them in it. It is well known to require no very extraordinary talents to learn, in the space of a year, or two at most, the language of any people upon earth.[21]

Carey was confident that the means of language learning would serve the ends of communicating the gospel of Jesus Christ. As early as 1792, Carey acknowledged that any culture could understand and come to the knowledge of the truth. The challenge was that the people were held by false religions, ungodly customs, and ignorance of the way of salvation.[22]

The fourth section of Carey's *Enquiry* is titled: "The Practicality of something being done, more than what is done, for the Conversion of the Heathen."[23] This section of his writing acknowledges distances of geography and culture that must be overcome. According to him, men motivated by commercial interests have made this adjustment. Therefore, ministers of the gospel must do no less. Carey was not interested in weak excuses that would keep ministers in England. He points to Paul as an example of suffering and reminds the church of his day that they were to be soldiers willing to endure hardship.[24]

Carey's writing in *The Enquiry* provides a clear window into his own biblical, theological, and missiological motivations before drafting the SFA. Ward's *Farewell Letters* provide a glimpse into the post-agreement outcomes as he reflects theologically on his own experiences and observations.

---

[21] William Carey, *An Enquiry into the Obligations of Christians to Use Means for the Conversion of the Heathens* (Leicester: Ann Ireland, 1792), 74.
[22] Carey, *An Enquiry*, 62-65.
[23] Carey, *An Enquiry*, 67
[24] Carey, *An Enquiry*, 71-73, 81-82.

Statement Two

Commitment to Converse Intelligently

The second statement of the SFA agreement contains only 130 words, but twice in this short section, the missionaries state their commitment to "conversing." The first mention concerns the ability of the missionaries to converse in an "intelligible manner." This will only come by careful study of the culture and acquisition of the language. The second mention refers to how their knowledge of customs and religion will come "by conversing with sensible natives, by reading some parts of their works, and by attentively observing their manners and customs."[25]

The focus on conversing acknowledges the need for dialogue because an important message must be accurately communicated. The Serampore team's commitment to conversing was a means of fostering relationships to gain an understanding of the local cultural and religious context. Their faith in the gospel and the urgent need for unbelievers to hear and believe led them to prioritize intentional listening and learning. While Carey and his colleagues did not use the term contextualization, that is what they sought to do. Contextualization is the process whereby the messenger seeks to faithfully communicate the gospel's message in an understandable way to the audience. Scripture is the anchor, and the message must remain faithful to this singular authority. The goal of gospel proclamation is that the audience would hear, believe, and respond in worship and obedience. Ward's eleventh Farewell Letter addresses young missionary students who may soon enter foreign fields. He lays out a plan for dialogue once these students gain a basic grasp of the language. In the following portion of the letter, Ward highlights simple dialogue as a critical component of missionary entrance by stating,

> When you can understand the natives, endeavor to obtain from them an account of their religion; its theory, ceremonies, &c. Statements made by themselves will be more correct than what you can find in books; and, in gaining the relation from one upon whom the system has made a strong impression, you will find matter for thought, for sermon, and for prayer, which you could obtain by no other process.[26]

---

[25] Statement Two.
[26] Ward, *Farewell Letters*, 195.

The Serampore Form of Agreement

Ward, Carey, and the other Serampore missionaries were not simply academics interested in learning for the sake of learning. Learning would not come primarily from books but through intentional time and relationships with Indians. Learning and dialogue served the missionary impulse—gospel proclamation for personal and societal transformation.

Commitment to Dispersing Knowledge

Statement Two expresses a missionary motivation to acquire cultural, linguistic, and religious understanding. This understanding was helpful for their efforts around the central activity of Bible translation. However, the missionaries also utilized the printing press at Serampore to circulate other literature. Daniel Potts summarized their achievements by stating:

> They systematized many languages, enlarging their scope to express a wide variety of ideas; compiled and printed grammars, dictionaries, and schoolbooks which gave a tremendous foundation for literary development; printed the first vernacular newspaper which set a worthy example to its many successors; and, among still other things, established presses which made possible a hitherto unprecedented circulation of their own and others' productions.[27]

Carey and his associates worked to gain an audience for themselves and the gospel but were simultaneously committed to the transformation and improvement of Indian society. Carey had an aptitude for botany, and his botanical garden at Serampore was well known. He wrote to botanists worldwide and was instrumental in the foundation of The Agricultural Society of India.[28] Carey also contributed to forestry by printing an article in the *Asiatick Researches* about the types of trees that might thrive in Bengal.[29] While contributions of this sort were subsidiary to gospel advance, they were part of the missionaries' overall desire to promote the flourishing of the society where they served.[30]

---

[27] Potts, *British Baptist Missionaries*, 113.
[28] Potts, *British Baptist Missionaries*, 70-74.
[29] William Carey, "Remarks on the State of Agriculture, in the District of Dinajpur" *Asiatick Researches*, X (1808), 1-27.
[30] Potts, *British Baptist Missionaries*, 75.

Statement Two

The previously mentioned study by Ward, *A View of the History, Literature, and Mythology of the Hindoos*, was the most robust phenomenological study of Hindu culture and religion of the time. Potts acknowledges that a modern reader of Ward's text "might feel that *Hindoos* is an overly-critical and biased study encompassing only the Hindus of Bengal and hardly able to fulfill its claimed object of the time, that of correcting 'the mistaken notions, that too many individuals had been led to form' of Hinduism's 'simple, mild and virtuous' character."[31] Admittedly, Ward's tone and limited perspective are weaknesses. Nonetheless, Potts provides a tempered yet appreciative evaluation of Ward's book:

> Despite its undoubted flaws the descriptive parts of Ward's *Hindoos* remain unrivalled as a repository of detailed information, and it is an indispensable work on early nineteenth-century society and religion in Bengal, as seen by a highly literate non-official European of the time, who had intimate contact with the society about which he wrote.[32]

Ward's descriptions and eyewitness accounts provide invaluable insights that show how the Serampore missionaries accomplished the stated objective of Statement Two—namely, observing and conversing with the people. Pott's evaluation of Ward's "intimate contact with the society" reinforces this claim.

---

[31] Potts, *British Baptist Missionaries*, 93. Abbé Dubois was a contemporary who took a similar phenomenological approach. His book *Hindu Manners*, based on his manuscripts, was published posthumously. Abbé Dubois, *Hindu Manners, Customs, and Ceremonies*, 2nd edn., trans. Henry K. Beauchamp (Oxford: Clarendon Press, 1899). For the Serampore missionaries' interaction with Dubois see, Marshman, *Life and Times*, II, 294-295. Abbé J.A. Dubois, *Letters on the State of Christianity in India; in which the Conversion of the Hindoos is considered as impracticable. To which is added A Vindication of the Hindoos, Male and Female, in answer to a severe attack made upon both by the Reverend ****** (London: Longman, Hurst, Orme, Brown, and Green, 1823). For Joshua Marshman's response to Dubois, see "Letters of the State of Christianity in India." *Friend of India* (Quarterly), X (1824), 187-392; James Hough, *A Reply to the Letters of the Abbé Dubois on the State of Christianity in India* (London: L.B. Seeley & Son, 1824).

[32] Potts, *British Baptist Missionaries*, 94.

The Serampore Form of Agreement

In achieving their Bible translation objectives, the Serampore missionaries contributed to advancing many Indian languages. Carey and his colleagues contributed dictionaries, grammars, and translations that aided Indian society and the British government. In addition, Carey's role as a professor at the College of Fort William provided him with the credentials, influence, and opportunities to promote the Bengali language.[33] While Carey was not welcomed initially by the British, their need for civil servants to learn local languages led to an unlikely partnership.

Literature rolling off the press at Serampore was not merely religious. In the opening decades of the 19th century, Baptist missionaries were key contributors of educational materials in the Bengali language.[34] Felix Carey contributed translations in history, science, and philosophy. While missionaries alone should not be credited with the health and revitalization of Bengali literature, their writing contributions and printed distributions are noteworthy.

Commitment to Indigeneity

The second statement of the SFA reveals the missionaries' concern for their acceptance and, even more importantly, the acceptance of the gospel itself. The missionaries positively stated their concern to "gain their attention to our discourse." The error they sought to avoid was "being barbarians to them."[35] The third statement of the SFA explicitly states their plan to curb any manners or customs that would unnecessarily hinder their relationships or the gospel's advance. It commends the Moravians and Quakers' methods, who followed Paul's pattern by adapting to cross-cultural contexts to win others to Christ (1 Cor 9:19–23).

Central to missions is the reality that God sends ambassadors who invite those separated from God to be reconciled by the person and work of Christ (2 Cor 5:14–21). Missionaries, such as the Serampore team, operate in an environment of cross-cultural tensions as they cross linguistic, geographic, and cultural boundaries to proclaim a universally trustworthy and

---

[33] Potts, *British Baptist Missionaries*, 94–96. Timothy George, *Faithful Witness: The Life and Mission of William Carey* (Birmingham, AL: New Hope, 1991), 145–148.
[34] Potts, *British Baptist Missionaries*, 98.
[35] Statement Two.

relevant message. The stated challenge that Statement Two seeks to avoid is the perception by nationals that the message and messengers are foreign and irrelevant.

The Serampore missionaries followed the example of Paul by placing the primary responsibility upon themselves to learn, adapt, and communicate effectively. The repeated statements about dialogue and understanding explicitly show this commitment. First, missionaries work to remain faithful and accurate to the gospel because salvation depends on the veracity of the message. Then that message must be communicated in a way that is clearly understood. For men and women to respond to God's revelation of himself humbly and obediently, they must understand what he has said and how they should respond.

The Serampore Baptists' desire to avoid alien and barbarian status is consistent with the indigenizing principle popularized by Andrew Walls in the late 20th century. The indigenizing principle recognizes that the gospel may be faithfully lived out in culturally distinct contexts. Walls explains, "God accepts us as we are, on the ground of Christ's work alone ... God accepts us together with our group relations; with that cultural conditioning that makes us feel at home in our part of human society and less at home in another."[36] Furthermore, Walls notes that each person "has been formed by his own culture and history, and since God has accepted him as he is, his Christian mind will continue to be influenced by what was in it before. And this is as true for groups as for persons."[37] Timothy Tennent adds, "The indigenizing principle is the particular force of the gospel that reminds us that the gospel really does penetrate and become rooted in the specific particularities of our cultural life. We live out our Christian lives within specific contexts, each of which has its own peculiar challenges and opportunities."[38]

Another way of understanding this part of the SFA statement is to appreciate how the gospel is at home in many different contexts. Cultural

---

[36] Andrew F. Walls, *The Missionary Movement in Christian History: Studies in the Transmission of Faith* (Maryknoll, NY: Orbis, 2000), 7.

[37] Walls, *The Missionary Movement*, 8.

[38] Timothy C. Tennent, *Theology in the Context of World Christianity: How the Global Church Is Influencing the Way We Think about and Discuss Theology* (Grand Rapids, MI: Zondervan, 2007), 12.

differences between the messenger and recipients of the gospel have sometimes led to the imposition of foreign cultural values on new believers. These extra-biblical requirements have been impediments to the gospel. Foreigners may unnecessarily reject parts of culture they do not understand or value. Differences that may be morally neutral may be rejected by the cultural outsider, alienating the intended audience. Paternalism is the ugly side of missions where foreigners are treated as children and expected to conform to the norms of the cultural outsider.

The indigenous principle that says the gospel should feel at home is in tension with the pilgrim principle that says this world is not our true home. This tension is present in Statement Two because the Serampore missionaries wanted to avoid being "barbarians" while acknowledging that the worldview of the Indians was alien to them. The missionaries unabashedly worked for worldview, cultural, and religious transformation. The judgment of the Baptists, based on the authority of Scripture, is that they are dealing with unbelievers caught up in idolatry. Therefore, removing all tensions is not the goal of Statement Two. Furthermore, peace and understanding cannot come at the expense of theological compromise.

The pilgrim principle reminds believers that their true citizenship is in heaven, and we are only sojourners on earth, awaiting the kingdom of God. Walls clarifies that the pilgrim principle "whispers to [the pilgrim] that he has no abiding city and warns him that to be faithful to Christ will put him out of step with his society."[39] Because the primary allegiance of Christians is to Christ, disciples will reject aspects of their old culture and worldview that are inconsistent with Scripture.

The Apostle Peter reminds believers that God calls them and constitutes them as a new people, called out of darkness to proclaim his excellencies (1 Pet 2:9-11). Likewise, Paul reminds the church at Ephesus of their situation before Christ by stating, "remember that you were at that time separated from Christ, alienated from the commonwealth of Israel and strangers to the covenants of promise, having no hope and without

---

[39] Walls, *The Missionary Movement*, 8.

God in the world" (Eph 2:13). While the word "heathen," may sound uncouth to modern ears, the evaluation of the spiritual condition of unbelievers by the Serampore missionaries is consistent with Scripture.

The commitment to learning and communication reveals the overarching goal of the Serampore group's mission. They wanted to say with Paul, "So then you are no longer strangers and aliens, but you are fellow citizens with the saints and members of the household of God, built on the foundation of the apostles and prophets, Christ Jesus himself being the cornerstone" (Eph 2:19-20). While the gospel may be lived out in various contexts without imposing a mono-cultural framework, this broken world is not the final home for the children of God. Walls summarizes, "The faith of Christ is infinitely translatable, it creates 'a place to feel at home.' But it must not make a place where we are so much at home that no one else can live there. Here we have no abiding city."[40]

Conclusion

The second statement of the SFA rests upon theological convictions about the centrality of the gospel message and salvation in the name of Christ alone. This foundation undergirded the Serampore missionaries' commitment to learning the language, culture, and worldview of the Indian people. Their purposeful acquisition of the language and culture was an intentional strategy to garner trust to communicate the gospel successfully. The Serampore team's commitment to observation and conversation shaped the trajectory of their ministry and continues to offer an example for cross-cultural missions today.

---

[40] Walls, *The Missionary Movement*, 25.

STATEMENT THREE

Abstaining from Whatever Deepens Prejudice Against the Gospel

Johnson Thomaskutty

Though often overshadowed by the glorious names of William Carey (1761–1834) and Joshua Marshman (1768–1837), William Ward (1769–1823) contributed remarkably to the history of Protestant missions in India. Formulated by Ward, the *Serampore Form of Agreement* (SFA)[1] constitutes one of the most important parts of that contribution. The SFA connects the past, present, and future of Christian missions in India. It laid out the principles, philosophies, and strategies of the Baptist Missionary Society.[2] In the process, it opened a new perspective for missionary activities in a multicultural, multireligious, and pluralistic context. As a result, it can be taken even today as a manual for mission practice.

The third of the eleven statements that compose the SFA focuses on principles for building relationships between the missionaries and the local communities while avoiding damaging prejudices.[3] This chapter's task is threefold: to understand the relationship between the foreign missionaries and the native communities, to analyze the meaning of the Third Statement of the SFA, and to describe the significance of the Third Statement in the context of the Serampore Mission's history and the future of missions. The following questions require special attention. First, how did the

---

[1] Also known as the Serampore Covenant.
[2] Zane Pratt, M. David Sills, and Jeff K. Walters, *Introduction to Global Missions* (Nashville: B&H Publishing, 2014), 118.
[3] See E.A. Payne's introduction in the "Serampore Form of Agreement," *Baptist Quarterly*, 12.5 (Jan 1947), 125.

The Serampore Form of Agreement

Serampore Mission minimize prejudices between the foreign missionaries and the local community? Second, what are the ways and means through which missions in India can be advanced?

Background

Indian history in the early nineteenth century requires some exploration to acquire a broader understanding of the Serampore Mission and the influences behind the SFA.[4] Colonial discourse dominated the Indian subcontinent, and local voices were submerged under those from the West.[5] While foreign colonials considered India a fertile land for entrepreneurial, ideological, and missional engagement, colonial structures subjugated the people of the land. The people of India did not readily receive the Westerners' religious ideologies, political systems, and cultural practices; they faced the dilemma of accepting or rejecting the imposed ideologies.

Missionaries brought their own Western prejudices to the mission field—they had to overcome their own heart issues. European prejudices might be dealt with in two categories: first, the overt racism shown by Westerners not associated with the mission, and second, the errors made in speaking against idol worship and polytheism and other concerns that the missionaries made despite good intentions. This was further complicated because Indians viewed Westerners through their own filter of prejudices. Ward's initiative in developing the SFA marked a historical milestone in confronting these prejudices.

Pratt, Sills, and Walters comment, "It was a document influenced by history yet contemporary and forward thinking."[6] This missional mandate, incorporating past influences, present significance, and future hope, was necessary for the people of God. Western missionaries from various

---

[4] For more details about the rise of Protestant Missions, see Anthony L. Chute, Nathan A. Finn, Michael A. G. Haykin, *The Baptist Story: From English Sect to Global Movement* (Nashville: B&H Publishing, 2015), 115-134.

[5] Brian K. Pennington, *Was Hinduism Invented? Britons, Indians, and the Colonial Construction of Religion* (Oxford: Oxford University Press, 2005), 13-14.

[6] Pratt, Sills, and Walters, *Introduction to Global Missions*, 118.

Statement Three

movements conceived the East as a heathen world.[7] In 1706, under the leadership of Bartholomäus Ziegenbalg (1682-1719) and Heinrich Plütschau (1677-1752), the first Protestant mission began in Tranquebar in Tamil Nadu.[8] Following the Lutheran Pietist missionaries from Germany, the second great Protestant missionary endeavor came under William Carey in 1793. This second effort marks the beginning of the modern missionary movement, which had its roots in the evangelical awakening in America and Europe. William Carey's motto, "Expect great things from God... Attempt great things for God," can be linked to the Calvinian theological framework that produced the great revivals.

Christopher Smith considered the SFA as "a theology of evangelism."[9] The Serampore missionaries came from the English-speaking world to evangelize the so-called barbarian societies. The evangelical initiatives of the Moravian and Baptist missionaries in Serampore and the surrounding areas,[10] the effects of colonialism in the Indian subcontinent,[11] and the underdeveloped situation of the country produced a complex situation requiring the missionaries to proceed with care. The missionaries investigated conditions in India and prepared themselves to take steps with much caution and historical awareness. It became a Magna Carta for future missions in India.

Though the local Indians viewed the foreign missionaries through their own prejudices, the Serampore missionaries took the cultural situation of India seriously. The Serampore missionaries actively protested sociocultural and religious practices such as Brahmanical domination, female in-

---

[7] William Carey, *An Enquiry into the Obligations of Christians to Use Means for the Conversion of the Heathens* (Leicester: Ann Ireland, 1792), 69-70.

[8] Pratt, Sills, and Walters, *Introduction to Global Missions*, 108-109.

[9] A. C. Smith, "William Ward (1769-1823)," in Michael A.G. Haykin, ed. *The British Particular Baptists, 1638-1910*. Vol 2. (Springfield, MO: Particular Baptist Press, 2000), 263-264.

[10] Jon Hinkson, "Missions among Puritans and Pietists," *The Great Commission: Evangelicals and the History of World Missions*, eds. Martin I. Klauber and Scott M. Manetsch (Nashville: B&H Academic, 2008), 43.

[11] For a classic work on colonialism, Percival Griffiths, *The British Impact on India*, Routledge Revivals (New York: Routledge, 1952). Andrew Porter, ed. *The Nineteenth Century - Oxford History of the British Empire*, Vol. III (Oxford: OUP, 1999).

The Serampore Form of Agreement

fanticide, and *sati*. William Carey and his colleagues joined hands with Indian reform leaders like Raja Ram Mohan Roy (1772-1833).[12] Carey and his colleagues believed in the equality of people irrespective of their caste, class, gender, ethnic and national backgrounds, and race. Though India was culturally rich, certain taboos created hurdles to the nation's development. Along with promoting social reform initiatives, the Serampore missionaries attempted to provide a buffer between the local people, rooted in their ancient culture and religion, and a newer generation of missionaries who came with more Western methods. Seen in this context, the publication of the SFA can be viewed as an attempt to establish certain standards and set patterns in missionary endeavors.

Though the Serampore missionaries were open to the new realities in India, the locals did not fully trust them because they considered them part of the colonial schema. They could not accept foreign missionaries' spiritual, religious, cultural, and ideological monopoly over them. This reticence of the Indian inhabitants also provides an essential context for understanding the SFA's attempt to standardize missionary endeavors in India.[13] William Carey and his companions took the Indian culture seriously and developed an inculturation method.

The Serampore missionaries placed infinite value upon immortal souls. They affirmed, "If all souls are infinitely valuable, then all humans are of equal value." This theology of equality was a driving force in their Christian witness in India.[14] The Serampore missionaries took active steps in accommodating the situations of the Indian people, and they laid out principles for the next generation of missionaries to India.

The people of the land often considered the missionaries with their own prejudiced mentality. On the other hand, the missionaries who came without knowledge of India created a clash of cultures. For example, tension existed between non-vegetarianism and vegetarianism, monotheism and

---

[12] Hendrik Kraemer, *World Cultures and World Religions* (Cambridge: James Clarke Co., 1960), 131-132.

[13] Robert Ivermee, *Hooghly: The Global History of a River* (London: C. Hurst and Co., 2020), 132.

[14] E. A. Payne, "The Serampore Form of Agreement," 130.

Statement Three

polytheism, the God of the heart and idolatry, individualism and community consciousness, and many others.[15] Though the missionaries espoused the concept of equality, they often found it challenging to implement at the grassroots level. At times, the worldview of the missionaries collided with that of native people.[16] Notably, Carey thought that caste, while an integral part of Indian culture, was incompatible with Christian principles.

Exposition with Examples

The Third Statement of the SFA provided a vital directive to those involved in Christian witness, mission, and evangelism in the pluralistic Indian context. It emphasized a dialogical approach to other religions in missional engagements. Statement Three cautions the missionaries to consider the cultural and social ethos of the Indian nationals. The following expressions from the Statement merit examination.

The expression *abstaining* can mean restraining from doing or enjoying something. The missionaries were instructed to adjust to India's socio-religious and politico-cultural circumstances to avoid offending the local people with the unusual aspects of European culture. For example, the missionaries should avoid denigrating other religious traditions, cultural practices, festivities, and rituals. If the missionaries abstained from offensive European practices, the natives would more quickly come to trust them. Rather than impose Western views upon the local communities, the missionaries were expected to be accommodative in their own life situations and inculcate a new way forward in developing Christian ethos in the nation.[17]

The expression *whatever* broadens the reach of the statement. The meaning here is that the missionaries should not impose customs from their own cultural and ideological backgrounds. Instead, it was preferable

---

[15] Cf. A. H. Oussoren, *William Carey, Especially His Missionary Principles* (Leiden: Sijthoff, 1945), 181-184, 264-265.

[16] Carey, *An Enquiry*, 69-70.

[17] George Smith, *The Life of William Carey: Shoemaker and Missionary* (London: John Murray, 1885), 132-156. Editor's note: The SFA shows cultural sensitivity to Hindus who disliked killing animals, in its avowal not to be cruel to animals. This statement was made several decades before the SPCA was founded in England and shows an awareness of Hindu sentiments. See William Ward, *A View of the History, Literature, and Religion of the Hindoos*, 2nd edn. (Serampore: Mission Press, 1815), II, 341-342

The Serampore Form of Agreement

to indigenize Christianity—to Indianize the Christian faith. In the Indian context, the missionaries needed to follow the same approach as Paul, who modeled a culturally sensitive approach to Christian engagement. Though the Serampore missionaries attempted to adapt to Indian ways, on certain fronts, they worked to transform politics, religion, and culture in company with other movements like the Brahmo Samaj. William Carey's involvement in the campaign against *sati* provides a noteworthy example. Nonetheless, for many years, Christianity was seen as a religion of the *Feringhis*[18] and failed to make significant inroads among the Indians.[19]

The expression *deepening* referred to the danger of aggravating the situation by hurting the feelings of the people. In some cases, breaking the cultural ethos may be counterproductive. The local people were already wounded due to prolonged subjugation by the colonial powers. The missionary practice of non-vegetarianism might deepen the wounds of the locals who were strict vegetarians. Religion is more sensitive than politics, so the missionaries are cautioned to walk carefully. This warning came in the context of zealous evangelical engagements by the Indians.[20]

The local communities approached the Western missionaries with certain preconceptions, but the missionaries were instructed not to deepen those prejudices further. According to the *Oxford Dictionary*, prejudice can mean "an unreasonable dislike of or preference for a person, group, custom, etc., especially when it is based on their race, religion, sex, etc." In a context where the British East India Company held political power, the Indians were suspicious of the missionaries and their religious agenda. Though the missionaries did not represent the East India Company, the locals saw both as entities controlled by Westerners.[21]

---

[18] Or *Parangis*, a derogatory term for Europeans and those of Portuguese-Indian descent, meaning meat eating, wine drinking, loose living and arrogant persons. C.B. Firth, *An Introduction to Indian Church History* (Delhi: ISPCK for Senate of Serampore College, 1998), 111.

[19] R. K. Pruthi, ed. *Brahmo Samaj and Indian Civilization*, Culture and Civilization Series (New Delhi: Discovery Publishing House, 2004), 49. Also see Suneel Bhanu Busi, "Who are We and What Constitutes Our Identity," *Religious Identity and Renewal in the Twenty-First Century*, The Lutheran World Federation (Leipzig: Evangelische Verlagsanstalt, 2015), 195.

[20] See Sharada Sugirtharajah, *Imagining Hinduism: A Postcolonial Perspective* (London: Routledge, 2003), 74-89.

[21] Penelope Carson, *The East India Company and Religion, 1698-1858* (Woodbridge: Boydell Press, 2012), 2-5.

Statement Three

The expression *against* conveys the potential polarity between the foreign missionaries and the local people. Rather than impose their alien culture and ethos upon the local citizens, the missionaries were supposed to accommodate the cultural and ethnic aspects of the various people groups. Statement Three challenges culturally insensitive practices implemented by previous foreign missionaries in different parts of India: "Nor is it advisable ... to attack their prejudices by exhibiting with acrimony the sins of their gods; neither should we upon any account do violence to their images, nor interrupt their worship."[22] This statement also served as a corrective for an overly confrontational style of evangelism practiced at times by members of the Serampore Mission.

The expression *gospel* concerns the Bible's unaltered message and its core substance. It is derived from the Greek expression *euangelion*, which means sharing good news or glad tidings of salvation. Statement Three uses the expression in relation to the demands of the time and place. When the missionaries engaged in witnessing for Christ in a pluralistic context like India, they needed to build trust among the people rather than developing a 'we' and 'they' linguistic pattern. By avoiding methods and principles of Christian mission and ministry imported uncritically from a Western context, the missionaries could hope to disciple Indian Christians in the full sense of both words: Christian and Indian.

The expression of the most successful preacher, "that he would not care if the people trampled him under their feet, if he might become useful to their souls"[23] underlines the importance of missionary selflessness in a foreign culture. The Serampore Missionaries had to be prepared to sacri-

---

[22] E. A. Payne, "The Serampore Form of Agreement," 131.

[23] Editor's note: The source of this quotation remains a mystery. In private correspondence, Dr. Bennie Crockett suggests Robert Hall, Jr (1764-1831) as the most likely candidate. However, Dr. Crockett states that a survey of Hall's published sermons has not yielded results. There is the possibility that Ward quoted Hall from memory, for as Potts has shown, Hall preached at George Street, Hull, before Ward's baptism there, on one Lord's Day from May to August 1796. (E.D. Potts, *Biography of William Ward*, Mss., CLRC, 19). But it is more likely Ward quoted some publication he had just read, perhaps *The Biblical Magazine*, or *Circular Letters of the Association*. However, it is also possible Ward meant someone else in the SFA.

fice when they traveled from distant England to share the Gospel in Bengal. Thus, the SFA placed Great Commission at the forefront of missionary endeavors.[24]

The Serampore missionaries did not just preach the gospel—like the Quakers and the Moravians, they actively sought to alleviate poverty. Scripture prioritizes concern for the poor, marginalized, and dehumanized sections of society. As Jesus took the side of the ostracized and neglected sections of society, the Serampore missionaries were encouraged to give preferential care to the poor. Like Jesus, in the Gospel of Luke, who started his ministry with an emphasis on the good news to the poor, the proclamation of release to the captives, recovery of sight to the blind, and freedom to the oppressed, the Serampore missionaries were equipped to do mission with an emphasis on new jubilee principles.[25] In a similar fashion to Paul, who went to the heathen preaching the gospel to people of every kind, the Serampore missionaries preached the message of the Bible among the people of India. In sum, like Paul's readiness "to become all things to all men, that he might by any means save some," the Serampore missionaries were challenged to not lay unnecessary stumbling blocks for the gospel by their conduct. The missionaries did their best to keep the rhythm of the Bible in their missionary endeavors.[26]

Analysis

Ernest Payne states the SFA has historical significance and "remains a moving and challenging statement of the main principles" foundational to mission among India's peoples.[27] The SFA is a crucial source for studying early nineteenth-century mission strategy. The insistence that equality and

---

[24] E.A. Payne, *The Serampore Form of Agreement*, 131.

[25] The idea of equality of missionaries and the local people was emphasized by the missionaries. See Samuel E. Masters, "'Will Anyone Say the Lord is not Among Us?' The Serampore Mission and Its Covenant." (Ph.D. diss., The Southern Baptist Theological Seminary, Louisville, 2020), 181, 184–186, 233.

[26] For more details regarding Ward's radical reform and mission, see A. Christopher Smith, "William Ward, Radical Reform, and Missions in the 1790's." *American Baptist Quarterly* 10 (1991): 218–244.

[27] E.A. Payne, "The Serampore Form of Agreement," 125.

Statement Three

fraternity should be sustained in missionary work was revolutionary. However, it was firmly rooted in the New Testament. As the Apostle Paul says, "There is neither Jew nor Greek, slave nor free, male nor female, for you are all one in Christ Jesus" (Gal 3:28).[28] Missionaries from the West should not treat Indians as inferiors; instead, they should consider them as equals to build trust. In the Second Statement, the emphasis falls on missionaries' acquaintance with people's minds. In a mission context, capturing people's minds in love is essential. Jesus's commandment of "love your enemies" can be a paradigm for all those involved in missions in an alien context (Matt 5:44).[29]

These themes run throughout the SFA. Statement Six further emphasizes the aspect of treating the people as equals. Mission is possible in a context where foreign missionaries and local inhabitants are on the same level. Rather than doing mission in a dominant/subjugated bipolarity, it should establish equality between the foreigners and the nationals.[30] In Statement Seven, the missionaries are encouraged to guard and build up the locals to elevate their standard of living. At this level, mission is not simply oral or written rhetoric, but includes practical and humanitarian concerns.[31] In Statement Eight, there is a call to understand the local people's worth in evangelization.[32] Thus, the theme of equality is integral to

---

[28] Elsa Tamez, "Galatians," *The International Bible Commentary: An Ecumenical Commentary for the Twenty-First Century*, ed. William R. Farmer (Bangalore: Theological Publications in India, 1998), 1739.

[29] Jeanne Stevenson Moessner, "The Self-Differentiated Samaritan," *Images of Pastoral Care: Classic Readings*, ed. Robert C. Dykstra (Danvers, MA: Chalice Press, 2005), 66.

[30] According to Domenic Marbaniang, "The social works that the Christian missionaries did in India presented a living and visible example of their view of human dignity and equality. In addition to educational Missions that gave an occasion for all to study (irrespective of caste, race, or gender, the very first time in India), medical Missions brought help to the missions of the common people of India, for whom no skilled assistance in the time of trouble and death was available." Domenic Marbaniang, *Secularism in India: A Historical Analysis* (Itarsi: Domenic Marbaniang, 2005, 2010, 2011), 59. Quote from J.N. Farquhar, *Modern Religious Movements in India* (London: MacMillan & Co., 1924), 20.

[31] See Marbaniang, *Secularism in India*, 59.

[32] John Mark Terry and Robert L. Gallagher, *Encountering the History of Missions: From the Early Church to Today* (Grand Rapids: Baker Academic, 2017), 243-257.

The Serampore Form of Agreement

the framework of SFA.³³ Statement Three should be analyzed in light of equality in every area of human life.

The SFA issued a call to unite missionaries and people of the land in a joint endeavor, but the missionaries did not help this cause by referring to the locals as "heathens." The expression "heathens" was used uncritically to address the non-Christian communities; however, this would not be appropriate in our contemporary context.³⁴ Even considering the evolution of cultural sensitivities since then, I feel it was the wrong starting point for the Serampore missionaries.³⁵ On the other hand, the missionaries' dedication, unremitting toil, constancy in prayer, cross-centered preaching, and brotherliness toward the Indian converts deserve praise.³⁶

Another criticism that might be leveled against the Serampore Mission involves their selection of a spiritually dry place like Serampore. Why did the missionaries choose a land like Serampore and the surrounding areas for their missionary endeavors? Even in the context of the bicentenary of the Serampore mission, we do not find significant church growth in

---

³³ Pratt, Sills, and Walters, *Introduction to Global Missions*, 115–134.

³⁴ Michael J. Altman, *Heathen, Hindoo, Hindu: American Representations of India, 1721–1893* (Oxford: Oxford University Press, 2017), 1-3. Editor's note: Altman explains that "heathen" were part of a customary fourfold taxonomy of the world: Christians, Muslims, Jews and Heathens. What might be regarded as offensive is Richard Baxter's (and Cotton Mather's) sweeping qualification of heathen people as "ignorant, sensual, brutish men," and that ignorance was to blame. Certainly, if the Serampore missionaries had only read Baxter, this would have been a wrong starting-point. However, it might also be noted that by the time the SFA was written, not ignorance, but oppression and idolatry were seen as the main hindrance to the message of Salvation.

³⁵ E.A. Payne, "The Serampore Form of Agreement," 129.

³⁶ Dwight P. Baker, "William Carey and the Business Model for Mission," *Between Past and Future: Evangelical Mission Entering the Twenty-First Century*, ed. Jonathan J. Bonk (Pasadena, CA: Evangelical Missiological Society, 2003), 189.

Statement Three

Serampore and the surrounding regions.[37] These questions remain a mystery in the minds of several historians and missionaries.[38] The primary reason for the selection of the location was the offer by the Danish colony at Serampore of protection from the British authorities.

Another criticism that might be advanced is that in our present postcolonial context, the expression "winning" reflects negatively upon the mission. The idea of "winning souls" has biblical roots (Proverbs 11:30). However, in our contemporary context, missionary works should avoid the perception that the prime agenda is "success" or "victory." The word "winning" might imply "victory" over the heathen cultures, religiosity, spirituality, and other aspects. The expression can be misunderstood in a multireligious and pluralistic context like India.[39] These sorts of biases should be carefully dealt with when interpreting the SFA in the contemporary context.

The gospel should be considered a means of inner conversion and holistic transformation. Paul's idea of accommodation in 1 Corinthians 9:20-22 provides a model in a pluralistic context like India. Paul writes: "To the Jews I became like a Jew, to win the Jews. To those under the law I became one under the law."[40] The apostle's cultural and contextual assimilation fits well in the Indian context.[41] Similarly, Johannine incarnate Christology

---

[37] Editor's note: A survey made in situ by Peter de Vries has located more than twenty indigenous congregations that still exist which are fruit of the Baptist work from the period of the Serampore Mission. Nonetheless, it is true that Christianity has not expanded in West Bengal like in other parts of India.

[38] If the Serampore missionaries had chosen a place in the southern part of India, would the destiny of the mission have been different 200 years on?

[39] Cf. Carey's remark that, "The first step towards winning the natives to our religion is to show them that we have one. This will hardly be done without a visible church." George Smith, *The Life of William Carey: Shoemaker and Missionary* (London: John Murray, 1885), 354.

[40] Jan Lambrecht, "First Corinthians," *The International Bible Commentary: An Ecumenical Commentary for the Twenty-First Century*, ed. William R. Farmer (Bangalore: Theological Publications in India, 1998), 1692.

[41] See Arren Bennet Lawrence, "Paul, Culture, and Sexual Immorality in 1 Corinthians 5 and 6," *One Gospel, Many Cultures: Doing Theology in Context* (Minneapolis: Fortress Press, 2022), 103-133.

can be paradigmatic—the Word becomes flesh and dwells among the people (John 1:14).[42] Without imposing the foreign cultural aspects upon the locals, the missionaries can adopt a model of becoming everything to everybody as a way forward in their Christian missional endeavors.

Statement Three highlights several important aspects concerning mission and evangelism in the Indian context. First, Westerners before the Serampore Mission often treated the locals as inferiors and uncivilized people, but Carey and his companions realized such treatments would not yield fruits in missions. Second, mission in India was best promoted based on a dialogical relationship between Western missionaries and unevangelized Eastern communities.[43] Third, Indian anti-British prejudices produced by imperialist domination complicated the relationship between the missionaries and the nationals. Fourth, Statement Three cautions the missionaries that despite prejudices against the foreign mission and British Raj in India, they should avoid any conduct that would deepen those prejudices. Fifth, with India controlled by foreign colonial authorities, the nationals struggled to accept missionaries representing a foreign mission association.[44] These points have general implications in today's context but are not directly applicable to Christian work in modern India, which is an independent republic. Nonetheless, local prejudices against the gospel still exist in today's context. Atrocities against the Christians in India amply demonstrate the continued discrimination of Indians toward Christians and Christian missionaries.[45]

The Serampore missionaries attempted to read the mindset of the people properly against the backdrop of British Rule. Their statements, including Statement Three, were realistic and emerged from their contextual

---

[42] See Johnson Thomaskutty, "Culture Dynamics in the Johannine Community Context," *One Gospel, Many Cultures: Doing Theology in Context*, ed. Arren Bennet Lawrence (Minneapolis: Fortress Press, 2022), 135-160.

[43] See Robin Boyd, *An Introduction to Indian Christian Theology* (Delhi: ISPCK, 1969/2000), 7-18.

[44] Porter, *Religion versus Empire?*, 64-135.

[45] For more details about atrocities against Christians in India today, see Chad M. Bauman, *Anti-Christian Violence in India* (New York: Cornell University Press, 2020).

Statement Three

realities. They realized the mindset of Indians was closed to foreigners because of imperialism and colonization in India, even before the British arrival.[46] At the same time, the local people were often hospitable to the foreign missionaries and open to accommodating them despite growing suspicion.

The SFA emerged at the right time to expand Serampore's mission influence in India. The agreement emphasized the necessity of planting indigenous churches in the country.[47] By considering concerns from both sides, the Serampore missionaries dynamically bridged foreign mission strategies and the indigenous realities of the people.[48] We can see the SFA as the outcome of their efforts to understand the culture.

The First Statement of the SFA focused on the immortality of the souls. Here, the missionaries emphasized sharing the eternal message of salvation for people's redemption rather than emphasizing dualistic expressions such as saved and heathen, winning and defeating.[49] As the second Statement of the SFA teaches, missionaries were to engage the people at their level without prejudice, learn their ethos and pathos, their religious scriptures and practices, and their thought patterns and cultural dynamics. The goal was to develop a dialogical missionary approach. This statement encouraged them to acquire a more in-depth understanding of the local community rather than impose their ideas without prior knowledge.[50] The fourth Statement encourages the missionaries to strive constantly to do

---

[46] See Emily Conroy-Krutz, *Christian Imperialism: Converting the World in the Early American Republic* (New York: Cornell University Press, 2015). Also, Jeffrey Cox, *Imperial Faultlines: Christianity and Colonial Power in India, 1818-1940* (Stanford, CA: Stanford University Press, 2002).

[47] John D. Massey, Mike Morris, and W. Madison Grace II, *Make Disciples of All Nations: A History of Southern Baptist International Missions* (Grand Rapids, MI: Kregel Academic, 2021), 45.

[48] C. Peter Williams, "The Church Missionary Society and the Indigenous Church in the Second Half of the Nineteenth Century: The Defense and Destruction of the Venn Ideas," Converting *Colonialism: Visions and Realities in Mission History, 1706-1914*, ed. Dana L. Robert (Grand Rapids, MI: Eerdmans, 2008), 86-111.

[49] George Philip, "The Centrality of Christ and the Hermeneutical Perspectives of the Serampore Mission," *Serampore Mission: Perspectives in Contexts*, ed. Johnson Thomaskutty (New Delhi: ISPCK, 2019), 164-181.

[50] James Patole, "The Modern Missionary Movement of the Serampore Trio: A Missiological Perspective," *Serampore Mission: Perspectives in Contexts*, ed. Johnson Thomaskutty (New Delhi: ISPCK, 2019), 232-258.

good to the people, and the fifth Statement affirms "Christ the crucified" as the focal point of evangelization and conversion.[51] The sixth Statement emphasizes equality between the foreign missionaries and the local people.[52] In the seventh Statement, attention focuses on building a community that includes women and socially vulnerable people.[53] By concentrating on cultivating the spiritual gifts of the nationals, the eighth Statement enables the community of God to be self-sufficient in the missionary works in the local and national contexts. In that process, Bible translation (Statement Nine), personal religiosity (Statement Ten), and complete dedication, even relinquishing personal possessions (Statement Eleven), are emphasized.[54] All these aspects enhance the witness of the missionary efforts and undermine the suspicions of the Indian nationals.

The Serampore missionaries had to develop a mission strategy that balanced competing influences such as the missionary zeal of the West in the nineteenth century, the colonial hegemony by British Rule in India, and the prejudices of the colonized nationals. Local prejudices would increase if the missionaries insisted on their own cultural behaviors, such as eating cow meat, killing animals, speaking abusively about other gods, idols, images, and icons, and distancing themselves from Indian cultural practices. The strategic attempt made by the Serampore missionaries yielded many results in the Indian subcontinent.

Influence

Statement Three enabled the missionaries to connect integrally with the local people. This open-minded strategy included adopting critical new

---

[51] K. Giri, "William Carey's Approach to the People of Other Faiths, Religious Practices, Caste System, and Conversion," *Serampore Mission: Perspectives in Contexts*, ed. Johnson Thomaskutty (New Delhi: ISPCK, 2019), 282-303.

[52] Woba James, "The Contribution of the Serampore Missions towards the Ecumenical Movement: A Historical Perspective," *Serampore Mission: Perspectives in Contexts*, ed. Johnson Thomaskutty (New Delhi: ISPCK, 2019), 141-151.

[53] Annie George, "Educational Principles of the Serampore Mission and its Implications for Contemporary Education," *Serampore Mission: Perspectives in Contexts*, ed. Johnson Thomaskutty (New Delhi: ISPCK, 2019), 123-140.

[54] J. Stanly Jones, "William Carey's Bible Translation Principles: Prospects and Challenges," *Serampore Mission: Perspectives in Contexts*, ed. Johnson Thomaskutty (New Delhi: ISPCK, 2019), 70-93.

Statement Three

methodologies in their linguistic work. Their use of Indian terminologies (derived from Sanskrit and Bengali) for Christian terms facilitated intercultural and interreligious dialogue. The Serampore missionaries developed a love for Sanskrit alongside a particular interest in Bengali.[55] They believed that the development of vernaculars would lead to the country's quick modernization.[56] With that aim in mind, they worked to develop Bengali language and literature. By developing a language study center in Serampore, the missionaries equipped the locals and themselves for growth.[57] These efforts also helped foster trust between the missionaries and the local communities.

Das Gupta links the Serampore missionaries' "great achievements in lexicography and grammar" to a global environment shaped by the European Enlightenment and its manifestation in language study.[58] The Indian subcontinent is popularly known for its diversity of languages and dialects. During the Enlightenment in the eighteenth century, there emerged in Europe a great interest in the grammar of Oriental languages.[59] As Das Gupta explains, this was the period in which "the educated middle classes had assumed leadership in society and when the vernaculars had become an effective instrument of communication for social change and intellectual progress."[60] As a product of Enlightenment, Carey elevated many Indian

---

[55] Indira Mukhopadhyaya, "William Carey's Contributions for the Promotion of Sanskritic Studies," *Carey's Obligation and India's Renaissance*, eds. J. T. K. Daniel and Roger E. Hedlund (Serampore: Council of Serampore College, 1993), 194.

[56] T. Johnson Chakkuvarackal, "The Serampore Mission and the Linguistic Renaissance in India," *Bangalore Theological Forum* 35/2 (2003): 127.

[57] Johnson Thomaskutty, "Re-reading the Gospel of John in the Light of William Carey's Linguistic Methods," *Serampore Mission: Perspectives in Contexts*, ed. Johnson Thomaskutty (New Delhi: ISPCK, 2019), 97.

[58] R. K. Das Gupta, "William Carey and Bengali Grammar," *Carey's Obligation and India's Renaissance*, eds. J. T. K. Daniel and Roger E. Hedlund (Serampore: Council of Serampore College, 1993), 188.

[59] The period of Enlightenment was marked by the intellectual and philosophical conviction that truth could only be obtained through the powers of human reason, observation, and experiment. See D. K. McKim, *Westminster Dictionary of Theological Terms* (Louisville/London: Westminster John Knox Press, 1996), 90.

[60] Das Gupta, 188. In addition, Delon comments that, "European Enlightenment thinkers were interested in diverse aspects of language and languages: their structure, their historical relationships, their 'moral' and philosophical qualities, the methods used to teach languages, their

The Serampore Form of Agreement

vernaculars from their primitive condition.[61] Of course, the emphasis on vernacular versions of the Scriptures also had roots in the Protestant Reformation. The Serampore missionaries considered language a powerful tool in bridging the relationship between the missionaries and the local communities.

In 1921 Rabindranath Tagore observed that "Carey was the pioneer of the revived interest in the vernaculars."[62] Carey realized the complexity of India's sociocultural problems due to its multiethnic and multilingual character. He strongly felt that the people should be aware of their mother tongues and conversant in other languages. The missionaries also needed to know several Indian languages to work in India. He envisaged the language study center in Serampore to facilitate this purpose, where new missionaries could acquire the vernaculars.[63]

An emphasis on language development began to lower the cultural barriers that separated the Serampore missionaries and the local people. The missionaries developed two books in a lucid and colloquial Bengali prose style: *Kathopakāthan* and *Ithihāsamālā*.[64] Depicting daily life, these works were intended to facilitate acquiring the Bengali language. As N. R. Ray states,

> The texts relate encounters experienced in recruitment of domestic hands, conversation between Sahib and his Moonshi, between moneylender and the debtor, gentry and gentry, between women and women, clergy and the parishioner, zemindar and the riot, besides

---

function in society, and their role in science and literature." See M. Delon, ed. "Grammar," *Encyclopedia of the Enlightenment*, Vol. 1 (London/New York: Routledge, 2001), 617.

[61] Vishal and Ruth Mangalwadi, *The Legacy of William Carey: A Model for the Transformation of a Culture* (Wheaton: Crossway Books, 1993/1999), 20. Also see Thomaskutty, "Re-reading the Gospel of John," 96.

[62] See S. Pearce Carey, *William Carey: 'The Father of Modern Missions.'* Edited by Peter Masters (London: Wakeman Trust, 1993), 203.

[63] S. K. Chatterjee, "Carey and the Linguistic Renaissance in India," *Carey's Obligation and India's Renaissance*, eds. J. T. K. Daniel and Roger E. Hedlund (Serampore: Council of Serampore College, 1993), 158-159. Also see Thomaskutty, "Re-reading the Gospel of John," 97.

[64] See Chatterjee, "Carey and the Linguistic Renaissance," 168-169.

market scene and the style of speech current among laborers, quarreling people, and gesticulating women.[65]

Ray further states, "The dialogues were meant to serve as a lingual bridge between the Englishmen and the so-called lower ranks of the Bengali people."[66] The texts were intended to emphasize colloquial expressions and to communicate human life in day-to-day affairs.[67] These pedagogical projects were the practical results of the SFA's insistence on doing everything possible to close the cultural gap between the foreign missionaries and the local people.

The Serampore missionaries developed a sociolinguistic approach to understanding the language system of Bengal.[68] They observed how the people combined different language forms to express their identity. This consisted of code-switching and diglossia of language systems in which a classical form of a language ('H' form) exists alongside another colloquial form or forms of the same language ('L' form).[69] In Carey's assessment, Sanskrit was at the center of Indian languages. Therefore, he approached other languages ('L' forms) through Sanskrit.[70]

The Serampore missionaries' linguistic work is just one example of numerous efforts to enhance relationships with the Indian people. The missionaries emphasized involvement in social advocacy, religious dialogue, humanitarian work, women's liberation, educational freedom, and more to change the discriminatory mentality of the locals and the missionaries.

---

[65] N. R. Ray, "William Carey—Linguist with a Difference," *Carey's Obligation and India's Renaissance*, eds. J. T. K. Daniel and Roger E. Hedlund (Serampore: Council of Serampore College, 1993), 155-156. Also see Thomaskutty, "Re-reading the Gospel of John," 97.

[66] Ray, "William Carey—Linguist with a Difference," 156. Also see Thomaskutty, "Re-reading the Gospel of John," 98.

[67] Ray, "William Carey—Linguist with a Difference," 156.

[68] For more details about socio-linguistics, see A. Jaffe, ed., *Stance: Sociolinguistic Perspective* (Oxford: Oxford University Press, 2009), 1-28.

[69] The term "code-switching" describes the mixing of different languages while communicating in bilingual setting. See P. Gardner-Chloros, *Code-Switching* (Cambridge: Cambridge University Press, 2009), 1-19.

[70] Chakkuvarackal, "The Serampore Mission and the Linguistic Renaissance in India," 131-132. Cf. Thomaskutty, "Re-reading the Gospel of John," 99.

The Serampore Form of Agreement

Ongoing Relevance

Statement Three of the SFA provides a significant paradigm for building a healthy relationship between mission agencies and the people of the land. The SFA, in its entirety, also provides a model for the ongoing mission of the Indian church. As most of the Episcopal churches, various evangelical bodies, and a considerable group of Pentecostal/free churches are affiliated with the Senate of Serampore College, the ethos of the Serampore mission continues to be implemented at the grassroots levels of the churches in their mission efforts.[71]

Following the principles of the Serampore mission and the SFA, the churches of India engage in inter-ecclesial and interreligious dialogue to facilitate ecclesial unity and religious harmony.[72] For example, the United Theological College, Bengaluru, India, one of the premier and autonomous theological institutions under the Senate of Serampore College, facilitates dialogical, ecumenical, and holistic mission endeavors.[73] The Serampore missionaries emphasized a holistic people-centric praxis. Drawing on the SFA, the theological curriculum of The United Theological College engages Indian society without prejudices.[74] Broadminded and inclusive missional practices in India's multireligious, multicultural, and pluralistic context must replace narrow-minded exclusivism.[75] The prejudiced mindset of the native people toward Christian missions should be considered, and both the missionaries and the people groups should engage in dialogical relationships.

Influenced by the Serampore Mission and Senate of Serampore College, the Protestant mission in India takes up a holistic mission concerned

---

[71] Prakash Abraham Mathew, "The Impact of the Bible through the Protestant Reformation and the Protestant Missionary Movement," *Serampore Mission: Perspectives in Contexts*, ed. Johnson Thomaskutty (New Delhi: ISPCK, 2019), 49-69.

[72] See Harold Coward, ed. *Hindu-Christian Dialogue: Perspectives and Encounters* (Delhi: Motilal Banarsidass Publishers, 1993).

[73] Johnson Thomaskutty, "Wider Ecumenism in John 17:1-26 in the Light of Theological Education in India," *Bangalore Theological Forum* LIV/1 (June 2022): 157-173.

[74] For the United Theological College, see https://www.utc.edu.in/, accessed on August 22, 2022.

[75] Giri, "William Carey's Approach," 294-295.

Statement Three

with humanitarian aspects such as the environment, disability, marginalization, and Dalit, Tribal, and Adivasi concerns.[76] Elements such as inter-religious dialogue, cultural interpretation, liberating reading, and other exercises in the Senate of Serampore College and their theological reflections and praxes at the ecclesiastical levels mostly emerge from the non-prejudiced and inclusive outlook of the SFA.[77] Even after two hundred years, the SFA widely influences the church and academic circles.[78] Statement Three and other critical SFA statements provide the basis for an unbiased approach to equipping people for a wider-contextualized Biblical spirituality.[79]

Conclusion

This chapter attempts to understand and analyze Statement Three of the SFA in isolation and association with other statements and aspects. The statement should be read over against the prevailing situation of the nineteenth century when the missionaries from the West and the natives from the East could not join each other on a common platform. The presence of the British East India Company, the colonial setting of the country, and past mistaken missional engagements formed this backdrop. However, in Statement Three, with its emphasis on dialogue, the SFA proved decisive in shaping the missional and ministerial scope of the Indian church.[80] The Serampore missionaries developed a new way forward by adopting accommodative strategies in mission. Statement Three facilitated a bridging between the missionary ethos and the Indian pathos that further invigorated Christian witness, mission, and evangelism. This statement touches on significant aspects of the Christian faith, bolsters dialogical interaction, facilitates unity, and encourages equality as a crucial element. Taken seriously, the principles of the SFA can shape Christian witness, mission, and evangelism and initiate transformation in the church and society. Statement

---

[76] Kaholi Zhimomi, "Beyond the Serampore Mission Historiography: Re-defining Ecumenism from the Context," *Serampore Mission: Perspectives in Contexts*, ed. Johnson Thomaskutty (New Delhi: ISPCK, 2019), 259-281.

[77] George, "Educational Principles of the Serampore Mission," 123-140.

[78] Giri, "William Carey's Approach," 141-151.

[79] Johnson Thomaskutty and Mathew Chandrankunnel, eds., *Wider Contextualized Biblical Spirituality* (New Delhi: Christian World Imprints, 2021).

[80] Smith, "William Ward, Radical Reform," 219-244.

The Serampore Form of Agreement

Three of SFA and its contextual interpretation should play a paradigmatic role in the ongoing mission and ministry of the church, not just in India but around the world.

STATEMENT FOUR

Dinner, Disease, and Duty

Myron Noonkester

Surveying the Governor-General's residence, the retired cordwainer knew that his life, and the world with it, had changed. Twenty-six years earlier, on February 10, 1779, the cordwainer, William Carey, had occupied a different side of the world and displayed a different state of mind. When George III proclaimed a Fast Day for Britain during the American Revolution, Carey, then a penurious draft-age apprentice, buried his anger in devotion.[1] He communed that day with Independents, Dissenters who rejected the established Church of England.[2] That act led him astray from the faith of his fathers, astray from his parish, and, eventually, astray from the country of his birth. Now, near the banks of the Hooghly River in India, he entered the residence where the Governor-General invited him to dine on this early February evening in 1805. He, formerly the humble cordwainer, was now vested with considerable power in the Christian missionary movement as one of the brethren of the Serampore Mission. Eight months later, that mission would issue the Serampore Form of Agreement

---

[1] Carey claimed to be a "cobbler," but there is a case to be made that he was a cordwainer, that is, a maker of shoes rather than a repairer of them only. For Carey the apprentice cordwainer's chronic poverty, see "William Carey, D. D. Poor Law Settlement Order." *Northampton County Magazine*. 4. 1931.

[2] Carey then "concluded that the Church of England, as established by law, was the camp in which all were protected from the scandal of the cross, and that I ought to bear the reproach of Christ among the dissenters..." George Smith, *The Life of William Carey: Shoemaker and Missionary* (London: John Murray, 1885), 14-16. Congregationalists seem not to have resented Carey's subsequent departure: "Biographical Sketch of The Rev. William Carey, D.D., Late Principal of Serampore College, Bengal." *The Congregational Magazine, for the Year 1835.* Vol 18. N.S. 121-122 (January 1835): 1-10; and (February 1835): 73-83.

The Serampore Form of Agreement

whose Statement Four responded to all the elements of social experience in British India: decadent inequality such as Carey found at the Governor-General's residence, disease and death, and aspirations for social betterment, reform, and evangelization in an improving age. And so, as Carey experienced the domestic graces, the rich food of one of the supreme representatives of everything he formerly despised in church and state, he was, for once, on the inside looking out.[3]

An Imperial Dinner

What did Carey see? In these surroundings, distinguished by classical European architecture modified into Indian elegance, Carey, now a Baptist missionary to India and honored guest on account of his linguistic abilities, could not help but be reminded of what it was to have imperial power. Like the Great King of Persia on the Royal Road or a Roman emperor on campaign, the Governor-General, Richard Colley Mornington, Marquis of Wellesley, commanded a residence teeming with symbols of victory. This Governor-General was notorious for display even among British sahibs. Wellesley's presumption was effortless and irksome. George III himself is said to have commented on how difficult it would be for Wellesley to return to England after having contrived such grandiose ceremony in India.[4] Having defeated one of the last great Indian warrior princes, Tipoo Sultan, at Seringapatam in 1799, Wellesley graced a medal on which the British Lion subdued Tipoo the Tiger.[5] Wellesley's successes after the trial of overcoming Tipoo were unbelievable. Every few weeks or months, Members of Parliament and ministers of His Majesty's Government had received intelligence of new princedoms and states with exotic-sounding

---

[3] E. Daniel Potts, *British Baptist Missionaries in India, 1793-1837: The History of Serampore and its Missions* (London: Cambridge University Press, 1967), 176 and n. 7. Carey to John Sutcliffe, February 8, 1805, cited in Eustace Carey, *Memoir of William Carey, D. D.: Late Missionary to Bengal; Professor of Oriental Languages in the College of Fort William, Calcutta* (London: Jackson & Walford, 1836), 477-478.

[4] Wendy Hinde, *George Canning* (New York: St Martin's Press, 1973), 156.

[5] Center for Study of the Life and Work of William Carey, D. D., 1761-1834, Wellesley Collection 2. Medal, Richard Colley, Marquis of Wellesley (1760-1842) as Governor and Captain General of India. Reverse side, commemorating Battle of Seringapatam, May 4, 1799; Wellesley Collection 4. Medal, white metal, Seringapatam. ca. 1800-1810.

Statement Four

names, Malabar, Orissa, Mysore, Maratha, and so on. Their representatives laid down decorated weaponry, acknowledged subordination to King George III, and (apparently at least) requested the favor of amalgamation into the Second British Empire under the gracious if distant eye of the Imperial Senate, the Parliament of Westminster.[6] Such news was received with astonishment in some quarters, consternation in others. It was dazzling. But there was a catch. What gave Wellesley the right to annex thousands of miles of territory and millions of new subjects, few of whom were Christian, and none of whom were English? It was a policy nightmare with predictable results. Like Caesar, Wellesley was too dangerous to be allowed to continue. Unlike Caesar, his Rubicon was thousands of miles of open ocean, and so he dared not cross it. Instead, in the aftermath of parliamentary accusations against him, he spent the rest of his life seeking vindication which was not bought as easily as the magnificence surrounding him.

Still, neither parliamentary accusers nor military opponents could deny that Wellesley was a world-changer. In the Maratha War of 1803–1805, Wellesley multiplied the British presence on the subcontinent into something more closely approximating comprehensiveness.[7] Fighting the Marathas to render their leader or peshwa a figurehead without taxing power and dependent on the favor of the British resident represented another step in the direction of direct British rule of India. That eminent and ancient capitalist-bureaucratic-international jobbery, the East India Company, expanded along with it.[8] Never mind that the expense of such lavish operations brought the East India Company to the brink of bankruptcy.[9] The Serampore Missionaries met these developments over time with Bible

---

[6] *Bengal, Also, Fort St George and Bombay Papers, Presented to the House of Commons... Relative to the Mahratta War in 1803. Printed by Order of the House of Commons, 5th and 22nd June, 1804* [London: House of Commons], 1804.

[7] William Dalrymple, *The Anarchy: The Relentless Rise of the East India Company* (New York: Bloomsbury, 2019), 368ff.; Sailendra Nath Sen. *Anglo-Maratha Relations 1785-1796*. Volume Two. (Bombay: Popular Prakashan, 1974 [reprinted 1994]).

[8] Stewart Gordon, *The Marathas 1600–1818, The New Cambridge History of India*, II, 4 (Cambridge: Cambridge University Press, 1993), 176.

[9] Margot Finn and Kate Smith, eds., *The East India Company at Home*, 1757–1857 (London: UCL Press, 2018).

The Serampore Form of Agreement

translations, grammars, and a dictionary in the language of perhaps the most warlike people on the subcontinent.[10] Their Gospel of Matthew coincided with the cessation of the Mahratta War.[11]

Born about a year apart, host and guest could not have been more different. Wellesley had followed the *cursus honorum* of social invincibility: Harrow, Eton (where he obtained the honor of donating a leaving portrait),[12] and Christ Church, Oxford. Carey was a self-educated Baptist pastor. Carey had written a manifesto and a constitution; Wellesley wrote letters to subordinates and letters of justification to superiors and colleagues. Wellesley, born into the rulers of the English settler-colony in Ireland, knew what it was to inherit rule over an alien, semi-hostile population. Carey knew what it was to write a new church constitution to compose squabbles of a tiny band of Particular Baptists in Leicester.[13] They welcomed one another to mission improbable: Wellesley could not hope to complete the cycle of conquering Hindus and Muslims, mollifying the bean-counters and ancient directors of the East India Company who feared Christianization efforts,[14] buying off or scaring off native princes, and Christianizing India, all the while surviving parliamentary scrutiny. But audacity was a family trait. Wellesley's family changed its name to preclude association with John Wesley, founder of Methodism. Wellesley himself accumulated titles on a staggering scale: Richard Colley Wellesley, Marquess Wellesley of Norragh, also called (from 1781) 2nd Earl of Mornington, Viscount Wellesley of Dangan Castle, or (from 1797) Baron Wellesley of Wellesley, of Dangan, County Meath, Ireland.

---

[10] [W. Carey], *The Holy Bible Containing the Old Testament and the New. Translated into the Mahratta [Marathi] Language by the Serampore Missionaries. Vol. V. Containing the New Testament* (Serampore: [Mission Press], 1811); W. Carey, *A Dictionary of the Mahratta Language* (Serampore: s. n., 1810).

[11] [W. Carey], [*Gospel of Matthew in Marathi*]. [Serampore: Mission Press], 1805.

[12] Linda Colley, *Britons: Forging the Nation 1707-1837* (New Haven: Yale University Press, 1992), 168-169.

[13] Church Covenant. March 24, 1793. Harvey Lane Baptist Church. Leicester Record Office, 24.D.71.II/1.

[14] Carey Center, East India Collection 24. Facsimile copy from The British Library, Add. ms. 39892 f. 61. Warren Hastings, "On the attempt to send missionaries to convert the Hindoos and Mosselmen" (endorsement by Col. S. Toone). Received from Mr. Hastings in 1807.

Statement Four

Carey had nothing to match that. Rather the opposite. He represented the Baptist Missionary Society headquartered in the market town of Kettering. Baptists summoned associations with social degradation, regicide in 1649, and military rule during the Protectorate of the 1650s. Their subsequent endurance of persecution in the days of John Bunyan in Bedford Gaol seemed to their betters a just recompense for the sin of Lucifer, rebellion.[15] The poet Robert Southey adopted the language of English caste to style them "low-born and low-bred mechanics."[16] Prejudice against Dissenters as king-killers, preachers of humbug, fanatics, and debauchers inspired the opposite of the diplomatic hospitality Carey received on the Governor-General's preserve. Such hateful stereotypes and the conspiracy theories that enveloped them justified everything from shunning and eviction to imprisonment.[17]

Carey's 26 years on the journey from angry radical to court linguist had witnessed the completion of the promise, such as it was, of the American and French Revolutions. The upshot of those revolutionary developments was to pit the Second British Empire, more South Asian than North Atlantic, against Napoleon. Consequently, the Carey-Wellesley qualified-mutual-appreciation dinner in 1805 took place while the world engaged in a multi-continental war. Months later, Napoleon won a crushing victory over his Alliance foes at Austerlitz, while by the end of October, Admiral Nelson had won at Trafalgar. With Napoleon ready to envelop the European continent in his own Continental System, thereby locking Britain out, India became ever more important to Britain with her still-powerful navy and international commercial and military interests. Accordingly, Wellesley and Carey, so cosmically different, came to share some attitudes, taking shelter in a common approach to government policy amid the international maelstrom of world war. They were both iconoclasts in a land teeming with living idols eager to thwart them. As Seramporians proceeded by Biblical

---

[15] Ronald Hutton, *The British Republic 1649-1660* (New York: St. Martin's Press, 2000), 30.

[16] [R. Southey], "Account of the Baptist Missionary Society," *Quarterly Review* (1809), I, 224.

[17] William Winterbotham, *The Trial of William Winterbotham, Assistant Preacher at How's Lane Meeting, Plymouth; Before the Hon. Baron Perryn, and a Special Jury, at Exeter; On the 25th of July, 1793 for Seditious Words Charged to Have Been Uttered in Two Sermons Preached on the 5th. and the 18th. of November, 1792*. Third Edn. (London: Printed for William Winterbotham, 1794).

The Serampore Form of Agreement

analogies, Wellesley operated according to analogies drawn from British society. For example, he had to be disabused of the notion that Maratha chiefs were to their Peshwa as the territorial aristocracy of England and Ireland were to George III.[18]

The dinner of Wellesley and Carey offered a parody of English willingness in a distant land, as opposed to their own, to transgress relations of social and religious caste. The power of the caste dining taboo, or at least the social prejudice against it, was as powerful in England even if it was somewhat less formal than in India. Its signal weakened to imperceptibility at this distance, where considerations of solidarity among the ruling minority became paramount. Dining formed a vital consideration at the Serampore Mission. The missionaries expected new converts not simply to be baptized by immersion in the Hooghly, deprived of its sacred powers. They also expected them to dine with the missionaries and leave caste forever.[19] Wellesley and Carey could break English caste together partly because they shared an aversion to the counting-house mentality and religious caution of the East India Company, the chartered monopoly of British India.

Dining with Wellesley carried a larger significance for the relationship between society and religion in British India as it was addressed months later in the Serampore Form of Agreement Statement Four. Dinner with Wellesley was a parody of the social disruption, the *feringhi* (pigeon Portuguese for foreigner) moment whereby the Serampore Missionaries insisted that new Christian converts dine with them to break caste and sever the thread that attached them to Indian society. Carey's mentally disabled wife, a sufferer of every problem that missionary endeavor could provoke, did not accompany him.[20] Carey was not always the most prominent, effective, or powerful of the Serampore Missionaries. But from the beginning, he was the avatar, icon, and celebrity influencer of the Serampore Mission, a performative role that he would have renounced, righteous in

---

[18] C. A. Bayly, *Empire and Information: Intelligence Gathering and Social Communication in India*, 1780-1870 (Cambridge: Cambridge University Press, 1996), 49.

[19] Carey Center, Ward Collection 2. Letter of William Ward to W. Hudson, October 8, 1801.

[20] James R. Beck, *Dorothy Carey: The Tragic and Untold Story of Mrs. William Carey* (Grand Rapids, MI: Baker Book House, 1992).

Statement Four

indignation and disgust, but which occasionally then and always since has formed the foundation of popular understanding of him.

How would Baptist missionaries respond to this cataclysm of opportunity? With Napoleonic Wars as cover, Wellesley had waged naked aggression and then spent the rest of his life justifying its extravagance and desolation.[21] It was truly apocalypse then.[22] The result was an imagined conjunction between nineteenth-century evangelization, British imperial prospects, and early Christian experience within the Roman Empire.[23] Still, Baptists were divided over Wellesley's conquests. Andrew Fuller expressed dislike for the Serampore Brethren's support of Wellesley's actions by pointing out that many in the British public thought Wellesley's actions were not so much different from Napoleon's.[24] And yet Fuller hoped Providence was at work, as in the Roman case, opening opportunities for evangelism. In ways, missionary motives diverged slightly from Baptist ones. The Baptist approach to state power was refined and precise, as had to be the case for Dissenters lobbying for a relaxation of laws that merely tolerated them without granting them religious freedom.[25]

There were limits to Carey's willingness to render honor to the subcontinental Caesar. Carey complained in 1804 that Fort William Vice-

---

[21] Center for Study of the Life and Work of William Carey, D. D., 1761-1834, Wellesley Collection 3. Letter marked "Private" from Marquis of Wellesley to "My Dear Sir," November 13, 1800; Robert Montgomery Martin, ed., *The Despatches, Minutes, and Correspondence of the Marquess Wellesley, K. G. During his Administration in India*, 5 vols., ed. Montgomery Martin (London: John Murray, 1836-1837); Richard Colley Wellesley, *Notes Relative to the Late Transactions in the Mahratta Empire. Fort William, 15th Dec. 1803* (London: John Stockdale, 1804); Marquis of Wellesley, *History of the All the Events and Transactions Which Have Taken Place in India: Containing the Negotiations of the British Government, Relative to the Glorious Success of the Late War* (London: John Stockdale, 1805).

[22] Andrew Fuller saw the apocalypse narrated in the pages of the infidel Edward Gibbon: M C. Noonkester, "Mr. Gibbon, Revd. Fuller and the Apocalypse," *Notes and Queries* 237 (1992): 486-489.

[23] As the French Revolution became the Napoleonic Wars, Baptists became, of all things, royalists: Robert Hall, *A Sermon Occasioned by the Death of Her Late Royal Highness The Princess Charlotte of Wales, Preached at Harvey-Lane, Leicester, November 16, 1817*. 3rd edn. (Leicester: Thomas Combe, 1818).

[24] E. Daniel Potts, "The Baptist Missionaries of Serampore and the Government of India, 1792-1813," *Journal of Ecclesiastical History* 15 (1964): 233.

[25] See, for example, "Paper of Reasons for Repealing the Test and Corporation Acts" of 1739. Bernard Lord Manning, *The Protestant Dissenting Deputies*, ed. Ormerod Greenwood (Cambridge: Cambridge University Press, 1952), 119.

The Serampore Form of Agreement

Chancellor Claudius Buchanan had altered his address to the governor-general "(the whole of the flattery is his)" without informing him before it was submitted. "Mr. B's design," wrote Carey, "was to bring our mission forward upon that public occasion."[26] Yet, Carey could not resist the opportunity provided by Wellesley's five-year plan that included the College of Fort William, his "Oxford of the East"[27]: to create an educated, linguistically versed bureaucratic order capable of ruling a polyglot, poly-cultural empire of millions. The recently constructed Government House hosted more than the Governor-General's banqueting. It staged annual disputations held in 1803, and on September 20, 1804, Carey addressed in Sanskrit an assemblage that included Wellesley, his brother, the future Duke of Wellington, the Supreme Court judges, the Supreme Council and "an envoy from Bagdad."[28] So it is hardly surprising that on that providential night when Carey dined with the Governor-General, he heard Wellesley say "he would rather have the testimony of a person like him...than the applause of a Parliament."[29] Wellesley likewise "expressed his satisfaction" with the Serampore Mission. For the moment, the government connection seemed, like the prayer of the righteous, to avail much.[30]

The predisposition of the Governor-General and the anxieties of the East India Company determined whether Baptist missionaries would enjoy the measure of toleration they enjoyed in Britain.[31] It was a measure of

---

[26] College Street Baptist Church Mss., Carey to John Ryland, 12 December 1804, cited in Allan K. Davidson, *Evangelicals and Attitudes to India, 1786–1813: Missionary Publicity and Claudius Buchanan* (Sutton: Courtney Press, 1990), 149, n. 34.

[27] Kenneth W. Jones, *Socio-Religious Reform Movements in British India*, The New Cambridge History of British India, III, 1 (Cambridge: Cambridge University Press, 1989), 26.

[28] S. Pearce Carey, *William Carey, D.D., Fellow of the Linnaean Society* (London: Hodder and Stoughton, 1923), 208.

[29] William Ward's *Journal* for February 10, 1805. "Bro. Carey being detained till late last night to dine with the Governor-General, he staid to preach at Calcutta. The Governor very graciously stopt [*sic*] & conversed with Bro. Carey for 5 minutes or thereabouts as he was walking with Mr Bown in the Levee Room. He asked how we were going on & thanked Bro. Carey for his Shanscrit Speech, & said he would rather have the testimony of a person like him respecting the College, than the applauses of a Parliament." Cited in Potts, *British Baptist Missionaries*, 176.

[30] Carey to John Sutcliff, February 8, 1805, cited in E. Carey, *Memoir of William Carey*, 477–478.

[31] J. S. Dharmaraj, "Serampore Missions and Colonial Connections," *Indian Church History Review* 26., no. 1 (1992): 21–35.

Statement Four

Wellesley's world-historical clout that he never lacked for enemies on multiple continents, and so he was ejected in August 1805 with cause, under protest, and in disgrace. His eastern star fell as quickly as it had arisen. For once, old, hard-bitten East India Company men could not have exaggerated. During Wellesley's administration, as it turned out, over 40% of government expenditures in Bengal were for the army.[32] The Wellesley phenomenon had raised East India Company from 17 million to 31 million in nine years and created a major trade imbalance because exports nosedived. For once, war was not good for business. Pitt the Younger, the Prime Minister, provided the final malediction, declaring that Wellesley had "acted most imprudently and illegally, and that he could not be suffered to remain in government."[33]

As a matter of course, the Serampore Mission spent time responding to events taking place elsewhere. Carey's dinner with Wellesley demonstrated that Statement Four of the Serampore Form of Agreement arose partly from the aftermath of epochal conquest. Caissons had rolled, elephants had charged. Seringapatam had happened. Yet, when Carey left the dinner in the residence that evening in February 1805, he could not have known that the occasion for the Serampore Form of Agreement in October would be the dismissal, at the height of his powers (and power) of Wellesley.

A few months after the diplomatic triumph of Wellesley's dinner, conditions had ripened for a societal approach to Christian missions in India. Wellesley, for his part, would not survive the political backlash occasioned by his ambitious territorial gains. The dangers involved in his approach seemed to be confirmed shortly after his departure in the Vellore Mutiny of 1806. So it was just as well that he abandoned the imperial mission and returned to England. Carey would again outlast one of his rivals by dint of survival. He would remain in India until his death almost three decades later. In the end, Wellesley would be undone not by the overwhelming

---

[32] P. J. Marshall, *Bengal: The British Bridgehead, Eastern India 1740–1828* in *The New Cambridge History of India*, II, 2, (Cambridge: Cambridge University Press, 1987), 135.

[33] Mary Drewery, *William Carey: Shoemaker and Missionary* (Grand Rapids, MI: Zondervan, 1978), 135.

number of his backbiting opponents but by the singularity of his Anglo-Irish brother,[34] the Duke of Wellington, who was destined to defeat Napoleon.

Disease

For the Serampore Mission, the distance from William Carey's imperial dinner in February to Carey's mission colleague William Ward's Serampore Form of Agreement in October was as vast as India's sunny plains. Wellesley's rise and fall opened and destabilized much of the Indian landscape. Even with a friend in the Governor-General's office, the task set for the Serampore Missionaries was daunting. True, the missionaries had no doubts about their goal. Socially marginalized back home, Serampore missionaries projected the Christianization of India. It was their burden, their bounden duty of handing Indians the Bible in their vernacular language.[35] Never mind that they confronted a treacherous imperial government. Never mind that the audience for their evangelism was distracted by poverty, resistant on the grounds of caste interest, uncomprehending of the alien nature of it, and pressed by hand-to-mouth concerns into perfect indifference. They dwelled in a world governed by a single imperative defined by William Carey's insistence that the "Great Commission" was binding on all generations of Christians, not just the Early Church. Anglicans took a different view. They measured the urgency of that Seramporian imperative according to its threat to revive seventeenth-century enthusiasm and fanaticism.[36]

The Serampore Mission had originated in William Carey's back-to-the-future insistence that New Testament exhortations to global evangelism were not limited to the early church. The Serampore Mission's growth occurred amid wildly varied circumstances: the vagaries of Danish

---

[34] Colley, *Britons*, 132; Iris Butler, *The Eldest Brother: The Marquess Wellesley* (London: Hodder & Stoughton, 1973).

[35] Miles Ogborn, *Indian Ink: Script and Print in the Making of the East India Company* (Chicago: University of Chicago Press, 2007), 206.

[36] Jon Mee, *Romanticism, Enthusiasm, and Regulation: Poetics and the Policing of Culture in the Romantic Period* (Oxford: Oxford University Press, 2003), 66.

Statement Four

foreign policy, travel aboard a ship of Danish registry called the *Kron Princesse Maria* and captained by Captain Christmas,[37] the crackbrained schemes of an East India Company surgeon, and local officials unable, in an age of religious mania and persecution, to tell the difference between English Baptists and French Catholic priests. The hallmark of the mission was its organization borrowed in whole or in part from the Central European Moravians with their Reformation that stretched back to the martyred Jan Huss.[38] Like their Moravian influencers, Seramporians exerted an impact well out of proportion to their numbers and possessions. Moravian communitarianism almost represented an insider language in which the various agencies with whom the missionaries had to deal were not only not conversant but entirely ignorant. Serampore communitarianism resembled its Moravian inspiration because it refused to accept defeat by a domestic religious establishment. It took the battle global. It engaged in lands distant in geography and belief, seeking to convert imperial triumphalism into Gospel opportunity. Furthermore, it produced a spiritual battle fought in multiple dimensions and different venues.

By the time of Wellesley's removal in 1805, the Serampore Mission had reached the intersection of two paths that lay through the thicket of polity, doctrine, and ritual. But the challenges it addressed to achieve that end were not only earthly, but subject to enormous complexity and risk. Trouble began with location. Proximity has often defined Serampore. It is located fifteen miles north of Kolkata (once Calcutta) on the banks of the Hooghly River. But distance has played a greater role in its history. Distant Danes ruled it as part of their entrepôt network[39] until 1845. The Danes possessed their own networked empire in Serampore and Tranquebar. Still, it was based on an earlier entrepôt model and unlikely to crave endless

---

[37] Providence in this case chose to work through Danish instruments. *Kron Princesse Maria*, Danish ship under Captain Christmas got them in. Daniel E. White, *From Little London to Little Bengal: Religion, Print, and Modernity in Early British India, 1793-1835* (Baltimore: John Hopkins University Press, 2013), 60.

[38] A. G. Spangenberg, *An Account of the Manner in which the Moravian Church of the Unitas Fratrum or United Brethren, Preach the Gospel and Carry on their Missions Among the Heathen* (London: H. Trapp, 1788).

[39] Donald Ferguson, "The Settlement of the Danes at Tranquebar and Serampore," *Journal of the Royal Asiatic Society of Great Britain and Ireland* (July 1898): 625-629.

The Serampore Form of Agreement

expansion in recognition of the modesty of national resources that were not shared with the upstart, overwhelmingly powerful, and insatiably grasping British.[40] There was a generational transition occurring. Colonel Olave Bie died May 18, 1805, while the Serampore Danish Church of Saint Olave dates from 1805. Afterward, the British who had always influenced it became its imperial rulers, acquiring it in a kind of imperial reversion, not unlike a nineteenth-century fellow of an Oxford college acquiring a parish. It became an odd staging ground, successful because effectively a city-state, a base for everything from the projected Christianization of India to a debt refuge and drug haven. Carey had to traverse an international boundary line as he commuted to work on the Hooghly from Serampore to Fort William in Calcutta. Passage there was not a foregone conclusion. Britain and Denmark lurched back and forth between armed conflict and peace, as Denmark unavailingly tried to remain neutral during the Napoleonic Wars.[41] In May 1801 began fifteen months of British rule of Serampore with the head of the Danish station there, Colonel Bie, under house arrest.[42] Such vagaries can only have reminded the Serampore Baptist Missionaries of the long history of persecution and war endured by the faithful and their friends.

Disease and death formed causes and effects of disorder in the body politic of Serampore. Global supply chain issues disturbed the sleep of the commercial interest. At the same time, colonial labor and raw material exploitation hardened urban and village life as the business cycle replaced the harvest cycle. Higher and higher levels of epidemic disease exacerbated social friction between groups and persons. Diseases of body, mind, and polity rendered the British presence in India deadly and debilitating. What for Indians were landscape and home became vertigo for Europeans. As foreigners, they were not subject to caste, village rules, or even European laws or norms. Statement Four proclaims that "life is short." *Vita brevis* is

---

[40] Tapan Banerjee, *The Mission of Danes from Tranquebar to Serampore* (Chandannagore, Hooghly: Sm. Sabita Banerjee, 2013), 24–35.

[41] Gareth Glover, *The Two Battles of Copenhagen 1801 and 1807: Britain and Denmark in the Napoleonic Wars* (Barnsley: Pen and Sword, 2018), 64–101.

[42] Timothy George, *Faithful Witness: The Life and Mission of William Carey* (Birmingham, AL: New Hope, 1991), 147.

Statement Four

usually coupled with "art is long." In Serampore's demography and mortality tables, the emphasis was on truncation. Life was short because of casualties, fevers, and deaths, which predominated with alternately alarming and numbing regularity in the years from the foundation of the mission at the turn of the nineteenth century.

For many missionaries to India, seasickness marked their long voyage to the subcontinent. The batch of missionaries sent out as replacements or reinforcements in 1804 was no exception. Missionary Joshua Rowe reported that fellow travelers, "of both sexes," found hymns, prayer, and even breakfast interrupted by indisposition. "The Captain has been sick, whilst "on my left hand is Mrs. Moore very sick, calling out lustily for a pot: bro: Moore holding her head and calling for a bucket. [Moore] Complains of being sick himself. Mary Biss vomiting upon her Mother." Moreover, "Bro: Mardon," ascending the ladder for fresh air, was "obliged to discharge the contents of his stomach before he could get on the deck." Lastly, "Mrs. Biss [was] very sick: bro: Biss holding her head..."[43]

Remedies in the British Indian pharmacopeia[44] were few, for medicine around the turn of the nineteenth century lacked antibiotics, of course, and so were limited in effectiveness.[45] Remarriages were inevitable and did not seem to have occasioned remark, as when William Ward married deceased Brother Fountain's widow, Mary Tidd.[46] Generation as life and metaphor applied to this situation and nourished its own peculiar form of creative tension, sometimes viewed in latter days as male propagandism.[47] The result of being surrounded by birth, death and illness, ever falling, relapsing,

---

[43] Joshua Rowe to John Sutcliff, January 3, 1804 in Timothy D. Whelan, ed., *Baptist Autographs in the John Rylands University Library of Manchester (1741-1845)* (Macon, GA: Mercer University Press, 2009), 116-118.

[44] Suman Seth, *Difference and Disease: Medicine, Race, and the Eighteenth-Century British Empire*. Edited by Sanjoy Bhattacharya (Cambridge: Cambridge University Press, 2018).

[45] David Arnold, *Science, Technology, and Medicine in Colonial India. The New Cambridge History of India* (Cambridge: Cambridge University Press, 2000).

[46] A. Christopher Smith, *The Serampore Mission Enterprise* (Bangalore: Centre for Contemporary Christianity, 2006), 31.

[47] Anna Johnston, *Missionary Writing and Empire, 1800-1860* (Cambridge: Cambridge University Press, 2003), 6-7.

and recovering, was a mortuary culture[48] defined by the prospect of famine and epidemics.[49] John Thomas, East India Company surgeon and initial colleague for Carey, had died in 1801.[50] William Grant died after landing in October 1799, John Fountain perished soon after, and Daniel Brunsdon fell two years later. Neither Grant nor Daniel Brunsdon survived long enough to "make any important impression,"[51] and Ward himself wondered at Grant journeying 15000 miles to convert Hindus only to die on the very cusp of beginning.[52] Significantly, herbal palliatives (the best that could be done in an age innocent of an antibiotic future) appeared in letters exchanged between William Carey and Serampore doctor, Nathaniel Wallich, a Danish converso.[53]

The demand for those missionaries sufficiently educated and committed was great. There were replacement delays amounting to missionary supply chain issues. Contrary to what is sometimes supposed, there was little or no honeymoon for the Serampore Mission. Moreover, as a project, it was contentious in a raucous way from the start.[54] Arguably, Serampore

---

[48] Mark Harrison, "A Dreadful Scourge: Cholera in early nineteenth-century India," *Modern Asian Studies* 54, no. 2 (March 2020), 502–553.

[49] J. G. Brooker, "Mission Burial Ground, Serampore." *Bengal Past and Present. Journal of the Calcutta Historical Society*. 47. Part 1. Serial no. 93. (January-March, 1934), 57–65; J. Higginbotham, *Men Whom India Has Known: Biographies of Eminent Indian Characters* (Madras: Higginbotham & Co., 1874); Holmes and Co. *The Bengal Obituary, or a Record to Perpetuate the Memory of Departed Worth, Being a Compilation of Tablets and Monumental Inscriptions from Various parts of the Bengal and Agra Presidencies* (Calcutta: J. Thomas, Baptist Mission Press, 1848); Cornelius Walford, *The Famines of the World: Past and Present* (London: Edward Stanford, 1879), 14. I am grateful to Professor Jon Brooke for this last reference.

[50] C. B. Lewis, *The Life of John Thomas, Surgeon of the Earl of Oxford East Indiaman, and First Baptist Missionary to Bengal* (London: Macmillan and Co., 1873); Arthur C. Chute, *John Thomas, First Missionary to Bengal, 1757-1801*. Introduction by A. J. Gordon (Halifax, Nova Scotia: Baptist Book and Tract Society, 1893); "On Wednesday the 20th Instant. A Sermon Will be Preached in the Harvey-Lane Meeting House. By the Rev. Mr. Thomas." *Leicester Herald*. Saturday, March 16, 1793.

[51] Potts, *British Baptist Missionaries*, 17, 22.

[52] Brian Stanley, *The History of the Baptist Missionary Society, 1792-1992* (Edinburgh: T&T Clark, 1992), 38.

[53] Carey Center, Carey Collection 7. Letter of William Carey to Nathaniel Wallich, April 20, 1824. John Fleming, M.D. [and William Carey], "A Catalogue of Indian Medicinal Plants and Drugs, with Their Names in the Hindustani and Sanscrit Languages," *Asiatick Researches*, 11 (London: J. Cuthell et al., 1812), 153–196; Edinburgh University Library, Special Collections. La.II.646/70.1. Letter to William Carey from Nathaniel Wallich (with reply) regarding treatment of patient with calomel. n. d.

[54] Stanley, *History of the BMS*, 39–43, 57–67.

Statement Four

was more than a Mission; it was a series of missions, a process, rather than an entity. The perpetual springtime of routine and order for Indians was a wild, hot, endless summer of chaos for European missionaries. The shifting power dynamic at Serampore affected internal politics, and not always for the better. Carey was more and more tied to the College of Fort William.

Meanwhile, factions formed as renegades, rogues, and deserters appeared, and disappointment sometimes became the order of the month.[55] Missionaries had hit commercial jackpots through their stake in the printing market. The result was a relative rise in their social status. Yet, they needed to treat both as external to the primary directive of their mission. Their community had to be self-regulating as it grew through marriage, birth, and conversion. Concerns of generation and gender often impinged on a patriarchal order.[56] Domestic demands of living in a missionary community produced unstated but extreme challenges for women and children. Women played a vital and yet, at times, half-visible role in mission societies.[57]

Statement Four addressed the personnel issues, mostly a matter of patriarchal uprightness, that arose as new arrivals did not always share the mutual sense of purpose characteristic of the founders of the Serampore Mission.[58] Personnel problems reflected the vagaries of cross-cultural adjustment to the Indian context. Even William Carey's commitments made him, without a shade of bitterness, a walking personnel problem himself.[59] His range of interests and occupations, from linguistics and botany to Bible

---

[55] [William Adam], *Correspondence Relative to the Prospects of Christianity, and the Means of Promoting its Reception in India* (Cambridge: From the University Press—Hilliard and Metcalfe, 1824).

[56] Center for Study of the Life and Work of William Carey, D. D. (1761-1834), Ward Collection 2. Letter of William Ward to W. Hudson, October 8, 1801.

[57] Sunil Kumar Chatterjee, *Hannah Marshman: The First Woman Missionary in India* (Hooghly: Sunil Kumar Chatterjee; S. K. Poddar, People's Little Press, Calcutta, 1987).

[58] Smith, *The Serampore Mission Enterprise*, 93-115.

[59] William Ward to Andrew Fuller, 7 October 1805, BMS, IN/17, conveniently cited in A. C. Smith, 34. Ward wrote, "Brother Carey is half his time in Calcutta, and his soul is in translation. He is cut out exactly for sitting doggedly to such an immense work. But he is not cut out for ... watching over and regulating 200 little things belonging to a Mission Settlement...not... for seizing opportunities, pursuing advantages, and pushing on a work with zeal."

The Serampore Form of Agreement

translation and college teaching, stretched the boundaries of the community. The Moravian model required, above all, a community of families. The death rate in India meant a constant need for replenishment, which brought inconstancy and vexations not uncommon among people on an interminable long-distance journey. The situation degenerated occasionally. Where the Moravian model prescribed a community of families unified in purpose, the Serampore reality could degenerate into frontier adventurism in certain unfortunate cases. It became an ongoing disruption, a polemic of sorts directed not at caste or empire or idolatry but inward toward the very constitution of Serampore itself. It vexed Carey and Ward, whose authority as "seniors" emerged largely in response to this distemper. John Biss, Richard Mardon, William Moore, and Joshua Rowe arrived as replacements in 1804. They were all in their twenties.[60] They required direction, but Serampore's fluid social and political situation permitted dissension and resistance to grow. A tight and often unpopular order was necessary to admonish young males journeying from a class society to an imperial frontier. But success in that area was more easily projected than effected.

1803 saw the arrival of the disputatious and unclubbable John Chamberlain.[61] Whatever one may think of his criticisms, and they were many, there can be no doubt that he refused to cooperate and went rogue.[62] In Chamberlain, disputatious tendencies turned inward. He was the godfather, as it were, of his biographer, William Yates, and the younger generation of missionaries whose existence was a rebellion against and an affront to the Serampore Mission of later years, becoming in a sense a splendid ruin of an idea supervised by its brilliant heir and caretaker, John Clark Marshman. In some respects, there was schism and secession from the beginning.[63]

---

[60] Potts, *British Baptist Missionaries*, 23, 246-247.

[61] Potts, 22-24; Smith, *The Serampore Mission Enterprise*, 101-103.

[62] [Anon.], *Sketches of India; or, Observations Descriptive of the Scenery, etc. in Bengal: Written in India in the Years 1811, 12, 13, 14; Together with Notes on the Cape of Good Hope, and St. Helena, Written at those Places, in Feb., March, and April 1815* (London: Black, Parbury, and Allen, 1816), 83-85.

[63] Baptist Missionary Society, IN/25, Richard Mardon to John Ryland, Cutwa, August 26, 1805.

Statement Four

There was also a question of strategy, which the Serampore brethren pursued at multiple levels. Would they lean toward the direct, village evangelism which the Christian world and the Mission's publicists craved, or would they move toward the more sedate and careful process of Bible translation for the ages, relying on—with the Renaissance, Reformation, and Enlightenment in mind—the printed press to multiply their impact beyond consciousness or comprehension of a human lifespan answering the problem of life expectancy in India?[64] The choice was neither simple nor simply binary. There were certainly tempting contemporary pulls in the latter direction,[65] particularly with the approach in 1804 of the British and Foreign Bible Society.[66]

Serampore needed reinforcements because competition loomed. Indeed, the façade of denominational cooperation in India, although of considerable value to evangelism, also threatened to become a zero-sum game at any moment. The resurgence of Anglicans and Catholics mattered in 1805 because their establishmentarian goals could not be assimilated into the vital concerns of Serampore Baptists regarding autonomy.[67] Anglicans, particularly, were on the march in the person of that Cambuslang-to-Cambridge-to Calcutta connection Claudius Buchanan, who pursued missions with all the fervor of a Scottish Anglican who had been jilted on the cusp of marriage.[68] Serampore Missionaries may have studied their way toward

---

[64] Serampore Missionaries, *Proposals for a Subscription for Translating the Holy Scriptures into the Following Oriental Languages: Shanscrit, Bengalee, Hindoostanee, Persian, Mahratta ... [etc.] and Chinese* (Serampore, Bengal: Printed at the Mission Press, 1806).

[65] Drewery, *William Carey: Shoemaker and Missionary*, 133.

[66] *Reports of the British and Foreign Bible Society, with Extracts of Correspondence, &c. Volume the Second, for 1811, 1812, and 1813* (London: J. Tilling, 1813); William Dealtry, *A Letter Addressed to the Rev. Dr. Wordsworth, in Reply to his "Reasons for Declining to Become a Subscriber to the British and Foreign Bible Society."* (London: J. Hatchard, 1810).

[67] Abbé J. A. Dubois, *Description of the Character, Manners, and Customs of the People of India; and of their Institutions, Religious and Civil. Translated from the French Manuscript* (London: Longman, Hurst, Rees, Orme, and Brown, 1817).

[68] Hugh Pearson, *Memoirs of the Life and Writings of the Rev. Claudius Buchanan, D.D., Late Vice-Provost of the College of Fort William in Bengal*. Second Edn. 2 vols. (Oxford: At the University Press for the Author, 1817).

The Serampore Form of Agreement

Christianization, but Buchanan was not bashful. While Carey plodded, Buchanan plotted.[69] He was performative through and through. He undertook a land voyage of discovery that amounted to a performative antiquarian tour of India suitable for publicity back in Britain.[70] Buchanan envisioned an Anglican empire in India made by scholarship boys and eager chaplains.[71] Buchanan, like T. B. Macaulay afterward, wanted to Anglicize India. This approach contrasted sharply with the model of indigeneity that the Serampore Missionaries followed.[72] Carey had reason to know because of his place in the command structure of the faculty of the College of Fort William.[73] And that was all before the Vellore Mutiny of 1806 brought contradictions within strategies for Christianization into the open air of missionary discourse, sometimes threatening even the possibility of evangelism.[74]

---

[69] On Buchanan as "promoter," "publicist," "organizer," and "explorer," see Davidson, *Evangelicals and Attitudes to India*, 108-163.

[70] Abel Holmes, "Indian Copy of the Hebrew Pentateuch, Discovered by the Rev. Claudius Buchanan, D. D.," *American Quarterly Register* 9, no. 1. (August, 1836): 59-67.

[71] Charles Grant, *A Poem on the Restoration of Learning in the East; Which Obtained Mr. Buchanan's Prize* (Cambridge: R. Watts at University Press, 1805). High Anglicans would come to regret cooperation, however tactical, with "Dissenters." H. P. Liddon, *Life of Edward Bouverie Pusey*, 4 vols. (London: Longmans, Green and Co., 1893), 1:285-286.

[72] Claudius Buchanan, *Memoir of the Expediency of an Ecclesiastical Establishment for British India Both as a Means of Perpetuating the Christian Religion among our own Countrymen and as a Foundation for the Ultimate Civilization of the Natives* (London: Cadell and Davies, 1805); William Tennant, *Thoughts on the Effects of the British Government on the State of India: Accompanied with Hints Concerning the Means of Conveying Civil and Religious Instruction to the Natives of that Country* (Edinburgh: Longman, Rees, Hurst, and Orme, 1807).

[73] British Library, India Office, IOR/F/4/364/9081, April-July 1811. Carey received an allowance of 150 rupees per month for an establishment to help him obtain transcripts of scarce and valuable Sanskrit works. Sunil Kumar Chatterjee, "William Carey and the Fort William College," in *Carey's Obligation and India's Renaissance*, Eds. J. T. K. Daniel and Roger E. Hedlund (Serampore: Council of Serampore College, 1993), 228-237.

Pearson, *Memoirs*, 1:324ff. For Buchanan on Fort William. *Essays by the Students of the College of Fort William in Bengal to which are Added the Theses Pronounced at the Public Disputations in the Oriental Languages on the 6th February, 1802.* (Calcutta: The Honorable Company's Press, 1802). [William Carey], "No. IX. Translation of a Speech in the Shanscrit Language, Delivered by the Shanscrit Professor, Acting as Moderator, at the Oriental Disputations on the 20th of September, 1804; Extracted from the Third Volume of the Primitiae Orientales" in *The College of Fort William in Bengal* (London: Cadell and Davies, 1805), 168-178; Sisir Kumar Das, *Sahibs and Munshis: An Account of the College of Fort William* (New Delhi: Orion Publications, 1978).

[74] Karen Chancey, "The Star in the East: The Controversy over Christian Missions to India, 1805-1813," *The Historian* 60, no. 3 (1998): 507-522.

Statement Four

Duty

In October 1805, William Ward, writing to and for his colleagues and addressing posterity amid the demands of an immediate tactical situation, tried once again to establish what the Serampore Mission was or ought to be. As a form of agreement, Ward's Statement Four proclaims neither law nor intent. Rather, Statement Four proclaims an attitude that is personal and ethical, bespeaking a series of applied virtues. It derived standards for missionary conduct from scriptural injunctions of various sorts. It displayed a rough and ready but informed awareness of conditions on the landscape and fitted them into a sustained, if implicit, social analysis. Sociability was to be prized, and a missionary must even be considered "culpable" if restricting ministrations to "preaching two or three times a week" in a "place of worship." Moreover, "conversations" with "natives almost every hour in the day" were necessary. That such conversations resulted in a missionary being "instant in and out of season" was not only scriptural but part of an approach to social totality in proclaiming "the glad tidings of salvation."

There is throughout Statement Four an awareness of the delimiting character of political, social, and cultural circumstances. But there is also a sense of "the opportunities of doing good," which, particularly in distant villages, owed something to Wellesley's military extravagances. Serampore, ballyhooed by Baptists as a medium of global influence,[75] remained a conjunction of jurisdictions, Denmark, Britain, Indian princes, village communities, castes, commercial nexuses, criminals, and occupations. Seramporians possessed the unassailable confidence that attends upon the security of purpose, despite a constant awareness that India was rife with gods. The ambiguity of the legal status of Serampore offered a perpetual stimulus to reinvention and a series of problems. Was Serampore a closed corporation, a wholly owned subsidiary, a colony? Uncertainty of tenure, sometimes amounting to a problem of legality, had made Wellesley's favor necessary. The apostrophization of "Serampore" has proven, then, the opposite of the historical reality experienced by Seramporians. Like Serampore, the Danish colony, the Serampore Mission occasioned

---

[75] Niall Ferguson, *Empire: The Rise and Demise of the British World Order and the Lessons for Global Power* (New York: Basic Books, 2003), 137.

The Serampore Form of Agreement

episodes and conflicts, changes and disavowals, dreams and nightmares, hope and despair. It was valuable in the spiritual and financial sense, so it was contested as much or more than it was constructed. Its insecurity of tenure, caught between the Baptist Missionary Society, the East India Company, the Danish government, and the British Empire, in a vast, crowded country was a provocation to nearly infinite forms of conflict, many of which distracted individual missionaries from their labors.

Seramporians were reviewers and expositors of texts, which they made and purveyed while, alternatively, baptizing with water in a river valley. They proposed to throw Christian water on Hindu fires while relying upon pre-Darwinian science and a received (and quite sophisticated) ethnography in which the Pashtuns in Afghanistan were descended from the Lost Tribes of Israel.[76] At times, it all seemed too much. As Andrew Fuller told Ward in September 1805, "I seem to view you all as a ship in a tempestuous sea ... some washed overboard ... others bruised ... and all frequently at their Wits end."[77]

Statement Four pointed to the need, perhaps the demand, to discountenance external political activity and impose unity by the consensus of the senior missionaries. So much is evident in Carey's letters to the Philadelphia Baptist Association in 1801 and 1805.[78] And that was to attend to the social situation at hand. Commitment to evangelism was pervasive. But commitment and implementation were two different things. Divine commandment called for implementation by human instruments. The Serampore Form of Agreement promoted the transition in tactics from direct, if diffuse and remote evangelism, to the creation of a Bible translation diaspora. The shift from far-flung evangelism to intensive Bible translation had begun, as was evident in an international push to that effect. There was no question that the Serampore Mission could adopt a two-track approach, but there was some question whether, given its personnel and resources, it

---

[76] Colin Kidd, *British Identities Before Nationalism: Ethnicity and Nationhood in the Atlantic World, 1600-1800* (Cambridge: Cambridge University Press, 2000).

[77] Baptist Missionary Society, H/2, Andrew Fuller to William Ward, September 12, 1805.

[78] A. D. Gillette, ed., *Minutes of the Philadelphia Baptist Association 1707-1807, Being the First One Hundred Years of Its Existence. Tricentennial Edition, 1707 to 2007*, Philadelphia Association Series (Springfield, MO: Particular Baptist Press, 2002).

Statement Four

could afford to do both. Amid the consistency of providential metaphor, messages and motives occasionally got mixed. In 1805 and 1806, Dr. Furman of Charleston "was active in raising funds for aiding the translations of the Scriptures by Drs. Carey and Marshman."[79] At the same time, the Serampore Brethren could conclude that knowledge of Hindu ways of thought, teaching, and practice "is of the highest consequence, if we would gain their attention to our discourse, and would avoid being barbarians to them."[80] It was a marketing challenge to convince people to commit the equivalent of social suicide for an invisible cause in a culture that permeated every aspect of life. Serampore missionaries were projectors imbued with an idea, jealous of its furtherance, and eager to adapt themselves to its demands as they perceived them each day.

Seramporians viewed Hinduism as a Brahmin plot and therefore chose not to attack "Brahminism" directly but to appeal to individual souls in contravention of it.[81] They applied stringent standards for conversion and no compromise with caste, which subjected them, in many cases, to disappointment. From a marketing standpoint, it was the treatment of inevitable failure as success. Dining with the missionaries appealed to the senses of real-world incarnation as spiritual truths loomed. But they also possessed control of the means of scriptural production. Liberating scripture from the Brahmins. The missionaries attacked the social doctrine of caste rather than Hindu gods themselves, not trying to apply European astringents of skepticism or indifference. Hostility centered on the missionaries' insistence upon sacrilege. Caste was an outgrowth of priestcraft like the European class system that developed under the Anglican and Catholic confessional states. Not so much a Long Reformation as Another Reformation, an end run around the semi-impregnable nature of Anglican and Catholic confessional power into a region where British power could be leveraged

---

[79] H. A. Tupper, *Two Centuries of the First Baptist Church of South Carolina, 1683–1883. With Supplement* (Baltimore: R. H. Woodward, 1889), 148.

[80] Statement Two, SFA in the *Periodical Accounts Relative to the Baptist Missionary Society* (London: J. W. Morris, 1806), III, 200.

[81] Jeffrey Cox, *The British Missionary Enterprise since 1700* (New York: Routledge, 2008), 125.

into opportunity. Instead of a "City on a Hill," it was a "Village in an Alluvial Floodplain." It is more than that they were saying one thing to Indians and another to the society-minders back home in Britain. It is that they were homeless and perceived it as their duty to attempt what was, viewed in cultural terms, an improbability.[82]

For Carey, one-way travel to India meant demotion, starting over in a return to peasant status. He was compelled to "go up into the Country; and build... a hut, and live like the Natives."[83] He was first among missionaries in that sense, and was so regarded by his colleagues. Collegiality formed them into a college before Serampore College happened over a decade later. Even the most rudimentary collegiality was a protection, a tactical acknowledgment of the realities of Christianity in the Global South. The usual Battle Royale for the Serampore Brethren with unpredictable resistance from the government and pushback from Hindus amounted to social and spiritual warfare.[84]

Confrontation with forces of resistance to the Christian message required steadfastness and willingness to adapt strategies of evangelization, a flexibility often implied rather than explicitly proclaimed in the text of Statement Four.[85] India was, for British interlopers, an imagined place, and even when located there, they adopted a Eurocentric perspective.[86] British interloping could not destroy the social citadels of village life. But it might Orientalize knowledge of Hindu and Muslim social customs.[87]

---

[82] Lata Mani, *Contentious Traditions: The Debate on Sati in Colonial India* (Berkeley: University of California Press, 1998), 121-157.

[83] Potts, *British Baptist Missionaries*, 13-14.

[84] Richard Fox Young, "Church Sanskrit: An Approach of Christian Scholars to Hinduism in the Nineteenth Century," *Wiener Zeitschrift für die Kunde Südasiens* 23 (1979): 205-231; Richard F. Young, *Resistant Hinduism: Sanskrit Sources on Anti-Christian Apologetics in Early Nineteenth Century India* (Leiden: Brill, 1981).

[85] See Geoffrey A. Oddie, *Imagined Hinduism: British Protestant Missionary Constructions of Hinduism, 1793-1900* (New Delhi: Sage Publications, 2006).

[86] Michael Wintle, *Eurocentrism: History, Identity, White Man's Burden* (London and New York: Routledge, 2021). For the premonitions and for "Asiatic Despotism", see Javed Majeed, *Ungoverned Imaginings: James Mill's The History of British India and Orientalism* (Oxford: Clarendon, 1992), esp. 28ff.

[87] British imperialists essentialized Muslims and Hindus. William Tennant, *Indian Recreations; Consisting Chiefly of Strictures on the Domestic and Rural Economy of the Mahomedans and Hindoos.* 2nd edn., 2 vols. (London: Longman, Hurst, Rees, and Orme, 1804).

Statement Four

The Christian insistence upon literacy, reading the scriptures, versus the Hindu emphasis on visuality, seeing a god, created a space contested not only spiritually but intellectually. Idolatry for the missionaries formed a local manifestation of a global problem. Objects, the missionaries insisted, were not to be worshipped but classified. It might be added that translating and printing did not bring or require vision.[88] It may seem that reading is knowing and seeing is believing. For the Seramporians, it was reversed: reading was believing and seeing was knowing. The Hindu and Muslim perspective is left on the implied margins.[89] Much of that consideration had already been traced in the various Orientalist works of empire-builders such as Warren Hastings, Charles Wilkins, Nathaniel Brassey Halhed, and Sir William Jones.[90] Myths of "Oriental despotism" under Mughal rule had long served Company purposes of conquest and usurpation and created skepticism in Indian populations.[91] That, in turn, raises the questions of to what extent the Agreement was interactive, and how Hindus or Muslims would have read it? Had subalterns seen the Serampore Form of Agreement, they may have read it with hostility. In the event, missionary mingling with the regnant culture had to become self-regulating because of the overtly sexual nature of certain Indian religious practices.[92]

Word choices in Statement Four apply Biblical analogy to a shifting, tricky set of social and cultural circumstances. "Doing good" is a term

---

[88] White, *From Little London to Little Bengal*, 57-63, esp. 65.

[89] S. V. Desika Char. *Hinduism and Islam in India: Caste, Religion and Society from Antiquity to Early Modern Times* (Princeton, NJ: Markus Wiener Publishers, 1993).

[90] A. Yusuf Ali, *A Cultural History of India during the British Period* (Bombay: D. B. Taraporevala, Sons & Co., 1940, reprinted 1976), 28-46. Two or three generations removed from the conquests that founded the Second British Empire. [William Jones], *Works of Sir William Jones. In Six Volumes* (London: Printed for G. G. and J. Robinson, Pater-Noster-Row; and R. H. Evans [Successor to Mr. Edwards], No. 26, Pall Mall, 1799).

[91] See John R. McLane, *Land and Local Kingship in Eighteenth-Century Bengal* (Cambridge: Cambridge University Press, 1993), 3-26.

[92] Brian Young, "'The Lust of Empire and Religious Hate': Christianity, History, and India, 1790-1820," in *History, Religion, and Culture: British Intellectual History, 1750-1950*. Edited by Stefan Collini, Richard Whatmore, and Brian Young (Cambridge: Cambridge University Press, 2000), 91-111

The Serampore Form of Agreement

used in the New Testament and was another aspect of social operation according to a Moravian model.[93] Wellesley had advanced ruthlessly. Missionaries must not imitate that example in any way. Nor must they become throwbacks to merchant adventurers, buccaneers, or those East India Company representatives known as "factors." And so, Ward had intuited cross-cultural communication almost by default.[94] In covenant and constitutional terms, "culpable" as applied to a missionary's neglect to perform a divine duty was a legal category with a suggestion of immediate sanction. It also appears in Genesis 44:32 as a matter of a surety bond, in Deuteronomy 22:8 as a form of liability for violation of a product warranty, and in Ezekiel 25:12 as a punishment for vengeance.

Reference in Statement Four to servants[95] and laborers was a shot at caste and a wedge. It certainly reflected the elementary social awareness that they were likely to be more promising targets of evangelism than cushy, well-appointed, and educated Brahmins enjoying the advantages that Indian society offered. The notion of making an itinerary into villages, markets, assemblies, and public places for indigenous Indians referred to going where no East India Company chaplain could go.[96] "Village to village" and "assembly to assembly": geography and a roving polemic for the gospel. Reprising the "lazy Englishman in a warm climate" motif clearly arose from their own experience. To be sure, the heat and humidity of India would have been something a European could endure only on-site on the subcontinent. This climatological realism stopped short of determinism but hinted at traits specific to regions of the world from Jamestown to Calcutta.

"Doing good," as referenced in Statement Four, distills New Testament language and the Gospel message. Association with idolatry had to

---

[93] August Gottlieb Spangenberg, *An Exposition of Christian Doctrine, as Taught in the Protestant Church of the United Brethren, or Unitas Fratrum* (London: W. and A. Strahan, 1784).

[94] Stanley, *The History of the BMS*, 48.

[95] Carey Center, East India Collection 28. "Servants of Bengal." Bound volume of thirteen Company Style paintings, gouache on mica, ca. 1840. Includes "Mace Bearer or Porter," "Bengalee Writer," "Aya or Nurse," etc. See Susan Bayly, *Caste, Society and Politics in India from the Eighteenth Century to the Modern Age. The New Cambridge History of India*, Vol. 4, No. 3. (Cambridge: Cambridge University Press, 1999).

[96] Daniel O'Connor, *The Chaplains of the East India Company, 1601–1858* (London: Bloomsbury, 2012).

be avoided and yet the trappings of idolatrous practice had to be engaged through study and observation for idolatry to be challenged and overthrown. What Hindus and Muslims thought of these approaches may be inferred from a lack of early success. At any rate, missionary encounter was more than a Eurocentric process. Indeed, its most dramatic achievements, translations, Indian conversions with renunciation of caste, and the publishing renaissance that shaped modern Bengal, were partnerships.

Serampore missionaries sought to respect what they considered social and cultural goods in a society that they regarded to be (in a manner not entirely unlike their country of origin) idol-ridden and depraved. They had to assess the likely results of immediate expenditure of evangelistic capital versus banking goodwill for posterity. Through a process of winnowing, they determined that stamina was to be valued above all. Statement Four, seen in context, reveals that Christian remedies must come slow and deep rather than fast and shallow. The Seramporians would have rejected alternating notions that they were missionary heroes or imperialist adjuncts; to accept either characterization obscures the creative tensions they faced. Seramporians proclaimed the gospel for everyone, and from that platform, inspired an indigenous nonconformity. The Christian communities they helped to originate would become an alternately tolerated and persecuted minority of believers. It is not ironic, therefore, that Christianity in today's fragmented Britain must still reflect on the example afforded by indigenous Christianity in India. Awareness of empire, environment, and duty as social considerations of evangelism exemplified in Statement Four of the Serampore Form of Agreement helped to make that Indian Christianity the example that it remains.

STATEMENT FIVE

"Christ the Crucified, the Great Subject of our Preaching."

Peter de Vries

The fifth statement forms the keystone of the ten mission principles of the *Serampore Form of Agreement*.[1] Expressed in William Ward's passionate language, the statement reflects the Serampore Associates' doctrinal convictions on the centrality of Christ's sacrifice for Gospel preaching that "constantly nourished and sanctified the church."[2] In its singular focus, Statement Five is the most precise theological expression of the SFA and calls for careful analysis to understand it in its missiological and cultural context.

Having established the necessity of preaching as the primary means of evangelization in the previous statement, the fifth statement of the SFA focuses on the core of the Gospel message. As with the first four statements, Ward points to biblical and historical precedents to formulate his forthright conclusion. The statement begins, "we must keep to the example of Paul and make the great subject of our preaching, Christ the crucified." It ends emphatically with "Oh! then may we resolve to know nothing among Hindoos and Mussulmans but Christ and him crucified." Ward

---

[1] The original version of the *Serampore Form of Agreement* has a clear structure: a preamble, ten statements ("First ... Tenthly") and an epilogue ("Finally"). The long title: *Form of Agreement, respecting the great Principles from which the Brethren of the Mission at Serampore think it their duty to act In the Work of Instructing the Heathen, agreed upon at a Meeting of the Brethren, at Serampore, on Monday, October 7, 1805* (Serampore: The Brethren's Press, 1805), hereafter SFA. As shown earlier, it is attributed to William Ward.

[2] Twice reflected by the emotional outburst "Oh!" typical for Ward's writing.

frames his statement with the Apostle Paul's audacious avowal to the Corinthians: "but we preach Christ crucified."[3]

For Ward, the crux of the doctrine of the atonement is the cross—the same cross that stood at the heart of the sermons of Luther, Whitefield, Wesley, the Puritans, and the Moravians.[4] By appealing to the Apostles, church history, and mission practice, Ward points to the priority of crucicentric preaching in mission work. Moreover, he asserts that the missionaries' experience at Serampore confirmed this since every Hindu convert had "been won by the astonishing and all-constraining love exhibited in our Redeemer's propitiatory death." Thus, Ward and his associates place Christ, the cross, and the atonement at the heart of the SFA, making it the center of their mission praxis. Seventeen years later, writing a devotional work while at sea, Ward had not changed his mind: "What is the Bible, if we take Christ out of it? What is preaching, ... without him? What is the doctrine of God without the Mediator? ... What would heaven be without a Redeemer ... How important then in the scheme of christian doctrine is the vicarious sacrifice of Christ! ... Without this, it loses all its virtue and energy."[5]

In the following, we will explore the background of this theme, its impact on the Serampore Mission, and its relevance for global mission today.

Paul's Cross-centeredness
In the face of religious Jews seeking miracles and intellectual Greeks impressed only by skillful oratory, Paul writes that the Gospel does not give into cultural forces but focuses on "Christ and him crucified" as the central truth of the Gospel (1 Cor 1:22–23, 2:2). Though the Gospel seemed mere foolishness (or folly) in the world's eyes—because Jews and Greeks alike rejected the Apostles' teaching on Jesus as the crucified Savior—for

---

[3] 1 Corinthians 1:23 and 2:2.
[4] SFA, 7. Secretary Andrew Fuller, who was averse to Methodism, rephrased the reference to Whitefield, Wesley and the Puritans with: "most useful men in the eighteenth century." *Periodical Accounts Relative to the BMS* (1806), III, 202. Hereafter, *PA*.
[5] William Ward, *Reflections on the Word of God, for Every Day in the Year* (London: Simpkin & Marshall, 1825), 163–164.

Statement Five

Paul, the person and work of Christ is the "sum and substance of the gospel." His sole modus operandi was its proclamation.⁶ Though crucifixion as a form of punishment was utterly abhorrent to Jews, Romans, and Greeks, it became the hallmark of early Christian teaching, and the cross its treasured symbol. It would not have evoked such a strong reaction among people unfamiliar with this cruel instrument of slow death.⁷ However, the ideas of punishment, unjust suffering, sacrifice, and reconciliation are universal. So, although the crucifixion of the Son of God completely defies human reason, Paul continues to point to the cross as the full and final expression of God's love in Christ. With its Hebrew root of a sacrificial lamb slain to cover the "mercy-seat" of the ark of covenant, the cross has become the place where God "once for all" shows his mercy, inaugurating a new order (Lev 17:11, Rom 3:24-25, Heb 9:5, 10:10). Moreover, Paul asserts that for those who believe, the truth of Christ's redemption through the cross holds tremendous power (1 Cor 1:18, 24). And this central doctrine of "Christ crucified" became the secret of the early church's growth, a truth that the Protestant Reformers Luther and Calvin rediscovered. A doctrine so crucial that the English coined the term *atonement* (being or becoming "at one" or "at-one-ment") to convey its insights. This truth pervades the entire SFA.⁸

The Age of Atonement

The emphasis of Statement Five reflects the warm evangelical convictions of British Particular Baptists who were impacted by Jonathan Edwards' Evangelical Calvinism, who taught a "finely-struck balance between divine

---

⁶ *Matthew Henry's Commentary on the Whole Bible*, vol. VI (New York & London: Fleming H. Revell, 1721), 512.

⁷ Though legends drew parallels between Krishna and Christ, Hindus had no word for crucifixion. Poles, stakes and trees were used as gallows or gibbets, on which criminals were impaled or hung. F. Wilford, "Origin and Decline of the Christian Religion in India," in *Asiatick Researches*, vol. X, (1811), 61.

⁸ SFA, 7. Ward, *Reflections*, 84. "In contemporary theological usage atonement has come to mean the process by which reconciliation with God is accomplished through the death of Christ. Its earlier usage tended to have as well the wider meaning of the end sought through the atoning process, as in reconciliation, redemption... and salvation." William J. Wolf, "Atonement: Christian Concepts," in *The Encyclopedia of Religion*, ed. Mircea Eliade, vol. I (New York & London: Macmillan, 1987), 495.

The Serampore Form of Agreement

sovereignty and human responsibility."[9] From their origins, Baptists taught a fervent "religion of the heart" and particular doctrinal convictions expressed in the London Confession of Faith (1644).[10] Adhering closely to the biblical text, Particular Baptists actively preached that everyone needs conversion and emphasized Christ's sacrifice as the means of salvation. This was a priority they shared with other Evangelicals such as the Puritans, the Moravians, Methodists, evangelical Anglicans, and Presbyterians.[11] So significant was this evangelical influence on English-speaking society that Boyd Hilton argues the first half of the nineteenth century was the "Age of Atonement."[12] A flurry of Christian activities marked the period, transforming the British Isles through voluntarism expressed in denominational cooperation around societal issues like the abolition of slavery, temperance, Bible distribution, Sunday schools, and mission societies. At the same time, the second half of the 18th century saw the rise of scientific discovery and sociopolitical and philosophical discourse, typified as the "Age of Improvement."[13] The Serampore missionaries who came of age at this time of scientific, technological, commercial, and political expansion naturally shared the intellectual curiosity typical of the age. Alongside their missionary work, they did research in agriculture, astronomy, botany, cultural practices, linguistics, and religious thought, and they took great care to classify, describe, and publish their observations for an Indian and British audience.[14] They operated from a Calvinist work ethic that valued practical service, or "Christian usefulness," which was synonymous

---

[9] Brian Stanley, *The History of the Baptist Missionary Society, 1792-1992* (Edinburgh: T&T Clark, 1992), 3-6. esp. 4.

[10] William H. Brackney, *The Baptists* (New York & London: Greenwood, 1988), 71. This document was superseded by the 1689 Second London Confession of Faith.

[11] David W. Bebbington, *Evangelicalism in Modern Britain: A History from the 1730s to the 1980s* (Grand Rapids, MI: Baker Book House, 1992), 2-3; Boyd Hilton, *The Age of Atonement: The Influence of Evangelicalism on Social and Economic Thought, 1795-1865* (Oxford: Clarendon, 1988), 8-9.

[12] Hilton argues how (British) society from 1785 to 1865 was marked by a "dominant mode of thought, an amalgam of enlightenment rationalism and evangelical eschatology, and its core or 'hinge' was the Christian doctrine of Atonement." Hilton, *Age of Atonement*, 3.

[13] Popularized by Asa Briggs, *The Age of Improvement, 1783-1867*, 2nd edn. (London & New York: Routledge, 2000).

[14] For an overview of scientific and technological advances during the missionaries' life, Keith Farrer, *William Carey: Missionary and Botanist* (Kew, Vic: Carey Baptist Grammar School, 2005),

with being "fruitful" and "profitable."[15] Though their "vital religion" contrasted with the dry rationalism (and rigid hyper-Calvinism) of their forebears, all their evangelical efforts—including preaching—are best viewed in the light of this deep desire for progress and improvement.[16] Therefore, both Atonement and Improvement, expressed in a desire to save and an urge to improve, pervades the entire SFA.

The Christ-centered Emphasis in Carey's Preaching

In his methodical yet passionate *Enquiry*, William Carey held up the examples of Eliot, Brainerd, and the Moravians for mission because they were well-known, and their exceptional evangelistic efforts were beyond dispute among Evangelicals.[17] After commenting on John Eliot's success planting churches and establishing schools in New England, Carey refers to David Brainerd's ministry of prayer and preaching among American Indians, where "an extraordinary work of conversion was wrought."[18] For Carey, these cross-cultural conversions proved that obedience to Jesus' command "to go and teach the nations" (Matthew 28:19) would certainly be blessed.

69-74. For specific scientific achievements, Sujit Sivasundaram, "'A Christian Benares': Orientalism, Science and the Serampore Mission of Bengal," *The Indian Economic and Social History Review* 44, no. 2 (2007): 111-145.

[15] "Another part of our work is the forming our native brethren to usefulness, fostering every kind of genius, and cherishing every gift and grace in them. In this respect we can scarcely be too lavish of our attention to their improvement." SFA, 10. Ward's letters often extoll the virtues of benevolence, piety and usefulness. Samuel Stennett, *Memoirs of the Life of the Rev. William Ward*, 2nd edn. (London: Simpkin & Marshall, Holdsworth, 1825), 63, 104, 105, 115-122, 260; Matthew M. Reynolds, *The Spirituality of William Ward* (West Lorne, Ontario: H&E Academic, 2023), 118-121. The idea is perhaps based on John 15:1-8 and Eph 2:10.

[16] This should not be taken too far, however. A recent study argues that Serampore Baptists' "failure" to spiritually and morally "improve" Bengali converts resulted in them turning "towards projects of temporal improvement... [which helped] advancing the colonial project... promoting the 'otherization' of Indians who needed to be improved by superior Britons." Laura Tavolacci, "Agriculture as Redemption: Baptist Missionaries, Bengali Elites, and the Agri-Horticultural 'Improvement' of India, 1793-1840" (Dissertation, Davis, University of California, 2018), 5.

[17] Bebbington, *Evangelicalism in Modern Britain*, 40-41.

[18] William Carey, *An Enquiry into the Obligations of Christians, to Use Means for the Conversion of the Heathens: In Which the Religious State of the Different Nations of the World, the Success of Former Undertakings, and the Practicability of Further Undertakings Are Considered*, New facsimile edn. with intro by E. A. Payne (Leicester, London: Ann Ireland; Carey Kingsgate Press, 1792, 1961), 36. Carey in his *Enquiry* refers five times to "Elliot" [*sic*] and Brainerd.

The Serampore Form of Agreement

Carey and his associates continued to hold up their example throughout their missionary careers. His *Journal* notes the encouragement received by re-reading Brainerd's *Journal* during his early years of preaching among the Bengalis.[19] Brainerd, in his reflection on the success of his ministry, had remarked that Christ crucified was the "centre and the mark ... the principal scope and drift" of his preaching, which gave him great boldness and freedom.[20]

> And this was the preaching God made Use of for the Awakning [*sic*] of Sinners, and the Propagation of this Work of Grace among the Indians. - And, it was remarkable, when I was favoured with any special freedom in discoursing of the Ability and Willingness of Christ to save Sinners, and the need they stood in of such a Saviour, there was then the greatest Appearance of Divine Power in awakening secure Souls, promoting Convictions begun, and comforting the Distressed.[21]

Carey's *Journal* records the challenges of preaching among the Bengalis while still a language learner. With limited proficiency, he reveled in preaching the Gospel, "the very element of [his] soul,"[22] expounding concepts of sin, repentance, faith, and salvation.[23] His journal entries from 1792-1795 reflect his identification with Brainerd's experience. On one especially encouraging Lord's Day, he rejoices that his hearers remember the name of Jesus Christ and understand the need for forgiveness to receive

---

[19] April 19, 1794. *Carey's Journal* in Terry G. Carter, ed., *The Journal and Selected Letters of William Carey* (Macon, GA: Smyth & Helwys, 2000), 25, 26. For Brainerd's influence on Carey, see A. De M. Chesterman, "The Journals of Brainerd and Carey," *Baptist Quarterly* 19, no. 4 (1961): 147-156.

[20] David Brainerd, *An Abridgment of Mr. David Brainerd's Journal among the Indians. Or, the Rise and Progress of a Remarkable Work of Grace among a Number of the Indians in the Provinces of New-Jersey and Pennsylvania* (London: For John Oswald, 1748), 92. Jonathan Edwards, *The Life of the Rev. David Brainerd, Missionary to the Indians*, new edn. (London: Burton and Smith, and E.W. Morris, 1818), 416.

[21] Brainerd, *Abridgement of Brainerd's Journal*, 95.

[22] June 14, 1795. *Carey's Journal* in Carter, *Carey's Journal and Letters*, 59.

[23] For a typical outline of a Serampore Gospel presentation, see "The Substance of a Sermon to the Hindoos" by Felix Carey in John Rippon, ed. *The Baptist Annual Register for 1801 and 1802*, vol. II (London: Sold by Button and Conder, 1803), 840-844.

salvation. On another, he "endeavoured to preach, and had more enjoyment than some time past ... enabled to speak to them of the necessity of a Sincere union with Christ."[24] After preaching to a large congregation on God's forgiveness to "save sinners in a Way in which Justice and Mercy could Harmonize, Carey felt his "soul warmed with the opportunity and hope for Good, [and] ... greater concern for the Salvation of the heathen," he notes it caused him to pray more fervently. But a year later, after his hearers had grown tired, he confided to his sisters, "I preach every Day to the Natives, and twice on the Lord's Day constantly, besides other itinerant labours; and I try to speak of Jesus Christ and him crucified, and of him alone, but my soul is often much dejected to see no fruit."[25] However, not witnessing powerful responses, as in Brainerd's audiences, did not deter him.[26] Rather, it emboldened him. That same month, he confided to a friend how he addressed deeply entrenched harmful Hindu customs with argumentation, only to conclude with Paul, "My great Weapon is, and shall be Jesus Christ and him Crucified."[27] In the face of strong cultural and religious resistance, Carey expressed his conviction that his weapons of warfare were not carnal, but spiritual (2 Cor 10:4–5).

Fast forward two decades and Carey continues to resolutely articulate this cross-centered emphasis to his son Jabez on a mission at Amboyna: "Consider this as your greatest work and labour to build up the people in Faith and Holiness but above all labour to lay Christ Crucified as the foundation on which you build for all that is not built on that foundation will fail."[28] To Carey, the doctrine of the Savior's death was not mere dogma but the core of the mission call.

---

[24] Feb 22 & April 30, 1795. *Carey's Journal* in Carter, *Carey's Journal and Letters*, 54, 57.

[25] Carey to his Sisters, Mudnabatty, April 10, 1796. B.M.S. Mss. Angus Library RPC, Copy CLRC.

[26] Compare Ward's sober reflection on the lack of visible fruit in 1818, "Either we have not hit the chord which touches the heart of a Hindoo, or it is our jargon, or something or other is amiss. Powerful impressions, as in David Brainerd's congregations, we have never seen." Ward to Ryland, Sep 4, 1818. *Baptist Magazine* XI (1819), 177. Hereafter, *BM*.

[27] Carey to Fuller, April 23, 26, 1796. *PA*, I (1796), 301.

[28] Carey to Jabez, Amboyna. Undated letter, but inferred late October 1815. WWC/Copy Appendix I.2B. Mss. Angus RPC, Copy CLRC. Cf. For a similar instruction to his second son on a mission to Dacca, Carey to Wm Carey Jr., 17 Sep 1816, Mss. Angus, RPC.

The Moravian Impulse

Ward notes in Statement Five that the Moravians attribute all their success to cross-centered preaching. While reading their accounts on his way to Bengal, he wrote, "I feel towards the first Greenland missionaries a most lively affection ... their testimony of the blood of Immanuel will I trust be mine."[29] Then, reflecting on their self-sacrifice, "Thank you, ye Moravians ... If I am ever a missionary worth a straw, I shall owe it to you under our Saviour."[30] Those impressions lingered. When Ward arrived at Serampore, he stumbled upon the place where the German missionaries Grassman and Schmidt had lived a decade earlier. He remarked, "I could almost kiss the ground on which they had trodden."[31] A month later, meeting animist Santals in the Rajmahals with Carey on his detour from Mudnabati to Serampore, Ward rejoiced in the effects of preaching on the suffering of Christ; "I longed to stay amongst these social strangers, & tell them of Jesus; & I had a strong persuasion that they might be won by his cross."[32] Three years on, itinerating among poor villagers, Ward's crucicentric focus remained apparent when he "had some pleasure in recommending our Saviour's sufferings as a balm for all their wounds."[33] Like the Moravians, Ward and his associates expounded Christ as the suffering servant, significantly impacting their Bengali audience.

---

[29] Lord's Day, June 16; Monday, July 1, 1799. William Ward, "Missionary Journal" (1799-1811), I, 17, 22. Cf. *PA*, II (1801), 5-6 (misprinted Larkell instead of Loskiel). Ward read Crantz's *History of Greenland*, the Brethren's *Periodical Accounts*, and Loskiel's *Mission among American Indians*. The testimonies of Zeisberger and Bochnish, along with Brainerd and Eliot, were high on Ward's list. Wednesday, July 3, 1799. *Ward's Journal*, I, 23. Cf. *Periodical Accounts Relating to the Missions of the Church of the United Brethren, Established among the Heathen*, vol. I (London: BSFG, 1790), 52-53, 62, 108.

[30] Friday, June 21, 1799. *Ward's Journal*, I, 18. This quote is wrongly attributed to Joshua Marshman in S. Pearce Carey, *William Carey, D.D., Fellow of the Linnaean Society* (London: Hodder and Stoughton, 1923), 183. For evidence on Moravian influence on Marshman, J. C. S. Mason, *The Moravian Church and the Missionary Awakening in England, 1760-1800* (Woodbridge, Suffolk; Rochester, NY: Boydell & Brewer, 2001), 169-70.

[31] Wednesday, Oct 23, 1799. *Ward's Journal*, I, 53. The location of the former Moravian Mission is not exactly known.

[32] Tuesday, Dec 31, 1799. *Ward's Journal*, I, 65. Cf. S. Pearce Carey's paraphrase, "the wounds of Christ having melted their hearts," which is not in Ward's original. Carey, *William Carey, D.D.*, 181-182.

[33] Monday, Oct 3, 1803. *Ward's Journal*, II, 330.

Statement Five

The Translation Principle

The translation of the Scriptures into the vernaculars was one of the fundamental Reformation principles the Associates adopted in the SFA. Their determination stemmed from a strong sense of obligation: "Unless heathen nations can obtain the oracles of God, they must perish without any knowledge of salvation. On the translation, therefore, ... the eternal destiny of millions of our fellow-creatures" rest, the task "a duty paramount to all others."[34] Bible translation called for a concerted effort—"we ought never to give up until accomplished."[35]

That the Gospel in the vernaculars belongs to every people group was demonstrated at Pentecost, where "a capacity of speaking in all foreign languages was bestowed upon" those gathered.[36] Carey, in his *Enquiry* pointed to what Andrew Walls called "the translation principle," which, like the incarnation of Christ—the Word translated into flesh (John 1:14)—lies at the heart of the *missio Dei*.[37] Just as the vernacular Bibles of Wycliffe, Erasmus, and Luther transformed European Christendom, the Associates' occupation with Bible translation introduced "a new Era into India."[38] Ward reasoned that, since Hindus and Muslims base their religion on divine revelation, "It was necessary ... to meet them on their own ground; and ... to give them the true shastrŭ," in their "native tongue," and Carey was uniquely gifted to do it.[39] They witnessed how Bengali evangelists received respect while speaking with the sacred book in their hand

---

[34] [Carey, Marshman, Ward], *College for the Instruction of Asiatic Christian and Other Youth, in Eastern Literature and European Science, at Serampore, Bengal* (London: Black, Kingsbury, Parbury and Allen, 1819), 28.

[35] Statement Nine "The Serampore Form of Agreement," *Baptist Quarterly* 12, no. 5 (1947): 136.

[36] Carey, *An Enquiry*, 14.

[37] Andrew F. Walls, "The Translation Principle in Christian History," in *The Missionary Movement in Christian History: Studies in the Transmission of Faith* (Maryknoll, NY: Orbis, 1996), 26–27.

[38] Smith, *The Life of William Carey*, 236–37; Carey to Ryland, Aug 17, 1800, *Carey's Journal and Letters*, 182.

[39] "Letter to Rev. Daniel Sharp," April 9, 1821. William Ward, *Farewell Letters to a Few Friends in Britain and America, on Returning to Bengal in 1821* (New York: Bliss & White, 1821), 145.

The Serampore Form of Agreement

and how the Scriptures built up new converts in the faith, the book itself becoming a means of conversion.

But transmitting divine meaning from one language to another was a complex process. Striving to be faithful to the original languages, Carey sought to transliterate "Christ" into the thought forms of Bengali culture as *Kreest*. But that term required explanations as to why the Incarnate was not another *avatar*, but "the full expression of God in human medium," for *Kreest* and Creeshnoo (Krishna) sounded similar but were clearly not the same.[40] In his early preaching, Carey was perhaps unaware of how his hearers (mis)understood theological concepts, which led him to despair about his inability to communicate. To the Hindu, *paap* (sin) was a breach of caste law, not personal sin, while *moksha* (salvation) meant release from the cycle of reincarnation.[41]

Finding the right balance between biblical faithfulness and cultural relevance would always be tricky. While situated in North Bengal and unable to find a suitable Bengali word for "cross," Carey finally settled on using the Portuguese term *cruz*, "that being well understood in ... Calcutta."[42] The communion phrase "to break bread" presented another difficulty, as Bengalis were unfamiliar with a loaf of bread.[43] Adopting such *firanghi* ideas carried unavoidable connotations of the foreignness of the Gospel. Yet, they noted how, despite these obstacles, the Gospel was able to penetrate people's hearts. Ward recorded how an enquirer named Gokool testified how, upon hearing the Gospel, his heart "seemed nailed to Xt,"

---

[40] Walls, "Translation Principle," 27. The Sanskrit for incarnation is *avatar*. Thursday, Dec 11, 1800. *Ward's Journal*, I, 121. Early translations of the Scriptures into Arabic, Persian and Urdu, as well as later translations into Hindi and Marathi (among others), avoided this confusion by transliterating the Aramaic *Yasou' Al Maseeh* into *Yeshu Masih*, Jesus Messiah, instead of the Greek Ἰησοῦς χριστός. Both titles mean Jesus (the) Anointed (One).

[41] S. K. Datta, *The Desire of India* (London: Baptist Missionary Society, 1908), 196.

[42] Carey to Ryland, March 7, 1801. *Carey's Journal and Letters*, 155.

[43] "The phrase *ruti bhangilen* [sounds] strange to a Bengali because this act of breaking bread is alien to Bengali society. From a linguistic standpoint, *ruti*, 'bread', never collocates with *bhangilen*, 'broke.'" Sisir Kumar Das, "Early Bengali Prose: Carey to Vidyasagar" (Ph.D. thesis, University of London, 1963), 83-84. Today Bengali Christians are comfortable with the idea.

gladly becoming his "slave" (*das*).[44] Gokool had interpreted foreign concepts into familiar categories. In the early Bengali converts, the Associates saw the translation principle at work through their preaching of the Gospel. In Walls's words, it was the beginning of "*inter*actions of the word of Christ with new areas of thought and custom ... a turning of the processes of language ... towards Christ."[45]

Bengali response to Christ-centered preaching

The first Bengali convert, Krishna Pal, a *soodra* (carpenter), testified how he heard the "tidings of Salvation through the death of Christ" on his way to (or at) the bazaar from Serampore missionaries Dr. John Thomas and John Fountain.[46] Though he had heard the message from the Serampore Moravians earlier, it struck him as the Word of God at this opportune time. He embraced the Christian faith being confronted with the love of Christ through the doctor's aid, "telling me that a father chastises the son he loves; using likewise another simile, that a father by making an incision in the arm of his child, saves it from the small-pox."[47] Thomas gave Krishna a *gayatri* to repeat: "Sin confessing,—sin forsaking—Christ's righteousness getting—freedom will be obtained." This was a true sacred saying instead of the secret mechanical mantra usually given to high-caste Brahmans, "which it would be sin for a Sooder to hear."[48] These four rhythmic

---

[44] Monday, Dec 22, 1800. *Ward's Journal*, I, 126. The Bengali name *das* (from Sanskrit *dāsa*—slave, servant) was often used for a devotee of a god.

[45] Walls, "Translation Principle," 29. Emphasis in original.

[46] Monday, Dec 22, 1800. *Ward's Journal*, I, 125-126. Fountain spoke at the bazar on January 5, 1800, *BM*, viii (1816), 344-345.

[47] Krishna to a Friend in England, *Quarterly Papers of the BMS*, No 7. July 1823 in [John] [Dyer], ed., *News from Afar, ... Being a Re-Publication of the Quarterly Papers of the Society from 1822-1832* (London: Baptist Missionary Society, 1832), 27-28. The cow-pox vaccine was discovered five years prior by Jenner. Thomas was familiar with small-pox inoculations, which are noted in *Ward's Journal*, 218, 354, 367.

[48] Tuesday, Nov 25; Saturday, Dec 27, 1800. *Ward's Journal*, I, 118, 128. Also spelled, guytre, gayutree, gayatri. William Ward, *Account of the Writings, Religion, and Manners of the Hindoos. In Four Volumes* (Serampore: Mission Press, 1811), I, 218, 316-318; Charles Bennett Lewis, *The Life of John Thomas, Surgeon of the Earl of Oxford East Indiaman, and First Baptist Missionary to Bengal* (London: MacMillan and Co., 1873), 332.

The Serampore Form of Agreement

Bengali phrases expressing the heart of the Gospel emboldened Krishna to overcome inevitable communal opposition.[49]

But Krishna's conversion did not occur instantly. He was familiar with the *gayatri* through his initiation into a religious Bhakti sect among lower castes, the Ghoseparowites, where he received his own "perfect mantra."[50] For sixteen years, he had been a disciple of Ram Doolal, who preached universal love and abolished caste distinctions. Effectively, this association had lowered the barrier for him to adopt Thomas' "truer mantra" of Christ and accept his invitation for a shared meal at Mission House. Thomas recognized the sincerity of his expression of individual sin and guilt, which enabled Krishna to overcome the fear of publicly breaching caste, his predestined place in society.[51]

Such culturally sensitive Christ-filled preaching also profoundly affected the writer Samdas, who testified upon his conversion that he heard the itinerating missionaries and "was led to think about the death of Xt. for sinners ... Jesus Xt. was God—nevertheless he became a man—he was fastened to the cross by nails thro' his two hands; he was crowned with thorns ... pierced in his side—all this sorrow he bore for us. Believing this he hoped; & he resolved to sin no more."[52] For him, Gospel preaching resulted in a personal revelation of the love of Christ.

Likewise, the evangelist Sebuk Ram wrote to a supporter, "I made known in the presence of many people ... the cross of Christ, and the sufferings he endured for sinners."[53] Imitating a traveling bard, Ram would

---

[49] Lewis notes that Thomas based these on Proverbs 28:13: *pap shikar korile, pap tyag korile, yeshur dhormmo paile, mukto hoy*. পাপ সিকার করিলে পাপ ত্যাগ করিলে যেশুর ধর্ম্ম পাইলে মুক্ত হয়। Lewis, *Life of John Thomas*, 364; John Clark Marshman, *The Life and Times of Carey, Marshman, and Ward: Embracing the History of the Serampore Mission* (London: Longman, Brown, Green, Longmans, & Roberts, 1859), I, 61-62.

[50] Also known as Karta Bhojas or Kurta Bhoojas, these were a Hindu dissenting sect at Ghosepara, 30 Miles northeast of Serampore, numbering about 20,000 practising a form of Deism. Claudius Buchanan, *The Works of the Rev. Claudius Buchanan L.L.D.* (New York: Whiting & Watson, 1812), 258. James Long, "The Banks of the Bhagirathi," *Selections from the Calcutta Review* (Aug 1881-Jan 1882), II, 332-333.

[51] Monday, Dec 22, 1800. *Ward's Journal*, I, 126.

[52] Friday, April 2, 1802. *Ward's Journal*, II, 222-223. Also spelled Syam Doss of the writer caste, Samdas was tragically robbed and murdered five months later. *PA*, II (1802), 303.

[53] Letter from Sebuk Ram to Mrs [Skinner] March 1811. *PA*, IV (1811), 241-242.

enter a village and sing his favorite hymn, "Salvation by the death of Christ." He would expound on the fifth chapter of Matthew and often received a warm welcome.[54] In Moravian-like fashion, the native evangelists utilized Jesus' ethical instructions of the Sermon on the Mount as a great "appetizer" of the Christian faith, appealing to the conscience of the hearers.[55] Thus, the Moravian emphasis on Christ's sacrificial death became a priority, central to the conversion experience of early Bengali Christians. Although utterly foreign, the suffering crucified Christ—for what other god had actually *died* for one's sins—became the missiological bridge, the key to unlocking the hearts of Bengali people.[56]

Fuller's Crucicentrism

How did the doctrine of Christ crucified take center place in the SFA? Ward's correspondence reveals that BMS secretary Andrew Fuller alluded to it before the SFA's publication. In October 1804, Fuller wrote Ward with warm urgency, "O that I may know him & the power of his resurrection. I have felt within the last half year an increasing attachment to Xt Crucified. Have preached ever since about nothing else in a manner. How sweet is the Way of Salvation thro' his name! I feel how much more useful I sh^d be if I were more imbued in this subject."[57] And again three months later: "My mind has of late been more impressed than ever on the importance of knowing, believing, loving, & preaching Christ; & may I know nothing but Christ & him Crucified."[58]

A decade earlier, Fuller had defended the centrality of this Reformation principle in his Letters against Socinian (or Unitarian) Dissenters. After

---

[54] *PA*, IV (1809), 28.

[55] J. E. Hutton, *A History of the Moravian Church* (London: Moravian Publication Office, 1909), 82.

[56] "He came down from heaven forsaking all his glory. He was led to the place of execution, bearing his cross to which he was nailed as one board is nailed to another ... What ... for? To rescue us from sin and hell. *This* is the Saviour. None of *your* Gods laid down *their* lives to save sinners. No. But this great and dear Saviour did." Felix Carey, "Sermon to the Hindoos," *Rippon's Register*, II, 842. Emphasis in original.

[57] Fuller to Ward, Kettering, Oct 27, 1804. BMS. Mss., Microfilm Reel 20.

[58] Fuller to Ward, Kettering, Jan 14, 1805. BMS. Mss., Microfilm Reel 20.

The Serampore Form of Agreement

affirming the Deity of Christ and the necessity of his atoning death as the only means of a sinner's salvation, he surmised:

> The doctrine of the cross is ... the grand peculiarity and the principal glory in Christianity ... it is the gospel itself. In fine, the doctrine of the cross is the central point in which all the lines of evangelical truth meet and are united. What the sun is to the system of nature, that the doctrine of the cross is to the system of the gospel: it is the life of it.[59]

In the face of Deist and Unitarian popular thought, Fuller reiterated his evangelical convictions before Baptist ministers in 1801 in even stronger language: "The doctrine we teach must be that of Jesus Christ and him crucified. The person and work of Christ have ever been the corner-stone of the Christian fabric: take away his Divinity and atonement, and all will go to ruins ... This was the doctrine by which the Reformation was effected ... the leading theme of the puritans and nonconformists."[60] Indeed, for Fuller, as for Luther, Brainerd, and Edwards before him, the saving and sanctifying cross was the crux of the Gospel, which needed a universal hearing.[61]

Ward felt the impact of Fuller's reflections and answered using another simile:

> I rejoice much that XI. the crucified has been your theme so much lately. I perceive now how much I have left my ministry unfulfilled by not having formerly perceived what is so plain in scripture, viz

---

[59] Andrew Fuller, *The Calvinistic and Socinian Systems Examined and Compared as to Their Moral Tendency; in a Series of Letters Addressed to the Friends of Vital and Practical Religion* (Market Harborough: W. Harrod for the Author, 1793), 190-191; Andrew Fuller, *Apologetic Works*, ed., Thomas J. Nettles and Michael Haykin, vol. 3 (Berlin/Boston: Walter de Gruyter, 2021). Cf. Andrew Gunton Fuller, *The Complete Works of the Rev. Andrew Fuller*, vol. I (Boston: Gould, Kendall, and Lincoln, 1836), 83.

[60] "God's Approbation of our Labours necessary to the Hope of Success," Sermon VII. Preached at the Annual Meeting of the Bedford Union, May 6, 1801. A month later at Oakham, he worded it as, "This all-important principle is a golden link, which, if laid hold of, draws with it the whole chain of evangelical truth." Fuller, *Complete Works*, I, 190, 411.

[61] Adam McClendon, "The Crucicentrism of Andrew Fuller (1754-1815)," *Churchman* 127, no. 4 (2013): 317.

that XI. is all & all. I recollect something of a sermon of Dr Doddridges on preaching XI. which gave some sermon ideas on this subject. I put some more in reading the Greenland Missionary Accounts... I do see that XI. is not only the substance of every thing; but he is the key that unlocks every thing & the telescope that enlarges any thing & brings it near. I do see that living to Him is the Xian life, that all the doctrines of the Gospel are savoury & profitable or explained in Him, and all the precepts, illustrated by His example & sweetened by his love, become an easy & pleasant yoke.[62]

The Cross and Incarnational Mission

By the Autumn of 1805, Ward was so convinced of the centrality of the doctrine that he made Christ crucified the core statement of the SFA. The following January, the BMS sent out new missionaries under Fuller's charge: "My dear brethren, know nothing but Jesus Christ and him crucified. Be this the summit of your ambition. For you to live must be Christ ... If you possess the savor of Christ ... you will be blessings in your generation."[63] Two years later, Richard and Rhoda Mardon[64] were sent out from Serampore to plant a new church with Ward's advice,

> Let your preaching be very simple: *"Exalt the Lamb of God, The sin-atoning Lamb."* Tell of his incarnation, miracles, sufferings, death, resurrection, and ascension. Never be tired of preaching Jesus. The

---

[62] Ward to Fuller, Sunderbunds, Oct 7, 1805. BMS. Mss. An edited version of this part of the letter was published in the *PA*, II (1806), 189-190, replacing Ward's shorthand XI with Christ. Though the letter is dated Oct 7, according to Ward's *Journal* it was written during his mission trip on November 6-29. The date October 7, 1805 was printed on the title page of the SFA, and Ward supervised its printing prior to this trip to Jessore and beyond. Perhaps he started the letter on that day, but did not sign it off until December 11.

[63] Fuller's charge to James Chater and William Robinson, in January 1806. Fuller, *Complete Works*, I, 79. Fuller too was impressed by the Moravians, see Fuller, *Complete Works*, I, 203.

[64] Richard Mardon (1776-1812) and Rhoda Brenham (1779-1811) were BMS Missionaries from Plymouth Dock, who sailed from Bristol in January 1804 via America, in company of the Biss, Moore and Rowe families. After learning Bengali, they moved to Goamalty, Malda district, in Feb 1808 to occupy the indigo factory of two European evangelicals, H. Creighton and W. Grant, who had died in Oct 1807. After planting a small church, Rhoda died during childbirth at Serampore on Dec 24, 1811, leaving four children behind. Richard returned to Goamalty, where he continued his itinerancy. The infant died in March, a daughter in April, and Richard on May 23, 1812. *PA*, IV, (1808-1810) 285, 312, 329, 350, 389-391; *PA*, V (1813), 29-30, 76, 78-79, 87-91 (Obituary).

The Serampore Form of Agreement

subject can never be old to you, and to the heathen, it is "good news from a far country."[65]

However, preaching was not the ultimate goal:
Yet do not be content with *preaching* merely—draw the natives to you—mix with them—become their servant, to win them—try to gain their affections—shew them that you can actually become their brother, and that though they may be hated of all men for Christ's sake, yet that you will never forsake them, nor be ashamed of them ... Never forget, dear brother, that your ministry is a "*winning* of souls." It is love alone that can dissolve the chains of the cast: it is the *love* of Christ alone, in dying for sinners, that has done whatever has already been done in the conversion of Hindoos; and there is no hope but in a ministry that shall be like that of the Great Head of the church whose love was stronger than death.[66]

Ward, being pastorally inclined, had made winning souls his priority. It required patience, long-suffering, and, above all, Christian love. As his biographer, Stennett would remark after his death, "The love of Christ was the predominant affection in his heart, and the glory of God in the good of immortal souls, the great aim of all his actions."[67] Ward was convinced that only preachers with an incarnational lifestyle, imbibed with the love of Christ as image-bearers of the Incarnate, could draw enquirers to faith.

In 1808, the Mardons attempted precisely that. They wrote of a plan to move from their isolated European estate to build a bungalow among the "native flock," thus lowering the threshold to reach them.[68] Richard often discoursed on the atonement, "a doctrine as delightful to [him] as ... important."[69] Using local converts as teachers, he established a Christian

---

[65] *Monthly Circular Letters relative to the Mission in India*, I (February 1808), 26. The peculiar vocabulary and style point to Ward as the author. He was also the editor of the *CL* at the time. From 1808 onwards, his Journal omits many events published in the *CL*.

[66] *CL*, I (1808), 26, emphasis original. Note the similarity to the Preamble and Statement Seven of the SFA.

[67] Stennett, *Memoirs*, 248; Reynolds, *The Spirituality of William Ward*, 98–105.

[68] The indigo factory was at quite a large distance of the newly planted Goamalty church. *PA*, IV (1808), 21–23.

[69] Mardon to Carey, Goamalty, April 15, 1812. *PA*, V (1813), 73.

Statement Five

presence through primary schools in the surrounding villages. He also deserves credit for highlighting the plight of the Paharias, the destitute tribal people in the Rajmahal Hills that Ward and Carey briefly encountered in December 1799. "Surely they have minds capable of receiving instruction as well as other men, and the soul of a Pahareea is as precious as a soul of a Hindoo, a Musulman, a Bhoteeya [Bhutanese], or a Burman. Why then may they not be furnished with the means of grace?"[70] Though they did not live long enough to see the fruit of their attempts "to flesh out" the Gospel, the Mardons deserve commendation for engaging closely with native people. Their efforts proved that the Gospel message is most compelling when the doctrine of atonement supplements the doctrine of incarnation.

The Extent of the Atonement

As noted before, Fuller had linked the doctrines of the cross and the atonement. Ward, in the SFA, also stated that the centrality of the cross points to Christ's priestly work of atonement, the sacrificial nature of his death for the propitiation of sins (Heb 2:17). "The doctrine of Christ's expiatory death and all-sufficient merits has been, and must ever remain, the grand mean of conversion."[71] So essential to Ward's thinking was the doctrine of substitutionary atonement theology that his *Reflections* in 1822 define it as, "The terms sacrifice, propitiation, atonement, all refer to the same doctrine: a sin-avenging God exalting the honours of his justice in the sufferings and death of Christ, the Victim pouring out his soul unto death."[72]

The word group Ward uses perhaps reflects that of the non-conformist theologian-writer Richard Baxter (1615–1691), who rejected the idea of limited (or definite) atonement and argued instead for unlimited (or gen-

---

[70] *CL*, III (1810), 162. E. Daniel Potts, *British Baptist Missionaries in India, 1793–1837* (London: Cambridge University Press, 1967), 31.

[71] Statement Five. SFA, 6. Interestingly, Ward uses the singular term "mean" here instead of the more common plural term "means" as Carey had used in the title of his *Enquiry*. This puts emphasis on the singular focus of the doctrine.

[72] Ward, *Reflections*, 203. Cf. Isaiah 53:12.

eral) atonement. At the time, limited atonement was advocated most vocally by fellow Puritan John Owen (1616–1683).[73] As a Particular Baptist, Ward affirmed with the Puritans that Christ's atoning work is sufficient for all, and that all who are called, trusting in the meritorious work of Christ, receive all his benefits. The prologue to the SFA states this clearly: "We are sure that only those who are *ordained* to eternal life will believe, and that *God alone* can add to the church *such as shall be saved.*"[74] But while Owen maintained that Christ died only for the sins of the elect, Baxter argued he died for the sins of both the elect and unbelievers. This distinction was important because of Baptist adherence to the Second London Confession of Faith (1689), which followed the so-called five points of Calvinism. It distinguished Particular Baptists from General Baptists, who leaned towards an Arminian position.[75] While Baxter rejected Arminianism (for denying special grace to the elect) and Calvinists like Owen (for denying 'general' grace to the world), his critics blamed him for being a universalist and taking a middle-ground position.[76] Consequently, Fuller, a great admirer of Owen, expressed strong anti-Baxterian sentiments.[77]

What was Ward's position on this issue? Ward's language in the SFA and his *Reflections* read at times more "Baxterian" than "Owensian."[78] However, writing to a broad audience, he avoided stating his own views on

---

[73] John Owen, *The Death of Death in the Death of Christ* (1648), a defense of limited (or better: definite) atonement against classical Arminianism, Amyraldianism (Baxter and others), and universalism (Thomas More). Though Ward was impacted by Richard Baxter's motivational writings, *Saints' Everlasting Rest* (1650) and *Call to the Unconverted* (1658), I found no evidence he read Baxter's polemical work.

[74] Preamble SFA, 1. Emphasis mine.

[75] General Baptists rejected the five points of Calvinism expressed at the Council of Dort (Dordrecht) in 1619: total depravity, unconditional election, limited atonement, irresistible grace, and perseverance of the saints. David W. Bebbington, *Baptists Through the Centuries: A History of a Global People*, 2nd edn. (Waco, TX: Baylor University Press, 2018), 52–53.

[76] J. I. Packer, *The Redemption and Restoration of Man in the Thought of Richard Baxter: A Study in Puritan Theology* (Vancouver, BC: Regent College Publications, 2003), 230.

[77] "A moderate Calvinist ... is half Arminian, or as they are called with us, Baxterians." Fuller, *Complete Works*, I, 77.

[78] Compare also Ward's mix of non-specific (general) and particular language: "the blood of atonement, ... possesses ... infinite merit; is efficacious to every purpose for which it is shed ... it was accepted by the Lawgiver as an equivalent for the personal obedience, or sufferings, of all who should believe." Ward, *Reflections*, 334.

Statement Five

the extent of the atonement.[79] Ward, who had a Methodist background before becoming a Baptist, studied for 15 months under the evangelical Calvinist John Fawcett. Though he undoubtedly would have re-evaluated his former Arminian belief system, there was hardly enough time to debate the finer points of Calvinism, and neither did he wish to entertain it.[80] Though Ward differed with Fuller on issues like closed or open communion, their correspondence gives no hint of their views on limited atonement.

Carey and Marshman had only a few days to respond to the draft SFA after Ward introduced it on October 5th. It was signed on the 7th, so they had little time to ensure the SFA was theologically wholly sound. Nonetheless, Fuller's edited version of the SFA, which omitted Ward's reference to Wesley, does not make any other changes to Statement Five, so presumably, he was comfortable with Ward's non-specific phrasing "all-sufficient merits ... grand mean," before introducing it to the general public.[81]

In his thesis, Matt Reynolds argues that Ward agreed with four of the five Calvinist points. Still, he concludes that Ward's writings perhaps remained intentionally ambiguous on limited atonement (or "particular redemption") to reach a greater audience.[82] In the closing words of Statement Five, Ward affirms that in his experience, every Hindu had been won through "the astonishing and all-constraining love of Christ exhibited in our Redeemer's propitiatory death." No-one could object to that testimony.

---

[79] Reynolds, *The Spirituality of William Ward*, 91-97. For an helpful overview of different viewpoints, see David L. Allen, *The Extent of the Atonement: A Historical and Critical Review* (Nashville, TN: B&H Academic, 2016). Allen rightly says the most challenging issue is phraseology, to clearly identify what each writer means.

[80] "The doctrines of the love of God, the atonement, the resurrection and kingdom of Jesus, are, I trust, more precious to me ... Yet I can part with the dogmas of enthusiasts - with the creeds of bigots, with the utmost ease. If I were asked for my creed, I could soon give it: *God is love.*" March 17, 1797. Stennett, *Memoirs*, 242.

[81] *PA*, III (1806), 198-211. See fn 4.

[82] Reynolds, *The Spirituality of William Ward*, 94.

Bengali Intellectual Responses

Just as Paul found Christ crucified to be a stumbling block to his Jewish hearers, many Bengali elites responded adversely to the missionaries' teaching on the atonement and its implication for the nature of the Godhead. In the person of the Hindu Reformer Rammohun Roy (1772-1833),[83] the spirit of inquiry and reason, which the missionaries had so carefully fostered, clashed with the doctrine of atonement. Before the controversy over Christ's divinity in 1820, the Serampore and Calcutta missionaries (represented by Joshua Marshman and William Yates) worked with Roy to abolish sati and improve society. Their subsequent strained communications and public controversy are well described elsewhere but deserve a brief mention in this context.[84]

Despite Marshman's sincere attempt to demonstrate the necessity of Christ as the mediator between God and people, they could never convince Roy of the scriptural basis for the Trinitarian doctrine expressed in the Nicene Creed. The stumbling block proved to be the missionaries' concession that the triune Godhead is incomprehensible.[85] As the debate increasingly revolved around the issue of faith versus reason, Roy fortified his defense by utilizing modern Unitarian apologetics.[86] While he identified with Jesus the man, the missionaries held up the Christ of faith. Both parties talked past each other. Roy raised complex hermeneutical questions about the Scriptures, both Hindu and Christian, which he resolved using common sense and reason. Rooted not in faith but in skepticism, this approach was not new. In Europe, Deists, rational Dissenters, and Unitarians had "acted as a solvent of Christian orthodoxy," liberalizing biblical thought.

---

[83] For a critical treatment, see Bruce C. Robertson, *Raja Rammohan Ray: The Father of Modern India* (Delhi: OUP, 1995). For a useful overview of Roy's theology, Robin H.S. Boyd, *An Introduction to Indian Christian Theology* (Delhi: ISPCK, 1975), 19-26.

[84] Potts, *British Baptist Missionaries*, 226-244. For a helpful recent treatment, Sean Doyle, "Prophetic Precepts or Divine Preeminence? Rammohan Roy vs. Joshua Marshman on the Significance of Jesus," in *Expect Great Things Attempt Great Things*, eds., Allen Yeh and Chris Chun (Eugene, OR: Wipf & Stock, 2013), 42-59.

[85] J. Marshman, *A Defence of the Deity and Atonement of Jesus Christ, in Reply to Ram-Mohun Roy of Calcutta* (London: Kingsbury, Parbury, and Allen, 1822), 228-229; Jogendra Chunder Ghose and Eshan Chunder Bose, eds., *The English Works of Raja Ram Mohun Roy* (Calcutta: Oriental, 1885), I, 195-196.

[86] Ghose and Bose, *Roy's English Works*, I, 266-288.

Statement Five

The missionaries, "wedded to orthodoxy," attempted to meet Roy on his own ground with reason but failed to find convincing hermeneutical keys.[87] Eventually, Roy laid the foundation of a reform movement that sought to "improve" Hinduism from within, advocating its monotheistic origins and rejecting idolatry. Roy borrowed the ethical teaching of Jesus but did not accept his miracles, resurrection, and claim to divinity.

A more successful attempt to engage the elites with the Gospel was made in the 1840s by a civil servant, the Scot, John Muir (1810-1882). Muir, who served with the Indian Civil Service, upon arrival, studied Oriental languages, perhaps, under Carey. Impacted by evangelicalism, Muir wrote a series of Sanskrit tracts and books to defend the Christian faith and regularly contributed to the *Friend of India*.[88] After reading a tract that extolled the cleansing power of the Ganges river, he composed a Sanskrit treatise subtitled, "The Inefficiency of the Ganges to Wash away Sin, with a Statement of the True Atonement."[89] This poetic "sketch" is a dialogue between teacher and disciple, in verse "for the learned of India into a form congenial to their national models."[90] With that firm contextual foundation, Muir countered the belief that a river wash removes sin, describing it as a "cheap and easy form of grace" and stating that "Atonement (*prāyaścitta*) for the sins of all men was accomplished by the sacrificial death of him who was sinless."[91] The term *prāyaścitta* originated from Carey's Sanskrit Bible and was adopted by Yates, who improved on Carey's style. Scholar Richard Fox Young wonders whether the term was

---

[87] Bebbington, *Evangelicalism in Modern Britain*, 50-51.

[88] On Muir's relationship with evangelicalism, Richard Fox Young, *Resistant Hinduism: Sanscrit Sources on Anti-Christian Apologetics in Early Nineteenth-Century India* (Vienna: Institut für Indologie der Universität Wien, 1981), 49-53.

[89] John Muir, *The Inefficiency of the Ganges to Wash Away Sin, with a Statement of the True Atonement* (Calcutta: Baptist Mission Press, 1840). Though the tract lacks the writer's name, a copy is bound in a volume with other tracts signed by John Muir, available at the CLRC, Serampore. Muir was well acquainted with Serampore. As reorganizer of Sanskrit College at Benares from 1844-1845, he would have met Superintendent George Nicholls, Headmaster of the English School, ex-student of Serampore College and Ward's son-in-law. Marshman, *Life and Times*, II, 280.

[90] "Notice of New Works in Sanskrit Verse," *Calcutta Christian Observer*, IV (1840), 16-17.

[91] Young, *Resistant Hinduism*, 61.

perhaps better understood to mean penance or expiation instead of atonement. He suggests that even if there was no better word, Muir should have explained its context better.[92] While scholars debate these issues, we recognize Walls' observation that translation is "interaction ... the turning of the processes of language ... towards Christ."[93] Muir's approach thought the mastery of Sanskrit verse promoted dialogue more than Marshman's previous diatribe against Roy. The result was a healthy debate that aided contextualized explanations of the Atonement and Divinity of Christ.

Conclusion

Perhaps Ward's finest expression of the cross, combining Pietist and Moravian insights with his Indian experience, is found in his *Reflections* (1822):

> The cross of Christ is a strong attractive to a broken-hearted sinner. While he meditates on the crucifixion, the burden of guilt is removed, the hard heart is melted, sorrow for sin is excited, his hope in God is strengthened, his zeal for Christ is inflamed, and his love to all the redeemed and to the whole human race is enlarged.[94]

So, for Ward, as for Carey and Marshman, the cross was the impetus for mission. But he did not stop there. The preaching of the crucified Christ included the complete person and work of Christ, not just his death but also his resurrection, exaltation, and future return.[95] Gratitude for Calvary motivated him to pursue sanctification. For him, as for Fuller, the cross promoted victory over sin. "The Christian [who] was once the chained ... is now enabled to conquer; ... It is the conquering banner of Christ which he carries."[96] Indeed, it is the resurrection power of *Christus Victor* poured out through the Holy Spirit, "the Sanctifier," who facilitates the disciples' righteous walk. In the Serampore missionaries' view, that power is the key to India's transformation.[97]

---

[92] Young, 62.
[93] Walls, "Translation Principle," 29.
[94] Sept 4. 1 Corinthians 2. "We preach Christ crucified." Ward, *Reflections*, 356–357.
[95] E.g. Lord's Day, April 25, 1802; Oct 23, 1803. *Ward's Journal*, II, 228, 339.
[96] Sept 12. Romans 8: 28-39. Ward, *Reflections*, 367; Bebbington, *Evangelicalism in Modern Britain*, 16.
[97] Ward, *Farewell Letters*, 179–180; Ward, *Reflections*, 271; Carey, *An Enquiry*, 7, 15.

Statement Five

In sum, in the SFA, the Associates' understanding of the Moravian three-fold emphasis on Christ's sacrifice, suffering, and resurrection took center stage in Serampore's soteriology, and Christ-centered preaching became Serampore's signature principle. Today, the relevance of this timeless principle is evident when one witnesses how the Indian Church thrives where ever Christ is put first, transforming the lives of individuals and communities. India's future depends on it. May He be glorified!

STATEMENT SIX

Hospitality, Counsel, Equality, and Respect

G. Landon Adams

William Ward (1769-1823) drafted the Serampore Form of Agreement (1805) as a declaration of ideal missionary principles.[1] As stated in his journal, Ward wrote the SFA for himself and his colleagues at the Serampore Mission. The declaration condensed thirteen years of experience (1793-1805) into eleven Statements. Its purpose was to set a pattern for their successors.[2] The commentary in this chapter features several minor characters from the story of the Serampore Mission to illuminate the SFA.

In his well-known summary of the SFA, S. Pearce Carey shortened Statement Six to the phrase: "To esteem and treat Indians always as our equals."[3] Carey's summary is reductionistic in its focus on the seemingly nebulous sentiment of "equality." Ward's actual words, taken from the middle of his Statement, read: "We ought to be easy of access, to condescend to them as much as possible, and on all occasions, to treat them as our equals..." In proper context, Ward's phrase, "to treat them as our equals," is complex. One cannot understand Statement Six's meaning or substance based on a single phrase isolated from its context.

Just as contemporary readers may be led astray by S. P. Carey's summary, some may also misunderstand Ward's use of "condescend." By

---

[1] Hereafter: SFA.

[2] "I wished much that we should leave to our successors something like this, & therefore drew it up, read it to the Brethren, & to-night gave to each a copy for their corrections & additions." *William Ward's Missionary Journal, 1799-1811* (hereafter: *Ward's Journal*), October 5, 1805. All references to Ward's Journal come from the four original volumes held at the Angus Library and Archive at Regent's Park College, Oxford: BMSA IN/16. I am indebted in part to the William H. and Kathryn E. Brackney Angus Travel Bursary for funding my research visit to Regent's Park College in June 2022.

[3] S. Pearce Carey, *William Carey D.D., Fellow of the Linnaean Society* (London: Hodder and Stoughton, 1923), 248.

The Serampore Form of Agreement

"condescend" Ward meant that someone was stooping from their high position to help someone in a lower position. Jesus himself was said to have condescended to the world through his incarnation, and the missionaries desired to follow his example.[4] Ward understood social inequality as a condition of the world, yet he advocated for treating others as equals through conscious acts of condescension.

Between the concept of English class and the concept of Indian caste, Ward lived in an inescapably hierarchical world.[5] Hierarchy alone was never the problem. Work relationships, organizations, and even family life require certain hierarchies. The Christian gospel challenged these preconceived notions, not in the practicalities of organization, but in the valuation of an individual's worth. Indian society in early nineteenth-century Bengal assigned value—socially and spiritually—to an individual based on their inherited caste. For ministers of the Christian gospel, this would not do. In the Bible, God's economy of salvation valued all people as sinful creatures needing salvation from their creator. This otherworldly message required the Serampore missionaries to place an "infinite value upon immortal souls" (Statement One), "though [missionaries] may know that [natives] are in many respects inferior to [Europeans]" (Statement Three).

Ward acknowledged the apparent inequalities between the missionaries and their Indian neighbors in external means, knowledge, skills, and abilities. Simultaneously, Ward and his colleagues upheld the doctrine of Christian equality in a social and cultural setting hostile to equality of any kind. Aware of the tension between these two competing concepts, the missionaries knew that their work would require "sacrifices" (Statement Six) of time, effort, comfort, and reputation.

Analysis of Statement Six

The full text of Statement Six appears below, divided into four sections. The first section showcases William Ward as a hospitable missionary. The

---

[4] William Ward, *Reflections on the Word of God, for Every Day in the Year* (London: W. Simpkin and R. Marshall, Holdsworth, 1825), 5.

[5] For English conceptions of class, see David Cannadine, *The Rise and Fall of Class in Britain* (New York: Columbia University Press, 1999), 26–35. For Indian conceptions of caste, see Susan Bayly, *The New Cambridge History of India*. Part 4. Vol. 3, *Caste, Society and Politics in India from the Eighteenth Century to the Modern Age* (Cambridge: Cambridge University Press, 1999), 3–10.

Statement Six

second section narrates early Christian converts' struggles and the missionaries' role in providing "fatherly" (Statement Seven) counsel. The third section features Unna, an early Christian convert who sought a more concrete application of salvific equality in her social relations. The fourth and final section tells the cautionary tale of John Chamberlain as he modeled attitudes and behaviors that were antithetical to the mission. Altogether, these stories provide a compelling case that the SFA reflected the concrete reality of the missionaries as they navigated the tension between the "infinite value" (Statement One) of souls under their care and the constant temptation to regard them as merely "inferior" (Statement Three).

Hospitality

It is absolutely necessary that the natives should have an entire confidence in us, and feel quite at home in our company ... we ought to be easy of access ...

While still learning Bengali, William Ward took a morning stroll with William Carey and John Fountain through the streets of Serampore.[6] On this walk, they held gospel conversations with strangers, and one expressed an interest in hearing more. Carey invited this man to attend their Sunday service, but this did not satisfy the man. He insisted upon living with the missionaries to "always hear them." Carey, who had already lived in India for seven years, shrewdly deduced that this man was "someone who had lived with a European" and was now "out of place." The man offered his services to them as a "durwan" or "gate-keeper" for their residence. Carey explained to Ward that a *durwan* was an almost universal feature of European living in India. Such gatekeepers not only lived by the entrance of a residence, but they "kept out improper persons." While this was a flattering proposal, this was not the Serampore Mission way.

Not hiring a gatekeeper was the first step toward providing ease of access to the public. Allowing open access to their premises was a calculated risk, but it was vital to their early work. This calculated risk of refusing an

---

[6] Lord's Day, March 23, 1800. *Ward's Journal*, I, 74.

experienced *durwan*'s services was part of the Serampore Mission hospitality strategy. It led to a constant barrage of uninvited, sometimes unwelcomed, guests.[7] Ward recorded many encounters with people who had come to Serampore to seek assistance from the missionaries. Sometimes, inquirers came to hear more about the gospel, sometimes they came to receive free literature, and sometimes they needed the basics of food and shelter.[8] Consequently, their openness to the public could have been one circumstantial factor that led to their first Christian conversion.

Krishna Pal, a local carpenter, dislocated his shoulder after falling at his home. Krishna's friend came to the mission house to seek the assistance of the physician, John Thomas.[9] Only after receiving medical aid did Krishna hear and respond to the gospel as the Serampore Mission's first Christian convert. There is no way to be certain, but without proper pecuniary motivation, a gatekeeper may have chased away the uninvited guest in this scenario. The absence of a gatekeeper was by no means why Krishna became a Christian, yet it seems that the missionaries' strategic choice paid off.

Beyond the lack of a gatekeeper, Ward sought to make people feel "quite at home in [his] company." He did this primarily by using his personal quarters as a space to entertain guests. As the only single adult male missionary at the Serampore Mission, Ward did not have to worry about the impropriety of inviting friends and strangers into his room.[10] In several journal entries, Ward mentioned his habit of holding conversations in his room with others late into the evening.[11] On several occasions, Ward's guests were Krishna and Gokol, who became the first Christian converts.[12]

---

[7] Monday, November 29, 1802. *Ward's Journal*, II, 270. Men with swords demanded access to the Mission premises looking for a runaway servant.

[8] Wednesday, April 7, 1802. *Ward's Journal*, II, 225.

[9] Tuesday, November 25, 1800. *Ward's Journal*, I, 119.

[10] Ward hosted thirty people in his room at once! Saturday, October 22, 1803. *Ward's Journal*, II, 339. Following his marriage to John Fountain's widow, Ward's room was turned into the "the public room." Saturday, January 7, 1804. *Ward's Journal*, II, 356.

[11] August 1, 1800; October 1, 1800; January 14, 1801; February 17, 1801; February 15, 1802. *Ward's Journal*, I, 92, 104, 135, 140; II, 210. Ward first used his private quarters for mentoring Felix Carey, William Carey, Jr., and John Fernandez.

[12] November 7, 1800; November 21, 1800; December 1, 1800; December 5, 1800; June 1, 1801; June 15, 1801; February 6, 1802; March 25, 1802. *Ward's Journal*, I, 112, 116, 119, 120, 155, 159; II, 207, 220.

Statement Six

These moments spent in evangelism and discipleship showcase Ward's willing use of personal space for pastoral work. Being "easy of access" and making Indians feel "at home" in his company were the driving forces behind his blending of personal and professional uses of time, space, and resources.

Beyond Ward's personal efforts, the missionary family extended hospitality in many ways. One of the most important avenues for hospitality was their dinner table. While the table may seem like a typical example of hospitality, it was one of the most challenging aspects of being hospitable in their Indian context. While the missionaries were perfectly happy to share their table with Indian neighbors, this was opposed by Indians and frowned upon by Europeans.[13] Such a seemingly harmless communal experience of sharing a meal had far-reaching implications for one's social and religious standing in Hindu Indian culture. As mentioned above, the Hindu system assigned a hierarchy of value to individuals that corresponded with their social rank. Eating with the wrong person could cost an Indian their caste in nineteenth-century Bengal. This loss of caste entailed social ostracization for such Hindu apostates.

In a bold move, Krishna and Gokol ate lunch with the missionaries and "thus publicly threw away their cast."[14] This communal dining in full daylight was a momentous occasion for the converts and the missionaries. Both parties knew there would be repercussions from this public trampling of tradition, but it is unclear if either party anticipated how swift and severe it would be. Ward considered it "astonishing news" when Gokol reported that a mob of 2,000 people had assembled at Krishna's house, dragged him before the Danish magistrate, and made false accusations.[15] Although the

---

[13] "Creeshnoo's wife & sister were to have been with us in the evening, but the women have many scruples to sit in the company of Europeans." Lord's Day, December 7, 1800. *Ward's Journal*, I, 120.

[14] Monday, December 22, 1800. *Ward's Journal*, I, 125.

[15] Tuesday, December 23, 1800. *Ward's Journal*, I, 126.

The Serampore Form of Agreement

Danish Governor promptly released him, Krishna faced further persecution from his neighbors in the ensuing months.[16] All this resulted from losing caste through eating with European missionaries as a public display.

Apart from the Serampore missionaries, Europeans refused to eat with Indians,—even Christian Indians who had lost caste.[17] Ward recorded his frustrations with some of the most faithful European friends of the Mission. While these friends would not openly ridicule the Indian converts—as did many European merchants—they would not change their own attitudes or behaviors toward them. On one occasion, Ward lamented the actions of his friend, Mr. Ellerton, who refused to show hospitality to two Indian Christians:

> I was ... very sorry that though our two native brethren went up twice to Mr Ellerton's, yet they got nothing to eat. It is not merely Hindoos who are bound by the chain of cast. Europeans when amongst Hindoos, even good men, mind the cast also. I was afraid this circumstance would hurt the minds of our brethren ... it seems a cruel thing that persons who profess to wish to gather them as one family in Xt. should refuse them an occasional place at their table, or a little food ... Tho' they said nothing I know they felt it.[18]

In contrast to these "good men" who "mind caste," Ward, Carey, and Marshman were determined to uphold a different, more hospitable example for their Indian and European brethren.

---

[16] August 1, 1801: Krishna's wife, Rasamayi (Rasoo) was beaten by her landlord. April 7, 1802: Krishna's neighbors attempted to force him to wear different clothes to show his loss of caste. Gokol struggled to find employment as noted by Ward on February 21, 1803: "When a man loses cast he not only is excluded his father's house, but he cannot obtain employment amongst the heathen." November 24, 1804: "Bro. Futick... was lately seized by the chief Bengalee man there dragged from his home; his face, eyes & ears clodded up with cow-dung, his hands tied, & in this state confined several hours in this man's house." *Ward's Journal*, I, 165; II, 225, 283, 398.

[17] Friday, June 19, 1801. *Ward's Journal*, I, 160.

[18] Monday, October 10, 1803. *Ward's Journal*, II, 334.

Statement Six

Pastoral Counsel

> *To gain this confidence we must on all occasions be willing to hear their complaints; we must give them the kindest advice, and we must decide upon every thing brought before us in the most open, upright, and impartial manner...*

Krishna's and Gokol's conversions opened the way for more Indian seekers to become Christians. Ward expressed that the numerical growth turned their "anxiety for converts" into "anxiety about them."[19] Ward and his fellow missionaries intended to be actively involved in the lives of their converts. Sometimes, this pastoral concern led to frustrations for the Indians, and often, it led to frustrations for the missionaries. Nevertheless, the events illustrate the reciprocal process of discipleship in which the paternal missionaries and their perceived children in the faith learned about following Christ in a culture hostile to the gospel.

The spirit of Ward's plan for pastoral counsel included hearing Indian Christian complaints "on all occasions" giving them the "kindest" advice, and making decisions "in the most open, upright, and impartial manner." One can see that Ward insisted upon the right actions as much as the proper disposition in which the actions were to be performed. Moreover, Ward insisted on "willingness" to hear, advise, and rule—not just an obligatory or begrudging service. This descriptive language reflects the seriousness with which the missionaries understood their fatherly role in the discipleship of converts (Statement Seven). As early as January 1800, the missionaries agreed on how best to merge their nuclear families into one large mission family.[20] One year later, the missionaries were learning how to include the families of new converts in meaningful ways. Accountability for Christian growth was one of the most important aspects of life within this extended multicultural family.

The corporate counterpart of individual pastoral counsel was church discipline. The church service was the main arena where the missionaries

---

[19] Lord's Day, April 3, 1803. *Ward's Journal*, II, 291.
[20] Saturday, January 18, 1800. *Ward's Journal*, I, 66-67.

The Serampore Form of Agreement

handled such discipline because the Lord's Supper required personal holiness through repentance of sin. Transitioning from life as a Hindu to a Christian in India was no easy task. Consequently, converts were often excluded from the ritual communion of the church for weeks or months. In several instances, the lifestyle choices and interpersonal strife among converts caused the missionaries to lament. At a low point in the lives of several recent converts, Ward admitted that: "The depravity & base principles we have to contend with, & the conduct of one or two of the baptized, is more difficult to bear than the deaths of so many of our friends."[21]

One example shows that the missionaries were not quibbling over Puritanical customs. An early issue that gave the missionaries minor grief was cannabis smoking amongst their recent converts. Interestingly, both Krishna and Gokol shared the habit, yet the missionaries did not make a blanket policy against it. Early on, Ward suggested that Gokol's habit caused mood swings, but Ward did not mention Krishna's use until two years later.[22] Toward the end of 1804, this habit had become an annoyance, and Ward "brought before the Brethren a practice too much followed by Creeshnoo & a few more of our native brethren, viz. the smoking of an intoxicating herb called Ganja."[23] It is unclear from Ward's journal how problematic this habit had become for the mission, but he said it was "too much followed," implying excess. The missionaries recommended "leaving of it ... very strongly to [their] brethren."

Depending upon the viewpoint of contemporary readership, the preceding example could be regarded as a sin, a crime, or a harmless bad habit. Despite the seriousness or flippancy with which one might regard marijuana use today, the missionaries should be commended for their pastoral discernment and care. More important than these lifestyle issues loomed

---

[21] Wednesday, October 20, 1802. *Ward's Journal*, II, 262-263.

[22] "We fear [Gokol] smokes hemp..." Monday, April 5, 1802. *Ward's Journal*, II, 224-225. See Jonathan Brooke, "'We may have read—but the reality!': Narrating Baptist Missions in Bengal, 1800-1855," (Ph.D. diss., University of London, 2005), 84-113. Though they were both early converts in 1800, Krishna and Gokol did not progress in sanctification at the same rate. Brooke argues that in the rhetoric of Ward, Krishna became the model Christian convert while Gokol remained the perfect counterpoint against missionary optimism.

[23] Saturday, December 8, 1804. *Ward's Journal*, II, 399.

Statement Six

the recurrent interpersonal conflicts within the extended Christian family at Serampore. The missionaries spent much more time and effort calming the "passionate" tempers of their Indian brethren and solving interpersonal conflict than other issues combined.

Ward called "heat and passion" the "national sins" of India.[24] The missionaries expected the Hindu public to show this mark of sinful immaturity, but they held their converts to a higher standard. The missionaries regarded Indians as generally more "passionate" or prone to anger than themselves. Krishna first displayed his "passion" against a Brahman employed at the mission. While the missionaries rebuked him for this foolish display of anger, they secretly found it humorous.[25] Dissimilarly, Gokol's anger against fellow Christians was no laughing matter.

Gokol first displayed anger in the dispute between Unna and Krishna (see next section). As a result of his participation in this factious dispute, he was suspended from participating in the Lord's Supper. In response, Gokol exhibited unrestrained emotion in threatening to kill himself if disallowed to participate.[26] Thankfully, he survived his own rage, but this was not the end of the matter. Two months later, he attempted to shock the missionaries by bursting into the Bengali school room and stamping upon the New Testament "with a stick in his hand."[27] What were the missionaries to do? They sent for him to come to their house, listened to him, and "talked to him very much."

Despite the longsuffering of the missionaries, Gokol went "from bad to worse." He even tried to raise a friend named Samdas from the dead and "kicked up dust with Bro. C[arey]," when rebuked.[28] At this point, Ward regarded Gokol as "worse than dead" because he had caused "the most sensible pain."[29] Despite such morose reflections, neither the missionaries

---

[24] Wednesday, May 19, 1802. *Ward's Journal*, II, 232.
[25] "His hatred to Brahmanism almost exceeds ours." Tuesday, August 18, 1801. *Ward's Journal*, I, 167.
[26] Monday, February 1, 1802; Lord's Day, March 7, 1802. *Ward's Journal*, II, 207, 215.
[27] Monday, April 5, 1802. *Ward's Journal*, II, 224.
[28] Lord's Day, October 3, 1802. *Ward's Journal*, II, 259.
[29] Friday, October 8, 1802; Monday, November 1, 1802. *Ward's Journal*, II, 260, 265.

nor Krishna gave up on Gokol, who was readmitted to the church on March 5, 1803.[30]

Compared to Gokol, Krishna was much more self-controlled, but he was not perfect. During his first seven years as a Christian, Krishna lashed out in anger on several occasions, especially when the missionaries attempted to interfere in the marriages of his two daughters. To be fair, the missionaries' involvement may have been smothering for a man like Krishna, who was older than Ward and Marshman. Indeed, the fatherly self-perception of the missionaries was not always perceived in the same way by their converts. After all, the missionaries were interfering in his fatherly role in finding husbands for his daughters.

Kollador and Bhyrub arrived at Serampore in 1803, and both were eventually married to Krishna's daughters. Problematically, Kollador was promiscuous with several female members of Krishna's family upon his arrival. Though this was an understandable frustration for Krishna, the missionaries' anxiety over the two suitors was warranted. Though the missionaries addressed this with Krishna, he would not listen. Instead, he "went into a dreadful passion, & would hear nothing," making the "the most dreadful expressions of vengeance against us."[31] Krishna's anger lasted for approximately one month before his repentance and return to good standing in the church.[32]

One year later, the same pattern can be observed. Krishna wanted to marry his second daughter to Bhyrub, but Ward knew that Bhyrub had the rumored reputation of secretly going "to see a bad woman."[33] This made Ward suspect Bhyrub's character, and he told Krishna. Despite the missionaries' disapproval of the marriage, Krishna performed the ceremony as a "new way" of "opposition" to them.[34] Ward reported that "Creeshnoo said there was no love amongst us & therefore he did not wish to be

---

[30] While at Dinajpur, Ward received word that Gokol died and was buried as a Christian. Monday, October 24, 1803. *Ward's Journal*, II, 340.

[31] Thursday, June 30, 1803. *Ward's Journal*, II, 310. [Editor's note: alternative spelling the more common, Holladhor, or Hollodhar].

[32] Saturday, August 6, 1803. *Ward's Journal*, II, 317.

[33] Monday, October 3, 1803. *Ward's Journal*, II, 330.

[34] Thursday, July 19, 1804. *Ward's Journal*, II, 379.

Statement Six

amongst us ... The mission is in the deep waters now. This is our only hope, God is at the helm."[35] Ward's apprehension seems linked to the twelve Indian Christians disallowed to participate in the Lord's Supper on August 4, 1804. Perhaps Krishna's influence had grown to cause realistic fears of a church split along ethnic lines. Thankfully, it did not come to this, and the next day, the church added two new converts through baptism.[36]

That same week, Ward discovered Bhyrub's secret betrayal of Krishna and the Mission. He had been forging bills against the Mission's credit with Krishna's signature to a local sircar.[37] Before sending Bhyrub away, the missionaries confirmed Krishna's innocence to the sircar and the Mission family. Though disillusioned and wounded, Krishna took time to heal. A month later, he rejoined the church.[38]

A final example may clarify the sensitivity with which they approached their task. In the case of both Gokol and Krishna, the missionaries did not avoid hard conversations in passivity. Despite months of mutual frustrations, they maintained their ideals of pastoral counsel by being approachable, honest, and impartial in their decisions. Moreover, this final example shows the trust that they built with Indian Christians by persevering through difficult seasons.

One of the earliest converts, Unna, caused a yearlong rift within the church (see next section). After her repentance and restoration to the church, she brought a personal matter before the missionaries. Her daughter's husband wanted to join the church, but there was a potential problem. He had two wives. Until this point, the male converts were unmarried or married to one wife. Ward wrote: "We have some concern about acting

---

[35] Thursday, July 19, 1804. *Ward's Journal*, II, 380.
[36] Saturday, August 4; Lord's Day August 5, 1804. *Ward's Journal*, II, 381.
[37] Monday, August 6, 1804. *Ward's Journal*, II, 381-382. A *sircar* or *sarkar* (several spellings exist) "denotes a native servant who keeps the household accounts and receives and disburses money for his employer, a sort of house-steward; also any writer or accountant." H. H. Wilson, *A Glossary of Judicial and Revenue Terms, and of Useful Words Occurring in Official Documents Relating to the Administration of the Government of British India* (London: Wm. H. Allen and Col., 1855), 466. https://repository.library.georgetown.edu/handle/10822/707745. Accessed August 9, 2022.
[38] Lord's Day, September 2, 1804; Friday, November 2, 1804. *Ward's Journal*, II, 384-385, 391.

right in these circumstances. If a man have two wives I suppose we should not advise him to abandon either; but say – 'GO & sin no more'. There are many heavy burdens in the Mission; without grace to support us according to our day we should shrink."[39]

While Ward neglected to record the outcome, several key takeaways exist. First, the missionaries were sensitive to custom as they had been in the case of other lifestyle habits. They were not laissez-faire with the marital lives of their converts and seekers.[40] Secondly, the missionaries never expected automatic trust between themselves and others. As Unna's case (next section) will demonstrate, the missionaries did not give up on their Indian friends. Third and finally, the missionaries did not expect automatic Christian maturity from their early converts. As these examples have shown, the missionaries were patient and diligent in their discipling and advising.

The missionaries exercised pastoral authority in guarding the communion of the church. Their use of authority was evident in their pastoral counsel. Still, it is important to note that they did not use force to correct the defects of character and immaturity of converts. Instead, they thought it best to lead "by example" and "by grades" so that conviction could occur rather than merely "leave off that which is wrong while in our presence ... and of doing that out of our presence which they dare not do in it" (Statement Eight). In their hospitality and counsel, they had to wait patiently for the voluntary responses of their Indian friends. In the cases of Krishna, Gokol, and Unna, they were not disappointed in the end.

Equality

> *We ought to be easy of access, to condescend to them as much as possible, and on all occasions, to treat them as our equals ...*

---

[39] Monday, July 19, 1802. *Ward's Journal*, II, 245.
[40] In the same journal entry concerning Unna's son-in-law, Ward lamented "young Petumber's" quarrel with his wife. Monday, July 19, 1802. *Ward's Journal*, II, 245.

Statement Six

On February 22, 1801, William Ward reflected on the baptism of two Indian women, Rasamayi (Rasoo) and Unna, claiming that "they found much joy in putting on Xt."[41] This phrase, "putting on [Christ]," occurs in the New Testament twice (cf. Romans 13:14), but it appears only once in relation to baptism. The baptismal passage appears in Galatians: "For as many of you as have been baptized into Christ have put on Christ. There is neither Jew nor Greek, there is neither bond nor free, there is neither male nor female: for ye are all one in Christ Jesus" (Galatians 3:27-28).[42]

The apostle Paul's powerful statement challenged first-century Christians and nineteenth-century Christian converts from Hinduism.[43] While Rasamayi and Unna joined the Serampore church as equals, Unna remained a servant in Rasamayi's (wife) and Krishna's (husband) house. The drama that unfolded following their baptisms was a learning opportunity for the Serampore missionaries and their Indian converts.

Trouble began six months after Unna's baptism. Ward recorded in his journal that a "foolish quarrel" broke out between Unna and her employer, Krishna. Ward wrote, "Unna got it into her head that as she was a holy sister, it was not right to be Creeshnoo's servant."[44] Though Ward seemed surprised by this occurrence, he and the other missionaries were not ignorant of radical social applications of the Christian gospel. In fact, the missionaries rejoiced at their converts' publicly discarding caste or challenging the oppression of "Brahmanism" as evidence of their Christian conversions.[45] Though the suddenness of this conflict regarding Unna seemed to take Ward by surprise, there is ample evidence that the missionaries sent her mixed signals. On several occasions, the missionaries at-

---

[41] Lord's Day, February 22, 1801. *Ward's Journal*, I, 141. Rasamayi or Rasoo was Krishna's wife. Unna was Krishna's in-house servant.

[42] All Scriptural quotations will come from KJV.

[43] There is evidence that Galatians 3:27-28 was a favorite baptismal passage at Serampore. See the baptism of the Pittmans. Lord's Day, October 11, 1807. *Ward's Journal*, III, 604.

[44] Saturday, August 29, 1801. *Ward's Journal*, I, 168.

[45] "These men who despise the cast secretly are not much nearer the kingdom of God than others." Saturday, December 8, 1804. *Ward's Journal*, II, 399.

The Serampore Form of Agreement

tempted to demonstrate their idealistic commitment to the equality of Indians of both high caste and low caste.[46] They did not foresee their converts applying the notion of Christian equality in their households.

In abstract ideals, the Serampore missionaries committed themselves to Moravian-like cooperation and equality.[47] Moreover, they were Baptists who had a congregational heritage in church polity. So, Unna's conclusion that it would not be right to continue as a servant within her newly constituted spiritual family is not at all outside the realm of plausibility. More concretely, Unna reached her conclusion about not being a servant only after the missionaries made it possible for Unna to move out of her master's home![48]

Unna's choice illustrates the inherent tension between God's salvific economy and the realities of social inequality. The tension caused by Unna's choice became the precipitating cause of Gokol's rebellious outbursts (see previous section). Gokol's family and Unna spent most of the following year estranged from Krishna and the missionaries. Although the missionaries became frustrated, they did not quit on Unna, and she eventually returned to both Krishna's household and the church.[49]

Unna's choice and Ward's frustration revealed the tension in which the Serampore missionaries operated. As Baptists, the missionaries believed in the spiritual equality of those who had "put on Christ," and they bore this out in their ecclesiology and missiology. As nonconformist, middling-sort Englishmen, the missionaries were realistic in understanding social inequality.[50] In Unna's case, they seem to have taken their own social

---

[46] Friday, November 7, 1800; Tuesday, October 13, 1801. *Ward's Journal*, I, 114, 175.

[47] John Clark Marshman, *The Life and Times of Carey, Marshman, and Ward. Embracing the History of the Serampore Mission*, vol. 1 (London: Longman, Brown, Green, Longmans, and Roberts, 1859), 402. Brian Stanley, *The History of the Baptist Missionary Society*, 1792-1992 (Edinburgh: T&T Clark, 1992), 39-43.

[48] December 28, 1800; February 22, 1801; August 25, 1801; March 27, 1802. *Ward's Journal*, I, 130, 141, 168; II, 220.

[49] Lord's Day, March 28, 1802. *Ward's Journal*, II, 221.

[50] As Englishmen, the missionaries represented the middle class who had to navigate social relationships between the higher and lower orders. As Baptists, they represented the nonconformists/dissenters in matters of religion. Both the middle class and nonconformists were growing in numbers, respectability, and influence in nineteenth century England. Despite this

Statement Six

sensibilities for granted. They unfairly expected their Indian converts to possess the same social savvy they possessed in being selectively socially disruptive with their gospel witness. When Unna asserted her Christian equality against her subservient employment status, she made a mistake. In time, however, she repaired her relationship with Krishna's family and the missionaries.[51]

Unna's example provides a negative case study in attempting to apply a Christian spiritual concept in the real, broken world. The Serampore church family was an oasis amid the desert of hostility. While Unna may not have found social equality within the household of her new Christian brother and sister, she found a measure of support and equality spiritually within the church. Rules, discipline, help, and support applied to both Unna and her employers in the same measure.

On October 6, 1805, the day after Ward drafted the SFA, the Serampore Mission celebrated the thirteenth anniversary of the founding of the BMS with a momentous church service. William Ward and Joshua Marshman were ordained co-pastors of the Serampore church. Four European and three Indian Christians were ordained to create a seven-member diaconate (Acts 6:1-7). Following ordinations, William Carey preached in English and Bengali for the morning service. In the evening, Carey and Ward preached explicitly to the newly ordained deacons in English and Bengali. After baptizing two new converts, the church celebrated the Lord's Supper, allowing European and Indian deacons to distribute and facilitate the observance. Ward reflected on this service: "Such a day was never seen at the Mission house before. All seemed happy."[52]

While these bilingual services with multicultural participation might seem commonplace in today's globalized society, this was a new occurrence in Bengal. The next day, Ward wrote: "There seems to be a stirring amongst our unbaptized. Those who have been for years under the gospel, sometimes hardened & sometimes despising, these seem to feel anxious to

---

eventuality, the Serampore missionaries experienced social disadvantages back home, and they knew how to navigate the complexities of social hierarchy and ecclesial antipathy.

[51] Saturday, March 27, 1802. *Ward's Journal*, II, 220.
[52] Lord's Day, October 6, 1805. *Ward's Journal*, II, 441.

The Serampore Form of Agreement

be found in Xt ... All these want to join the church, & Golook wants to be restored."⁵³ Though Ward does not explicitly connect these services on Sunday and the "stirring" that occurred on Monday, there seems to be more than mere coincidence in the timing. Perhaps, Indian seekers saw the way forward as converts because their fellow Indians participated in the church's service.

Though becoming Christians would entail real sacrifices for Indians, seekers and converts caught a glimpse of equality in the Serampore representation of the eschatological new creation (Rev. 5:6–10). The multicultural church at Serampore invited the oppressed Indian converts to experience the joy of Christian community as they awaited future reward for their sacrifices (Matt. 19:29).

Respect

All passionate behaviour will sink our characters exceedingly in their estimation. All force, and every thing haughty, reserved, and forbidding, it becomes us ever to shun with the greatest care. We can never make sacrifices too great, when the eternal salvation of souls is the object, except, indeed, we sacrifice the commands of Christ.

A contemporary reader may be caught off guard or taken aback by Ward's eschewing of all "passionate behaviour" in Statement Six of the SFA. By "passionate behaviour," Ward referred to losing one's temper. Ward clarified that the opposite extreme of "reservedness" or "forbidding" was equally problematic. He prohibited hot-headedness and cold-heartedness alike. Unfortunately, John Chamberlain (1777–1821) exhibited both emotional extremes to the detriment of his legacy and the Serampore Mission.

In 1803, Carey, Marshman, and Ward began to refer to themselves as "senior brethren" when fresh missionary recruits arrived at Serampore. John Chamberlain, one of the first missionaries to be considered a "junior" missionary, arrived in January with his wife. After learning the Bengali language, the Chamberlains launched out of Serampore in July 1804 to pioneer the first outpost mission station at Katwa. Though optimistic about

---

⁵³ Monday, October 7, 1805. *Ward's Journal*, II, 441.

Statement Six

expanding the mission's reach and influence, personal tragedy struck when Chamberlain's wife died unexpectedly in November 1804. This was the beginning of trouble.

Chamberlain's life became a nightmare. He lost two infants and two wives within two years and was isolated from his fellow missionaries at his station in Katwa. Moreover, he continued the work of the mission single-handedly while poorly managing entrepreneurial trade.[54] These circumstances warrant historical empathy; however, personal tragedy does not exempt him from responsibility for his bad actions.

At first glance, Chamberlain's physicality and personality may seem positive. He was "a man of robust form, great energy of character," and could spend hours in "intense application and labour."[55] In his cultural context, however, these traits inhibited his effectiveness. His size and energy gave his preaching a "thundering & vehemence of stile" that "rather frightens the natives than convinces them."[56] This intensity aided him as a pioneer, but it led to his disgrace as a missionary.

John Clark Marshman described Chamberlain as "impetuous and overbearing," lacking "any touch of judgement or prudence" or self-control.[57] Chamberlain was aware of his character flaws, but his self-awareness did not translate into changed behavior.[58] The first indicator of a problem appeared in Ward's description of Chamberlain as "a wild bull in a net: going to the grave & crying, roaring & groaning ... beating his servants, so that they were all about to run away from him."[59] Even Chamberlain's written communication contained expressions that were "almost like derangement."[60] He was an emotionally erratic man who was grieving the death of his wife, but he had begun to take his problems out on other people through physical assault. Chamberlain's grief cycle reached a new low when he

---

[54] March 30, 1805; April 11, 1805; August 22, 1805; September 3, 1805. *Ward's Journal*, II, 414, 415, 432, 435; William Yates, *Memoirs of Mr. John Chamberlain, Late Missionary in India* (London: Wightman and Cramp, 1826), 151.

[55] Marshman, *Life and Times*, I, 178.

[56] Lord's Day, November 3, 1805. *Ward's Journal*, II, 449.

[57] Marshman, *Life and Times*, I, 430, 479.

[58] Yates, *Memoirs of John Chamberlain*, 22, 56.

[59] Wednesday, December 19, 1804. *Ward's Journal*, II, 400-401. Emphasis added.

[60] Saturday, January 12, 1805. *Ward's Journal*, II, 406.

The Serampore Form of Agreement

shamefully lashed out against an Indian Christian brother named Bydenaut.

One of the core convictions of the Serampore Missionaries was that Indian Christian preachers were necessary for the evangelization of India (Statement Eight).[61] As such, the hopes of forming a church at Katwa depended upon Bydenaut's relocation to aid Chamberlain.[62] Unfortunately, when Bydenaut arrived with his companion Kangalee, Chamberlain had a "passionate" outburst:

> When I asked him this evening why he did not stay at Cutwa with Bro. Chamberlain, he related that when he went with Kangalee from hence they proceeded to Cutwa; that they staid there all the first day almost without his asking them to eat, & when they began to cook a little for themselves near his house he came, ordered them to take the pot off the fire & kicked it to pieces. This was because they had omitted to ask his leave to cook upon his ground. Oh! Brethren, I hope you will never think again that zeal without love will make a Missionary to the Hindoos.[63]

The senior missionaries took this opportunity to rebuke Chamberlain for his shameful act.[64] In sum, the mission station venture was not off to a good start because Chamberlain was modeling the behavior of the heathen rather than that of a Christian missionary.

Six weeks later, the Serampore missionaries held the special church service in Serampore on October 6, 1805 (see previous section). The night before the momentous occasion, Ward presented to his fellow missionaries the document that is the subject of this book, calling it "a Form of Agreement respecting the Principles upon which we think it our duty to act in instructing the heathen."[65] Ward explained in his journal that it was primarily "that we should leave to our successors something like this." Joshua Marshman, likewise, composed "a plan of Union for the family

---

[61] "I am ready to doubt whether Europeans will ever be extensively useful in converting souls by preaching, in this country." Monday, November 13 [15], 1802. *Ward's Journal*, II, 268.

[62] Tuesday, June 25, 1805. *Ward's Journal*, II, 425.

[63] Monday, August 5, 1805. *Ward's Journal*, II, 429.

[64] Thursday, August 22, 1805; September 3, 1805. *Ward's Journal*, II, 432, 435. They also wanted a report of his expenditures, which he refused to give them.

[65] Saturday, October 5, 1805. *Ward's Journal*, II, 440.

Statement Six

which will accompany the family rules, as this agreement will accompany the Station Rules." Two things become evident from Ward's stated intentions: 1) the SFA communicated the senior brethren's principles to junior brethren, and 2) the SFA pertained to the outer mission stations.

Unsurprisingly, John Chamberlain was the fourth signatory to the SFA under Carey, Marshman, and Ward.[66] He was the first junior brethren and the first missionary stationed at a distance. Considering these contextual details, John Chamberlain certainly factored into Ward's authorial intentions—especially for Statement Six. While it would be improper to characterize the entire SFA as a reactionary document to a problematic missionary, certainly, several elements pertained directly to Chamberlain. Statement Six, read alongside Ward's missionary journal, provides a compelling case for this understanding.

Following the autumn of 1805, Chamberlain calmed down and found happiness through marriage to his second wife, the widow, Mrs Grant.[67] All seemed hopeful until seven months later. Chamberlain lost this second wife to childbirth on the boat ride between Katwa and Serampore.[68] His newborn son, William Grant Chamberlain, died exactly three weeks later.[69] This double misfortune disturbed both missionaries and the public alike. While Ward pondered the providence of it all, Europeans at Calcutta spread the rumor that Chamberlain had murdered his wives.[70] As uncharitable and evil as this rumor may seem, Chamberlain's infamous outbursts did not help his reputation, and on May 20, 1807, he struck another Indian in an argument.[71]

Ward's prohibition against "all force and everything haughty" seems prophetic when considering the case of another junior missionary, William Robinson (1784-1853). This last outburst of Chamberlain in 1807 confirms

---

[66] Lord's Day, October 27, 1805. *Ward's Journal*, II, 446.
[67] Saturday, December 28, 1805. *Ward's Journal*, II, 465.
[68] Wednesday, September 17, 1806. *Ward's Journal*, III, 511.
[69] Wednesday, October 8, 1806. *Ward's Journal*, III, 515.
[70] Sister Robinson refused to go up to Katwa with her husband to assist Chamberlain out of fear. Tuesday, February 24, 1807. *Ward's Journal*, III, 539.
[71] Wednesday, May 20, 1807. *Ward's Journal*, III, 549.

the ease with which a European could take for granted their privileged status among their perceived "inferior" Indians. This was a more significant problem than John Chamberlain.

On Friday evening, September 25, 1807, the senior missionaries received a complaint that Robinson attempted twice to force a servant to lose caste.[72] As a result, William Carey rebuked the much younger Robinson, who evidenced no repentance. This was not an isolated incident of "haughtiness" or "force." Ward described Robinson as "infinitely obstinate, and capable of shaking down the whole Mission House."[73] The senior missionaries proposed to pair the "haughty" Robinson with the "passionate" Chamberlain and cut them off from Serampore. Chamberlain protested, and Ward foresaw that they "would live like two cats tied together by the tails."[74] After a brief stint working together, each man went his own way.[75]

Robinson later proved to be teachable despite his false start as a missionary. Left unchecked, his attitude and behavior could have gone from bad to worse. Instead, he changed his behavior to such a degree that John Clark Marshman characterized him as "one of the ablest men whom the Society had sent out to India since 1799."[76] John Chamberlain was not so, and "his life was a constant succession of disputes and difficulties."[77]

The stories of these two men are instructive in understanding the proclivities of Europeans in their Indian context. Partly due to the imperialistic power dynamics and partly due to human nature, the temptation to use force and privilege was an ever-present struggle for Europeans in India. This temptation was not an external feature of European society as much as it was an internal struggle to inflate one's self-worth by devaluing someone else. The senior missionaries knew all this, which is why Ward's SFA contained such a pointed statement against it. The Serampore Mission was

---

[72] Robinson demanded that his servant handle dirty drinking water and carry a candle made of animal fat. Lord's Day, September 27, 1807. *Ward's Journal*, III, 598.

[73] Lord's Day, October 18, 1807. *Ward's Journal*, III, 606.

[74] Saturday, October 3, 1807. *Ward's Journal*, III, 600.

[75] Stanley, *History of the BMS*, 54.

[76] Marshman, *Life and Times*, I, 408.

[77] Marshman, *Life and Times*, I, 479.

to be a beacon of hope for a lost and dying world. Carey, Marshman, and Ward lived out their principles and put them in writing.

Conclusion

Though concise, Statement Six was one of Ward's clearest guideposts for future missionaries to India. When surveying how European merchants and soldiers regarded and treated Indians, there is no comparison to the Christian missionaries at Serampore. Statement Six of the SFA reflected both their convictions and experiences of self-denial. As imperfect as this self-denial was, the pattern of Christ's condescension toward the world was the driving force behind their action. Not only did they lead their converts into spiritual maturity, but they had to hold one another accountable to the biblical standard of humility and sacrifice. Contemporary readers should commend the Serampore missionaries for their emulation of the example of Christ (Philippians 2:1–11) and the early church (Acts 2:44; 4:32) in hospitality, counsel, equality, and respect.

STATEMENT SEVEN

"Caring for the Gathered Souls"

Peter de Vries, Samuel Masters, and Matthew M. Reynolds[1]

"A real missionary becomes in a sense a father to his people." While this formulation may sound dated to contemporary ears, the Bible is the proper framework for understanding Ward's intentions. The Serampore partners consciously drew on the missionary example of the Apostle Paul,[2] who wrote to the Corinthians, "For though you have countless guides in Christ, you do not have many fathers. For I became your father in Christ Jesus through the gospel."[3]

The image of a father implies an affectionate familial relationship critical to new believers' growth. According to Ward, if the missionary "feels all the anxiety and tender solicitude of a father; all that delight in their welfare and company that a father does in the midst of his children, they will feel all that freedom with, and confidence in him which he can desire." The example also implies a generational relationship. It runs counter to certain contemporary theories of mission that require a rapid cycle of engagement and disengagement as opposed to the lifelong mentorship suggested by the analogy.

This does not mean the Serampore missionaries envisioned Indian believers remaining in a perpetual state of dependency. The final paragraph

---

[1] The section on the Christian magistrate composed by Reynolds. The section on women composed by de Vries. The remainder by Masters.

[2] See the Preamble to the SFA, and William Carey, *An Enquiry into the Obligations of Christians, to Use Means for the Conversion of the Heathens* (Leicester: Ann Ireland, 1792), Title Page.

[3] 1 Corinthians 4:15, ESV.

The Serampore Form of Agreement

of Statement Seven makes it clear that only a relationship of "mutual esteem" would induce the Indians "to open their minds" to the missionaries and allow him to lead them in "regular and happy manner." What is more, the SFA explains that just as a loving father wants to see his children grow into healthy adulthood, the purpose of the missionary was to guide the believers into Christian maturity and to occupy positions of leadership in the church.[4]

Gathered Souls

The first sentence of Statement Seven reads, "Another important part of our work is to build up, and to watch over, the souls that may be gathered." Here, "Watching" and "building up" are fatherly responsibilities. The final clause of the sentence carries significant weight as well. First, Ward has already shown the importance of souls in the first statement of the SFA: "it is absolutely necessary that we set an infinite value upon immortal souls." These immortal souls are to be built up and cared for.[5] This perspective forced the missionaries to overcome any prejudice they may have harbored.

Second, though not explicitly stated, the use of "gathered" implies that Ward saw the church—as understood in Baptist ecclesiology—as the proper venue for this work. As congregationalists, Baptists have historically referred to the local body of believers as the gathered church. Their understanding of the local church as a self-governing "gathered assembly" distinguished their ecclesiology from other protestant traditions. Two of Particular Baptist's most important confessional statements spoke of the church in these terms.

The First London Confession advised, "Thus being rightly *gathered*, established, and still proceeding in Christian communion, and obedience of the Gospel of Christ, none ought to separate for faults and corruptions, which may, and as long as the Church consists of men subject to failings, will fall out and arise amongst them, even in true constituted Churches,

---

[4] See Statement Eight.
[5] See Statement One in this book for further development of the theme of the eternal value of souls.

Statement Seven

until they have in due order sought redress thereof."⁶ The Second London Confession established that "To each of these churches thus *gathered*, according to his mind declared in his word, he hath given all that power and authority, which is in any way needful for their carrying on that order in worship and discipline, which he hath instituted for them to observe; with commands and rules for the due and right exerting, and executing of that power.⁷ The Second London Confession continues, "A particular church, gathered and completely organized according to the mind of Christ, consists of officers and members; and the officers appointed by Christ to be chosen and set apart by the church (so called and gathered), for the peculiar administration of ordinances, and execution of power or duty, which he intrusts them with, or calls them to, to be continued to the end of the world, are bishops or elders, and deacons."⁸

Statement Eight of the SFA makes obvious this framework provided by Baptist ecclesiology. Statement Eight continues themes from Statement Seven regarding the importance of developing Indian leaders. Here again, it seems clear that the Serampore missionaries developed a working philosophy within the framework provided by their ecclesiology. Statement Eight explains, "It is only by means of native preachers that we can hope for the universal spread of the Gospel throughout this immense continent." The second paragraph speaks of "the native brethren" forming "separate churches" and choosing "pastors and deacons from amongst their own countrymen." The purpose was "that the word may be statedly preached, and the ordinances of Christ administered, in each church, by the native minister." This was to be done "without the interference of the missionary of the district." However, this missionary would not abandon them but rather "Constantly superintend their affairs" as he focused on planting new churches. Exactly how the missionary was to "supervise" without "interfering" is not spelled out. Latitude must be granted since the Serampore Mission represented the first large-scale Baptist missionary

---

⁶ "The First London Confession (1644)," in *Baptist Confessions of Faith*, by William L. Lumpkins (Valley Forge, PA: Judson Press, 1969), 168. Article XLVI. Emphasis added.

⁷ "The Second London Confession (1689)," in *Baptist Confessions of Faith*, by William L. Lumpkins (Valley Forge, PA: Judson Press, 1969), 286-287. Chapter XXVI, Paragraph 7. Emphasis added.

⁸ "The Second London Confession of Faith (1689)," 287. Chapter XXVI, Paragraph 8.

endeavor ever attempted. Baptist Associational life in Great Britain might have offered some helpful parallels, but no Baptists had ever attempted evangelizing a foreign nation on this scale.

The missionaries dedicated time to the inquiries of seekers and believers. Carey, for example, spending most of his week in Calcutta, rejoiced in the growing fruitfulness of Indian evangelists such as Krishna Pal, "The number of inquirers constantly coming forward, awakened by the instrumentality of these brethren, fills me with joy. I do not know that I am of much use myself, but I see a work which fills my soul with thankfulness. Not having time to visit the people, I appropriate every Thursday evening to receiving the visits of inquirers. Seldom fewer than twenty come."[9] Back in Serampore, Ward handled many of the inquiries at the Mission.[10]

At times, this fatherly care required the exercise of church discipline. However, they relied primarily on the ministry of the word taught from the pulpit and in personal discipleship. In Statement Seven, Ward writes, "We must be willing to spend some time with them daily, if possible, in this work. We must have much patience with them, though they may grow very slowly in divine knowledge." Ward was so convinced of the importance of this fatherly work that he wrote to a friend, "I have been thinking of looking out for some spot for my future retirement, where I may erect a bungalow and have a Christian village, and devote my remaining days to the instruction of inquirers and the formation of young Hindoos for the ministry."[11]

The missionaries placed great importance on the ministry of the Word, whether in personal ministry or public preaching. Ward described what he considered the most effective approach, "Study - yes, study to be quiet—but above all, study to get at the affections, the consciences, and the false

---

[9] George Smith, *The Life of William Carey, D.D.* (London: John Murray, 1885), 161.

[10] Ward wrote to Fuller, "The might of the Mission as it respects foresight, directing the things put in motion, watching over all, hearing all, advising with all—all this falls on me. The enquirers cases are all regulated by me. Neither they nor our baptised carry their complaints or wants, or affairs before Bro Carey or Brother Marshman." Ward to Fuller, Mission Boat, Sunderbunds, Oct 7, 1805. BMS, Mss., Reel 44.

[11] John Clark Marshman, *The Life and Times of Carey, Marshman, and Ward: Embracing the History of the Serampore Mission* (London: Longman, Brown, Green, Longmans, & Roberts, 1859), II, 161.

refuges of sinners: —study to be useful—then you will become a spiritual father ... If you become a useful, you will first be (as the Puritans said) a painful preacher of the gospel.[12]

The task was larger than that of creating Baptist churchmen. The question was how to form a Christian society in the larger context of a culture dominated by Hinduism. Statement Seven attempted to provide answers in three areas critical to helping Indian believers make their way in the world. First, faith and work, or more prosaically, how to make a living as an Indian believer. Second, how to relate to secular authorities. And third, how to understand the role of women.

Christian Faith and Work in a Hindu Society

New Christians faced a profound dilemma. Union with the church at Serampore meant expulsion from the web of relationships required to make a living. Baptism at the mission church, and more importantly, participation in the Lord's supper and sharing communal meals, meant the rejection of caste. New believers became social pariahs. Statement Seven states, "We ought also to remember that these persons have made no common sacrifices in renouncing their connections, their homes, their former situations and means of support, and that it will be very difficult for them to procure employment with heathen masters. In these circumstances, if we do not sympathize with them in their temporal losses for Christ, we shall be guilty of great cruelty."

The Serampore missionaries believed part of the solution involved inculcating a protestant work ethic: "We ought also to endeavour as much as possible to form them to habits of industry." But this was not sufficient. They also had to "assist them in procuring such employments as may be pursued with the least danger of temptations to evil." The missionaries, at times, sought employment of the new converts among Europeans. For example, Krishna Pal worked for James Rolt, a cabinetmaker, and the governor of Serampore hired him to work on the town's new church building.[13]

---

[12] Ward to Stennett, May, 1803, quoted in Samuel Stennett, *Memoirs of the Life of the Rev. William Ward*, 2nd ed. (London: Simpkin & Marshall, Holdsworth, 1825), 118-122.

[13] Edward S. Wenger, *The Story of the Lall Bazar Baptist Church Calcutta: Being the History of Carey's Church from 24th April 1800 to the Present Day* (Calcutta: Edinburgh Press, 1908), 15.

The Serampore Form of Agreement

Some converts found teaching in the Lancastrian schools begun by the Marshmans. A cooperative established in the Sunderbans employed Indian believers in indigo production, "Then they sublet the plots to peasants on reasonable terms, especially to the Christians of a dozen villages there, freeing them from oppressive landlords, and at the same time providing an endowment for the college."[14]

As much as the missionaries might have liked for new believers to be able to continue to live close to their Hindu neighbors, Christian villages became a necessity:

> A Christian village has lately been established, for the purpose of promoting the general comfort of our native brethren, and also facilitating the communication of religious instruction to them. It now consists of 13 dwelling houses, with a small chapel in the centre; and will, we trust, be considerably enlarged during the present season, as several families are desirous of removing to it from the town, from which it is distant but a very short way, on an open and elevated spot of ground. Pran Krishnu, one of the native preachers resides in it, and conducts daily worship in the chapel, and in other ways seeks the edification of the people under his charge. On Tuesday, Saturday and Sabbath evenings, also worship is conducted by one or other of the missionaries; and an adult school is held on Sabbath in the chapel by Mr. Buckingham, a pious and active young man, who has been with us since before Mr. Ward's lamented death, from whom he received his first instruction in religion.[15]

The Serampore missionaries had probably not anticipated all the issues arising from the gospel. They certainly envisioned Indian believers gathered into native churches. But these believers were also in the world, even if they were not of the world.

---

[14] S. Pearce Carey, *William Carey, D.D., Fellow of the Linnaean Society* (London: Hodder and Stoughton, 1923), 383.

[15] *Periodical Accounts of the Serampore Mission*, XVII (1827), 2-3 (152-153). John Mack in his report on Jan 1, 1827, *Annual Report of the BMS* (1827), Appendix II, quoted in, Charles Williams, *Missionary Gazetteer* (London: F. Westley and A.H. Davis, 1828), 440-441.

Statement Seven

Relating to the Civil Magistrate

As previously stated, Statement Seven's primary aim was to set forth how the missionaries should relate to native brethren and sisters as they strove to see Christ's character formed within them and manifested in every area of life. Proper relations with the British Government posed a particular challenge in this quest. In the section of Statement Seven that deals with proper relations to the government, Ward sets forth three reasons the native brethren should "honour the civil magistrate." First, Scripture taught honor for rulers and, as such, was binding for Indian and British Christians alike. Second, such honor was a commensurate act of gratitude for the "liberal protection" they had experienced from the East India Company. And third, such honor would demonstrate to the British authorities that they had "nothing to fear from the progress of Missions."

Ward also gave two reasons the authorities had nothing to fear from the progress of missions in India. First, since disobedience to the human magistrate would constitute disobedience to their heavenly Lord, the natives would surely abide by British authority in their quest to obey their Lord and Savior, Jesus Christ. Second, if properly instructed in the Christian faith, native Christians would become better citizens, for their Christian faith would prompt them to love and be more devoted to their British rulers than citizens of other religions.

Before they departed for India, pastor Samuel Pearce of Birmingham had written to the missionaries who joined Carey in India in 1799:

> Since that kingdom which we, as the disciples of Jesus wish to establish, is not of this world, we affectionately and seriously enjoin on each missionary under our patronage, that he do cautiously and constantly abstain from every interference with the political concerns of the country where he may be called to labour, whether by words, or deeds; that he be obedient to the laws in all civil affairs; that he respect magistrates, supreme and subordinate; and teach the same things to others: in fine, that he apply himself wholly to the all-important concerns of that evangelical service to which he has so solemnly dedicated himself.[16]

---

[16] *Periodical Accounts Relative to the Baptist Missionary Society*, 1 (1799), 519. Hereafter *PA*.

The Serampore Form of Agreement

Despite the clarity of Pearce's statement, its application in concrete situations left the missionaries sometimes feeling pulled in opposite directions. On the one hand, some Scripture passages teach that Christians are to honor and obey the civil authorities—even if they are ungodly and oppose the cause of Christ (cf. Rom 13:1-8; 1 Tim 2:1-6; 1 Pet 2:17; Matt 22:21). These passages teach that Christians are to honor and respect those that are in authority over them, to be subject to their jurisdiction—because to resist their authority is to resist the authority that God has appointed—to pay taxes owed to them, and to pray for them. On the other hand, other passages require allegiance to God *above* the civil magistrate when obedience meant breaking a divine law (cf. Acts 4:18-20; 5:27-29).

The Serampore missionaries were Particular Baptists. But like Presbyterians and Congregationalists, they were Dissenters or Nonconformists, rejecting the authority and forms of worship of the Established Church of England. For Baptist forefathers like John Bunyan, dissent meant jail time. In Carey, Marshman, and Ward's day, Dissenters could not study at Oxford or Cambridge. In India, Carey could not serve as a full professor at Fort William College in Calcutta (or receive a full professor's pay), and none of the Trio could preach in Anglican chapels in Calcutta. However, they shared fellowship and communion with Anglican chaplains David Brown and Claudius Buchannan. Here also, the missionaries were torn.

Chapter 24 of their doctrinal statement (the *Second London Confession of 1689*) affirmed the Bible's teaching on submission to authorities. Baptists were allowed to participate in the government. They could accept the office of magistrate to maintain the peace and promote justice—even by war, provided the occasion was just and necessary.[17] But, when British demands seemed to oppose the call of God, these Baptist Dissenters were more likely to, well, dissent. At the same time, living in East India Company dominions in India, they were more aware of the consequences of arousing the ire of the civil magistrate than those holding the ropes in England.

---

[17] "Second London Confession (1689)," 283-284. Chapter XXIV.

Statement Seven

Following the commands of Scripture concerning the civil magistrate in Bengal was challenging for the missionaries, but teaching native Christian converts how they should relate to the colonial government was perhaps even more challenging. If, in relating to the magistrate, foreign missionaries failed to give the East India Company the respect and obedience they felt was due, at worst, they would be sent home to England. If native converts to Christianity fell out of favor with the British government, they were likely to receive more severe treatment. Before the renewal of the East India Company's charter in 1813, The British government took great pains not to offend the religious sensibilities of Hindus and Muslims. Their *sepoy* armies were comprised of such, and the British could little afford any offense that might compromise the allegiance of their native military. But Indian converts to Christianity—precisely because of their conversion—had fallen out of favor with all their native relations. So, if the British perceived disobedience or threat from these native fruits of British missionary labor, they would have no scruples against a more severe response.

The SFA sets forth principles the Serampore missionaries felt they *should* adhere to. However, it does not resolve every tension produced in pursuing these principles. Should the government's position directly oppose their core calling of gospel preaching, what then? How would they resolve this tension? And to what extent were they ready to be disobedient for the sake of the gospel?

The British Government in India

Though Englishmen ruled certain strategic areas of India when William Carey arrived in Bengal in 1793, it was not the British government, but the East India Company (EIC) through the governors of three "presidencies"—one in Bengal, one in Bombay, and one in Madras. This British commercial enterprise, begun in 1600, had morphed into a sovereign power over parts of the Indian subcontinent. It would continue until 1858 when, following Indian *sepoy* mutinies that began in Barrackpore (Bengal) and spread beyond Delhi, it was brought under the direct control of the British crown by the Government of India Act. So, it was not the British government that opposed the missionaries but rather a commercial interest—in the form of a joint-stock company.[18]

The EIC recognized that India was filled with deeply religious peoples and that the surest way to endanger its profits was to offend their religious sensibilities. Vastly outnumbered, the EIC depended on its native army to protect its commercial interests. So, while a public offense of a religious nature might cause a riot, an affront to the native soldiers that comprised their army could result in the loss of all their interests in India. Because of this, the EIC decided to pursue a policy of non-interference in the religious affairs of the people. They represented a Christian country but were committed to a religiously neutral policy.[19]

For this reason, when William Carey and John Thomas came to Bengal in 1793 as missionaries, they entered Calcutta clandestinely.[20] When Ward and Marshman arrived with their fellow missionaries in 1799, they adopted a different course, openly declaring they were Baptist missionaries. They were likely only just saved from immediate expulsion thanks to refuge given them by the governor of Danish-controlled Serampore.[21] In such an environment, the Baptist missionaries had to respect the magistrate and show them they had nothing to fear from the progress of missions in their dominion. But as the Serampore Mission expanded, many events would put their principles to the test.

The Persian Pamphlet Affair[22]

On September 2, 1807, Ward records in his journal that "Mr. Krefting, our [Danish] Governor, sent for our perusal an official letter signed by Lord Minto [Governor General of India], Sir Geo. Barlow & Mr. Lumsden,

---

[18] Ian Copland, "East India Company," *An Oxford Companion to the Romantic Age*, eds. Iain McCalman, et al. (Oxford: Oxford University Press, 1999).

[19] Penelope Carson, *The East India Company and Religion, 1698-1858* (Woodbridge, Suffolk; Rochester, NY: Boydell, 2012), 8.

[20] Marshman, *Life and Times*, I, 61.

[21] Marshman, *Life and Times*, I, 111.

[22] For a more detailed account of the Persian Pamphlet Affair see Matthew M. Reynolds, *The Spirituality of William Ward* (West Lorne, Ontario: H&M Academic, 2023), 188-199.

Statement Seven

complaining of one of our Persian pamphlets as very inflammatory & calculated to inflame the Musulmans."[23] As they later learned, the "inflammatory" remarks were made by a *moonshee*, or native language teacher, who had converted to Christianity from Islam. He had been tasked with translating a "short abstract (in the Bengalee [Bengali] language,) of the life of Mahomet taken almost verbatim [*sic*.] from Sales' preliminary discourse prefixed to his translation [of] the Koran, desiring him to translate it into Persian."[24] But in his Christian zeal, he had not rendered the translation verbatim, but had "repeatedly referred to the Prophet Muhammad as a 'tyrant' and to the *Qur'an* as an 'imposture'—i.e., a work which is intended to deceive."[25]

Following the letter, Carey received a summons to appear immediately before the Governor General, Lord Minto. Then, a few days later, an express letter from the Company Government arrived for Carey expressing concern that their pamphlet might disturb the natives' free exercise of their respective religions.[26] To prevent this, they demanded the closure of the house of worship in Calcutta. And more devastating for the Mission's work, they demanded the press be transferred to Bengal Presidency control in Calcutta.

This was a dire situation indeed. Did the missionaries feel compelled to honor and obey the magistrate at the expense of a place of worship—at the cost of their press with which William Ward and his associates printed the Bible in numerous Indian languages? They had come to India for this purpose. Was their obligation still binding to respect the authorities God had placed over them? Or were they bound by a higher law? And what would be the cost if they disregarded the authority of the Company? They had to

---

[23] Wednesday, September 2, 1807. William Ward, *Journal*, III, 579. Mss. *BMS Missionary Correspondence; William Ward; Transcript of Diaries in 2 Books Comprising 4 Volumes; Book 1 (Vols. 1 & 2) 1799-1805; Book 2 (Vols. 3 & 4) 1806-1811*, microfilm; reel 44, publication No. 5350 (London: Baptist Missionary Society Archives), 1981. Hereafter, *Ward's Journal*.

[24] Tuesday, September 8, 1807. *Ward's Journal*, III, 583-584. The *Qur'anic* translation mentioned here is that of George Sale who translated the *Qur'an* from Arabic to English in 1734. This translation contained a defense of Muhammad that earned him a "reputation as a secret Muslim convert, or at least as a freethinker." Ann Thomson. "North Africa and the Levant," *Encyclopedia of the Enlightenment* ed. Alan Charles Kors. 4 Vols (New York and Oxford: Oxford University Press, 2003), III, 190-192.

[25] Reynolds, *The Spirituality of William Ward*, 187.

[26] Friday, September 11, 1807. *Ward's Journal*, III, 588.

respond, but what would they say? What principles would they employ in this impasse of conscience? After serious thought, Ward penned a letter to his colleagues, recommending what he felt was the best course.

In this letter, recorded in his Journal, we gain insight into Ward's reasoning as he pondered how to practice the principles he had penned roughly two years earlier concerning the civil magistrate.

> We should entreat their clemency, & try to soften them. Tender words, with the consciences of men on our side, go a long way. We can tell them to take the press to Calcutta would involve us in a heavy and unbearable expence, break up our family, &ca. &ca. &ca. and that we will give them every security which they would wish, by subjecting our press to the absolute control and inspection of the Government here, nay that we are willing to do every thing they wish us, except that of renouncing our work and character as Ministers of the Saviour of the world. To this Mr. Krefting can add what he likes. If they listen to this we are secured, with all the advantages of their sufferance. If they are obstinate, we are still at Serampore. I entreat you dear Brethren, to consider these things, and give them all the attention that our awful circumstances [require].[27]

Carey and Marshman heeded Ward's counsel. They presented Lord Minto with a gift of an English translation of the Hindu mythology, the *Ramayana*. Later, Marshman wrote and sent the "supplicatory and explanatory address" Ward had recommended.[28] After a couple of weeks of waiting, the Danish Governor's secretary delivered a letter from Governor Minto "revoking their decree about the press."[29] This was a major victory and an answer to prayer; however, it came at a cost. Going forward, they would be bound by certain restrictions and have to submit "to the inspection of the Officers of the British Government" before publishing.[30]

---

[27] Monday, September 21, 1807. *Ward's Journal*, III, 595–596.
[28] Thursday, September 24–25, 1807. *Ward's Journal*, III, 596–597.
[29] Saturday, October 10, 1807. *Ward's Journal*, III, 600–601.
[30] Saturday, October 10, 1807. *Ward's Journal*, III, 601–602.

Statement Seven

John C. Marshman attributed the "favourable change" to the "peaceable and judicious conduct of the three at Serampore in bending to the necessity of circumstances, and endeavouring to conciliate those who possessed despotic power, and were at one time disposed to use it tyrannically. It was the irresistible might of Christian meekness which carried them safely through this crisis."[31] Ward's pacific counsel had won the day.

But what if BMS colleagues in England saw things differently? What if they felt the Trio had sacrificed too much on the altar of government appeasement? In the unpublished candor of his Journal, Ward told Fuller,

> It may be right to take Bro. Fuller's advice, to go to gaol, when the putting one man in gaol will not be putting the whole cause at once in gaol, but in present circumstances I think it much better that we should give way in some instance, to secure objects which we may retain. Any *one* of us, I suppose, is ready to go to gaol, but we are none of us willing to put the whole Gospel interest in Bengal in gaol at once. I suppose, for the sake of preaching at the bull-ring in the market-place, you would not think it right to quarrel with the mayor of Northampton, if you knew that the result of this quarrel would be the silencing of all the Gospel Ministers in England. "If they persecute you in one city, flee", &c. Mr. Brown concurred in the idea of our softening Government.[32]

The dilemma in the Persian pamphlet affair is one incident in the history of the Serampore Mission where the principles of the Serampore Form of Agreement (SFA) regarding behavior toward the civil magistrate were tested. The Serampore Trio endeavored to live up to their principles. They were grateful to the Danish governor of Serampore, Krefting, who had boldly declared, "if they came to compel him, he would strike the flag & surrender himself a prisoner, but that he would not give up the press."[33] Accordingly, the Serampore missionaries desired to relieve him of any pressure that he felt from the British on their account. And they were strongly motivated to alleviate the fears the inflammatory pamphlet caused the Company officials.

---

[31] Marshman, *Life and Times*, I, 327.
[32] Thursday, September 24, 1807, *Ward's Journal*, III, 596.
[33] Monday, September 21, 1807, *Ward's Journal*, III, 594.

The Serampore Form of Agreement

In the Persian pamphlet affair—because the existence of a church and the Mission's press were at stake—the Trio faced the dilemma of how to honor the magistrate while holding fast to their calling as missionaries and servants of Christ. In the end, the Company's ire was appeased, and the Mission kept its press, but only by relinquishing some of the freedoms of expression they previously enjoyed. By what principle did the Trio yield ground to the Company? In short, they perceived that the cost of remaining out of favor with Company authorities was greater than the cost of submitting to increased scrutiny of their press. In correspondence with his colleagues, Ward foresaw disastrous consequences for the Mission if they could not mollify the magistrate's wrath.

> They may deprive us of Bro. Carey's salary, with which we can hardly get on now, & without which we must put an end to the translations, and go to gaol in debt; they can shut up the new meeting at Calcutta; they can stop the circulation of our grammars, Dictionaries and every thing issued from this press in their dominions; they can prohibit our entering their territories, &c.[34]

How much were the missionaries willing to sacrifice in this line? Ward maintained that they should do everything in their power to conciliate them and that they should be ready to "give them every security which they would wish, by subjecting our press to the absolute control and inspection of the Government here, nay that we are willing to do every thing they wish us, except that of renouncing our work and character as Ministers of the Saviour of the world ... If they listen to this we are secured, with all the advantages of their sufferance."[35] In Ward's estimation, they could afford to lose this battle to live and fight another day. Such compromise did not, in his mind, constitute a betrayal of their Lord or calling.

The reader may or may not agree with Ward's reasoning. He distinguished between the ministry environments of England and Bengal, and he felt that context must have some bearing on decisions. Clearly, the Trio strove to adhere to the principles of the Serampore Form of Agreement.

---

[34] Monday, September 21, 1807, *Ward's Journal*, III, 595.
[35] Monday, September 21, 1807. *Ward's Journal*, III, 595–596.

Statement Seven

Women as Co-laborers

The third section of Statement Seven sets out the Serampore missionaries' attitudes towards women. In earlier statements, they lamented the societal degradation and the sad plight of women around them. The section begins with the hope that gospel preaching would make native women an "ornament to the Christian cause." The idea was that outward ornaments that marked the Oriental woman were being transposed to "ornaments of grace," signifying inner transformation, expressed in beauty of character (Prov 1:9; 4:9; 1 Pet 3:4).[36] But men could not do this alone.

In his *Enquiry,* Carey wrote that no mission could occur without missionary wives. For Carey, women had an indispensable, albeit domestic role in missions. After stating he thought it best missionaries should be married men, their wives "would be necessary for domestic purposes."[37] For him, a missionary was by definition male, and wives came out not as independent agents but as "helpmeets" to support their husbands and make a home for their families.[38] As a non-conformist, he followed a Puritan understanding of the role of women, which emphasized the family union under the male parental head.

Carey's *Enquiry* acknowledges women's roles in God's economy throughout the book of Acts and in primitive Christianity. There was a woman of Joppa, raised to life by Peter, "which was an occasion of the conversion of many in that town;" Lydia of Thyatira, "who was converted and baptized, and her household with her" and a young Christian woman who was "being taken captive by Iberians ... and so much regarded that they sent to Constantine for ministers to come and preach the word to them."[39] He was familiar with evangelical writers such as Hannah More (1745-1833) and Henrietta Neale (1752-1802), who had pioneered female

---

[36] "Sister Grant and... Hannah Marshman... are great ornaments to the cause in which they are engaged." Carey to Ryland, June 29-30, 1802, in Terry G. Carter, *The Journal and Selected Letters of William Carey* (Macon, GA: Smyth & Helwys, 2000), 109. W. Ward, "Religious Tracts Anecdotes," *Baptist Magazine,* XIII (1821), 524.

[37] Carey, *An Enquiry,* 74.

[38] From Genesis 2:18b. "I will make him a help meet for him." KJV.

[39] Carey, *An Enquiry,* 19, 23, 31.

education in England.[40] Baptists would send their daughters to girls' schools, and women (often older widows) were occasionally appointed as deaconesses. The Broadmead Church at Bristol—home of Hannah and Joshua Marshman—was known for its stance on women in leadership.[41] But generally, public roles for Baptist women were few. Missionary correspondence, however, testifies that public and private roles of women on the field were much more fluid.

Realizing the need to attract a female hearing, Andrew Fuller published several of Hannah Marshman's letters in the *Periodical Accounts*. Hannah was an experienced teacher, and her letters fueled great interest in female education. These letters provided a window into the day-to-day affairs of the Serampore Mission.[42] Her pioneering role in education is described elsewhere. Over time she achieved an almost heroic status as an advocate for girls' education.[43] Later, mission leaders acknowledged that wives, in their role as co-laborers, were missionaries in their own right.[44] Yet it would not be until 1866 that the BMS actively recruited single *women* missionaries.[45] In the following, we trace the fluidity of missionary roles at the Serampore Mission. These roles changed as circumstances demanded.

---

[40] Karen E. Smith, "Female Education among Baptists in the Eighteenth Century: Martha (Smith) Trinder (1736-1790) and Henrietta Neale (1752-1802)," *Baptist Quarterly* 48, no. 4 (2007): 168-180. Hannah Marshman to Mrs Clarke, January 5, 1805 in *PA*, III (1805), 85-86.

[41] John Briggs, "She-Preachers, Widows and Other Women: The Feminine Dimension in Baptist Life Since 1600," *Baptist Quarterly* 31, no. 7 (July 1986): 338-339.

[42] E.g. *Periodical Accounts Relative to the BMS*, II (1801), 153; 527-528; *PA*, III (1806), 83-85; *PA*, IV (1810), 169-170. *Evangelical Magazine*, xiv (1806), 41. *Baptist Magazine*, XVI (1824), 541.

[43] George Smith, *Twelve Pioneer Missionaries* (London: Thomas Nelson and Sons, 1900), 67-87; Sunil Kumar Chatterjee, *Hannah Marshman: The First Women Missionary in India* (Sheoraphuli: Laserplus, 2006), preface. A. Christopher Smith, "The Legacy of William Ward and Joshua and Hannah Marshman," *International Bulletin of Mission Research* 23, no. 3 (1999): 122-123; Sutapa Dutta, *British Women Missionaries in Bengal, 1793-1861* (London: Anthem Press, 2017).

[44] Cox names the following "woman missionaries" in 1841-1842. At Calcutta: Mrs Yates, Thomas, Wenger and Evans, Pearce, and Small. At Howrah: Mrs Morgan. At Monghyr: Mrs Leslie, Lawrence, Parsons. Francis A. Cox, *History of the Baptist Missionary Society from 1792 to 1842* (London: Ward and Dyer, 1842), II, 394, 401.

[45] Brian Stanley, *The History of the Baptist Missionary Society, 1792-1992* (Edinburgh: T&T Clark, 1992), 227-229; Clare Midgley, "Can Women Be Missionaries? Envisioning Female Agency in the Early Nineteenth-Century British Empire," *Journal of British Studies* 45, no. 2 (April 2006), fn 11.

Statement Seven

Singles and Married Couples

As early as 1796, observing the difficulty of reaching high-class women living in secluded quarters (*purdah*) in Bengal, Carey pleaded for a more active role for women: "the necessity of females, well qualified, to communicate the gospel of Christ in a situation where superstition secluded all the women of respectability from hearing the word, unless from their own sex."[46] At the time of writing, Carey would have reflected on his own family experience with a wife who struggled with their cross-cultural experience. That Dorothy suffered so much remains the biggest enigma of Carey's legacy. As Carey's wife and mother of four surviving sons, Dorothy must be remembered as an indispensable part of Carey's life and work.[47]

Among Baptist missionaries, the common practice was that of the Moravians, who had sent married couples to the field. While in 1796 he envisioned single missionaries,[48] in 1812, talking to an American missionary, Carey had changed his mind. As was later reported, "Dr Carey... would hardly admit the possibility of a missionary being so situated, as not to make it expedient that he should be married. As a general rule, he urged marriage upon missionaries as an indispensable duty."[49] And that, preferably before coming out! Though William Ward went as a single missionary,

---

[46] Carey to Society, Hooghly River, Dec 28, 1796. *PA*, I, 347. E. Daniel Potts, *British Baptist Missionaries in India, 1793-1837: The History of Serampore and its Missions* (Cambridge: Cambridge University Press, 1967), 38.

[47] Chris Chun, "The Sacrifices of Dorothy Carey and Ann Judson: Two Sides of the Same Coin," in *Expect Great Things, Attempt Great Things: William Carey and Adoniram Judson* (Eugene, OR: Wipf and Stock, 2013), 125-136.

[48] "... let the Missionaries be either married or single as they may be procured... and the Missionaries' wives are as much impressed with the missionary spirit as they [husbands] themselves are..." Carey to Society, Hooghly River, December 26, 1796. Carter, *Carey's Journal and Letters*, 133.

[49] *Panoplist and Missionary Magazine*, XI (1815), 180. That person was most likely the single Congregational missionary Luther Rice, who arrived in August 1812, and who—like the Judsons before him—was baptized at the Serampore Mission. Upon hostility from the Calcutta authorities, he returned to America in November to become a representative of the newly formed American Baptist Missionary Society. John Clark Marshman, *The Life and Times of Carey, Marshman, and Ward: Embracing the History of the Serampore Mission* (London: Longman, Brown, Green, Longmans, & Roberts, 1859), II, 57-60.

he was one of few, and he dutifully married Mary, the widow of John Fountain, so that he could provide for her. This set a pattern of bereaved male missionaries marrying widowed missionary wives.[50]

Carey did not object to mixed marriages. But he was concerned that Britons would fully commit to their alliance with local women, and not keep them as concubines. His concern stemmed from practical reasons. He lamented the tragic consequences of his son Felix's marriage to a Burmese woman after being widowed. When Felix was forced to leave Burma, he had to leave her behind. Subsequently, the Burmese authorities declared this marriage illegal because of her Catholic faith, enabling Felix to marry a fourth time.[51] Undoubtedly, Felix's decisions caused Carey a lot of heartache. But Carey's main concern stemmed from the sad plight of children born from mixed marriages. In 1809, the missionaries founded the Benevolent Institution in Calcutta to alleviate the plight of these "country-born," who were often left to their own devices. With their multi-cultural background, the missionaries realized their potential as bilingual evangelists, some becoming celebrated missionaries.[52]

Single women were rarely sent to the field, and Carey noted later of a Miss Chaffin, "although 'an excellent woman' she was not 'of any use to the Mission.'"[53] This sounded harsh, but the Mission consisted of a large community of young single women, including three daughters of the Marshmans, two of the Wards, and several orphans. These young women were engaged in the domestic affairs of the Mission and at the girls' schools

---

[50] John Chamberlain (widowed in 1804) married Ann, widow of William Grant (who died shortly after their arrival in 1799) in 1805; Hannah, widow of John Biss (died in 1807) married William Moore (widowed in 1812) in 1813; Amelia, widow of Felix Carey (died in 1822) married James Williamson (who was single) in 1821.

[51] Charlotte Atlee White Rowe's *Journal*, Mss. Yale Divinity School Library, *Special Collections*, New Haven, CT., 39. With thanks to Reid S. Trulston for the reference; B.R. Pearn, "Felix Carey and the English Baptist Mission in Burma," *Journal of the Burma Research Society* xxviii, no. I (1938): 37-41.

[52] For the background, Marshman, *Life and Times*, I, 422-426; John Statham, *Indian Recollections* (London: Samuel Bagster, 1832), 368-378; Potts, *British Baptist Missionaries*, 128-129.

[53] Carey to Ryland, n.p. May 30, 1816. Carter, *Carey's Journal and Letters*, 135. Miss Chaffin was the daughter of a pharmacist in London, a trained nurse, who came out in 1812 with the Lawsons and Johns'. She was perhaps the first missionary nurse. Potts, *British Baptist Missionaries*, 38, 65.

Statement Seven

at Serampore. They were immersed in the vernaculars from childhood and excelled in teaching children. Unless specially gifted, new missionaries often took years to become fluent in the vernaculars, as Miss Chaffin hopefully eventually became.[54]

Wives as Managers

Functioning as a Moravian-type community, with all tasks divided between them, the missionary wives managed the Serampore Mission. Initially, they all took turns in "presiding" over the table.[55] From the start in January 1800, Hannah Marshman and Mary Ward, as well as Ann Grant and Ann Brunsdon, took turns keeping the monthly accounts. They painstakingly noted the expense of supplies and payments made to the boatmen, tailors, and washermen.[56] Hannah's diary and surviving letters testify of exhausting days looking after children and visitors, overseeing domestic servants, and organizing communal meals "all in the English way, except the curry."[57] The wives functioned as house mothers on a monthly rotation basis, overseeing the schools and domestic affairs. Their example inspired newly arrived missionaries, who requested their advice.[58] This relieved their husbands so they could engage in pastoral oversight, translation, College, and press work. Over time, Hannah took on a more senior role, which she shared with Mary. Carey fondly commented in 1820, "It

---

[54] Little is known about the course of events after Chaffin's arrival. She joined the Lawsons at Calcutta and was involved with the Junior missionaries' school in 1817. Her presence is noted at the Calcutta Missionary Society in 1829. She died on 19 Jan 1835, and was buried next to Mrs Leslie. *Baptist Magazine*, xxvii (1835), 438; E.S. Wenger's notes on John Lawson, CLRC, Mss., "g."

[55] "Sister Tidd, presides at breakfast & tea, & I at dinner." June 14, 1799. Ward's *Journal*, 15.

[56] *Housekeeping Accounts 1801-1804*, 2 Vols. Mss., CLRC, Serampore.

[57] Hannah Marshman to Mrs Clarke, Jan 5, 1805 in *PA*, III (1806), 85-86. Rachel Voigt, "Memoir of Hannah Marshman's Earlier Years," n.d., n.p., typed Mss., CLRC, Serampore.

[58] "any instructions relative to the establishment of European or native schools, [and] the management of domestic affairs... will be gratefully received." Letter from Rachel F. Bradwell *et al.* to Mrs Marshman and Mrs Ward, Mar 14, 1816 in *American Baptist Magazine* (1817), 1:103-104.

The Serampore Form of Agreement

would be superfluous to mention the large, faithful, and disinterested labours of our Dear Sister."[59] She was praised for her "extraordinary prudence."[60] And manage she could. To give one example:

> My first business in the morning, is to see that the children are bathed and dressed, for the day; at seven o'clock the writing-school begins; at eight worship and breakfast; at nine, school begins again, and continues till the bell rings for dinner, at half past one; at three, school again, which ends half past five; and by the time every thing is put in order, tea is ready; and after tea, worship immediately. By the time all is over, and the children are in bed, it is generally nine o'clock; after which time is my holiday, to read, write, or work; but I am often overcome with fatigue and the scorching heat of the day, that I feel neither will nor power to do anything at all; and when I sit down to converse with you, it is with a weary body, a stupid soul, and dim eyes; but I am sure of having all my faults lightly passed over, and all covered with love.[61]

However, that Hannah is often singled out as the "First Woman Missionary" seems unfair.[62] Serampore produced other "Mothers of Israel." Mary stepped in when the pressure of overseeing an expanding Mission while constantly bearing children was too overwhelming. In July 1812, while Hannah was managing her schools, a visitor commented, "Mary Ward has the care of providing for the whole mission family... a motherly woman, very active and kind."[63] And this was five months after the Wards lost their beloved five-year-old daughter and an adopted child. Again, after

---

[59] Carey to Society, January 7, 1820. B.M.S. Mss.

[60] Carey, *William Carey, D.D.*, 187. Cf. Carey's praise for Mary Johns who briefly resided at Serampore, before being expelled by the EIC. "Sister Johns I consider as one of the best women you ever sent out; She was beloved by every one, and her whole conduct shewed her to have a true missionary spirit." Carey to Fuller, August 4, 1814. BMS. Mss.

[61] Mrs Marshman to Mrs Clark, Baldwin Street, Bristol, Serampore Jan. 1805, in *PA*, III (1806), 83-89.

[62] Cf. "The formidable Mrs Hannah Marshman was 'the only missionary wife who took a constantly active part in the (Serampore) Mission's work,' where the Form of Agreement included a hope that work in female education might be undertaken for 'a European sister may do much for the cause by promoting the tidiness and stirring 'up the' zeal of the native female converts.'" Briggs, "She-Preachers," 343.

[63] H. Newell, *Memoirs of Mrs Harriet Newell, Wife of the Rev. S. Newell, American Missionary to India, Who Died at the Isle of France, Nov 30. 1812, Aged Nineteen Years*, 6th edn. (Edinburgh: Ogle, Allardice and Thomson, 1818), 154, 164-166.

Statement Seven

she returned from furlough in England to recover her health in August 1817, she looked after the child of bereaved brother Sutton. During Hannah's subsequent furlough (1820-1821), Mary, as the most senior female at the Mission, would have been in charge, aided by her eldest daughter.

The Mission's deep concern for the welfare of the wives was not always fully appreciated at home, as the "Bonnet affair" testifies. In 1805, Fuller reprimanded Mary for mentioning the "extraordinary" expense for the purchase of an imported straw bonnet to show how the American War had affected prices. A few years earlier, her husband had also complained of the high expense of a black hat at Calcutta without any issues. The cost of the bonnet had come out of their personal allowance, but Fuller felt it necessary to caution her, as such comforts would cause "great injury" to the cause.[64] Hannah too was questioned by a Committee member about the use of porcelain and silver cutlery to entertain visitors of her boarding schools.[65] Such scrutiny from a male-dominated BMS Committee was unhelpful and unjustified, causing pain and animosity.

Women as Counsellors

William Ward advocated a much more active role for women. Native women, in particular, were greatly undervalued. With his journalistic background, Ward reported in detail on the church's female members, their conversion, their testimonies, and contributions. In his writings, which Fuller faithfully published, he gave voice to native women, thereby removing prejudices against them. "Bro. C[arey] talked & the women appeared to have learnt more of the Gospel than we expected. They declared for Xt. at once. This work was new even to Bro. C. [:] a whole family *desiring* to have the Gospel & declaring in favour of it; & their great joy in hearing it. Creeshnoo's wife said, she had received great comfort from it."[66] A few days later, they were astonished to hear Krishna's wife's sister's account; "they both acknowledged that Xt's words had made their minds tender,

---

[64] Marshman, *Life and Times*, I, 211. E. Daniel Potts, "William Ward: A Biography" (Lismore, NSW 1994), 129-130, Mss., CLRC Serampore.
[65] Marshman, *Life and Times*, II, 218.
[66] Saturday December 6, 1800. *Ward's Journal*, I, 120. Emphasis in original.

The Serampore Form of Agreement

had removed their sins, & that he was all to them; that the *debtahs* were nothing, & the curse or the blessing of a brahman nothing."[67] These encouragements had immediate results. Joymoona and Unna were baptized and soon after visited Chandernagore to testify to three of Krishna's sisters.[68] The following Lord's Day, they reported that two sisters promised to come to Serampore and that many women in the French town had heard the gospel.[69]

Soon after it became apparent that cultural sensitivities greatly limited the ability of the men to counsel these zealous but inexperienced female converts. Missionary wives were encouraged to learn Bengali so they could minister to them. Though we have no records to prove they received formal lessons, as we have of their husbands, we can assume they spoke the vernaculars fluently. They naturally interacted with domestic servants of the Mission and were aided by two bi- (or tri-) lingual Portuguese women in the School.[70] Statement Seven formalized the Mission's intention "to afford to our European sisters all possible assistance in acquiring the language, that they may... become instrumental in promoting the salvation of the millions of native women... that they do much for the cause in this respect, by promoting the holiness, and stirring up the zeal, of the female native converts." The SFA, therefore, anticipated a new form of mission by women to women, the so-called "Zenana missions," first attempted by BMS missionaries Elizabeth Sale in 1854, and advocated by Marianne Lewis' *A Plea for Zananas* in 1866.[71]

In 1807, Ward commented on Hannah Marshman overseeing a separate "experience meeting" with the native sisters "for the keeping up of vital religion in our own family ... This is what I have long urged & longed for. I cannot bear that our sisters should be mere house-wives."[72] A close

---

[67] Monday December 22, 1800. *Ward's Journal*, I, 126. A *debtah* is a demigod.
[68] Friday October 30, 1801. *Ward's Journal*, I, 126
[69] Lord's Day November 1, 1801. *Ward's Journal*, I, 185.
[70] "I have two Portuguese women, who have been with me ever since the school commenced. They bathe and dress the scholars, make beds, and do a little sowing." Mrs Marshman to Mrs Clark, Bristol. Serampore Jan. 1805. *PA*, III (1806), 83-85.
[71] Stanley, *History of the BMS*, 229.
[72] Tuesday May 25 [26], 1807. *Ward's Journal*, III, 550.

reading shows that both Hannah and Mary counseled serious enquirers and helped destitute women enter the Mission compound.[73] Ward recognized the untapped potential of the women—native and European, and his writings highlighted their valuable contribution to the Mission effort.

Women's roles in the Church

In the early years all missionary wives fulfilled roles in church life by rotation. However, when Hannah became increasingly occupied in her schools, and Mary was on furlough during crucial years 1815-1817, by 1818 the Serampore and Calcutta congregations had to rely on local lay women for leadership roles. E.S. Wenger, the historian of the (Baptist) Lall Bazar Chapel in Calcutta, noted that in December 1825, "two *new* deaconesses were elected ... for the better superintending of the female part of the church ... viz. Mrs Lish and her servant Sally, clearly indicating that there had been Deaconesses previously."[74] Sally was most likely "Country-born," proof that there was no prejudice towards Eurasians. He notes that he could find no names of earlier (or later) deaconesses. Typically, these developments were not reported back home and only came to light in 1908 through Wenger's research. Another widow, Mrs Peacock, was sent to manage a female school in Dhaka in 1825. Perhaps she was the first single woman supported by the Mission.[75] At Serampore, too, female members had specific roles in church life. They had a vote in church meetings, gave

---

[73] See for example, *PA*, IV (1810), 186.

[74] Mrs Lish married Rev. William Robinson in April 1827. Her son Alexander Burgh Lish attributed his conversion to "the serious discourse of "Sally Ayah," who worked at the Lish household until her death in May 1828. A.B. Lish became missionary among the Khasis. "Brief Memoir of Rev. A. B. Lish of Agra" in *The Oriental Baptist*, VI (1852), 363-367. Edward S. Wenger, *The Story of the Lall Bazar Baptist Church Calcutta: Being the History of Carey's Church from 24th April 1800 to the Present Day* (Calcutta: Edinburgh Press, 1908), 190, 201-202, 554.

[75] As widow she served as an early female missionary, supported by a pension. The Benevolent Institution in Calcutta also supported her for some time (*Report of the Benevolent Institution*, 1828). "Rev. Henry Peacock" in Edward S. Wenger, *Biographical Sketches*, II, 38. Mss. CLRC, Serampore. Joshua Marshman, *Statement Relative to Serampore, Supplementary to a "Brief Memoir." With Introductory Observations, by John Foster* (London: Parbury, Allen & Co., 1828), 77. M. H. Langley, "The B.M.S. and its Story" in *The Codex*, XXX No 1. (Sept 1942), 4-6.

counsel, and signed as witnesses at marriage services of European and Native members.[76] They could speak in public during "experience meetings" but not preach.

Women as Translators

The Serampore Mission employed women not only as teachers but as translators as well. This matter was considered too delicate to be published in the early days. In December 1813, when Carey began translating into Khasi, he wrote, "This week we have obtained a person to assist in the translation of the Scriptures into the Kassai language, and I believe the only one in that whole nation who can write or read."[77] He gives no details. But twenty years later, when Carey and Marshman published their *Second Appeal* for funds, mention is made of the completion of the Khasi New Testament. It stated that Carey was aided by an Assamese pundit and "a very intelligent woman, the widow of one of the Rajas or Chieftains of the country."[78]

This correlates with remarks of Mr Smith of Sylhet in July 1813 in which he endorses a letter of Krishna Pal, who had been instrumental in baptizing the first tribals;

> I have [the pleasure of] enclosing you a letter from that good man Krishna-pal; and beg to observe, that there is not a better person to be got, to explain the ... Kasia language, than the woman mentioned in Krishna's letter. She has two Kasai sons and one daughter: these children she will not leave behind her, should she agree to go to Calcutta, but of this we are not certain as yet.[79]

---

[76] Cf. Signatures of Misses Derozio, Mrs Douglas, Mrs Rebecca Deacon, and Margaret Marshman, in *Marriage Register Vol I*, Mss. CLRC, Serampore.

[77] [Serampore Missionaries], *Brief View of the Baptist Missionary Society and Memoir of Translations* (Serampore: Mission Press, 1814), 31.

[78] [Serampore Missionaries], *Second Appeal on behalf of the Serampore Mission* (Serampore: Mission Press, 1833), 2.

[79] Letter from a Gentleman in Silhet to brother Carey, July, 1813. *Circular Letters of the Serampore Mission*, VI, (1813), 135. This was most likely Matthew R. Smith, resident of Sylhet, who corresponded with Carey about Botany and geography of the Hills.

Statement Seven

The *First Report of Serampore College* (1819) confirms that two Khasi students studied at the College. They most likely were the princess' sons, proving that she indeed made the move to Serampore.[80] It is extraordinary that Krishna identified and promoted a *woman* to be the most suitable candidate as a Khasi translator. It shows that Krishna was impacted by the example of women missionaries at Serampore and overcame societal prejudices. It is to the credit of Smith that he unequivocally supported Krishna in this recommendation. Carey would not have doubted his judgment, and so a tribal woman who communicated in both Bengali and Khasi joined the Serampore Mission family. That this information was not made public until 1833 shows that this was a most sensitive matter; the missionaries had felt to protect the identity of this widowed princess until well after the event.[81]

In 1992, the Baptist historian Brian Stanley wrote that Hannah Marshman's active role in the Mission was perhaps "unique in its day." Still, he suspected that "later missionary wives did as much, but without public acknowledgment that she received."[82] Scrutiny of primary sources proves he was right. Since then, the contribution of women missionaries has become an essential field of mission studies.

And our lenses do matter. Though men write this commentary, it is hoped that it will stimulate female historians to delve deeper into these sources to complete the picture.

Conclusion

Discipling new converts in India was more complicated than in Britain. By the early nineteenth century, Christianity had held sway in the British Islands for more than a millennium. This influence shaped the culture with biblical values and conditioned the conduct of even non-believers. This

---

[80] College Committee, *First Report of the College, for Asiatic Christian and Other Youth, Instituted at Serampore, August, 1818, under Patronage of the Most Noble the Marquis of Hastings, K.G. &c.* (Serampore: n.s., 1819).

[81] Another example of a female translator was Mrs Charlotte H. White from America, who married Joshua Rowe at Digah in 1817, and was engaged in Hindustani translation work. Peter de Vries, "William Carey's Advocacy for the Tribal People", in Subhro Sekhar Sircar and Sanjoy Mukherjee, eds., *William Carey: The Multifaceted Genius. A Carey Day 2018 Celebration Committee Publication* (Serampore: Council of Serampore College, 2018), 71-82.

[82] Stanley, *History of the BMS*, 228.

was, obviously, not the case in India. Here, discipleship required attention to issues that a British pastor might take for granted. These included matters dealt with in Statement Seven of the SFA. How was the church to be gathered? What was the role of work in the believer's life? How were they to relate to the government? And what was the role of women in the family, the church, and society?

"We should remember the gross darkness in which they were so lately involved, having never had any just and adequate ideas of the evil of sin, or its consequences. We should also recollect how backward human nature is in forming spiritual ideas, and entering upon a holy self-denying conversation." As a result, great patience was required. "We ought not therefore, even after many falls, to give up and cast away a relapsed convert, while he manifests the least inclination to be washed from his filthiness." While church discipline was practiced on various occasions, the missionaries were patient even in cases that might have shocked British churches if they had been made aware.

Much would be taught by words, both spoken and written. More would be taught by deed, by example, by faithful, consecrated living. Ward noted that the consequences of a poor example in Europe were not as devastating "because there the word of God always commands more attention than the conduct of the most exalted [C]hristian." However, in India, "those around us, in consequence of their little knowledge of the scriptures, must necessarily take our conduct as a specimen of what Christ looks for in his disciples. They know only the Saviour and His doctrine as they shine forth in us." Like parents, the missionaries were never off duty. Ward was right, "A real missionary becomes in a sense a father to his people."

STATEMENT EIGHT

The Serampore Mission's Principle of Indigeneity

Michael Chatterjee

The Serampore Form of Agreement (SFA), authored by William Ward and signed in 1805 by nine Serampore missionaries, made several foundational contributions to modern missiological thought. Among these, none were more important than its statements on the principle of indigeneity. The SFA clearly outlined The Mission's strategy, which strongly emphasized fostering local Christians' growth and promoting indigenous Christianity in Bengal. In almost all their activities involving education, translation, printing, opening Mission Stations, local churches, and so on, they aimed to support the indigenous character of the work. Statement Eight highlights the activities of the Mission in developing indigenous ministers and ministry and the challenges of conversion under East India Company (EIC) rule in Bengal.[1]

Understanding the Term Indigenization
Indigenization is the process of adapting the Christian message to a specific native culture and people to foster the growth of the Christian religion in that setting.[2] Therefore, it might be described as an effort to make Christianity acceptable to a population such as the Indian people. Indigenization

---

[1] This article highlights the 8th statement of the SFA. It states, "Another part of our work is the forming our native brethren to usefulness, fostering every kind genius, and cherishing every gift and grace in them." Ernest A. Payne, "Serampore Form of Agreement," *Baptist Quarterly* 12.5 (Jan 1947): 125-138.

[2] Since 1850, missionaries such as Henry Venn (1796-1873) and Rufus Anderson (1796-1880) advocated for the establishment of indigenous churches because they believed that colonial missionaries would not be effective in building "colonial churches" in British occupied territories.

is also the process of creating an indigenous theology that enables Christians in India to carry out the Christian mission using native materials in an Indian style of worship and witness so that the Indian population can comprehend the Christian message.[3] In the words of the Danish theologian Kaj Baago, "Indigenisation is evangelisation. It is the planting of the gospel inside another culture, another philosophy and another religion."[4]

The Indian scholar K.V. Mathew indicates a threefold purpose of indigenization:

1. To establish one's own faith in a new cultural setting.
2. To fortify one's own faith in the face of resistance in a new cultural context.
3. As an apologetic and missionary response to a new cultural context, it becomes a way of sharing one's faith.[5]

In summary, indigenization is the process of adapting the communication of a foreign gospel to a local culture and the traditions of the natives.

A helpful understanding of the Serampore Associate's view of indigenization can be found in A. H. Oussoren's comparison of William Carey and Count Zinzendorf, the founder of the Moravians. Oussoren quotes Zinzendorf: "I don't acknowledge any difference between the nations in matters relating to the heart. A Hottentot must lead exactly just the same life as an Englishman or German."[6] However, Oussoren states that Carey's approach was to "guide the native life in such a way that it really makes the missionaries superfluous and that all the treasures of the native culture

---

There is a need to develop a group of indigenous workers for indigenous churches to grow. In general, there are three levels of indigenization: structural, cultural, and contextual. Wilbert R. Shenk "After Bosch: Toward a Fresh Interpretation of the Church in the World of East Asia in the Twenty-first Century." Paper presented at Union Biblical Seminary, Pune, 21st August 2003. *UBS Journal* 2.2 (2004), 1-16. The SFA precedes the work of Venn and Anderson by nearly half a century.

[3] Potana Venkateswara Rao, "New Wineskins: A Study on Indigenous Christian Missions Theory," *IJR* 3/8 (2014): 169-170.

[4] Kaj Baago, *Pioneers of Indigenous Christianity* (Madras: CLS, 1969), 85.

[5] K.V. Mathew, "Indigenisation: An Old Testament Perspective," *IJT* 32/1-2 (1983): 7-8.

[6] A.H. Oussoren, *William Carey: Especially His Missionary Principles* (Leiden: A.W Sijthoff, 1945), 265.

Statement Eight

are Christianized."[7] Oussoren states Carey attempted to "lead their culture to the cross." The goal was not a copy of European culture but a new culture, uniquely Indian and Christian.

Of course, a commitment to indigenization implies a commitment to understanding the culture. The Serampore Associates worked arduously to grasp the nuances of Indian life. They studied India's languages and literature. Additionally, they traveled to gain first-hand knowledge of Indian life. They took evangelistic journeys to Chandernagore, Chinsurah, Hooghly, and other places near Serampore, preaching the word at villages en route while distributing books and pamphlets.[8] They often scheduled trips during the Hindu festivals. Ward used these trips to disseminate the Gospel and to survey Bengali culture and religion. Afterward, he included his observations in his works on Hindu culture.

One example of the Associates' cultural sensitivity was their dealing with native names. For example, the first Hindu baptized at the Mission was named Krishna Pal. Carey wrote Fuller, "I thought there was no connection between baptism and giving names but principally because it does [not] appear to have been the primitive practice to change the names of those who believed. For among the primitive Christians we have Sylvanus, Olympus, Hermes, Nereus, Fortunatus and others which are evidently Heathen names. Our Brethren convinced in the opinion that it is unnecessary and, therefore, we have not proposed it. This we should recommend to them not to name any more children with Heathenistic names."[9] So Krishna kept his name and continued to dress like a Hindu. The Serampore missionaries were committed to understanding the socio-religious context of the Bengali people and to developing their missionary project accordingly.

---

[7] Oussoren, *William Carey: Especially His Missionary Principles*, 264.

[8] [Andrew Fuller], *Brief Narrative of the Baptist Mission in India* (London: Button and Burditt, 1808), 25, 33, 37-38; John Clark Marshman, *The Life and Times of Carey, Marshman, and Ward. Embracing the History of the Serampore Mission* (London: Longman, Brown, Green, Longmans, & Roberts, 1859), I, 153, 188-190.

[9] Carey to Fuller, Aug. 4, 1801 in Terry G. Carter (ed.), *The Journal and Selected Letters of William Carey* (Macon, GA: Smith & Helwys, 2000), 172-173. Cf. SFA, 136.

The Serampore Form of Agreement

Developing an Indigenous Ministry

As a community, the Serampore Mission welcomed converts, irrespective of their caste. The Associates foresaw the necessity of providing for the native Christians who would need to live at the Mission compound. Carey opted for a common stock and a common dining table. He writes, "This is the more necessary as should any natives join us, they would become outcasts immediately, and must consequently be supported by us. But if the Stock is common so would the labour in that case, and of Consequence every addition of members to our Society would be an addition to our Stability, by superseding the necessary number of Servants, Labourers, &ct., which are the great sink of money here."[10]

The Associates understood that it was difficult for European workers to work in India, although they might adjust over time. Still, they faced challenges learning the language, culture, and habits of the Indians. As a result, Carey concluded only Indians could reach India. In 1802, Ward confessed, "I am ready to doubt whether Europeans will ever be extensively useful in converting souls by preaching in this country. God can do all things. Paul could become a Jew to win the Jews, & as Gentile to win Gentiles; but, however needful, we cannot become Hindoos to win them, nor Mussulmans to win Mussulmans."[11] Carey, in his *Enquiry*, mentioned the hindrances faced by Europeans in a foreign land, "As to the difficulty of procuring the necessaries of life, this would not be so great as may appear at first sight; for though we could not procure European food, yet we might procure such as the natives of those countries which we visit, subsist upon themselves."[12] The missionaries needed to develop indigenous native workers. This vision might not bring immediate results, but it would lay the foundation for the future of the Mission.[13]

---

[10] Carey to Ryland, Nov. 26, 1796, from Mudnabati, in Carter, *Carey's Journal and Letters*, 137.

[11] Monday, Nov. 13 [15], 1802. William Ward, *Missionary Journal 1799-1811* in 4 Vols, transcribed by E. Daniel Potts, B.M.S. Mss., Angus Library, Regent's Park College, Oxford, II, 268. Hereafter, *Ward's Journal*.

[12] William Carey, *An Enquiry into the Obligations of Christians to Use Means for the Conversion of the Heathens* (Leicester: Ann Ireland, 1792), 71.

[13] Joe L. Coker, "Developing a Theory of Missions in Serampore: The increased Emphasis upon Education as a 'Means for the Conversion of the Heathens,'" *Mission Studies* 17/1 (2001): 45.

Statement Eight

The Baptist Missionary Society (BMS) committee also advised the missionaries to be sensitive to the natives:

> However gross may be the idolatries, and heathenish superstitions that may fall beneath a missionary's notice, the society are nevertheless persuaded that both the mutual respect due from man to man, together with the interests of the true religion, demand, that every missionary should sedulously avoid all rudeness, insult, or interruption during the observance of the said superstitions; recommending no methods but those adopted by Christ and his apostles, namely, the persevering use of scripture, reason, prayer, meekness, and love.[14]

In their early years, the Mission and the BMS were committed to raising an indigenous body of native Christians to carry forward the work. The SFA gave special attention to the role of European women who accompanied their husbands in their missionary roles. They were not called missionaries. However, the SFA recognized that only women could reach women in India. The mission showed great concern for female converts, and they may have encouraged them to share with other women. Ward's Journal described how Joymooni publicly testified that "she had found a treasure in Christ greater than anything else in the world." and "constantly spoke" about Christ to her neighbors.[15] While Krishna itinerated with Ward in October, Joymooni and Unna "made known the word of life to many other women at Chandernagore."[16] While there is little evidence that they were officially appointed or employed at this time, they may have served as the prototype for a later generation of missionaries. Notably, missionary societies at the beginning of the 19th century subordinated the women who worked in their own societies. They went unrecognized as missionaries. Single female missionaries, as such, do not appear in India

---

[14] S. Pearce to A. Fuller, May 2, 1799. *Periodical Accounts Relative to the Baptist Missionary Society*, I (1799): 518-519. Hereafter, *PA*.

[15] Lord's Day, February 22, 1801. *Ward's Journal*, I, 141-142.

[16] *PA*, II (1802), 221.

The Serampore Form of Agreement

until the late 19th century. In due time, it became impossible for Protestant historians to ignore the role of women missionaries.[17]

Developing a Strategy for Native Itinerants

From their arrival, the missionaries witnessed societal evils such as infanticide, Sati, and Hook Swinging (*Churuk* or *Charak Puja*). They understood the people needed to be reached with the gospel. In this connection, Ward wrote to Ryland in 1803 on the need for native missionaries:

> Be assured that whatever Europeans may say about the impossibility of converting the Hindoos, there, wants nothing more, as it respects human means, but a few men of gifts and real powerful godliness. ... It will be vain to expect that the Gospel will ever spread widely in this country, till God so blesses the means as those native men shall be raised up, who will carry the despised doctrine, brought into the country by the Mleechas, into the very teeth of the Brahmins, and prove from the Scriptures that this is indeed the Christ that should come into the world. We hope we see the dawn of this. I have constantly made it a point of recommending the making of native preachers as soon as possible; and I hope we may soon see two or three, who are at least more able and eloquent than some good men who are employed in England.[18]

John C. Marshman commented that from the time of this letter, the Mission's attention was directed to training native brethren as Christian itinerants who were encouraged to preach in their mother tongue in the "simplicity of their national habits.... It was to this agency they looked for naturalizing Christianity in India."[19]

---

[17] Frederick S. Down, "Women in the History of Christianity," *Women Re-Shaping Theology: Introducing Women's Studies in Theological Education in India,* ed. Lalrinawmi Ralte (Delhi: ISPCK, 1998), 17-20.

[18] Ward to Ryland, April 11, 1803, in *PA*, II (1804), 426-427. *Mlechas* or "M'leeches, is a name by which [Hindus] designate all who are not of cast." [Fuller], *Brief Narrative,* 58.

[19] Marshman, *Life and Times,* I, 182-183.

Statement Eight

But itinerating itself would only be effective if the Mission could expand. So, the following year, Marshman proposed a "Plan for the subordinate Mission stations" modeled after Serampore. As each station would need to be self-supporting, new converts would find employment and protection at these new stations. "The advantages we would hope from this plan are, the more effectual as well as wider distribution of the Gospel throughout the country—the training up of a number of native brethren as itinerant missionaries."[20]

In August 1805, Marshman reminded Fuller of the advantages of "a body of native Christian brethren" who could accompany newly arrived European missionaries in bazaar preaching. The partnership of native brothers in personal evangelism would greatly increase the effectiveness of the foreign missionaries and aid them in language learning. Naturally, funds were needed to put this idea into practice. Marshman proposed to Fuller, "A hundred rupees per month... would nearly support ten of them, with their families, and a greater number of single brethren."[21]

By 1805, European missionaries had increased to where the Mission could begin planting new mission stations. To execute this plan, in the Serampore Form of Agreement, they described the principles by which the Mission wished to operate. These principles reflected six years of team experience and another seven years of Carey's solo experience in India. They stated that only through native preachers could the dissemination of the gospel take place in India. This implied the planting of native churches led by Indian pastors and deacons.[22] Ward states in the Eighth Statement of the SFA:

> It is only by means of native preachers that we can hope for the universal spread of the Gospel throughout this immense continent. Europeans are too few, and their subsistence costs too much, for us ever to hope that they can possibly be the instruments of the universal diffusion of the word amongst so many millions of souls, spread over such a large portion of the habitable globe. Their incapability of bearing the intense heat of the climate in perpetual itinerancies, the

---

[20] Marshman, *Life and Times*, I, 195-196.
[21] Marshman to Fuller, Aug. 28, 1805, in *PA*, III (1806): 171 (169-171).
[22] SFA, Statement Eight. Marshman, *Life and Times*, I, 226-230.

heavy expenses of their journies, not to say anything of the prejudices of the natives against the very presence of Europeans, and the great difficulty of becoming fluent in their languages, render it absolute duty to cherish native gifts, and to send forth as many native preachers as possible. If the practice of confining the ministry of the word to a single individual in a church be once established amongst us, we despair of the Gospel's ever making much progress in India by our means. Let us therefore use every gift, and continually urge on our native brethren to press upon their countrymen the glorious Gospel of the blessed God.[23]

The following year, the Associates formalized their plan to send out native itinerants:

1. It was the duty of the native brethren individually and collectively to communicate the truth of the gospel to the people, and they needed to be supported by the Church.
2. It was decided that two itinerants should be sent together.
3. The itinerants should not give up their national character and habits.
4. A committee was formed for the above works, and three senior missionaries were appointed to coordinate the endeavor. They choose twelve "active and intelligent" converts for the work.[24]

In 1809, the Mission began plans for employing young missionaries of "European habits born and educated in the country" (i.e., of mixed descent). They aimed to reduce dependence upon Europe because opposition from the EIC made the expansion of the European missionary force doubtful. Ward's own sense of European racial superiority becomes evident in the following expression: "For the army of labourers to be employed in assaulting the bulwarks of Hindooism, we ought to look to England only for a few superior officers. The non-commissioned officers and rank and file we must raise in the country." The Associates believed that

---

[23] SFA, 134; quoted in a footnote of "Extracts from Mr. Ward's Journal. From Oct.1, to the end of the year 1805," in *PA*, III (1806): 182-183 (180-187).

[24] J. Marshman to Dr. Ryland. Serampore, Aug. 18, 1806, in *PA*, III (1806): 261-264; Marshman, *Life and Times*, I, 257-258.

the country-born evangelists might "not possess the energy of the European character; but this defect was, in some measure, compensated by their thorough knowledge of the habits and feelings of the people, and their familiarity with the vernacular tongue."[25] Despite this view, the Mission saw the need to develop an indigenous body of native and Eurasian missionaries who would help plant churches across India.

Native Missionaries: Equals among Equals

The policy of the Mission from the beginning was that missionaries should be equals and companions to the people they are sent to serve.[26] Additionally, the missionary should be self-supporting. In other words, the missionary needed to understand and learn the language, culture, and traditions of the native people and to earn their livelihood while in the ministry. In 1794, after receiving an offer of 200 Rupees per month to supervise an indigo plantation, Carey informed the BMS that he no longer needed the help of the Society as he could subsist with the amount.[27] In 1799, Carey wrote to the Society, "Missionaries ought to follow some secular employ; both for their own support, and also ...[to allow] a Magistrate to make a return of all Europeans in his district... not to conceal our real work... to keep an unblemished conscience."[28] This indigenous policy was essential to the Mission because they wanted to raise native workers who would also be self-sufficient.

The Attitude of the Mission towards Cross-Cultural Identity

Unlike the Tranquebar Mission in South India, the Associates opposed the practice of the caste system within the church.[29] The missionaries did not

---

[25] Marshman, *Life and Times*, I, 413–414.

[26] "The plan laid down in my little piece [i.e. in his *Enquiry*] I still approve, and think it the best that can be followed. A missionary must be one of the companions and equals of the people to whom he is sent." Carey to Society, Bandell, December 16-26th, in *PA*, I (1793), 69.

[27] Carey to Society, Mudnabati, Aug. 5, 1794, in Eustace Carey, *Memoir of William Carey D. D. Late missionary to Bengal, Professor of Oriental Languages in the College of Fort William, Calcutta.* 2nd Edn. (London: Jackson & Walford, 1836), 190.

[28] Carey to Society, Hooghly River, near Plassey, Jan. 10, 1799, in E. Carey, *Memoir of William Carey*, 332.

[29] Marshman, *Life and Times*, I, 177.

discriminate against any converts based on their caste. Early converts like Krishna Pal and Gokool publicly gave up their caste by eating with the missionaries.[30] The missionaries were open to native converts dining with them at the table, a practice that did much to gain the confidence of the new believers and to undermine Hindu rules of commensality.

At the same time, the Associates showed a nuanced cross-cultural sensitivity. In 1803, Krishna Prasad, a Brahmin, was baptized. The missionaries allowed him to wear his "holi thread" (*poita*) "as they considered as much a token of social distinction, as of spiritual supremacy." He wore the thread for three years and then voluntarily gave it up.[31] They were not ready to tamper with cultural practices that did not have clear implications for the Christian faith. The Associates understood the sacred thread as a marker of cultural rather than a religious identity.[32] Soon, however, the Hindu priests complained to the magistrate about the practice of the converts wearing the "holi thread," and the missionaries had to end the practice.

The Mission encouraged inter-caste marriages as early as 1803 when the Brahmin Krishna Prasad of the writer caste married Onunda, the second daughter of Krishna Pal, who was of the laborer caste. Ward wrote jubilantly, it was "a glorious triumph over caste. A Brahmin married to a soodra, and in a Christian form."[33] Inter-caste marriage was taboo in Hindu society, but the missionaries were undeterred in their opposition to the caste system.

The missionaries worked to remove the apprehension of caste from the native believers. In 1803, when Gokool, one of the native converts died, Carey and Marshman, together with native believers, carried the casket to a grave dug in a plot of land especially purchased as a burial ground. "The missionaries had set themselves the task of breaking down these distinctions and prejudices of caste, both in life and death, and they were anxious

---

[30] [Fuller], *Brief Narrative*, 27; Geoffrey A. Oddie, *Religious Conversion Movements in South Asia: Continuities and Change, 1800-1900* (Richmond, Surrey: Curzon, 1979), n. 41, 76.

[31] Monday, June 6, 1803. *Ward's Journal*, II, 305; Marshman, *Life and Times*, I, 176-177.

[32] A. Christopher Smith, *The Serampore Mission Enterprise* (Bangalore: Centre for Contemporary Christianity, 2006), 197-198.

[33] Marshman, *Life and Times*, I, 180-181.

Statement Eight

to establish a conviction in the minds of the native Christians that they were all one blood, whatever might have been their previous rank in the circle of idolatry."[34] As the Mission discouraged caste practices, they allowed the converts to have similar food habits to the Europeans. In 1804, the Assamese Brahmin convert, Pudmu Nabhu, was chastised by his Brahmin friend for "Throwing away his cast eating beef," and left him in anger.[35] The native Christians enjoyed their newfound freedom, but struggled to navigate the uncertain cultural context.

The Mission faced challenges regarding caste-related issues, and there were reports of few reconversions. M. M. Ali, writing on Bengal's Missionary activities during the nineteenth century, states that there were attacks on missionaries and native preachers.[36] Atrocities were carried out against the converts, and there was a common practice of drugging and kidnapping new converts.[37] Ward recorded that serious enquirers were lured away by their families, never to return. Converts like Krishna, Gokool, and others

---

[34] Marshman, *Life and Times*, I, 186.

[35] Marshman's Journal (from Jan to Dec 16, 1803) sent to Dr. Ryland, in *PA*, II (1803), 423.

[36] Muhammad Mohar Ali, *The Bengali Reaction to Christian Missionary Activities 1833-1857* (Chittagong: Mehrub Publications, 1965), 137-142; Joshua Marshman, *Reply to "Missionary Incitement, and Hindoo Demoralization: Including Some Observations on the Political Tendency of the Means Taken to Evangelize Hindoostan"* Originally printed in the *"Friend of India"* (Serampore: Mission Press, 1822), 311.

[37] There were persecutions against the Mission converts, such as the Muslim convert Muhammad Bakur, a native of Shiraz in Persia. During his stay at Calcutta, he met Petruse, a local Armenian evangelist who introduced him to Carey. As there were voices raised by the Muslim community against his conversion in Calcutta, he had to take shelter in Mission House for 2 to 3 months. One day, on a visit to Calcutta to collect money owed to him by a local Muslim, Bakur was offered drugged tobacco. After smoking the tobacco, he fell unconscious. His clothes were cut into pieces, and he was conveyed on a ship traveling to Muscat. When he regained consciousness, he was forced to labor on the ship. He was tied up and tortured to renounce his belief in Christ, which he refused. During a storm, Bakur managed to escape at night and reach land. Here a Portuguese man sent him to Bombay. From here, he traveled to Madras and finally, with the help of the "Friend-in-need Society," reached Calcutta, where he joined the Mission again and was baptized in June 1814. In a violent attack by armed men upon the Baptist Mission at Sadamahal near Dinajpur in 1840, the missionary in charge, Rev. H. Smylie's life was endangered while the native preacher Buddha was badly beaten. He later succumbed to his injuries. Ten other local preachers were also attacked and wounded. In another incident in 1842, Rev. J. Campbell, a missionary preaching to the people at Bhawanipur (Calcutta) during the Charak puja festival, was attacked by the people with bricks and sticks and badly hurt. Non-violent persecution was also prevalent in Bengal when for example, barbers in Jessore, pressured by Hindu zamindars, were unwilling to shave native converts. F. A. Cox, *History of the Baptist Missionary Society from 1792 to 1842* (London: T. Ward & Co. and G. & J. Dyer, 1842), I, 248-249.

faced opposition from the community for giving up their caste. Gokool could not stay in his rented house, and while preaching, he and Krishna were jeered. In 1804, Futick was dragged from his home, "his face, eyes and ears clodded up with cow-dung, his hands tied and in this state confined several hours," and the village headman tore up his New Testament. But they saw these occasions as opportunities to display Christian character.[38] As such, it was always a challenge for the Associates to protect their few converts in a society opposed to conversion.

Conversion: Developing an Indigenous Group of Converts

Beginning in December 1800, the Mission began seeing native conversions.[39] These included such early converts as Krishna Pal (1764–1822), Pitamber Singh (1745–1805), Raghunath (1748–1808), Futika (–1808), and Krishna Prasad (1786–1806).[40] All worked with the Mission but died early, except Krishna Pal. Pitamber Singh, after his baptism, became a teacher in a Bengali school. Krishna Pal started the first native church in Bengal opposite his own house. He is considered the first native indigenous missionary in North India and was sent as an evangelist to Calcutta, where he itinerated for five years. Afterward, he was sent to preach to Jessore, Sylhet, Dacca, Cutwa (Katwa), Birbhum, and Berhampore. Then he was sent to Malda to open a mission station there, which was unsuccessful. He died in

---

[38] July 21, 1801; March 20, 1802, November 24, 1804. *Ward's Journal*, II, 165, 216, 398, 400.

[39] The total number of converts of the Mission from 1800 to 1821 were 1,417. Of these 700 were native converts, 400 soldiers and the remainder country-born. "Reply of the Serampore Missionaries to the Attack made in No. III of the Oriental Magazine." *Friend of India* (Monthly), VII (1824), 11-12. Sengupta is clearly mistaken that the total number of converts in Bengal between 1793-1833 was only 1,406. As he claimed, "The figure, gathered solely from missionary sources, is not beyond doubt. [For] the private records of the missionaries contain 'exaggeration and untruth' on this question." Kanti Prasanna Sengupta, *The Christian Missionaries in Bengal 1793-1833* (Calcutta: K.L.M., 1971), 192-193.

[40] For the testimonies of Pitamburu Singhu, Rughoonath, Futika and Krishna Prisada, see [William Ward], *Brief Memoirs of Four Christian Hindoos, Lately Deceased* (Serampore: Mission Press, 1816); For Krishna Pal, see William Ward, *Brief Memoir of Krishna-Pal. The First Hindoo, in Bengal, who Broke the Chain of the Cast, by Embracing the Gospel*, 2nd Edn. (London: John Offor, 1823); "Account of Krishna Pal, late Hindoo Preacher at Serampore, as given by himself, in a letter addressed to a Friend in England." *Annual Report of the BMS* (1823), 33-36; "Letter from the Rev. Wm. Ward of Serampore, to a Friend in Edinburg, dated 10th May, 1820," *Annual Report of the BMS* (1820), 35.

Statement Eight

1822.[41] The first Hindu female convert was Joymooni, Krishna's sister-in-law, who was baptized in early 1801. His wife Unna followed a month after.[42]

The Associates encouraged educated converts like Krishna Pal and Pitamber Singh to produce evangelistic literature for the people. Krishna's hymns were often sung in the early Bengali churches.[43] Pitamber Singh wrote three pieces, "Good Advice," "The Enlightener," and "The Sure Refuge." This last tract led to the conversion of several Bengalis and went through several reprints.[44]

The Mission practiced church discipline with the native converts. If any converts were found seriously wanting in personal holiness, they were excluded from "communion" and only restored after an observation period. Missionaries were also strict on the issue of polygamy among converts. Converts with more than one wife before becoming Christians were prohibited from participating in the ministry. In these ways, the Mission set the tone for developing the indigenous church.[45]

The first two mission centers were at Serampore and Dinagepore. When translations progressed in other languages, the Associates looked to expand their missionary activities to other parts of the country, even though this required permission from the Governor-general. For example, in 1803, a station began at Cutwa and a few years later at Jessore.

---

[41] Ward, *Brief Memoir of Krishna-Pal*, 26; *The First Hindoo Convert: A Memoir of Krishna Pal, a preacher of the Gospel to his countrymen more than twenty years* (Philadelphia: American Baptist Publication Society, 1852), 91.

[42] Marshman, *Life and Times*, I, 140.

[43] Andrew R. Bonar, ed., *Incidents of Missionary Enterprise; illustrative of the Progress of Christianity in heathen countries, and of the researches, sufferings, and adventures of Missionaries.* Third edn. (Edinburgh: T. Nelson, 1842), 114.

[44] [Ward], *Brief Memoirs of Four Christian Hindoos*, 23, 25-26; John Murdoch, *Catalogue of the Christian Vernacular Literature of India: With Hints on the Management of Indian Tract Societies* (Madras: Caleb Foster, 1870), 5.

[45] [Fuller], *Brief Narrative*, 41. Cf. George Smith, *The Life of William Carey D.D.: Shoemaker and Missionary* (London: John Murray, 1885), 144.

The Serampore Form of Agreement

Evangelism in the Native Language

In 1798, Carey wrote John Sutcliff, "I also maintain the worship of God, and expound in Bengali every morning; when about twenty people attend...When at home I constantly preach to them twice on the Sabbath. I now preach at Dinagepore once a month...."[46] The Associates translated the Bible and attempted to preach in the native Bengali language. They preached in the streets and marketplaces as well as the in the church congregation. They believed that the Bible needed to be preached in the native language.

They fed the poor physically and spiritually. With twenty rupees, they freed an enquiring young woman who was held in a "bad house" for a debt she could not pay.[47] When the news spread, other native communities became interested in hearing the gospel. In 1802, a man named Moorad came to the Mission meeting and asked the missionaries to go with him to his place to preach the gospel. Marshman, with native preachers Petumber and Bharut, went with Moorad to Luckphool and found a very attentive hearing. Though subsequent visits did not produce any fruit, through these evangelistic tours, the Associates trained native converts for evangelism.[48]

Within a few years, their focus on indigenous preaching became very effective. Carey wrote,

> There are two native preachers of the name of Krishna. One of them, the first Hindu who was baptized, is settled in Calcutta and the other with John Peter, at Ballasore. The first labours at Calcutta with great success. Krishna is now a steady, zealous, and well-informed, and I may add, eloquent minister of the gospel, and preaches, on an average, twelve or fourteen times every week, in Calcutta and its environs. Sebuk-ram, another honourable minister of the gospel, is also employed in and about Calcutta, and preaches nearly or quite as often. We preach in English at the jail every Lord's-day, the jailor being one of our deacons, and did preach in the fort till a military order stopped us. Our brethren Krishna and Sebuk-ram, however, preach

---

[46] E. Carey, *Memoir of William Carey*, 323–325.
[47] Wednesday, September 5, 1804. *Ward's Journal*, II, 385.
[48] [Fuller], *Brief Narrative*, 37–40, 42.

Statement Eight

once or twice a week in the fort, in the jail, in the house of correction, at Ali-poora, a village south of the jail, at ten or twelve houses in different parts of Calcutta, at a large factory, north of Calcutta, where some hundreds of men are employed, and at other places.[49]

The Beginning of the Indigenous Church in Bengal

Krishna Pal had begun the first recorded indigenous church of Bengal in Serampore, when, "on his own accord," he constructed a meeting house on a plot of land opposite his own home. Here, on August 16, 1801, Carey preached a sermon to "about twenty natives besides the family of Kristno."[50] The missionaries continued to preach at this place strategically located along the primary (pilgrim's) road to the Jagannath temple nearby. On August 25, they purchased a piece of land for Gokool and his family, which had a simple thatch chapel that eventually grew into a Christian settlement.

Upon his return from Europe in October 1821, Ward reported that "At Serampore, at the Mission Chapel, and also at the Danish Church, at Krishna's Chapel, and across the Ganges at the Barrackpore Chapel, during the Sabbath, there are seven services, and parties of Native converts visit and preach in the streets of neighbouring villages."[51] When the number of Bengali believers increased, they could no longer stay at the Mission compound. Eventually, facing persecution, they settled on land outside the town, where a "Christian Village" was established in 1826.[52] The following year the missionaries report,

---

[49] Carey to Sutcliff, Calcutta, March 27, 1812, in E. Carey, *Memoir of William Carey*, 516-517.

[50] Lord's Day, August 16, 1801. *Ward's Journal*, I, 167; *PA*, II (1802), 185. Cf. Lord's Day, December 23, 1810. *Ward's Journal*, IV, 742.

[51] "Circular Letter of William Ward," *Baptist Magazine*, XV (1823), 38. The Serampore (Baptist) Church, usually called 'Mission Church' was begun on April 24, 1800, with Carey as pastor. Marshman, *Life and Times*, I, 128, 130. Barrackpore was a military cantonment Station, and a residence of the Governor-General, opposite Serampore. In 1814, the Mission was invited to begin weekly church services here at the invitation of some "non-commissioned" officers. *PA*, VI (1815), 13-14; Cox, *History of the Baptist Missionary Society*, I, 246.

[52] Tuesday, August 25, 1801. *Ward's Journal*, I, 168; *PA*, II, 185; Cox, *History of the BMS*, I, 70; Smith, *Life of William Carey*, 140-141. There is evidence that 'native' informal worship carried on by others after Krishna Pal moved to Calcutta, Sylhet, and later Malda.

The Serampore Form of Agreement

This village has lately been established, for the purpose of promoting the general comfort of our native brethren, and also facilitating the communication of religious instruction to them. It now consists of 13 dwelling houses, with a small chapel in the centre, and will, we trust, be considerably enlarged during the present season, as several families are desirous of removing to it from the town, from which it is distant but a very short way, on an open and elevated spot of ground. Pran Krishnu, one of the native preachers, resides in it, and conducts daily worship in the chapel, and in other ways seeks the edification of the people under his charge.[53]

By 1855, the chapel in this "Christian Village" was known as Jannagore (Jannagar, Johnnugger) Church, named after John Clark Marshman, who helped to establish it. Until then, the Serampore Missionaries had pastored the Church with the help of a local evangelist living on site.[54] After 1874 it became an independent church. Thus, the Mission implemented the vision to raise indigenous Bengali churches.

Planting an Indigenous Church in Calcutta

Around 1802 the Mission sent Krishna Pal and other native converts to itinerate in Calcutta, which gave them a foothold in this metropolis, the nerve center of British power and a great cultural crossroads. The following year they began worship in Bengali and English in enquirer's homes.[55] The response among the Armenian and Portuguese communities was particularly encouraging. An Armenian who lived on Chitpore Road in North Kolkata refurbished his home to build a worship hall. The welfare of the city's residents was always on the Associates' minds. In 1806, Marshman wrote, "At Calcutta, among the million [*sic*] of natives, there seems to be the best prospect that has ever presented itself. A congregation, from four

---

[53] John Mack's Report in *Periodical Accounts of the Serampore Mission*, xvii (1827), 2-3 (152-153).

[54] See "Appendix, No. II. Account of the Stations connected with the Serampore Mission. Serampore," *Annual Report of the BMS* (1827), 35; Marshman, *Life and Times*, II, 353; *The Missionary Herald* (May 1, 1855), 163-164.

[55] Apart from Krishna Pal, native converts like Sebukram, Bhagavat, Neelo and Manik were preaching at different houses in Calcutta. *PA*, V (1813), 352; Cox, *History of the BMS*, I, 246-247.

Statement Eight

to six hundred, constantly attend, and patiently and attentively hear that their shasters, their religion, their gods, are nothing; and that there is but one way to eternal life—Jesus Christ and him crucified."[56]

Despite opposition to constructing an edifice in the center of Calcutta, the missionaries got permission. The Anglican chaplains Brown and Buchanan assisted them in getting a license to build a chapel, and in 1806 a plot in the center of town was purchased, and a temporary shed erected. On January 1, 1809, the Lall Bazar Chapel was opened, and Carey preached the first sermon.[57] Lall Bazar was notorious for prostitution, liquor shops, and other social evils.[58] The new chapel allowed the Mission to extend its outreach to the poor and marginalized, especially the Portuguese and "Country-born."

By 1810, the Mission had five independent churches in Bengal. Carey's original Baptist church, which he began in Malda, was divided into two branches, Serampore and Calcutta; Dinajpur led by Ignatius Fernandez; Cutwa by John Chamberlain; Goamalty by Richard Mardon, and Jessore, overseen by C. Carapeit Aratoon.[59] While the missionaries, together with the native itinerants, faithfully preached the gospel, held regular church services, and met with enquirers, the number of converts was still small.

Establishing Mission Stations with Native Workers

The Mission committed to a strategy of starting native churches with native converts in roles of responsibility:

> It is highly probable, dear brethren, that, from the churches in India God will raise up a supply of men to publish his Word throughout

---

[56] Marshman to Ryland, Serampore, August 18, 1806, in *PA*, III (1806), 261–262.

[57] The Lall Bazar Chapel was initiated as a joint venture between the Mission and Nathaniel Forsyth of the LMS. The church is regarded as the first Non-conformist church in Calcutta. The church gave them a base from where they did reform work as well. See [J. Marshman and W. Carey], *Statement Relative to the Administration of the Funds Entrusted to the Serampore Missionaries* (Serampore: s.n., 1820), 6-7. Signed Pamphlet, CLRC, Serampore. Edward S. Wenger, *The Story of the Lall Bazar Baptist Church Calcutta: Being the History of Carey's Church from 24th April 1800 to the Present Day* (Calcutta: Edinburgh Press, 1908), 21-25.

[58] Wenger, *The Story of the Lall Bazar Baptist Church*, 26–30.

[59] Besides five churches in Bengal, James Chater pastored a church in Rangoon, Burma. "Review of the Mission," *PA*, VI (1810), 110.

The Serampore Form of Agreement

Hindostan, and prevent the necessity, except in a few instances, of sending out European brethren for that purpose. These, however, will be necessary for the occupying of stations of great importance, and for the commencement of new missions.[60]

The government's hostility, the cost of maintaining European missionaries, and the language and culture barriers underlined the importance of native workers. The Mission proceeded with a plan of founding stations throughout North India. They organized this missionary work under the designation of "The United Missionaries in India." The area covered Bengal, Orissa, Bhutan, Hindustan, and Burma, which, as noted before, involved stations in Bengal in 1810: Serampore, Calcutta, Dinajpur, Saddamahl, Goamalty, Cutwa, and Jessore. One station was established in Balasore (Orissa), one in Rangoon (Burma), and two in the Upper Provinces (Patna, Agra). The Bhutan mission was unsuccessful and given up in 1811.[61]

By 1815, the number of stations in Bengal had grown to ten: Malda, Dinagepore, Sylhet, Berhampore, Cutwa, Bansberia, Serampore, Calcutta, Jessore, and Chittagong. There were Digah, Patna, Agra, Sirdhana, and Allahabad in Hindustan. In other provinces, they began stations at Surat, Nagpore, and Cuttack.[62] Though not all these stations survived, this growth in the wake of the 1813 Charter Act Renewal, which allowed new missionaries into India, was mainly achieved by utilizing Indian, Eurasian, and English missionaries raised in India (i.e., Carey's sons).[63]

Growth continued until 1827, when because of a controversy with the BMS, several stations broke away from Serampore under the management of the "Junior Brethren" of the Calcutta BMS. From this time, the BMS

---

[60] To the Society, Serampore, December 21, 1809, in *PA*, IV (1809), 90.

[61] *PA*, IV (1811), 214; Cox, *History of the BMS*, I, 95-203.

[62] "Review of the Mission ... at the beginning of 1815." *PA*, V (1815), 629-649. Outside India, stations were formed in Ceylon, Rangoon, Ava, Isle de France [Mauritius], Java, and Amboyna; Marshman, *Life and Times*, II, 98.

[63] "Besides the situations of our brethren in the army, in Mahratta [Nagpur], and Java, and the Isle of France, there are now fourteen stations, and only three of them occupied by brethren sent out as missionaries from England; namely, Serampore [& Calcutta], Digah, and Columbo. All the rest are occupied by men raised up in India." *PA*, V (1813), 173.

Statement Eight

stations in Bengal controlled four: Calcutta (Lall Bazar and Circular Road), Cutwa (Katwa), Sewry (Suri), and Berhampore (vacant). In Hindustan three: Digah (& Patna), Monghyr and Ajimere. as well as the stations in Colombo, Java, and Sumatra.[64] The Serampore Mission continued to manage six stations in Bengal: Serampore (& Dum Dum), Jessore, Dinagepore (& Sadamahl), Dacca, and Chittagong in East Bengal (now Bangladesh). Four in Hindustan: Benares, Allahabad, Muttra, Delhi, and one on the island of Akyab (Arracan).[65] These ten stations were overseen by five European, ten Asiatic, and fifteen native brethren. The churches consisted of three to four hundred native members.[66]

Brian Stanley observes that no accurate information on the sizes of the churches existed of the stations and the substations. In most cases, the records were in "tens rather than hundreds."[67] According to Christopher Smith, "William Carey did not visit, nor was he present at, the opening of most of the stations between 1794 and 1809. He never visited any of the Stations opened between 1809 and 1817."[68] Carey concentrated on producing Bible translations. After Ward died in 1823, Carey, Marshman, John Mack, and John C. Marshman managed the missionary activities. They remarked, "but the divine blessing has so extended these missionary operations that without aid from the friends of religions at home, it is impossible for them to be carried forward."[69] With the Serampore Mission's separation from the BMS in London, it became increasingly challenging for the Mission to fund its expansion on all fronts.

These stations were the result of a plan Carey had to extend indigenous churches across India:

> My plan relative to spreading the gospel has for several years past, been, to fix European brethren at the distance of 100 or 130 miles for

---

[64] *Annual Report of the BMS* (1827), 17–24, 35–41.

[65] *Annual Report of the BMS* (1827), App. II, 35–41. Rangoon (Burma) was transferred to the American Baptists.

[66] J. Marshman, *Statement relative to Serampore, supplementary to a "Brief Memoir" with introductory observations by John Foster* (London: Parbury, Allen & Co., 1828), 169.

[67] Brian Stanley, *The History of the Baptist Missionary Society, 1792-1992* (Edinburgh: T&T Clark, 1992), 56.

[68] Smith, *The Serampore Mission Enterprise*, 180. (Map of North India with Mission Stations).

[69] Marshman, *Statement Relative to Serampore*, 170.

each other, so that each one should occupy the centre of a circle of 100 miles diameter or less; and that native brethren should be stationed within that circle as preachers, schoolmasters, readers, &c at the proper distances, as circumstances may make convenient; and that he, as a brother, not as a lord, should visit and superintend them, so as to stir them up to zeal, correct their mistakes, explain the divine things to them, and in short, be as the soul of that circle. By following this plan, the brethren now crowded together in Calcutta would occupy a space of 400 miles in length by 100 in breadth, and had they all stayed in Bengal, could, with those already there, have completely occupied the province of Bengal. The proportion of expense necessary to carrying this plan into execution throughout India, might perhaps be borne by contributions from England and America, till brethren raised up in the country were sufficiently established in divine things, and sufficiently informed.[70]

By its nature, the plan required a diligent focus on preparing native evangelists and church planters.

Conclusion

At the dawn of the modern missionary movement, the work of the Serampore Mission was crucial in establishing the principles and practices required to establish an indigenous church. All the endeavors of the Associates aimed to uplift the indigenous population, including education, translation, printing, banking, and evangelism. They carefully drafted a plan based on the principles outlined in the Serampore Form of Agreement and considered the need and the context of Bengal. They were good planners. They aimed to create a body of indigenous Christians for starting stations and churches. This attempt was largely successful. Their fruit endures today in the Christian community of Bengal and in the countless missionary endeavors that beginning in the 19th century, have spread to every corner of the globe.

---

[70] Carey to Dyer, July 15, 1819 in J. Marshman, *Letters from the Rev Dr. Carey, relative to certain statements contained in three pamphlets lately published by the Rev. John Dyer, W. Johns, and Rev. E. Carey and W. Yates* (London: Parbury, Allen & Co., 1828), 15.

STATEMENT NINE

Scripture Translation: A Road to Cross-cultural Relationships

Pratap Chandra Gine

"To labour unceasingly in Biblical translation"

Statement Nine of the Serampore Form of Agreement (SFA) constitutes the heart of the Serampore Mission's strategy. Signed by seven Serampore missionaries on Monday, October 7, 1805,[1] it committed them "To labour unceasingly in Biblical translation." William Carey had labored over a Bengali translation almost from his arrival in India in 1793. However, his work accelerated with the arrival of teacher Joshua Marshman and printer William Ward. Serampore's efforts in translation have usually been analyzed through the lens of Carey's efforts. This is natural because of his centrality in these efforts, but the other missionaries played equally significant roles. In this chapter, emphasis will be given to Ward's perspective as the author of the SFA and as a printer and translator in his own right.

Rationale Behind the Translation of Scripture

The question arises whether it was altogether a fresh idea of the Serampore missionaries to translate the Christian Scripture into the local languages. Before the arrival of the Serampore missionaries in Bengal, there were at least two sets of protestant missionary bodies working in different parts of India – the Tranquebar Mission in Tamil Nâdu (Southern India) and the Moravian Mission in Bengal (Eastern India). Both missions were aided by

---

[1] They are William Carey, Joshua Marshman, William Ward, John Chamberlain, Richard Mardon, John Biss, William Moore, Joshua Rowe, and Felix Carey.

The Serampore Form of Agreement

the Danish East India Company (DEIC), which had already made its presence felt in India. The Tranquebar Mission, headed by Bartholomeus Ziegenbalg and Heinrich Plütschau, pitched its tent in India in 1706. The Moravian Mission, led by Br. Johannes Grassman and Br. Karl Friedrich Schmidt, was established in 1777.[2]

Both missions took up the challenge of Scripture translation. They sought help from scholars from the high-caste community, and many Indians welcomed their translations. The Tranquebar Mission could reap the harvest of their hard work. However, the Moravians struggled to maintain a foothold in the country: "Patna was closed at once, the Nicobar Islands later, and Serampore in 1792. In 1795, the Moravian Church reluctantly withdrew entirely from the East Indies, with the last missionaries returning home by 1802."[3] This does not mean, however, that the Moravians had an unsuccessful mission to India. The seed sown among people such as Krishna Pal produced fruit even after they departed from India.

The divine plan for Bengal followed a course the Moravians could not anticipate. The Moravians left Serampore in 1792, the same year the Baptist Missionary Society was founded. In early 1800, invited by Ole Bie, the Danish Governor at Serampore, Carey came to Serampore in the company of Ward. The land, which the Moravians abandoned, was reestablished as God's land. It became the center of Scripture translation, not only for India but also for the whole of Asia. The God of Carey, Marshman, and Ward wrote the mission history of Bengal from its beginning.

Why the insistence on Scripture translation? Did Christ ever command his disciples to be engaged in academic exercises alongside preaching? Is Scripture translation not a scholarly work? Were these missionaries academically equipped to be engaged in Scripture translation? Did they know or could even formulate principles and techniques of translation? Were they ever told by the Spirit to engage in the translation of Scripture, prioritizing it over preaching and baptizing? How could they know whether

---

[2] J. E. Hutton, *A History of Moravian Missions* (London: Moravian Publication Office, 1922), 165, 188; S. Pearce Carey, *William Carey, D.D., Fellow of the Linnaean Society* (London: Hodder and Stoughton, 1923), 191; E. Daniel Potts, *British Baptist Missionaries in India, 1793-1837: The History of Serampore and its Mission* (London: Cambridge University Press, 1967), 5.

[3] https://www.wmcarey.edu/carey/wmward/Misc%20html/moravian.html (Accessed on June 7, 2023).

Statement Nine

their translations were understandable to their recipients? Did all the Serampore missionaries agree unanimously to proceed with the translation work? Questions like these and many more arise. We ought to appreciate that the missionaries were not impeded by the event of the Tower of Babel but instead were encouraged by the experience of Pentecost.

Translation as a Cross-cultural Bridge

Knowing languages apart from one's mother tongue provides great benefits. In some cases, language learning becomes essential for interaction with specific disciplines or streams of knowledge. Whether for socio-practical life or academic engagement, the primary task of translation is to bridge the cross-cultural gaps between people of diverse backgrounds. Translation facilitates inquiries, complaints, and even compliments from both sides. Translation is a life-long journey. It attempts to span the gap of miscomprehension, always aiming to close the distance. As translation opens closed doors, it widens the horizon of hope, and makes relationships across cultural barriers possible.

Surprisingly, the College of Fort William, founded in Kolkata in 1800 by the Governor-General of India, Lord Wellesley, took a particular interest in Bible translation. One of the primary aims of this college was to equip young English clerks with knowledge of Indian languages and culture. As the Department of Bible Translation was introduced, local pandits were appointed. "By 1805 a beginning had been made in five languages, Persian and Hindustani, Western Malay, Oriya and Marathi. In 1806, however, the directors of the East India Company decided to discontinue the translation work and to confine the work of the college within more modest limits."[4] We note, however, that William Carey was appointed in 1801 as the Professor of Bangla (i.e., Bengali),[5] Sanskrit, and later in Marathi at the same College of Fort William.

---

[4] J. S. M. Hooper, *Bible Translation in India, Pakistan and Ceylon*. 2nd edn. Revised by W. J. Culshaw (London: Oxford University Press, 1963), 15–16.

[5] The anglicized spelling and pronunciation of Bangla (i.e., Bengali) is avoided throughout this piece of writing, since "Bangla" is the original language, and not "Bengali." The Democratic Republic Bangladesh has never used a different spelling for their national language Bangla.

The Serampore Form of Agreement

Carey's appointment at the Fort William College gave financial stability to the Serampore Mission. It also broadened Carey's capacity to translate the Scriptures. The decision of the governing body of the College of Fort William to close the Department of Bible Translation must have challenged him and his colleagues at Serampore to redouble their efforts. However, the college's decision might be perceived, it ended a unique department at the College of Fort William, one that might have eventually been imitated at other colleges.[6]

Genesis of the Serampore Missionaries' Scripture Translation Project
Before analyzing the purpose and method of Scripture translation at Serampore, it is necessary to examine what prompted the missionaries to focus on. When William Ward drafted the SFA,[7] two primary commitments played significant roles. First, the Serampore missionaries constituted a family destined to look after the well-being of each other and not individual selfish desires. Second, they agreed to engage unceasingly in translating the Scripture.[8]

The Serampore missionaries' translation project built on an essential insight regarding Sanskrit. In a letter in 1816, Carey reported that "the number of languages into which the sacred Scriptures are translated, or under translation, are nearly forty."[9] In response to the potential objection that such a number of different languages might seem incredible, Carey

---

[6] We note with wonder how it took nearly two hundred years for the Theology Department of Serampore College to open an office of Bible translation to offer diploma and degrees in Bible translation, namely, Dip. B.T. [Diploma in Bible Translation]; B.B.T.S. [Bachelor in Bible Translation Studies]; M.B.T.S. [Master in Bible Translation Studies]) under the Senate of Serampore College (University).

[7] John Clark Marshman, *The Life and Times of Carey, Marshman and Ward* (London: Longman, Brown, Green, Longmans & Roberts, 1859), I, 229-230.

[8] As in the SFA, William Ward refers to "Scriptures", so also Carey in his translations, particularly in Bangla translation, always preferred to use "Scripture." We note that in the Bangla translation of the "Sacred Scriptures," Carey had never used the term/word "Bible". His preferred term was the Sanskrit *Dharmasastra* and later *Dharmapustaka*. This term was used till 1974. Since then, the Bible Society of India adopted the term "Bible" in its transliterated form replacing the term *Dharmapustaka*. In the current writing both the terms ("Scripture" and "Bible") would be used simultaneously for convenience.

[9] A letter from William Carey to Dr. Baldwin, Calcutta, July 23, 1816, in *The American Baptist Magazine and Missionary Intelligencer* 1, no. 2. (Boston: James Loring, 1817), 65.

Statement Nine

responded, "This will not, however, appear so extraordinary when it is recollected, that, three or four languages accepted, every language in India is so entirely derived from Sangskrit, that, making a proper allowance for local variations of spelling and pronunciation, one dictionary may with propriety suffice for all these languages." This did not remove all difficulties, "Yet owing to diversity of termination and other circumstances, it is a fact, that those languages in India, which come nearest to one another, are as distinct as any two languages in Europe, which are derived from the same source."[10]

Carey's central role in the translation efforts at Serampore is well known, but the publishing work depended on the entire team, and the other members also translated. In his journal, Ward wrote, "The Memoir of Old Petumber only waits till Bro. Marshman can find time to translate the three pieces which the Old Man wrote in Bengalee verse."[11] Ward's primary role was as a master printer. J. B. Middlebrook, who was the General Home Secretary of the Baptist Missionary Society (BMS), describing Carey's need for much-needed printing staff, reported that, "A skilled printer was available in the person of William Ward, who had come to India as the result of Carey's personal and prophetic invitation to him some years before. He remained till his death in 1823 in charge of the press."[12] Andrew Lalhmangaiha rightly observed, "Carey did the translation, and William Ward finished them into books."[13] At the same time, Ward's work demanded significant linguistic competency.

One of Ward's primary responsibilities was proofreading everything printed at the Serampore Press. For example, during June and July 1808, Ward records that he did Persian exercises and proofread works in Hindustani, Bengali, Mahratta, Persian, and Sanskrit. At times, he did this with Carey and sometimes alone.[14] Carey wrote in a letter to Andrew Fuller,

---

[10] "A letter from William Carey to Dr. Baldwin," 65.

[11] Saturday, November 30, 1805. William Ward, *Missionary Journal 1799-1811* in 4 Vols, transcribed by E. Daniel Potts, Mss., BMS Archives, II, 460. Hereafter, *Ward's Journal*.

[12] J. B. Middlebrook, *William Carey* (London: The Carey Kingsgate Press, 1961), 69.

[13] Andrew Lalhmangaiha, *Holistic Mission and the Serampore Trio*. The ISPCK Tercentenary Publication (Delhi: ISPCK, 2010), 45.

[14] July 1-August 10, 1808. *Ward's Journal*, IV, 662-664.

The Serampore Form of Agreement

"Ward reads every sheet,"[15] which is a significant role before printing but also a responsibility of a good translator.

Ward translated as well. In 1801, he mentions, "I read to the Brethren tonight a small catechism, which I have drawn up for the use of children, & which Felix & I shall try to translate into Bengalee."[16] Felix, Carey's son, spoke Bangla like a native. In 1808, Ward wrote, "I have begun to translate the Baptist Confession of faith into Bengalee for our native brethren."[17]

Ward also contributed to the Serampore Mission's philosophy of translation. Ward shared Carey's focus on the centrality of Sanskrit, writing in his journal, Friday, June 6, 1806. "We have begun to print the Shanscrit Testament. I have urged Bren. C. & M. to urge this forward, as a faithful translation into the Shanscrit will render all the translations into the other Eastern languages easy & certain; for all the eastern pundits know the Shanscrit; & making the Shanscrit the original, every real pundit in the East could make from this a good translation into his own tongue."[18]

The missionaries considered language a bridge of communication and a means to commune with the people. William Ward realized they needed to understand the local religion and socio-religious practices well. He also understood that the heart of India's languages is found in India's own scripture. Studying their religious texts would lead the missionaries into the language of the people and the customs that shaped their lives. Therefore, to attain knowledge of their sacred texts, it was necessary to translate them into English. Hence, William Ward emphasized a reverse method of translation. Carey's translation of the Ramayana, an ancient Sanskrit work, shows that he agreed with the general premise. Ward translated Indian texts as part of his larger project describing Indian culture and customs in his multivolume work *History, Literature and Mythology of the Hindoos*.

---

[15] Carey to Andrew Fuller, Serampore, 20 April 1808. BMS. Mss. As quoted in E. Daniel Potts, *British Baptist Missionaries*, 82.
[16] Saturday, June 6, 1801. *Ward's Journal*, I, 157.
[17] Thursday, July 1 [June 30], 1808. *Ward's Journal*, IV, 665.
[18] Friday, June 6, 1806. *Ward's Journal*, III, 489.

Statement Nine

Reviewing Ward's *Hindoos*, Prafulla Chattopadhyay writes, "Though Carey thought that Ward 'does not learn the language so quickly,' it is amazing to note how within the short span of ten to twelve years Ward succeeded in learning the language, social history, philosophy and religion of the Hindus inhabiting the then Bengal Presidency."[19]

The translation and printing work took on monumental proportions. The Bangla New Testament, for example, went through multiple revisions. To his surprise, William Ward discovered that Carey's first translation of the Bangla New Testament "was wholly English [in] construction, which is the very reverse of the Bengalee."[20] Ward got this knowledge from a Christian planter who did his own Bangla translation:

> The present perfection of the translation of the Bengalee, as it respects construction, is to be attributed to a friend of mine (Mr. Ellerton of Malda) also in a letter to me pointed out the fault in the construction of the first edition of the Bengalee Testament. The first edition was wholly English construction, which is the very reverse of the Bengalee. So convinced is Bro Carey now of the importance of altering the construction that he had the Psalms & Isaiah wholly reprinted on this account, & he has recommended that the Pentateuch should be reprinted on this account whole.[21]

The Bangla translation went through eight revisions before Carey passed away in 1834. The last revision was in 1832.

Ward understood the difficulties of achieving clarity in a new translation. In 1806, he expressed concerns that the Serampore team was overreaching, "I think, however, that a person is in a great measure disqualified for becoming a translator into a new language unless he know the force & bendings both of that *from* which he translates & that *into* which he translates."[22] He was concerned about the quality of their work in some of the languages they attempted:

---

[19] William Ward, *History, Literature and Mythology of the Hindoos* (Delhi: Low Price Publication, 1990). 4 Vols. 3rd edn. Reprint. (First published 1817-1820). Reviewed by Prafulla Chattopadhyay in *Dharma Deepika*, Vol. 1, no. 2, (1995), 81.

[20] Ward to Andrew Fuller, Sunderbunds, Oct. 7, 1805, as quoted in Potts, *British Baptist Missionaries*, 84.

[21] Ward to Fuller, Mission Boat, Sunderbunds, Oct 7, 1805. BMS. Mss.

[22] Lord's Day, April 27, 1806. *Ward's Journal*, III, 484. Emphasis in original.

The Serampore Form of Agreement

Perhaps it is enough to justify the work that the substance of the divine will would be made known in such a translation. I know that these translations will be, & must be worse than the first Bengalee, because in the Bengalee Brother Carey knew something of the language but in these comparatively little can be known; respecting the construction, shades of meaning, words to convey spiritual ideas, &c. &c. great dependence must be placed on the pundits.

He continued by recommending Carey and Marshman concentrate on translations

which we, with our hands, can distribute, & which may be fitted for stations which we ourselves can occupy. As to making Bibles for other Missionaries, into languages which we ourselves do not really understand, I recommend them to be cautious; lest they should be wasting time & life on that which every vicissitude may frustrate.[23]

No doubt, this was sound advice, but the vast needs of the Indian sub-continent weighed on the hearts of the Serampore team.

Translation Principles

An analysis of the ninth article of the Serampore Form of Agreement provides certain translation principles of the Serampore Trio. The SFA was signed on Monday, October 7, 1805. Interestingly, in March of 1806, the Serampore missionaries issued a publication titled *Proposals for a Subscription for Translating the Holy Scriptures into Oriental Languages*.[24] This proposal was distributed in different countries and to potential subscribers to raise funds for the distribution of the Christian Scriptures. The uniqueness of this publication, however, is that it stated distinctly the languages in which they intended to translate the Scriptures and the principles they would follow in their translation. It mentioned fifteen languages, including

---

[23] Lord's Day, April 27, 1806. *Ward's Journal*, III, 485.
[24] William Carey *et al.*, *Proposals for a Subscription for Translating the Holy Scriptures into the following Oriental Languages: Shanskrit, Bengalee, Hindoostanee, Persian, Mahratta, Guzerattee, Orissa, Carnata, Telinga, Burmah, Assam, Bootan, Tibet, Malay and Chinese* (Serampore: Mission Press, 1806).

Statement Nine

Chinese, Burmese, Bhutanese, and Persian. S.K. Chatterjee identified the following stages of translation in this publication:

1. Learning the language and preparation of grammatical notes and vocabularies.
2. Starting translation initiated by the pundits.
3. Appeal for the subscription for printing.
4. Checking and comparison.
5. After response to appeal, preparation of type fonts.
6. When sufficient funds available, translation was [to be] put to press for printing.
7. Checking and correcting [to be] continued during printing.
8. After printing, opinions of reliable scholars [to be] collected.[25]

Comparing these two sets of principles of translation, readers can detect certain dissimilarities between them, though both focus on the translation of the Scriptures as a whole. First, the SFA statement is an agreement among the Serampore missionaries to translate the Scripture, whereas the *Proposal* is an appeal to the public to contribute. Second, the SFA statement emphasizes the commitment among the missionaries, while the *Proposal* promotes translation for the benefit of the common people. Third, the SFA does not speak of principles of translation *per se*, while the *Proposal* speaks of general principles and specific translation methods. The *Proposal* further emphasizes circulating the translation among the common people and using it in vernacular schools for the local children. Nonetheless, these dissimilarities disappear under close examination of Statement Nine. Both publications focus on similar points from different perspectives. Statement Nine establishes the following ten principles of Scripture translation.

First, to Labour with All Our Might

The first expression, "to labour with all our might," necessarily focuses on the essential element of the ninth principle of the SFA, i.e., a strong determination to work unitedly without any distraction. Since scripture

---

[25] Sunil Kumar Chatterjee, *William Carey and Serampore*. Third enl. edn. (Serampore: The Author, 2008), 190.

translation involves multiple interdependent tasks, everyone involved should work with oneness of mind. As Phillip Butler writes, "Scripture calls for believers to work together in unity... . Consider John 17:20-23, where twice in four verses Jesus prays that His followers may be one ... Except for the Great Commission itself, this is *one of the strongest comments Jesus made on missions.*"[26] Scripture translation is a fundamental activity of world mission. Even before starting his journey to India, William Carey realized this simple truth. Therefore, even before he boarded the ship, he could pronounce a prophetic word to William Ward that they would soon need his talent for their mission in India. And labour, Ward did. Joyfully. Putting the Scriptures in the hands of the people was his calling and "blessed work." Before the Bengali New Testament appeared, he wrote with eager anticipation, "It may, it will, enlighten the ignorant, convert the froward, raise the ruined, comfort the distressed, and support the dying. Blessed Book! In India it shall be said and sung, 'The Gospel bears my spirit up!'"[27]

Second, to Translate the Sacred Scriptures Into the Languages of India

The second expression: "to translate the Sacred Scriptures in the languages of India." In 1806, there was "an explosion of translation" at Serampore. Whether such a state was desirable may be assessed historically. According to E. Daniel Potts, "William Ward disapproved of this scheme, on the realistic grounds that none of them knew enough of the 'construction, shades of meaning, words to convey spiritual ideas, &c. &c.' of the languages concerned."[28] Potts supports the arguments of William Ward when he says that "Serampore should render translations only for those areas occupied by Baptists; reminded his colleagues of the Jesuits who had 'made grammars, dictionaries & translations in abundance'

---

[26] Phillip Butler, "The Power of Partnership," in Ralph D. Winter and Steven C. Hawthorne, eds., *Perspectives on the World Christian Movement: A Reader*. Third edn. (Pasadena, CA: William Carey Library, 1999), 754. Emphasis in original.

[27] Ward to friend at Hull, September 15, 1800 in *Periodical Accounts Relative to the BMS*, II (1800), 70-71. Hereafter, *PA*.

[28] Lord's Day, April 27, 1806. *Ward's Journal*, III, 484, as quoted in Potts, *British Baptist Missionaries*, 81.

which were 'now rotting in the Libraries at Rome'; and cautioned against spending so much time on translations so as to leave the Mission at the time of their deaths in such an unestablished state that all may come to nothing.'"[29] Ward's view was supported by Andrew Fuller and at a later stage by Marshman.

Ward shared Carey's conviction that the Scriptures must be translated into every language: "The necessity that the translation of the Holy Scriptures should make a part of the work of the Indian missionary, will appear, if we consider that the Hindoos and the Mahometans have always been taught, that their systems are founded on divine revelations."[30] Referring to the prophetic vision in the Book of Revelation, Cameron Townsend connects the Great Commission to translation work and the diversity of language groups in the world: "... all of them must hear the message of God's love, for they are included in both the Great Commission and in the prophetic vision of the vast throng of the redeemed recorded in Revelation 7:9, 'After this I beheld and lo, a great multitude which no man could number of all nations and kindreds and peoples and TONGUES, stood before the throne and before the Lamb, clothed with white robes and palms in their hands.' They can get there only if they hear the Word in a language they can understand."[31]

Third: To Help in the Work of Translation

Scripture translation is a complementary job in which God plays a significant role. The reader will recollect that before Carey sailed for India, he met Ward and said, "If the Lord bless us, we shall want a person of your business to enable us to print the Scriptures: I hope you will come after us."[32] And Ward joined Carey after five years. The history of Serampore

---

[29] Potts, *British Baptist Missionaries*, 81, fn. 2; A. Christopher Smith, *The Serampore Mission Enterprise* (Bangalore: Centre for Contemporary Christianity, 2006), 319-320.

[30] William Ward, "Letter XIII to the Rev. Daniel Sharp, Boston" in *Farewell Letters to a Few Friends in Britain and America, on returning to Bengal in 1821* (New York: Bliss & White, 1821), 144.

[31] Wm. Cameron Townsend, "Tribes, Tongues and Translators," in Ralph D. Winter and Steven C. Hawthorne, eds., *Perspectives on the World Christian Movement: A Reader*. Third edn. (Pasadena, CA: William Carey Library, 1999), 310. Emphasis in original.

[32] "Memoir of Rev. William Ward: One of the Serampore Missionaries," *American Baptist Magazine*, n.s. V. no 1. (January 1825), 6.

and the history of Scripture translation throughout India demonstrate how Carey and Ward united for this great cause. The question, however, remains whether the SFA only referred to human help!

John R. Stott provides two perspectives regarding language and revelation. First, "What strikes us immediately is the greatness of God's condescension. He had sublime truth to reveal about himself and his Christ, his mercy, ... justice, and his full salvation. And he chose to make this disclosure through the vocabulary and grammar of human language, through human beings, human images, and human cultures." And then he continues, "Yet through this lowly medium of human words and images, God was speaking of his own Word. Our evangelical doctrine of the inspiration of Scripture emphasizes its double authorship. Men spoke, and God spoke. Men spoke from God (2 Peter 1:21), and God spoke through men (Heb. 1:1). The words spoken and written were equally his and theirs. He decided what he wanted to say, yet did not smother their human personalities. They used their faculties freely, and yet did not distort the divine message."[33] This is what the task of Scripture translation is. This is where both the divine and human meet.

Fourth, to Go Forward

The translation work should extract energy and encouragement from every bit of work achieved. When the first page of Matthew's gospel came out of Serampore Press, no doubt, it was a meager work to celebrate, but the Serampore Trio rejoiced. Ward wrote to England saying, "I love England, I love you, and many more friends at Hull; but to give a man a New Testament, who never saw it, ... this, this is my blessed work. If it should be long on the earth, it will bear a precious crop, sooner or later. If a man should not know the value of it immediately, a leaf, a verse, may some time be more precious to him than a load of hay."[34] Challenges and threats are sure to come, yet an optimistic viewpoint and strong determination can overcome these obstacles and go forward to achieve the goal.

---

[33] John R. W. Stott, "The Bible in World Evangelization," in Ralph D. Winter and Steven C. Hawthorne, eds., *Perspectives on the World Christian Movement: A Reader*. Third edn. (Pasadena, CA: William Carey Library, 1999), 23-24.

[34] Ward to friend at Hull, September 15, 1800, in *PA*, II (1800), 70-71. Quoted in Hooper, *Bible Translation*, 34-35.

Statement Nine

Fifth, to Learn the Languages with Diligence

How beneficial it is for a translator to learn the target language diligently, bit by bit! Ward desired to establish a bond with Indian society through his communication skills. He understood communication as not merely knowing each other through expressions of thoughts and feelings but as an act of interdependence. To him, communication became a "means to commune with the community at large with competence and compatibility."[35]

William Ward made great efforts to learn Bangla proficiently. He sought out the Pandits, who were linguistically gifted, to understand the local language and culture. His learning became the foundation of his literary output and translation of the Christian Scriptures. Once he could express his thoughts clearly in Bangla, he dedicated himself to communicating the message of the Bible in Bangla. The process and content of Scripture translation should enable the production of other literature for the church. "The Trio also demonstrated the importance of scholarly research for mission strategy and action, producing linguistic materials needed by all, and taking the leadership in the study of Hinduism."[36]

Sixth, to Acquire the Languages

Language learners aim to acquire proficiency in speaking and writing a new language. Ward advanced sufficiently to engage in Scripture translation. Additionally, with his colleagues, he began two Bangla periodicals: the *Dig Darshan* (The Signpost) and the *Samachar Darpan* (News Mirror), a monthly periodical of a broader nature. In addition, he contributed to another Serampore Press publication, the English-language *Friend of India*. These publications became more than a form of communication; they provided a means of feedback. People's remarks helped Ward and his colleagues to improve their communication skills as writers and translators.

---

[35] Pratap Chandra Gine, "Preface," in *Communication in Theological Education: New Directions*. Edited by Michael Traber (Delhi: ISPCK, 2005), xi–xiii.

[36] R. Pierce Beaver, "The History of Mission Strategy," in Ralph D. Winter and Steven C. Hawthorne, eds., *Perspectives on the World Christian Movement: A Reader*. Third edn. (Pasadena, CA: William Carey Library, 1999), 247.

The Serampore Form of Agreement

Seventh, to Publish the Divine Word Throughout India

Learning the language was only the first step. Translating the Scriptures was a more significant challenge, yet this was only part of the even larger project of publishing the Bible for language groups across India. As we have seen, the Serampore Trio recognized the importance of Sanskrit in the context of eastern and northern Indian languages. Carey and Ward realized that although Bangla and Hindi have the same roots in Sanskrit, their morphological and syntactic structures differ.[37] Therefore, it remained a painstaking exercise to do justice to the publication of the divine Word in such languages.

The challenges extended beyond translation. William Ward became selective about the quality of paper used by the Serampore Press. Initially, the Serampore Press used "Patna" paper for printing. This paper, however, was porous and rough and attracted bookworms and white ants.[38] The Trio, notably Carey and Ward, decided to manufacture paper themselves. Daniel Potts writes that in their attempts to improve the process, "in a letter to the *Calcutta Post*, Ward asked readers for information regarding the making of strong and clear sizing for paper."[39] They erected a treadmill where forty men would work. Later, the Trio ordered a steam engine from Lancashire, England. The product of their efforts became known as Serampore Paper and gained a reputation for its high quality.[40]

Eighth, to Explain and Distribute the Divine Word on All Occasions as the Message for All

It is not sufficient to translate the Word of God. Efforts were also required in publishing and distribution. And this demanded money. The BMS committed a thousand pounds annually from England, but this was insufficient. Carey's salary as a Professor in the College of Fort William and profits from the printing press were added to the common fund of the Serampore

---

[37] Quoted from Carey's *Grammar of the Bengalee Language* (1801), iv, in Muhammad Abdul Qayyum, *A Critical Study of the Early Bengali Grammars: Halhed to Haughton* (Dhaka: The Asiatic Society of Bangladesh, 1982), 136.
[38] Middlebrook, *William Carey*, 70.
[39] Potts, *British Baptist Missionaries*, 111.
[40] Marshman, *Life and Times*, II, 223-225. Chatterjee, *William Carey and Serampore*, 50-61.

Mission. According to Herbert Marsh, the Serampore Trio's contributions "amount to more than *three thousand* [pounds] a year. Such facts deserve to be recorded."[41]

Ninth, to Preach the Message of Salvation in Large Assemblies of the Natives

Beginning March 2, 1823, for four consecutive days before his death, Ward preached in Calcutta and Serampore: "He spoke Bengalee with the fluency and ease of a native, and was thus enabled to acquire a powerful influence over the people. He commanded the attention of a native audience by the flow of his language, and his apt allusion to their habits, feelings, and allegories."[42] On the evening of March 6, he went to bed exhausted and went to glory on March 7. Of course, he was not the only preacher from the Serampore Mission. All the missionaries shared this responsibility, and they prepared Indian evangelists for the same task. Ward's dedication to evangelism is underlined by his commitment to it almost to his final breath.

Tenth, to Establish Native Free Schools for the Future Conquest of the Gospel

The Marshmans took on the responsibility of starting native schools. The concern for education went beyond simple social benevolence. While they believed education was a positive good for the people of India in its own right, they also understood that spreading the Gospel through Bible translations and the printed word depended on encouraging literacy. William Ward supported the free schools in and around Serampore and published relevant books for the children of these schools. These schools were established to communicate the 4Rs (i.e., Reading, Writing, Arithmetic, and Religious Studies). "He [Ward] and his colleagues had always acted on the principle that a native Christian mother must, at the least, be qualified to

---

[41] Herbert Marsh, *A History of the Translations: Which have been Made of the Scriptures, from the Earliest to the Present Age, throughout Europe, Asia, Africa and America. The British and Foreign Bible Society* (London, Cambridge: Rivingtons, Deighton, Nicholson and Barrett, 1812), 48. Emphasis in original.

[42] Marshman, *Life and Times*, II, 279

teach her children to read the Bible, and that female ignorance and Christianity could not exist together. But they were anxious to extend the blessing of knowledge also to heathen families, and, after Mr. Ward's return, he took the department of female education into his own hands, and established numerous schools in and around Serampore, which were vigorously maintained after his death."[43]

Conclusion

The Serampore Form of Agreement found its fulfillment in the ministry of the Serampore Trio. William Ward became the first to say goodbye to the Serampore Family. He had achieved his goal. Sixteen months after his return to the mission, Ward died of cholera. His own hymn describes the struggles of the Serampore work—and its infinite rewards:

> Yes, we are safe beneath Thy shade,
> And shall be so midst India's heat:
> What should a missionary dread,
> For devils crouch at Jesus' feet.
>
> There, sweetest Saviour! let Thy cross
> Win many Hindoo hearts to Thee;
> This shall make up for every loss,
> While Thou art ours eternally.[44]

---

[43] Marshman, *Life and Times*, II, 303.
[44] Last couplets of a hymn attributed to Ward. George Smith, *The Life of William Carey D.D.: Shoemaker and Missionary* (London: John Murray, 1885), 119. Vinita Hampton Wright, "William Ward (1769-1823) Radical, and 'spiritual father'," https://christianhistoryinstitute.org/magazine/article/rest-of-the-serampore-trio (accessed on September 3, 2023).

STATEMENT TEN

Prayer and the Cultivation of Personal Religion

Peter J. Morden

On 5 April 1806, Andrew Fuller, founding secretary of the Baptist Missionary Society (BMS), penned a letter to two missionary couples, James (1799-1829) and Anne Chater (d. 1820), and William (1784-1853) and Elizabeth Robinson (1784?-1810). The Chaters and the Robinsons were about to depart the British Isles for Bengal to augment the BMS work at Serampore. Fuller expressed his admiration for the new recruits and offered counsel as they embarked on their risky venture. He placed special emphasis on the vital importance of prayer and personal godliness, declaring:

> There is the greatest necessity for us all to keep near to God, and to feel that we are in that path of which he approves. This will sustain us in times of trial. The want of this cannot be supplied by anything else. Beware of those things which draw a veil between him and you, or that render a throne of grace unwelcome. If God be with you, you shall do well.[1]

In the BMS secretary's thinking, prayer and godliness were not only essential, they were inextricably linked: "communion" with God nurtured

---

[1] Andrew Fuller to James and Ann Chater, William and Elizabeth Robinson, April 5, 1806, in John Ryland Jr., *The Life of Andrew Fuller*, ed. C. Ryan Griffith (Berlin / Boston, MA: Walter De Gruyter, 2022 [1816, 1st edn.; 1818, 2nd edn.]), 236. For the phrase "throne of grace" and its connection to prayer, see Hebrews 4:16. For Fuller, see Peter J. Morden, *The Life and Thought of Andrew Fuller (1754-1815)* (Milton Keynes: Paternoster, 2015).

The Serampore Form of Agreement

through prayer was the spring from which godly living would flow. If communion were maintained, the missionaries would possess a "savour of Christ" wherever they went and whatever trials they experienced.[2] The apostle Paul's expression "savour of Christ" was highly appropriate, for the phrase was originally used in the context of pioneering cross-cultural mission.[3] Fuller did not reference the Serampore Form of Agreement (SFA) in his communication, but he would have been aware that his advice was in line with the core principles set out in its Statement Ten by William Ward (1769-1823) on behalf of William Carey (1761-1834), Joshua Marshman (1768-1837), and the younger missionaries based at Serampore.[4] The Robinsons and the Chaters eventually arrived in India on 23 August 1806, almost a year after the SFA had been formally adopted.[5] Yet, they had already been inducted into some of its leading tenets thanks to Fuller's letter.

This chapter examines Statement Ten of the SFA with its dual focus on "prayer and the cultivation of personal religion." It offers an exposition of the statement and highlights the different factors—theological and "spiritual"—which shaped its general argument and particular wording. Finally, its outworking in the lives of a sampling of early missionaries is considered. The BMS personnel sometimes struggled to live up to the high ideals the statement set out. Even so, the maintenance of their faith under great and repeated trials was remarkable. The chapter will argue that Statement Ten was shaped decisively by forces associated with the eighteenth-century Evangelical Revival. It further argues this single paragraph was crucial to the SFA as a whole and, more broadly, that it contains emphases foundational to the work of the BMS.

---

[2] Fuller to Chaters and Robinsons, Ryland, *Fuller*, 236-237.
[3] To Troas and Macedonia. See 2 Corinthians 2:12-17.
[4] For Ward's authorship of the SFA, see editor's introduction. Although the SFA was signed by all the male missionaries based at Serampore, it especially expressed the mind of Carey, Marshman, and Ward. For the authoritative history of the BMS up to his time of writing, with much biographical material on the Serampore Trio, see Brian Stanley, *The History of the Baptist Missionary Society*, 1792-1992 (Edinburgh: T&T Clark, 1992).
[5] Francis A. Cox, *History of the Baptist Missionary Society. From 1792 to 1842*. 2 vols. (London: T. Ward and Co., and G. & J. Dyer, 1842), I, 156.

Statement Ten

Exposition

The statement bears the hallmarks of William Ward's rather colorful journalistic style of writing described, not unfairly, as "fervid" by Joshua Marshman's son, John Clark Marshman (1794-1877).[6] The language is by turns overblown ("famish these idols"), repetitious (the overuse of the phrase "let us"), and, on occasion, both ("these laborious and unutterably important labours"). The argument is not as clear and progressing as it might be. The comment on the need for a "knowledge of the languages current where a missionary lives" is particularly awkward: it breaks the flow of thought and is, in any case, redundant since the argument for language learning had already been made in statement nine. Carey would have written the paragraph in a more straightforward, linear fashion. Even so, its essential thrust is clear enough, and Ward's passionate rhetoric reminds us of the extent to which the Serampore Trio was committed to the principles laid out. As already noted, the statement revolves around prayer and personal godliness.

Intercessory Prayer

The stress on prayer is the dominant one in the statement. The missionaries were to be "instant in prayer," give themselves to "secret, fervent, believing prayer," and be "united" in prayer. The example of David Brainerd (1718-1747), cross-cultural missionary to Native Americans, is offered explicitly to encourage them to pray. They were to be "fervent in spirit," earnestly wrestling with God in prayer.[7] This was spoken prayer rather than quiet contemplation and intercession rather than praise, thanksgiving, or confession. The missionaries practiced all these forms of prayer, but the statement is focused on asking God to intervene for people and situations.[8] We can be more specific still: this is prayer for the "salvation" of those who were "perishing" in India. The idols the missionaries believed

---

[6] John Clark Marshman, *The Life and Times of Carey, Marshman, and Ward. Embracing the History of the Serampore Mission.* 2 vols. (London: Longman, Brown, Green, Longmans, & Roberts, 1859), I, 229.

[7] Colossians 4:12.

[8] For examples of the missionaries practicing other dimensions of prayer, see Cox, *BMS*, I, 67, 99, 104 (thanksgiving / gratitude to God); 91, 123 (praise); 40, 323 (confession / lament).

held the people in thrall were to be removed—"famished" in Ward's journalistic rhetoric—and replaced by the worship of the one they believed was the only true and living God. This was urgent intercession springing from deeply held evangelical Christian convictions and focused on their particular mission.

How was such prayer to be practiced? There is a strong emphasis on individual, personal prayer, which was extempore rather than liturgical. As Brainerd pleaded alone from his heart for those he was seeking to reach, so the individual missionaries were to pray for those they worked among in their own regular times of personal prayer—described in the statement as "closet religion."[9] But prayer was not to be limited to these daily devotions. The phrase "instant in prayer" indicated a readiness to turn to pray at a moment's notice should a situation require it, for example, with an enquirer or a new convert, or when a ship was about to sail with mission personnel aboard. The *Periodical Accounts* of the BMS contain many examples, recorded in the missionaries' journals and letters, when they prayed both at set times and more spontaneously.[10]

Prayer, then, could be practiced alone, one-to-one, with a smaller group, or in the context of a more formal meeting or time of corporate worship. So corporate prayer was a vital stress alongside "closet religion." There were particular occasions when the missionaries would join together in prayer. For example, the day the SFA was read and first adopted, 6 October 1805, began at 6.00 a.m. with a prayer meeting.[11] 6 October was a significant date for the missionaries, as it was the day the BMS had been founded in England. Important anniversaries were often marked with a time of prayer, but there were also regular weekly meetings for intercession, held in both English and Bengali.[12] The aim in 1805 was to establish new mission stations away from Serampore and so there was an awareness BMS personnel would not always be able to meet together physically. Even

---

[9] Cf. Matthew 6:6, KJV.
[10] See, e.g., *Ward's Journal*, November 8, 1801 (before a ship sailed), February 2, 1802 (one-to-one). *Periodical Accounts Relative to the Baptist Missionary Society*. Vol. II (1802), 221, 242. Hereafter *PA*.
[11] *Ward's Journal*, Lord's Day, October 6, 1805. *PA*, III (1806), 181.
[12] See, e.g., *Ward's Journal*, December 22, 1801. *PA*, II (1802), 225, for the missionaries' regular Bengali prayer meeting.

Statement Ten

so, they could still be "united in prayer" whatever "distance may separate" them and praying together at set times could keep them connected despite geographical separation. At this crucial juncture, as the missionaries made plans to expand their work across the Indian subcontinent, they sought to formally embed the culture of intercession, which had been part of their modus operandi from the beginning. The very first number of the *Periodical Accounts*, which covered the formation of the BMS and its early progress up to 1794, contained 47 explicit occurrences of the words "pray," "prayer," and their derivatives in the space of 86 printed pages.[13] The edition for 1806 had 55 references in 125 printed pages.[14] What the 1806 *Periodical Accounts* called "a spirit of importunate prayer" had been at the heart of the mission from its inception.[15] Ward, Carey, and Marshman were determined it would remain so as the mission developed.

Personal Godliness

Alongside prayer, the "cultivation of personal religion" was also stressed. "Personal godliness" was indispensable. What did the missionaries understand by these phrases? They certainly meant a commitment to the "means of grace." As well as prayer, these means of grace included bible reading, which was a staple of both individual personal devotion and also "family worship." Carey's own practice was to read a chapter of the Bible in Hebrew first thing in the morning (between 5.45 and 7.00 a.m.) before engaging in family worship in Bengali at 7.00 a.m. His typical day would then close with him reading a chapter of the Greek New Testament at 11.00 p.m.[16] For all the missionaries, the Scriptures were "the precious fountain of truth" and could not be neglected.[17] Such personal devotion was vital, and, as with prayer, it was to be practiced corporately as well as privately. A visitor described their experience of Serampore thus:

---

[13] *PA*, I (1800), 1-86.

[14] *PA*, III (1806), iii-xiii; 14-125. This number of the *PA* is 152 pages long but page 126-152 is a list of subscriptions, collections and donations to the Society.

[15] *PA*, III (1806), Preface: vii.

[16] S. Pearce Carey, *William Carey, D.D., Fellow of the Linnaean Society*. Rev. edn. (London: The Carey Press, 1934), 258-259. Carey was recording a "sample day," June 12, 1806, in a communication with Ryland Jr. Cf. E. Daniel Potts, *British Baptist Missionaries in India, 1793-1837* (London: Cambridge University Press, 1967), 19.

[17] John Chamberlain to John Ryland Jr, September 3, 1804. *PA*, III (1806), 61.

The Serampore Form of Agreement

We were met by Dr Marshman and Mr Ward, who, with their wives, received us very cordially. The three families [including Carey's] live in separate houses but eat together in a large hall. The buildings stand close to the river [Hooghly]. The bell rings at 5 for the boys to rise for school; at 8 for breakfast, and immediately after breakfast for prayers in the large and elegant chapel: a hymn, Bible chapter and prayer. On Sunday, English worship 11 to 1; Bengali in the afternoon, and English again in the evening. Monday evening, a conference for the native Christians, Tuesday evening, an hour spent in examining difficult Scriptures; Thursday and Saturday evening, conferences.[18]

Corporate worship included celebration of the Lord's supper and sung worship.[19] Some hymns sung were composed by the missionaries themselves. Marshman's "Hail, precious Book divine!" included the stanza:

Deign, gracious Saviour, deign
To smile upon Thy Word;
Let millions now obtain
Salvation from the Lord:
Nor let its growing conquests stay,
Till earth exult to own Thy sway.[20]

Worship was addressed directly to Christ, their "gracious Saviour" for the "precious Book divine," which revealed their Lord and his gospel to them. The theology was Christocentric, with a high view of the Bible as the word of God, and missional. If God "smiled" on his "Word," then salvation would flow—for millions. Here was a big vision.

Indeed, while the missionaries certainly believed the cultivation of holy habits was crucial, they were deeply concerned with how a godly life was lived out in practice. Their approach to what they termed elsewhere "real

---

[18] Ann H. Judson to her Sister, Mid-June 1812, in S. Pearce Carey, *William Carey, D.D., Fellow of the Linnaean Society* (London: Hodder and Stoughton, 1923), 294.

[19] *Ward's Journal*, December 28, 1800, notes the first celebration of the Lord's supper in Bengali. See S.P. Carey, *William Carey* (1934), 209. *PA*, II (1802), 127.

[20] "Hail, precious Book divine!" S.P. Carey, *William Carey* (1934), 212. For Joshua Marshman's authorship, see *PA*, II (1802), 166-167. Cf. https://hymnary.org/text/hail_precious_book_divine (accessed Oct 1, 2023).

Statement Ten

religion"[21] or "true religion"[22] encompassed both the ways a relationship with God was nurtured and expressed (the means of grace) and the ways that relationship was worked out in transformed living (personal holiness). Hence, the important reference in Statement Ten to a "mild and winning temper." Ward himself was acutely aware of how vital this was for community living, for it was difficult indeed for men and women of strong personalities and different temperaments to live in proximity with each other. Writing to Fuller in 1800, he declared: "So much depends on a man's disinterestedness, forbearance, meekness, and self-denial. One man of the wrong temper could make our house a hell."[23] And, as always for the Trio, godly living had to have a missional edge. For them, it was not credible to speak of godliness and then fail to engage wholeheartedly in the missionary task. In "Hail, precious Book divine!" Marshman expressed it this way: "Now shall the Hindus learn / The glories of our King."[24] Not only was the intercession they were to offer outwardly focused, but their pursuit of godliness was also full of missional intent. This is the nature of the personal godliness insisted on in the SFA.

Before considering the factors which provide essential background to Statement Ten, it is important to underline its importance to the SFA as a document. The missionaries were called to "unutterably important labours"; they were "instruments of God in the great work of human redemption" in a pioneering missional context. Their strategy for fulfilling this high calling was set out in the successive statements of the SFA, but Statement Ten insisted that without prayer and godly missional discipleship that strategy would fail. This was quite explicit: "a mild and winning temper, and a heart given up to God in closet religion" was more important than knowledge and gifts; however great the missionaries' attainments might be. Statement Ten is therefore a keystone of the whole of the SFA.

---

[21] *PA*, IV (1817), 42.
[22] *PA*, IV (1817), 42, 120, 178.
[23] William Ward to Andrew Fuller, 1800, in S.P. Carey, *William Carey* (1934), 192.
[24] "Hail, precious Book divine!" S.P. Carey, *William Carey* (1934), 212. *PA*, II (1802), 167.

The Serampore Form of Agreement

Influences

A range of influences shaped this statement, and these are treated here under two headings, theology and spirituality. There is a significant overlap between these two sections, and it is helpful to think of them as two intersecting circles. Even so, the use of these headings helps us identify the key factors shaping this crucial statement of the SFA.

Theology

At first sight, the statement might appear to contain little theology. Yet, it was shaped by theological principles which were at the core of the missionaries' worldview. Their leading principles had already been laid out in the preamble to the SFA. Foundational was the belief that God is sovereign in salvation. This was stated plainly: "We are sure, that only those who are ordained to eternal life will believe, and that God alone can add to the church such as shall be saved." The SFA is underpinned by a Calvinistic theology and Statement Ten is no exception. The missionaries were all Particular Baptists: they believed in particular redemption and their denomination could trace its theological lineage to the five points of Calvinism articulated by the Synod of Dort in 1618–1619. This was expressed in, for example, the resolutely Calvinistic 1689 London Confession.[25] The Particular Baptists had grown out of English Puritanism and separatism as practiced by men like John Bunyan (1628–1688). Their continuing Calvinistic commitments were expressed by the denomination's leading late-eighteenth-century figures in many places, for example, by John Ryland Jr. (1753–1825) in his biography of Fuller.[26] For the Particular Baptists, these convictions were non-negotiable.

The theology underpinning Statement Ten is also evangelical, steeped in the missional priorities which characterized the eighteenth-century

---

[25] A discussion of these movements is beyond the scope of this chapter. For a useful summary of this background and the unfolding Baptist story in context, see Anthony L. Chute, Nathan A. Finn, and Michael A.G. Haykin, *The Baptist Story: From English Sect to Global Movement* (Nashville, TN: Broadman and Holman, 2015).

[26] Ryland, *Fuller*, 87–88.

Statement Ten

Evangelical Revival.[27] God alone could save, but he would work through people to accomplish his saving purposes. In the preamble to the SFA, the apostle Paul was held up as an exemplar of someone who held these two complementary principles together and put them into action. He was "the great champion for the glorious doctrines of free and sovereign grace" and, at the same time, "was the most conspicuous for his personal zeal in the work of persuading men to be reconciled to God." "In this respect," the preamble continued, "he is a noble example for our imitation." The missionaries stressed both divine sovereignty and human responsibility.

This understanding of how God's sovereignty operated in salvation had been hard won. In the first half of the nineteenth century, many English Particular Baptists had espoused high Calvinism, which exalted the divine decrees to such an extent and in such ways that human responsibility was greatly minimized. So, Andrew Fuller's boyhood pastor at Soham, Cambridgeshire, John Eve (d. 1782), refused to urge the unconverted to trust in Christ when he was preaching; indeed, according to Fuller, Eve had "little or nothing to say to the unconverted" in his pulpit ministry.[28] The BMS secretary was himself a central figure challenging high Calvinism in Particular Baptist life, especially through his treatise *The Gospel Worthy of All Acceptation*, first published in 1785.[29] In the *Gospel Worthy*, Fuller affirmed all the leading Calvinistic doctrines but struck at the heart of high Calvinism by insisting that the gospel should be "offered" freely to all. Fuller grounded his argument in the detailed theological and philosophical reasonings of the New England Congregationalist Jonathan Edwards (1703–58). Edwards's *Freedom of the Will* distinguished between "natural" and "moral" inability, arguing that although people were incapable of responding to the gospel without the regenerating grace of God,

---

[27] The eighteenth-century Evangelical Revival and what is often termed "modern evangelicalism" provides vital background for Statement Ten of the SFA. For different perspectives, see David W. Bebbington, *Evangelicalism in Modern Britain: A History from the 1730s to the 1980s* (London: Unwin Hyman, 1989); Michael A. G. Haykin and Kenneth J. Stewart, eds., *The Emergence of Evangelicalism: Exploring Historical Continuities*. (Leicester: IVP, 2008).

[28] Ryland, *Fuller*, 96.

[29] Andrew Fuller, *The Gospel Worthy of All Acceptation*. 1st edn. (Northampton: Thomas Dicey, 1785).

The Serampore Form of Agreement

they were still morally culpable if they failed to do so.[30] Fuller's debt to the Edwards was considerable, but he did not simply repeat his arguments. Rather, he contextualized them to serve his own purposes, insisting it was the duty of all to believe and, therefore, the duty of Christians—especially pastors—to preach invitational evangelistic sermons.[31] The Edwardsean evangelical Calvinism of the *Gospel Worthy* was the theology that drove the early work of the BMS and which underpinned the SFA.

As far as Statement Ten was concerned, the "great work of human redemption" was God's alone, and it followed that prayer was indispensable. Yet, God would not just use their prayers but also their Christian character—their godliness actively worked out in evangelistic mission—to bring about conversions. The important words in the statement were "instruments" and "means": devotion to prayer and the cultivation of personal godliness were the means God provided for them to become fit instruments for him to use. "Means" was an especially crucial word for the BMS missionaries and one of the leading ways they expressed the dynamic of their evangelical Calvinism. It was particularly prominent in Carey's *An Enquiry into the Obligations of Christians to Use Means for the Conversion of the Heathens*, published in 1792.[32] The words "obligations" and "means" in the title convey the thrust of his argument.[33] Christians were obligated to use means to take the gospel to those who had never heard it. The sovereignty of God in salvation was not in dispute, but God used faithful missionaries to accomplish his saving purposes. This understanding shaped his outlook and actions and that of his colleagues. To cite just one example, on an evangelistic tour, Marshman shared the gospel through preaching, debate, and literature distribution. Yet, he was absolutely clear that it was

---

[30] Jonathan Edwards, *Freedom of the Will*, in *The Works of Jonathan Edwards*, vol. 1, ed. Paul Ramsey (New Haven: Yale University Press, 1985 [1754]).

[31] Edwards's original purpose was to challenge Arminian concepts of human freedom.

[32] William Carey, *An Enquiry into the Obligations of Christians to Use Means for the Conversion of the Heathens. In which the Religious State of the Different Nations of the World, the Success of Former Undertakings, and the Practicability of Further Undertakings, are Considered* (Leicester: Ann Ireland, 1792).

[33] Stanley, *History of the BMS*, 12.

"the Lord alone" who could cause the gospel seed to "take root."[34] Statement Ten cannot be understood without an appreciation of Edwardsean evangelical Calvinism.

Spirituality

The commitment to prayer for the cause of world mission was also deeply embedded in eighteenth-century Particular Baptist spirituality. The "Prayer Call of 1784" and the movement it spawned encapsulated this commitment, and it is especially appropriate to consider the call to prayer here, given its importance to the founding of the BMS. Once again, a book by Jonathan Edwards is essential background. *An Humble Attempt to Promote Explicit Agreement and Visible Union of God's People in Extraordinary Prayer* was originally published in 1748.[35] Edwards's treatise was rooted in the effort to establish regular prayer meetings for Revival, which had begun in the 1740s and subsequently crisscrossed the Atlantic. At these meetings, participants offered "fervent and constant" prayer for the outpouring of the Holy Spirit and the rapid extension of God's kingdom around the world.[36] Fuller and his friends Ryland Jr. and John Sutcliff (1752-1814) read the work in 1784 and wasted no time in establishing monthly prayer meetings in their respective churches along the lines proposed. At these meetings, information on mission at home and abroad was shared before extempore prayer was offered for the worldwide extension of God's kingdom. In 1789, the Particular Baptists reprinted the *Humble Attempt* with a new Preface written by Sutcliff with the "avowed design" of further "promoting" prayer for mission. The Call to Prayer had birthed a dynamic movement.

Phrases in the *Humble Attempt*, such as "the promised glorious and universal outpourings of the Spirit of God," need to be read against the back-

---

[34] *Joshua Marshman's Journal*, March 12, 1803, in *PA*, II (1804), 395.
[35] For Edwards' *Humble Attempt*, see *The Works of Jonathan Edwards*, ed. Edward Hickman. 2 vols. (Edinburgh: Banner of Truth, 1974 [1834]), 2:280-312.
[36] Edwards, *Humble Attempt*, 312.

The Serampore Form of Agreement

ground of Edwards's optimistic postmillennial eschatology, with its accompanying belief in the imminence of "the latter-day glory."[37] Broadly speaking, Fuller and Sutcliff shared this eschatology, as did the early BMS missionaries. Carey's famous dictum, "Expect great things, attempt great things," is imbued with postmillennial optimism,[38] as is the hymn already quoted, "Hail, precious Book divine!" It was not just the conversion of a few, but of "millions" that was aimed for and the growing "conquests" of salvation were to continue until earth itself "exulted" in the reign of Christ.[39] Once again, we should note that here was a big vision, one driven by a hope-filled spirituality fired by intercession for the world and postmillennial eschatology.

A further comment on David Brainerd is warranted, given his example is explicitly cited in Ward's text.[40] His influence was mediated to the English Calvinistic Baptists through Jonathan Edwards's *Life of Brainerd*, and so he stands as another example of evangelical influence in general and Edwardsean influence in particular.[41] All the BMS pioneers revered Brainerd, with Fuller as big an enthusiast as any.[42] This appreciation was shared by the new wave of missionaries who followed Carey, Marshman, and Ward to Bengal. John Chamberlain (1777-1821) wrote: "Read dear Brainerd's Life, especially part the 8th of his diary: experienced an alteration in my mind ... I long to be like him. Surely, if ever I arrive at the heavenly world, I shall be eagerly desirous of seeing him."[43] Brainerd, as presented by Edwards in his spiritual biography, was Calvinistic, evangelical, and unshakably committed to the missionary task. What is more, he prioritized prayer

---

[37] Edwards, *Humble Attempt*, 306.

[38] From a sermon Carey preached on Isaiah 54:2-3 at Friar Lane, Nottingham, on 30 May 1792. His motto has passed into Baptist folklore as "Expect great things from God; Attempt great things for God," but probably the shorter title, "Expect great things; Attempt great things" is strictly accurate. See Morden, *Fuller*, 119, n. 109.

[39] "Hail, precious Book divine!" S.P. Carey, *William Carey* (1934), 212. *PA*, II (1802), 167.

[40] For biographical detail, see John A. Grigg, *The Lives of David Brainerd: The Making of an American Evangelical Icon* (Oxford: Oxford University Press, 2009), 3-127.

[41] *The Life of David Brainerd*, in *The Works of Jonathan Edwards*, vol. 7, ed. Norman Pettit (New Haven: Yale University Press, 1985 [1749]).

[42] Cf. Morden, *Fuller*, 59-60.

[43] William Yates, *Memoirs of Mr. John Chamberlain, Late Missionary in India* (London: Wightman and Cramp, 1826), 66.

Statement Ten

and personal godliness. Ward's holding him up as an example to be emulated is one further sign that Statement Ten was shot through with evangelicalism. Of course, the Serampore missionaries were Baptist as well as evangelical. They held to certain Baptist principles, for example, the importance of believers' baptism and the gathered church community. Their patterns of devotion were also shaped by their Reformed and Puritan heritage, with the emphases on private prayer and family prayer a staple of Puritan spirituality. And yet, as far as Statement Ten is concerned, forces associated with the Evangelical Revival, especially Jonathan Edwards and New England evangelical Calvinism, were dominant.

Outworking

The vision, then, was for fervent prayer for conversions and personal godliness nurtured by close communion with God, all worked out in a pioneering missional context which would be full of trials. How did the missionaries live up to the ideal? Three individuals will be examined here: William Robinson, a representative of the missionaries who came out to India as the SFA was being written; Joshua Marshman, a representative of the original Trio; and his wife, Hannah Marshman (1767-1847), who was a crucial member of the community-based at Serampore for nearly fifty years.

William Robinson

As already noted, William and Elizabeth Robinson (née Walker) sailed for Bengal in 1805, the same year the SFA was adopted. William was originally from Olney, Buckinghamshire, and had been tutored by the pastor of the Baptist church there, Andrew Fuller's friend John Sutcliff. Elizabeth had been converted under Fuller's ministry and was later baptized by Sutcliff. Thus, both William and Elizabeth were shaped by the ministries of two of the founding fathers of the BMS. Elizabeth died of a debilitating fever at Dinagepore in 1810. She was only 26 years of age.[44] William himself struggled with severe illness in his early years as a missionary and was close to death on several occasions. Surprisingly, he went on to have a long career and outlived all his contemporaries. He worked in Java and Sumatra before

---

[44] William H. Carey, *Oriental Christian Biography*. 3 vols. (Calcutta: Baptist Mission Press, 1850-1852), 3:90-91.

The Serampore Form of Agreement

pastoring the Lal Bazaar Chapel in Calcutta for 13 years. He remarried on four occasions: as well as Elizabeth, three other wives—Margaret (née Gordon), Mrs. Sophia Knaggs, and Mary (née Burgh)—predeceased him. With his fifth wife, Eliza (née Sturgeon), he worked, from 1839, in Dacca until his death.[45]

The story of William Robinson and that of his five wives is one of commitment and great sacrifice. But there is more that needs to be said, for Robinson exhibited what Francis Cox described, rather quaintly, as some "apoplectic tendencies of constitution."[46] Put simply, Robinson struggled to control his temper, especially in his early years in India. According to Ward, he was capable of "shaking down the whole mission house" at Serampore through his shouting.[47] He was reluctant to take direction from the Trio. For example, he initially refused their instruction to go to Bhutan to pioneer work there, believing they were being impractical and unreasonable.[48] Robinson eventually acquiesced, but the mission to Bhutan failed, with the Serampore Trio suspecting that their new recruit —for all the difficulties he encountered—could have tried harder.[49] Fuller, with his information on Robinson coming mainly from the Trio, came to believe the new man had shown himself "unsuitable" for the life of a Christian missionary because of his temperament and unwillingness to submit to the senior figures at Serampore.[50]

---

[45] For details in this paragraph, see Cox, *BMS*, I, 234, 253, 405; John Robinson, "Memoir of the Rev. William Robinson" in *The Missionary Register August 1855* (London: Seeley, Jackson, and Halliday, 1855), 329-334; A. Christopher Smith, "British Recruits for Serampore, 1800-1825," *The Baptist Review of Theology* 2.2 (Fall 1992), 12-13. Sophia was of Dutch descent (Ceylon), and married James Knaggs at Batavia. She was baptized by Robinson and both being widowed, he married her in 1824 at Bencoolen, Sumatra. Edward S. Wenger, "The Rev. William Robinson," *Missionary Biographies*, II, 31-35. Mss. CLRC, Serampore; Ernest A. Payne, *South-East from Serampore: More Chapters in the Story of the Baptist Missionary Society* (London: The Carey Press, 1945), 7-14, 26-37, 44-45, 48, 55-56.

[46] Cox, *BMS*, I, 333.

[47] S.P. Carey, *William Carey* (1934), 280.

[48] Eustace Carey, *Supplement to the Vindication of the Calcutta Baptist Missionaries Occasioned by Dr. Carey's "Thirty-two Letters," Dr. Marshman's "Reply to the Rev. J. Dyer" and Mr. John Marshman's "Review."* (London: George Wightman, 1831), 75.

[49] Ward, cited by E. Carey, *Supplement to the Vindication*, 76. Cf. Smith, "British Recruits for Serampore," 13.

[50] "Poor Robinson ... His democratic notions of I know not what liberty and equality are utterly unsuitable for a Christian missionary." Payne, *South-East from Serampore*, 11. In 1811

Statement Ten

Robinson had some credible reasons for his unwillingness to go to Bhutan. He felt, for example, that the efforts he had made to learn Bengali would be wasted if he began work among a people who spoke a different dialect.[51] The problems were not all on one side. However, there is little doubt that he was a difficult colleague in the years immediately following his arrival in Bengal. The senior missionaries believed he was unwilling to live sacrificially, wanted to stay close to Serampore rather than pioneer, and—possibly—had designs on having a leading role at the mission base. Both Ward and Marshman spoke of his "covetousness."[52] There had been a major breakdown in trust. His volatile manner stands in marked contrast to the "mild and winning temper" advocated in the SFA. The ideal set out by Statement Ten and the reality of his conduct appear far apart. He was not following the advice given to him by Fuller in his 1805 letter or living by the framework for godliness outlined in the SFA.

Joshua Marshman

As already noted, there were two sides to William Robinson's early disputes with the senior missionaries. Robinson pleaded his case with Fuller in a letter dated 17 December 1807:

> I am sorry to have to say such a thing, but it is the truth, that the elder brethren have treated the younger with so much unkindness and severity, that they have weaned the affections of the younger, in a great measure, from them. There is not a younger brother in the whole Mission but what has been wounded to the very quick, with the conduct of the elder ones towards him. You must, dear Sir, before this, have had some hints given you relative to these things, in the letters of some of the junior brethren, though they may not have spoken very plainly on the subject. I had not been here many weeks before I was convinced that the conceptions which I and many others had formed of the Mission family were totally wrong. Brother Chater said on one occasion [...] concerning the elder brethren, these men

---

Fuller further wrote concerning Robinson: "I fear this man will do no good anywhere." See, E. Carey, *Supplement to the Vindication*, 77.

[51] Robinson, "Memoir of the Rev. William Robinson," 329.
[52] E. Carey, *Supplement to the Vindication*, 77.

seem to say, 'we are the men and wisdom shall die with us.' Brother Moore once wrote a letter to the brethren of the Mission, wishing them to dismiss him. Brother Rowe once told brother Marshman to his face that, if brother Carey was dead, he would not stay in the Mission another day.[53]

Robinson's comments indicate the problems were far wider than a disagreement between him personally and the Trio: there were significant issues between the senior missionaries and other "junior brethren." Regarding those he mentioned, William Moore (1776-1844) arrived in Serampore in 1804 but struggled to learn Bengali—he displayed an "incapability" with respect to languages, according to Cox—and his relationship with the original Trio became increasingly fraught.[54] James Chater, who had journeyed to Bengal with Robinson, and Joshua Rowe (1781-1823), also found it difficult to integrate into the tight-knit community at Serampore, dominated as it was by the high ideals and strong personalities of the Trio. That they were unhappy is significant, as they were far more irenic and peaceable than the hot-tempered Robinson. Tellingly, they both fared better away from Serampore. Rowe served at Digha, where he worked in apparent harmony with William and Eleanor Moore (1776-1812), and Hannah Biss (née Osmund) (1776-1818).[55] Chater went first to Burma and then settled in Ceylon (Sri Lanka), where he established Sinhala-speaking churches, labored in Bible translation, and pioneered educational establishments.[56]

The specific mention of Marshman respecting Joshua Rowe's unhappiness is worthy of further comment. Robinson and his colleagues certainly had problems with Ward and even struggled with the quiet, scholarly Carey, but it was Marshman whom they regarded as their bête noire. The

---

[53] Robinson to Andrew Fuller, December 1807, in E. Carey, *Supplement to the Vindication*, 155-156.

[54] Cox, *BMS*, I, 417.

[55] Cox, *BMS*, I, 203, 229; E.M. Jackson, "Joshua Rowe," in *Dictionary of Evangelical Biography 1730-1860* (DEB), ed. Donald M. Lewis (2 vols; Oxford: Blackwell, 1995), 2:957. William Moore married Hannah Biss in 1813. In 1818 he married Anne Clarke (1800-1843). Edward S. Wenger, "The Rev. William Moore," *Missionary Biographies*, II, 24. Mss. CLRC, Serampore.

[56] See Cox, *BMS*, I, 225, 231; *DEB*, 1:217.

primary issues were his unwillingness to listen to new ideas and be challenged, his general inflexibility, the high demands he placed on new colleagues regarding, for example, language learning and sacrificial living, and his intolerance of those who failed to meet his standards in every particular. Ward himself confided in Fuller that his friend and colleague was "too volatile and has too much quicksilver in him."[57] Carey, no stranger to hard work himself, described Marshman's "labours" as "excessive, his body scarcely susceptible of fatigue, his religious feelings strong, his jealousy for God great, his regard to the failings of others very little, when the cause of God is in question."[58] This is perceptive. Regarding Statement Ten of the SFA, Marshman could be regarded as exemplifying some of its clauses and as being deficient in others. There is ample evidence that he gave himself to prayer for the progress of the Mission, he had a more than "competent knowledge" of local languages, and he had many other gifts which were deployed in the service of the mission, for instance, in education.[59] He was willing to give his all for the cause and had the mindset of a missionary pioneer rather than a pastor: no bad thing given his particular calling. But the evidence also suggests that the "mild and winning temper" which Robinson failed to exhibit was not displayed by Marshman either. Perhaps he is the supreme example of a central contention of Statement Ten: godliness is more important than giftedness. It is important to stress that Marshman had a great heart for God and the gospel and that the younger missionaries, such as Robinson, were also at fault for their disputes with him. But his character was flawed, and he seemed unable to address the issues. One of the original signatories of the SFA struggled to live out one of its central tenets.

Reconciliation between Robinson and Joshua Marshman

There is a postscript to these stories of relational breakdown, however. Robinson eventually mellowed and became closer to the founding fathers of Serampore, a process that was facilitated by Marshman. The younger

---

[57] Ward to Andrew Fuller, October 7, 1805, as cited in Potts, *British Baptist Missionaries*, 20.
[58] Carey to Andrew Fuller, August 2, 1811, as cited in Potts, *British Baptist Missionaries*, 21.
[59] For evidence, see Cox, *BMS*, I, 196, *PA*, II (1804), 395 (prayer); *PA*, II (1804), 456; III (1808), 491 (translation); *PA*, II (1804), 498–499 (education).

The Serampore Form of Agreement

man returned to Calcutta in 1825 and was given the pastorate of Lal Bazaar Chapel, which had earlier been established by the Trio. That Marshman gave up some of his own responsibilities as co-pastor to accommodate Robinson suggests that the older man was changing his attitude toward his junior colleague. During Robinson's pastorate, there was a further rapprochement between him, Marshman and Carey (Ward had died before Robinson's return to Calcutta). Relations were increasingly warm: Carey even made Robinson an executor of his will, and he became "one of Carey's most valued coadjutors."[60] In fact, he established himself as Marshman and Carey's advocate as relationships soured not only between them and other recent recruits but also with the home committee after Fuller's death in 1815. Trust was gradually restored. If Robinson had desired a role at the heart of Serampore, then his wish had at last been granted.

A prayer meeting that took place when the Mission was struggling at the beginning of the 1830s is further evidence of the strong relationships which had developed by then. Serampore was troubled with some severe financial difficulties, and it was hard to see how they could continue to operate. Marshman, Carey, and Robinson came together with others to plead with God for the life of the Mission, especially for Serampore College, which had been established in 1818 and faced financial ruin. Robinson described the meeting thus:

> The two old men (Carey and Marshman) were dissolved in tears while they engaged in prayer, and Dr. Marshman in particular, could not give expression to his feelings. It was indeed affecting to see these good old men, the fathers of the mission, entreating with tears that God would not forsake them now grey hairs were come upon them, but that He would silence the tongue of calumny, and furnish them with the means of carrying on His own cause.[61]

At this crucial juncture, they were "united" in prayer as the SFA had envisaged many years previously.

---

[60] S.P. Carey, *William Carey* (1934), 431.
[61] Marshman, *Life and Times*, II, 424. Cf. S.P. Carey, *William Carey*, rev. edn., 386.

Statement Ten

Hannah Marshman

Although Hannah Marshman was present in Bengal as a "missionary wife" as far as the BMS home committee was concerned, she more than deserves the epithet "missionary." She had arrived in India in October 1799 along with her husband and served with distinction for nearly 48 years, despite the indifferent health which necessitated her one and only return to England in 1820-1821. Her work in women's education is quite rightly described as "pioneering" by George Howells.[62] By 1824 there were 160 Indian girls attending six schools, a ministry she developed while working alongside her husband in other schools and continuing to play a lead role in the running of the large and complex missionary household in Serampore.

She was deeply committed to prayer and personal devotion. In a letter to a friend in Bristol in 1804, she shared her hope that people in England would be stirred to pray for them, expressed her belief in God's sovereignty, and told of the progress made by her schools. She delighted in biblical preaching and new converts joining the church. The letter is full of Scripture references and allusions. Her commitment to "earnest prayer" "for his kingdom to come, and his will to be done on earth" is stated explicitly. She also speaks of the vital importance of "sanctification," with holiness and prayer explicitly linked: "we pray for sanctification."[63] Hannah Marshman is one of those who lived out the principles that took their place at the heart of the SFA.

Hannah's devotion was displayed in death as well as in life. On 3 March 1847, she lay on her deathbed, with the Principal of Serampore College, W. H. Denham, at her side. Though dying, Hannah managed to summon the strength to say, "Where is Bunyan's Pilgrim?" A copy of *The Pilgrim's Progress* by John Bunyan was close by, and Denham held it in front of her so she could see it. According to him, Hannah asked him to read from the section which describes how "Christian" crosses the "River of Death." This he proceeded to do. At Hannah's funeral service, which took place

---

[62] George Howells, *The Story of Serampore and its College* (Serampore/Cuttack: Orissa Mission Press, 1927), 11.

[63] Hannah Marshman to Mrs Clarke of Bristol, 4 June 1804, in *PA*, II (1804), 527-528. Cf. Matthew 6: 10.

on 14 March, Denham spoke of this incident, saying that the passage from *The Pilgrim's Progress*,

> which seemed to affect her most was the [one] where Christian begins to sink and Hopeful encourages him ... As I read I paused, for she occasionally spoke on the circumstances recorded ... At her wish we turned to Christian's removal and the remaining characters. That of Steadfast and his last words appeared to interest her greatly... I could read no more. I knelt down and prayed that her feet like his might stand fast in that dread hour.[64]

Thus, in death she was inspired by one of the works that was part of her spiritual heritage, surrounded by "fervent, believing prayer" as she faced this final challenge to faith, and displayed the deep "personal godliness" so prized by Statement Ten of the SFA.

Conclusion

Statement Ten, with its emphasis on intercessory prayer for the work in India and its concomitant stress on missional discipleship, is a keystone of the SFA. It was shaped decisively by the evangelical currents which had flowed into English Particular Baptist life from the middle of the eighteenth century onwards. Especially influential were the theology and spirituality of Jonathan Edwards. Unsurprisingly, the missionaries did not always live up to the ideals that were set out in this challenging section of the agreement. However, many of the BMS personnel maintained an evangelical missional spirituality, doing so over many years and often in extremely trying circumstances. Whatever mistakes they made, their faith and commitment were truly remarkable.

This story is relevant for those embarking on cross-cultural mission today and, indeed, for those who engage in any form of evangelistic mission. The BMS missionaries were sure that if they did not prioritize prayer and personal godliness, then God would not be glorified, and their pioneering

---

[64] W.H. Denham, "Memoir of the Late Mrs Marshman," in *Baptist Magazine* 39 (August 1847) (London: Houlston and Stoneman, 1847), 481–482.

Statement Ten

mission venture would fail. These core convictions are surely true today as they were then.

STATEMENT ELEVEN

Lives on the Altar

Johan Kommers

Write the vision; make it plain on tablets, so he may run who reads it.[1]

In 1793, when William Carey (1761-1834) anchored off India's shore, he was among the first of the thousands of illustrious, faithful servants of God who, throughout the nineteenth century, went out to China, India, and Africa. These men—and women—were mostly simple people, driven by an apostolic faith and love. The first decades of that century saw a wave of pioneering Christian missionary initiatives. This movement flowed from a deepening of spiritual life, a new flowering of the old religion in a society chilled by Enlightenment thought.

Students from prestigious universities gave up promising careers in response to God's call. Thousands of single women set out for the Far East and Africa: to "the regions beyond." Selfless and humble, they committed themselves entirely to God. They combined muscular Christianity with radiant godliness. What was their secret? They consecrated their lives to the Savior and His service in places worldwide. They were driven by a passion that the people to whom they were called might come to know their Savior.[2]

---

[1] Habakkuk 2:2 (ESV).

[2] For example: Hudson Taylor (1832-1905), the founder of the China Inland Mission, said "The sun has never risen upon China without finding me at prayer." Howard Taylor, *Hudson Taylor and the China Inland Mission* (London: The China Inland Mission, 1918), 624.

The Serampore Form of Agreement

"This glorious goal"

On January 10, 1800, Carey took up residence at Serampore. After several years in India, he knew he lived in a "Land of Darkness."[3] Despite many difficulties, he remained focused on the primary purpose of missionary work, the "glorification of God." They achieved this goal by striving "by every means possible to bring non-Christians to the knowledge of the Savior, to set an infinite value upon immortal souls, to spread the knowledge of the name of the Savior."[4]

In 1805, together with other missionaries at Serampore, Carey agreed upon eleven great statements formulated by William Ward to guide the Mission. This document is known as the *Serampore Form of Agreement* (SFA). The SFA built on an initial agreement in 1800 but provided a more solid spiritual basis than the original document. According to Brian Stanley, the SFA is the "covenantal basis for the Serampore mission community."[5] In the SFA, we find a passionate document full of Biblical gems that adorn the missionary's goals.

The eleven statements in the SFA are based on Biblical foundations and emphasize as a primary policy objective the use of the spiritual gifts of the Indian converts. For Carey, 1805 was "on several accounts the most successful year of the Mission, since its commencement." Native workers were beginning to engage in the work, and he could see "an increase of true piety among them."[6] In India, the Serampore missionaries followed practices that had earlier contributed to the rise of Nonconformity in England. In the 18th century, uneducated preachers in England clashed with the Anglican church by preaching without a license from the magistrates. Carey began his ministry among these evangelical dissenters. He joined a small dissenting congregation and underwent adult baptism. In 1785, without

---

[3] Terry G. Carter, ed., *The Journal and Selected letters of William Carey* (Macon, GA: Smyth & Helwys, 2000), 8.

[4] In A. H. Oussoren, *William Carey Especially His Missionary Principles* (Leiden: Sijthoff, 1945), 270–271.

[5] Brian Stanley, "Planting Self-Governing Churches: British Baptist Ecclesiology in the Missionary Context" *Baptist Quarterly* 34, no 8, (1992): 379.

[6] In a letter from Carey to Sutcliffe, January 1, 1806, in Carter, *Carey's Journal and Letters*, 158.

formal training, he was given an opportunity and a pittance to preach as a Baptist. Given this sacrificial approach to ministry, it is unsurprising that Carey was impressed by the mission work of the Moravians, who lived a very sober life and focused on preaching Christ.[7] Once on the field, the Serampore missionaries did not have a fixed salary, although native evangelists who went out as itinerant preachers received a monthly allowance.[8]

"Let us ... "

In every generation, missionaries ask which method is most relevant. Statement Eleven has five sentences starting with "Let us ... ." Herewith the Serampore missionaries express their readiness to fulfill their mission commitment in practice. Their missionary method was intentional, propelled by a longing to bring the Word of God to the hearts and homes of the Indian people. This method emphasized the role of native speakers as evangelists in overcoming barriers to the Gospel.

Craig Ott states, "Missionaries tend to be characterized by two qualities: theological conservatism and methodological pragmatism."[9] The SFA is constructed on sound Biblical principles. This includes the final article in which dependency upon God provides a foundation for mission work. At Serampore, there was no intention to do the work relying on short-sighted, quick fixes. It was not a choice between Biblical or pragmatic; instead, it was both biblical and practical.

Carey's description of a typical workday from August 1, 1800, provides a glimpse of the practical nature of the work: "Our labours for every day are now regularly arranged. About six o'clock we rise; brother Carey to his garden; brother Marshman to his school at seven; brother Brunsdon, Felix, and I, to the printing-office. At eight the bell rings for family worship: we assemble in the hall; sing, read, and pray. Breakfast."[10] The passage goes on to describe the affairs of the day. They were without a compositor in

---

[7] Cf. David A. Schattschneider, "William Carey, Modern Missions, and the Moravian Influence" *International Bulletin of Missionary Research* 22, no.1 (1998): 8–12.

[8] See Carey's letter to the Mission Society, August 5, 1807, in Carter, *Carey's Journal and Letters*, 185.

[9] Craig Ott and J. D. Payne, eds., *Missionary Methods: Research, Reflections, and Realities* (Pasadena, CA: William Carey Library, 2013), 265.

[10] George Smith, *The Life of William Carey, D.D.: Shoemaker and Missionary* (London: John Murray, 1885), 128.

The Serampore Form of Agreement

the print shop and had to make do without. Carey spent the day in translation. Marshman in teaching school. He mentions conversations with a Brahmin, meals spent together, the help of his son Felix in the office, preaching in Bengali, and many other details of the daily life of the mission.

The power behind their mission work came from the interposition of God answering prayer. In prayer, they toiled for the salvation of the people of Bengal. Surrounded by devilish practices, opposition, interpersonal conflicts, and family issues, they were aware of their need for God. In line with Count Zinzendorf (1700-1760), love for God and compassion for the people guided their lives. The Serampore missionaries joined Word and deed in seamless unity. Statement Eight of the SFA expressed this unity, "Let us therefore use every gift, and continually urge on our native brethren to press upon their countrymen the glorious gospel of the blessed God."

Earlier, on December 26, 1793, Carey had written that, despite the little success he had seen, he was far from being discouraged, "and should I never succeed, yet I am resolved in the strength of the Lord Jesus and live and Die persisting in this work, - and I never give it up but with my Liberty or Life."[11] The last statement of the SFA may leave the impression of overstressed activity. Still, precisely at this point, the SFA urges the missionaries to search their motives and "watch continually against a worldly spirit and cultivate a Christian indifference towards every indulgence." By failing here, they believed they "would be unable to glorify God with our bodies and spirits which are His."

"Praeparatio Evangelica"

Love and passion for the Gospel motivated the nine missionaries who signed the SFA. The document described how and why the glorious Name of Jesus Christ should be made known in India. The basic principles and values documented in the SFA guided the Serampore missionaries and were meant to be a training manual for future generations of missionaries.

In 1884, the historian George Smith claimed "That the agreement embodies the divine principles of all Protestant scriptural missions. It is still a

---

[11] Carey to Ryland, Bandel, Dec. 26, 1793. Carter, *Carey's Journal and Letters*, 69.

manual to be daily pondered by every missionary, and every Church and Society which may send one forth."[12] In 1891, Arthur T. Pierson (1837-1911) agreed with Smith's evaluation of the literary, educational, and societal achievements of the Serampore Mission. Pierson believed that as "indirect results of the work of Carey and his beloved associates, can be best expressed as the *Praeparatio Evangelica*," that enabled the Indian church to grow to "half a million souls" fifty years after Carey's death.[13]

For Pierson, the American Bible teacher and mission catalyst, the Agreement read "like an inspired paper. The marks of the Holy Ghost are upon it."[14] A passionately written covenant that boldly underlined their goals, nine missionaries of the British Baptist Missionary Society, committed themselves "unreservedly to this glorious goal"—to reach the unreached.

"All things through Him"

In comparison with the agreement of 1800,[15] the SFA of 1805 builds on a more solid spiritual basis:

> We know nothing in the history of missions, monastic or evangelical, which at all approaches this in administrative perfectness as well as in Christ-like self-sacrifice. It prevents secularisation of spirit, stimulates activity of all kinds, gives full scope to local ability and experience, calls forth the maximum of local support and propagation, sets the church at home free to enter incessantly on new fields, provides permanence as well as variety of action and

---

[12] Quoted from George Smith, *Short History of Christian Missions, from Abraham and Paul to Carey, Livingstone, and Duff* (Edinburgh: T. & T. Clark, 1884), in Arthur Tappan Pierson, *The Divine Enterprise of Missions. A Series of Lectures...* (New York: The Baker & Taylor Co., 1891), 220.

[13] Smith, *Short History of Christian Missions*, 164.

[14] Pierson, *The Divine Enterprise*, 222.

[15] John Clark Marshman, *The Life and Times of Carey, Marshman, and Ward. Embracing the History of the Serampore Mission* (London: Longman, Brown, Green, Longmans, & Roberts, 1859), I, 124-125. For a reference to "the original agreement made when we united in 1800, which recognized the support of the widow as one of its leading principles," see Joshua Marshman, *Statement relative to Serampore, supplementary to a "Brief Memoir" with introductory observations by John Foster* (London: Parbury, Allen & Co., 1828), 78-80. For its implications on finance, see below.

The Serampore Form of Agreement

adaptation to new circumstances, and binds the whole in a holy bond of prayerful co-operation and loving fellowship.[16]

The final statement in the SFA alludes to Philippians 4:1-19 and 2 Timothy 2:3, in which the missionary Paul gives us insight into his others-oriented life, e.g., a life in fellowship with Jesus. At Serampore, they remained dependent upon God's provision. They often felt the need for finances, food, and other materials. Carey had known severe poverty in England and the first years in India. When he was joined by William Ward,[17] a printer, and Joshua and Hannah Marshman, educators, the financial struggles diminished considerably. Ward took government printing contracts, the Marshmans opened schools, and Carey taught languages at Fort William College in nearby Calcutta.

Through their translation work and evangelism, the Serampore men and women established a method that became a model for 19th-century Evangelical missions. They were convinced that local men and women had to do the work. In their view, India could best be reached by Indians, who were ready to cooperate with the missionaries and take the lead in many circumstances. These missionaries were not—as often happens—as spiders in the mission web. They readily delegated work to their native colleagues.

From the beginning, the Serampore missionaries worked alongside their indigenous colleagues. They functioned as *dubashis*, "'go-betweens' or conduits for information flowing between two civilizations." They "constituted and constructed infrastructural networks necessary for two-way transmissions of information between India and the West."[18] All the

---

[16] Smith, *Life of William Carey*, 129-130.

[17] For Ward as the composer of the SFA, see A. Christopher Smith, "The Legacy of William Ward and Joshua and Hannah Marshman" *International Bulletin of Missionary Research* 23, no. 3 (1999): 125-126.

[18] Robert Eric Frykenberg, *Christianity in India: From Beginnings to the Present* (Oxford: Oxford University Press, 2008), 142. Editors' note: While the term *dubashi* (intermediary) was mainly used in South India, Calcutta was known for its *banians* who fulfilled a similar role as dubashis in trade relations. See Susan Neild-Basu "The Dubashes of Madras," *Modern Asian Studies* 18, I (1984), 1-31. For the sake of the author's argument, Hindu *munshis* like Ramram Basu (c1757-1813) and *pandits* like Mrityunjoy Vidyalankar (c1762-1819), who assisted Carey at Fort William College, and Christian traders such as Ignatius Fernandez (1757-1830), Michael Derozio (1742-

Statement Eleven

work, either teaching, translating, preaching, or literature, could not have been done without the faithful role of native non-christian and Christian *dubashis*. The origin of these Christian coworkers in Serampore and the Tranquebar mission can be traced to the German city of Halle, where Evangelical Pietism and Enlightenment thought were blended into an explosive missionary movement.[19] Zinzendorf and the Brüdergemeinde began the Royal Dänisch-Hallesche Mission, which gave rise to more individualistic forms of missionary voluntarism. The mission reached the shores of India in 1706. It settled in Tranquebar in 1730 and expanded to Travancore and Serampore in the 1770s and other parts of India after that.[20] Frykenberg concludes "that the functions and roles of *dubashi* Christians, whether Europeans or native Indians, were essentially, inherently, and intrinsically-infrastructural. [...] they 'were but intermediary agents.'" In later times, *dubashis* often were used "to bring literacy in the 'mother tongue access' to the humblest folk."[21]

The influence of the Christian *dubashis* had been encouraged by the Serampore missionaries, for they had observed that *dubashis* evangelized, taught, and trained local individuals or small groups.[22] They provided knowledge and elements from which a more truly indigenous form of

---

1809), Peter Lindeman (1771-1856), fulfilled the role of *dubashis* for the Serampore Mission. Sunil Kumar Chatterjee, "Ignatius Fernandez" in *William Carey and Serampore*, 2nd edn. (Sheoraphuli: S.K. Chatterjee, Laserplus, 2004), 134-164. Edward S. Wenger, *The Story of the Lall Bazar Baptist Church, Calcutta* (Calcutta: Edinburgh Press, 1908), 41-43. Sakti Sadhan Mukhopadhyay, *Derozio: His Background and Cultural Milieu. A Collection of Sources and Documents* (Kolkata: Kidderpore College, 2008).

[19] For the role of Halle, August H. Francke, Von Zinzendorf and the emergence of the Evangelical missionary movement see, Erich Beyreuther, *Geschichte des Pietismus* (Stuttgart: J. F. Steinkopf Verlag, 1978), 123-227, 331-350. Martin Schmidt, *Pietismus* (Stuttgart/ Köln: Verlag W. Kohlhammer, 1972), 93-108.

[20] J. E. Hutton, *A History of Moravian Missions* (London: Moravian Publication Office, 1922), 5, 165, 188, 202. The Moravians Johannes Grassman and Karl F. Schmidt ran a mission in Serampore beginning in 1777 which they abandoned in 1792 prior to Carey's arrival. Krishna Pal, the first baptized Bengali convert, was first introduced to the Gospel by them. E. Daniel Potts, *British Baptist Missionaries in India, 1793-1837: The History of Serampore and its Mission* (London: Cambridge University Press, 1967), 5. S. Pearce Carey, *William Carey, D.D., Fellow of the Linnaean Society* (London: Hodder and Stoughton, 1923), 186, 189, 194.

[21] In Frykenberg, *Christianity in India*, 166.

[22] Two converts from the Writers caste fit the term: Tara-Chand and his brother Mut'hoora of Bansberia, who ran a school to support themselves as evangelists, and functioned as an independent church. *PA*, V (1813), 197-198; 201-203; 215, 234; 336, 341.

The Serampore Form of Agreement

Christianity would emerge in India. "It was they whose conversions turned previous cultures and convictions. It was they whose conversions turned previous ways of life upside down, even if only for themselves."[23] Fifty years, after Carey's death, in 1884, the Protestant community in India numbered half a million "with ordained native pastors outnumbering the missionaries, and every decade witnessing an increase at the rate of eighty-six percent."[24]

Simplicity of Life: The New Testament Pattern

The SFA, which regulated the missionary brotherhood's social economy and spiritual enterprise, deserves a thorough study for its divine disinterestedness, lofty aims, and kindly common sense. Carey and his colleagues believed mission work should follow the New Testament pattern. This work required men and women who took the words of Jesus literally and heeded what the Holy Spirit was saying to the churches. This produced apostolic power and apostolic results. The missionaries understood there would be significant cultural differences, but they "observe[d] with admiration" the apostle Paul, "the great champion for the glorious doctrines of free and sovereign grace [...] a noble example for our imitation."[25] The apostle Paul's readiness to become all things to all men that he might by any means save some, and his willingness to abstain from necessary comforts so that he might not offend the weak, were a guiding beacon.

They understood their vocation as identification with Christ's suffering and the cross. The cross provided a standard for judging their motivations because God's mission is cross-shaped. They had come to India for His name. Through the cross, the door opened to a world in need. Carey admired the Moravians for their "God-like work of Mission," especially for their "Zeal-Labour-Perseverance-[and] success."[26] Since the Serampore Mission drew on the example of the Moravians,[27] it is not strange that in

---

[23] Frykenberg, *Christianity in India*, 168. In 2013 it was estimated that in India, missionary *dubashis*—numbered between 40.000 and 100.000—all native born Indians. Their work can "result in explosive new movements in the future," 168.
[24] Pierson, *The Divine Enterprise*, 222-223.
[25] In the introduction to the *Serampore Form of Agreement*.
[26] Carey to Society Dec. 9, 1797. Carter, *Carey's Journal and Letters*, 74.
[27] See below.

Statement Eleven

the Agreement, we see traces of Count Zinzendorf's prayer that "Christ would draw him into the 'fellowship of Christ's sufferings.'" The *raison d'être* of the Serampore Mission was the love of God in Christ and the devotion to the slain yet conquering Lamb of God, Jesus Christ. At Serampore, they offered people the simple life-changing Gospel, and in it, all other gifts.

The Spiritual Existence

Carey enjoyed an intimate fellowship with God. In dependence upon God, he derived his strength, hope, and perseverance from his heavenly Master, Who keeps His promises. Carey knew his imperfections; "My soul is in general barren and unfruitful."[28] Yet, he could balance this self-knowledge against his understanding of divine character; "O what a portion is God, and what a shame that I am not always satisfied with Him."[29] That understanding gave relief amid many difficulties, "Towards Evening had a pleasant View of the all sufficiency of God, and the stability of his promises which much relieved my mind—and as I walked in the Night, was enabled to roll my Soul, and all my Cares in some measure on God [...] What a mercy it is to have a God."[30]

The Serampore missionaries had crossed the sea, but an extended voyage was never enough to make a missionary of a man or woman. The goal of mission work cannot be reached if missionaries are not ready to give up everything for the Gospel. So many die daily without hearing the glorious Gospel tidings. In England, Carey had met the indifference of many to the need of the Indians for the Gospel. Driven by the passion for Christ, Carey believed no effort should be spared to reach the people. But workers with a Moravian spirit were needed, "We want more missionaries, Men of mild Temper, good sense, and genuine love to our Lord, and Zeal for his Glory."[31] As John Thomas—Carey's colleague—writing to Fuller put it, "Do send men full of compassion here, where many perish with cold, many for lack of bread, and millions for 'lack of knowledge.'" Vividly,

---

[28] Journal, Aug. 27, 1794. Carter, *Carey's Journal and Letters*, 39.
[29] Journal, Jan. 28, 1794. Carter, *Carey's Journal and Letters*, 14.
[30] Journal, Jan. 17, 1794. Carter, *Carey's Journal and Letters*, 9.
[31] Carey to Society, Hooghly River, Jan 10, 1799. Carter, *Carey's Journal and Letters*, 201.

Thomas described the scene, "Oh miserable sight! I have found the pathways stopped up by sick and wounded people, perishing with hunger and distress, and that in a populous neighbourhood, where plenty of people pass by, some singing, others talking, but none showing any more compassion than as though they were dying weeds, and not dying men."[32]

A worldly spirit would distract the Serampore missionaries from their first aim to glorify God with their bodies and spirit. While never distracted from the well-being of the people, they had their windows open toward Jerusalem and not the earthly city. Worldly entanglements were incompatible with spiritual power.

Oussoren remarks that the glory of God is not mentioned *expressis verbis* as the ultimate goal of mission. And that Carey "did not see the vertical line" in his missionary work, for his mission purpose seemed to be "more anthropocentric than theocentric."[33] However, his letters show that he not only focused on making converts and fostering a Christian society. As a Calvinist, Carey sought to glorify God in all he undertook.[34]

Faith and Finance: "Well, I have God."

Financial support has always been a complicated issue in mission circles. The American Mission statesman, Rufus Anderson (1796-1880) frankly

---

[32] C. B. Lewis, *The Life of John Thomas, Surgeon of the Earl of Oxford East Indiaman, and First Baptist Missionary to Bengal* (London: MacMillan and Co., 1873), 405-406. Cf. Amy Carmichael who wrote 150 years later, "Would people not be stirred to go and tell the Good News when they would know that in India alone, 28 000 people a day go to their death without Christ." And writing about Christians seeking an easy life: "Surely we should not deliberately leave so many to starve to death, because those who have the Bread of Life have strong desire for sweets. Oh, the spiritual confectionary consumed every year in England! … It is the utter earnestness of purpose to be wholly on the altar of our Lord that speaks to me, the earnestness in 'downing the I.'" Quoted in J. Hans Kommers, *Triumphant Love: The Contextual, Creative and Strategic Missionary Work of Amy Beatrice Carmichael in South India* (Eugene, OR: Wipf and Stock, 2020), 441.

[33] Oussoren, *William Carey*, 271.

[34] "In our Churches we have both encouraging and discouraging things and probably always shall. But our Lord Jesus Christ is head over all things to the Church, which is his Body, and I therefore have no doubt but he will so order all things that the final result will be the establishment of his own cause, and thereby acquiring a tribute of praise and glory to himself." Carey to his Sisters, Serampore, Feb 21, 1831. B.M.S. Mss. Angus Library, Regent's Park College, Oxford. Cf. Johannes Van den Berg, *Constrained by Jesus' Love: An Enquiry into the Motives of the Missionary Awakening in Great Britain in the Period between 1698 and 1815* (Kampen: J. H. Kok, 1956), 155-156.

Statement Eleven

admitted that among the missionaries themselves, "most of the questions that arise have more or less connection with finance."[35] Dire poverty marked William Carey's first years in India. When he took work as an indigo planter to provide for his family, some members of the Baptist Missionary Society were scandalized. Perceptions were shaped by the notorious profiteering associated with the British colonial enterprise. The temptation was always present. Private trade and preaching Christ seemed incompatible. Ward wrote in Statement Eleven that turning to private trade meant "the mission is from that hour a lost cause."

Nonetheless, given the inadequate support from home, the Serampore missionaries would see no other option than self-support. Each of the original members of the Serampore Mission contributed through their labor. Carey taught at Fort William College. The Marshman's schools provided another income stream. And Ward contributed by taking outside printing jobs. For this reason, when the Serampore community adopted the original set of rules in 1800, they included a statement on finances:

> This week we have adopted a set of rules for the government of the family. All preach and pray in turn; one superintends the affairs of the family for a month, and then another; brother Carey is treasurer, and has the regulation of the medicine chest; brother Fountain is librarian. Saturday evening is devoted to adjusting differences, and pledging ourselves to love one another. One of our resolutions is, that no one of us do engage in private trade; but that all be done for the benefit of the mission.[36]

In financial matters, the Serampore missionaries determined to live by a lofty standard: absolute dependence on the providence of God. This meant they abstained from going into debt, except for short periods when

---

[35] Rufus Anderson, *Foreign Missions: their Relations and Claims* (New York: Charles Scribner and Company, 1869), 159.

[36] Smith, *Life of Carey*, 127-128, quoted from entry Saturday, Jan. 18, 1800. *Ward's Journal*, I, 66.

The Serampore Form of Agreement

they purchased property.[37] Of the borrowing system among the native people in India, George Smith, Carey's biographer, wrote, "There is one evil which Carey never ceased to point out [...] the borrowing system of the natives."[38] Smith complained, "While 12 per cent is the so-called legal rate of interest, it is never below 36, and more frequently rises to 72 per cent."[39] Carey's solution was to encourage the practice of saving, and he and Marshman were prime movers in introducing savings banks in India.[40]

Statement Eleven of the SFA documents the missionaries' view of personal finances:

> Let us for ever shut out the idea of laying up a cowry[41] for ourselves or our children. If we give up the resolution which was formed on the subject of private trade when we first united at Serampore, the mission is from that hour a lost cause. A worldly spirit, quarrels, and every evil work will succeed, the moment it is admitted that each brother may do something on his own account. Woe to that man who shall ever make the smallest movement toward such a measure!

The Serampore missionaries were motivated by the example of David Brainerd (1718-1747) to give themselves unreservedly with heart and soul to missionary work. In April 1794, six months after he arrived in India, Carey wrote, "April 14: Still a time of Enjoyment of God; I feel that it is good to commit my Soul, my Body, and my all into the Hands of God, Then the World appears little, the Promises great; and God an all sufficient

---

[37] Marshman, *Life and Times*, I, 128. In the middle of the 19th century, James Hudson Taylor, the founder of the China Inland Mission, strongly advocated against borrowing money for mission work. The CIM (since 1951 OMF) never asked for money nor incurred debt.

[38] Smith, *Life of Carey*, 323-324. The failure of the Indian banks in 1830-1833 was largely due to "the rottenness of the system of credit on which commerce and banking were at that time conducted." (412).

[39] Smith, *Life of Carey*, 324.

[40] [J. Marshman], "Bank for Savings applied to India," *Friend of India* (Monthly) II (1819), 73-83. Marshman, *Life and Times*, II, 223.

[41] A *cowry* or *cowrie* is a small shell, the smallest form of exchange used in nations around the Indian Ocean.

Statement Eleven

Portion. [...] April 19: no Earthly thing to depend upon, or Earthly comfort; except Food and Raiment; Well I have God."[42]

Popularization of the Diakonia

Pietism influenced mission principles at Serampore. This movement, emphasizing spiritual renewal and holy living, was often at risk of neglecting social concerns. However, focusing on cultural issues, the Serampore missionaries developed an un-pietistic way of doing mission work.[43] They attempted to win souls for Christ, but also to touch the people's history, customs, habits, and thoughts. Carey understood the commission of the Lord as a command to seek individuals, but in relation to the nation and family in which God placed them.[44] As Carey explained in an address attended by the Governor-General, Lord Wellesley, "This close intercourse with the natives for so long a period ... has afforded me opportunities of information not inferior to those which have hitherto been presented to any other person. I may say indeed that their manners, customs, habits and sentiments, are as obvious to me, as if I were myself a native."[45]

The Dutch missiologist, J.H. Bavinck (1895-1964), agreed with Carey's approach when he wrote that "Mission is the activity of the church throughout the whole world, which in the deepest essence is an activity of Christ himself, through which it calls the nations in their diversity to faith and obedience to Jesus Christ."[46]

In the Victorian era, evangelism and social concerns were rarely divorced. In Germany, Johann Hinrich Wichern (1808-1881) and Theodor Fliedner (1800-1864) initiated a work of evangelism and social action in which many men and women participated. The term *diakonia* was popularized to refer to work among the delinquent, displaced, illiterate, and

---

[42] "From Carey's Unpublished Diary—1794." *The Banner of Truth*, Issue 177 (June 1978): 8-9. Carter, *Carey's Journal and Letters*, 25-26.

[43] Oussoren, *William Carey*, 1.

[44] Oussoren, *William Carey*, 189.

[45] Translation of Carey's Sanskrit Speech in 1804, extracted from [Claudius Buchanan], *Primitiae Orientalis: containing the theses in the Oriental languages; pronounced at the public disputations ... by students of the College of Fort William in Bengal with translations* (Calcutta: College Fort William, 1804), III, 116. In Smith, *Life of Carey*, 224; Oussoren, *William Carey*, 90.

[46] See the full text of Bavinck's definition in Paul J. Visser, *Heart for the Gospel, Heart for the World. The Life and Thought of a Reformed Pioneer Missiologist Johan Herman Bavinck, 1895-1964* (Eugene, OR: Wipf and Stock, 2003), 216.

sick. Houses were founded to train missionaries for evangelism and missions overseas. Fliedner especially emphasized the role of single women and widows to apply in this work. In America, women played a heroic role in the revolution. The world around them interested them—they sought education, and, in religious affairs, they often acted with more zeal than the men. These women were called to a worldwide gospel service. One great exemplar, Amy Carmichael of Dohnavur, India, said that God's work is not only to preach and to teach but also to work with one's hands: "God didn't make you all mouth."[47]

The work at Serampore anticipated these later trends. The fate of the women burdened the Serampore missionaries, and Carey crusaded against the practice of *sati* (the ritual of a Hindu wife burning herself at her husband's funeral).[48] The need for female missionaries was acute. In middle-class and higher-status families, it was uncommon for wives to live outdoors. They mostly remained confined to the women's quarters of the house, called the *zenana*, where only husbands or brothers could enter. Mission organizations saw that male missionaries could have no contact with these women. In 1866, Marianne Lewis, a Baptist missionary in Calcutta, wrote *A Plea for Zenanas*, an appeal for mission organizations to send women to work full-time in the zenanas. The Zenana Mission, established under the auspices of the Baptist Missionary Society in 1867, offered women unique opportunities to enter mission work.[49]

How their role was seen initially is revealed in the 1842 jubilee meeting in Kettering in the brusque explanation of a Mr Brock: "Ladies, it is not yours to be supreme, it is ours. It is yours to obey. But though it is ours to be supreme, yet it is a supremacy in which there is to be nothing capricious, nothing tyrannical. You are not to be our drudges today, and our toys tomorrow. You are our companions, you are our helpmeets."[50] Within fifty

---

[47] Amy Carmichael, *Gold Cord: The Story of a Fellowship* (London: SPCK, 1932), 42.
[48] For his description of *Sati*, Carey to Ryland, Mudnabati, April 1, 1799. Carter, *Carey's Journal and Letters*, 79-80.
[49] Brian Stanley, *The History of the Baptist Missionary Society, 1792-1992* (Edinburgh: T&T Clark, 1992), 229.
[50] Stanley, *History of the BMS*, 228.

Statement Eleven

years, this tone had disappeared: "By 1890 over 60% of the American overseas mission force was female."[51] In the second part of the nineteenth century, single women served as deaconesses in the Anglican Church, as preachers among the Quakers and the Primitive Methodists, and as officers in the Salvation Army. When a missionary call was first given at the Keswick Convention, "it was women who were first to respond."[52] Paradoxically, in an age when female social submission was axiomatic, the missionary call to total surrender, expressed in Statement Ten of the SFA, provided women with a revolutionary outlet for their gifts and energies.

Personal Examples of Total Consecration

In 1804 Dorothy Carey began to lose her grip on reality.[53] Carey wrote to his father: "I and my family am, through the good care of God as well as I ever remember, except my poor wife who continues in the melancholy situation which she has long been in. You seem to think that the climate of this country has contributed to her derangement. I have no such idea."[54] Dorothy's decline represents one of the great tragedies of the Serampore Mission. One of the signatories of the SFA, Joshua Marshman, also suffered from severe depression. After his return from his visit to England, he had three major bouts.[55] Carey's eldest son Felix, also one of the SFA subscribers, wandered far from his faith for a time. His father wrote of Felix: "His departure from God has nearly broken my heart, may God restore him."[56]

---

[51] David W. Bebbington, *The Dominance of Evangelicalism: The Age of Spurgeon and Moody* (Leicester: Inter-Varsity Press, 2005), 211.

[52] David W. Bebbington, *Evangelicalism in Modern Britain. A history from the 1730s to the 1880s* (London: Routledge, 1989), 175.

[53] For the story of the tremendous sacrifice made by a woman in the cause of the world evangelization who has been unjustly treated by mission historians, see James R. Beck, *Dorothy Carey, The Tragic and Untold Story of Mrs. William Carey* (Grand Rapids, MI: Baker Book House, 1992).

[54] Letter from William Carey to his father, September 11, 1804. Beck, *Dorothy Carey*, 140.

[55] Beck, *Dorothy Carey*, 129.

[56] Letter of William Carey to Jabez Carey, January 20, 1816, B.M.S. Mss. Angus Library, Regent's Park College, Oxford.

The Serampore Form of Agreement

Before Carey's death in 1834, Norris Groves met him at Serampore.[57] He described the aged Dr. Carey as "sinking into the grave after more than forty years' service, leaving the world as poor, as to temporal things, as when he entered it. He leaves his widow and children, without a shilling, to the loving care of their brethren."[58] Groves described another Baptist couple as "very devoted, living most simply and returning not a little of their salary to the Society."[59] In this, they followed the example of Carey, who had been a professor of oriental languages at Fort William College. Most of his salary, he gave away, keeping only a fraction for his daily needs. His grave in Serampore bears simple words, adapted from a hymn by Isaac Watts, recalling the Evangelical experience of his youth in the far-off village Paulerspury: "A wretched, poor and helpless worm in Thy kind arms I fall."[60]

Our individualistic society focuses on the self. However, spiritual growth requires examples, people who exemplify what it means to believe in Jesus Christ: "Let the missionaries be men possessed of Gifts [...] gift of utterance or rather eloquence [...] a readiness to communicate knowledge to others, inward Godliness, meekness, and Zeal, are the principal."[61] Our current generation needs these historical examples of total consecration.

---

[57] Anthony Norris Groves (1795-1853) followed with his family God's call to Baghdad and India. Often called the "Father of Faith Missions," he is mentioned alongside William Carey and Hudson Taylor. See Robert Bernard Dann, *Father of Faith Missions. The Life and Times of Anthony Norris Groves* (Waynesboro, GA, Bletchley, UK: Authentic Media, 2004).

[58] Harriet Groves, *Memoir of the Late Anthony Norris Groves, containing Extracts from his Letters and Journals, 2nd edn.* (London: James Nisbet Co., 1857), 295.

[59] After Serampore, Groves visited the Baptist missionary James Williamson at Suri, Birbhum, who married Amelia Carey (nee Pope), widow of Felix Carey. Williamson supported himself as a doctor. Groves, *Memoir*, 297. Cf. F. A. Cox, *History of the Baptist Missionary Society from 1792 to 1842* (London: T. Ward & Co. and G. & J. Dyer, 1842), I, 337, 415.

[60] David Lawrence Edwards, *Christian England* (London: William Collins Sons & Co., 1984), III, 110.

[61] In a letter of Carey to Society, Hooghly River, Dec. 28, 1796. Carter, *Carey's Journal and Letters*, 133.

Statement Eleven

Close to God's Heart

William Ward intended the Serampore Form of Agreement as a model for missionaries laboring at Serampore and mission stations across India. The sacrificial spirituality enjoined in Statement Eleven runs throughout the SFA. A sentence from Statement Ten offers a vivid summary of this call:

> Let us often look at Brainerd in the woods of America, pouring out his very soul before God for the people. Prayer, fervent, expectant, lies at the root of all personal godliness. A competent knowledge of the languages current where a missionary lives, a mild and winning temper, and a heart given up to God—there are the attainments, which, more than all other gifts, will fit us to become God's instruments in the great work of human redemption.[62]

The story of Serampore at the dawn of the nineteenth century is one of answered prayer. Today, many are ignorant of its existence. Carey, Marshman, and Ward seem to have tip-toed noiselessly through the pages of history and disappeared into oblivion. How they worked can help a new generation of mission workers who labor in complex cross-cultural situations where they may find opposition to the message. The example of the Serampore missionaries, with their Biblical and apostolic faith, should inspire us today. They plowed a lonely furrow, but we would short-change ourselves and miss essential Biblical insight if we laid aside the Serampore Form of Agreement. Their sacrificial willingness to live and work in often primitive circumstances for the sake of the Gospel speaks to us today. At times, their motives were mixed, but in their lives of courage, dedication, and self-sacrifice, it is undeniable that an exceptional love for God and the people was the *cantus firmus*. Theirs was a missionary work done close to God's heart, and their lives embodied Carey's timeless watchword: "Expect great things from God. Attempt great things for God."

---

[62] SFA, Statement Ten.

APPENDIX

FORM OF AGREEMENT,

RESPECTING
THE GREAT PRINCIPLES
UPON WHICH
THE BRETHREN OF THE MISSION AT SERAMPORE
THINK IT THEIR DUTY TO ACT
In the Work of
INSTRUCTING THE HEATHEN,

Agreed upon at a Meeting of the Brethren, at Serampore, on Monday, October 7, 1805.

SERAMPORE
PRINTED AT THE BRETHREN's PRESS
1805

FORM OF AGREEMENT, &c.[1]

THE REDEEMER, in planting us in this heathen nation, rather than in any other, has imposed upon us the cultivation of peculiar qualifications. We are firmly persuaded that Paul might plant and Apollos water, in vain, in any part of the world, did not God give the increase. We are sure, that

---

[1] Text of the SFA with original spelling and punctuation as found in the Serampore version of 16 pages, Angus Library, Regent's Park College, Oxford. For clarity, spacing has been introduced between the Preamble, and First Statement, and between Statement Eight and Nine.

only those who are ordained to eternal life will believe, and that God alone can add to the church such as shall be saved. Nevertheless we cannot but observe with admiration, that Paul, the great champion for the glorious doctrines of free and sovereign grace, was the most conspicuous for his personal zeal in the work of persuading men to be reconciled to God. In this respect he is a noble example for our imitation. Our Lord intimated to those of his apostles who were fishermen, that he would make them fishers of men, intimating that in all weathers, and amidst every disappointment, they were to aim at drawing men to the shores of eternal life. Solomon says "He that winneth souls is wise," implying, no doubt, that the work of gaining over men to the side of God, was to be done by winning methods, and that it required the greatest wisdom to do it with success. Upon these points we think it right to fix our serious and abiding attention.

FIRST. In order to be prepared for our great and solemn work, it is absolutely necessary that we set an infinite value upon immortal souls; that we often endeavour to affect our minds with the dreadful loss sustained by an unconverted soul launched into eternity. It becomes us to fix in our minds the awful doctrine of eternal punishment, and to realize frequently the inconceivably awful condition of this vast country, lying in the arms of the wicked one. If we have not this awful sense of the value of souls, it is impossible that we can feel aright in any other part of our work, and in this case it had been better for us to have been in any other situation rather than in that of a Missionary. Oh! may our hearts bleed over these poor idolaters, and may their case lie with continued weight on our minds, that we may resemble that eminent missionary, who compared the travail of his soul, on account of the spiritual state of those committed to his charge, to the pains of childbirth. But while we thus mourn over their miserable condition, we should not be discouraged, as though their recovery were impossible. He who raised the sottish and brutalised Britons to sit in heavenly places in Christ Jesus, can raise these slaves of superstition; purify their hearts by faith, and make them worshippers of the one God in spirit and in truth. The promises are fully sufficient to remove our doubts, and to make us anticipate that not very distant period when He will famish all the gods of India, and cause these very idolaters to cast their idols to the moles and to the bats, and renounce for ever the work of their own hands.

Appendix

SECONDLY. It is very important that we should gain all the information we can of the snares and delusions in which these heathens are held. By this means we shall be able to converse with them in an intelligible manner. To know their modes of thinking, their habits, their propensities, their antipathies, the way in which they reason about God, sin, holiness, the way of salvation, and a future state, to be aware of the bewitching nature of their idolatrous worship, feasts, songs, &c. is of the highest consequence, if we would gain their attention to our discourse, and would avoid being barbarians to them. This knowledge may be easily obtained by conversing with sensible natives, by reading some parts of their works, and by attentively observing their manners and customs.

THIRDLY. It is necessary, in our intercourse with the Hindoos, that, as far as we are able, we abstain from those things which would increase their prejudices against the Gospel. Those parts of English manners which are most offensive to them should be kept out of sight as much as possible. We should also avoid every degree of cruelty to animals. Nor is it advisable at once to attack their prejudices by exhibiting with acrimony the sins of their gods; neither should we upon any account do violence to their images, nor interrupt their worship: The real conquests of the Gospel are those of love: "And I, if I be lifted up, will draw all men unto me." In this respect, let us be continually fearful lest one unguarded word, or one unnecessary display of the difference betwixt us, in manners, &c. should set the natives at a greater distance from us. Paul's readiness to become all things to all men, that he might by any means save some, and his disposition to abstain even from necessary comforts that he might not offend the weak, are circumstances worthy our particular notice. This line of conduct we may be sure was founded on the widest principles. Placed amidst a people very much like the hearers of the apostle, in many respects we may now perceive the solid wisdom which guided him as a Missionary. The mild manners of the Moravians, and also of the Quakers towards the North American Indians, have, in many instances, gained the affections and confidence of heathens in a wonderful manner. He who is too proud to stoop to others, in order to draw them to him, though he may know that they are in many respects inferior to himself, is ill qualified to become a Missionary. The words of a most successful preacher of the Gospel still living "that he would not care if the people trampled him under their feet, if he might become useful to their souls," are expressive of the very temper we should always cultivate.

FOURTHLY. It becomes us to watch all opportunities of doing good. A missionary would be highly culpable if he contented himself with preaching two or three times a week to those persons whom he might be able to get together into a place of worship. To carry on conversations with the natives almost every hour in the day, to go from village to village, from market to market, from one assembly to another; to talk to servants, labourers, &c. as often as opportunity offers, and to be instant in season and out of season—this is the life to which we are called in this country. We are apt to relax in these active exertions, especially in a warm climate; but we shall do well always to fix it in our minds, that life is short, that all around us are perishing, and that we incur a dreadful woe if we proclaim not the glad tidings of salvation.

FIFTHLY. In preaching to the heathen, we must keep to the example of Paul, and make the great subject of our preaching, Christ the crucified. It would be very easy for a Missionary to preach nothing but truths, and that for many years together, without any well-grounded hope of becoming useful to one soul. The doctrine of Christ's expiatory death and all-sufficient merits has been, and must ever remain, the grand mean of conversion. This doctrine, and others immediately connected with it, have constantly nourished and sanctified the church. Oh! that these glorious truths may ever be the joy and strength of our own souls, and then they will not fail to become the matter of our conversation to others. It was the proclaiming of these doctrines that made the Reformation from Popery in the time of Luther spread with such rapidity. It was these truths that filled the sermons of the modern apostles Whitfield, Wesley, &c. when the light of the gospel which had been held up with such glorious effects by the Puritans, was almost extinguished in England.[2] It is a well-known fact that the most successful Missionaries in the world at the present day make the atonement of Christ their continued theme. We mean the Moravians.

---

[2] Fuller, who was averse to Methodism, rephrased the reference to Whitefield, Wesley and the Puritans as: "most useful men in the eighteenth century." *Periodical Accounts Relative to the BMS*, III (1806), 202.

They attribute all their success to the preaching of the death of our Saviour. So far as our experience goes in this work, we most freely acknowledge, that every Hindoo among us who has been gained to Christ, has been won by the astonishing and all-constraining love exhibited in our Redeemer's propitiatory death. Oh! then may we resolve to know nothing among Hindoos and Mussulmans but Christ and him crucified.

SIXTHLY. It is absolutely necessary that the natives should have an entire confidence in us, and feel quite at home in our company. To gain this confidence we must on all occasions be willing to hear their complaints; we must give them the kindest advice, and we must decide upon every thing brought before us in the most open, upright, and impartial manner. We ought to be easy of access, to condescend to them as much as possible, and on all occasions, to treat them as our equals. All passionate behaviour will sink our characters exceedingly in their estimation. All force, and everything haughty, reserved, and forbidding, it becomes us ever to shun with the greatest care. We can never make sacrifices too great, when the eternal salvation of souls is the object, except, indeed, we sacrifice the commands of Christ.

SEVENTHLY. Another important part of our work is to build up, and to watch over, the souls that may be gathered. In this work we shall do well to simplify our first instructions as much as possible, and to press the great principles of the Gospel upon the minds of the converts till they be thoroughly settled and grounded in the foundation of their hope towards God. We must be willing to spend some time with them daily, if possible, in this work. We must have much patience with them, though they may grow very slowly in divine knowledge.

We ought also to endeavour as much as possible to form them to habits of industry, and assist them in procuring such employments as may be pursued with the least danger of temptations to evil. Here too we shall have occasion to exercise much tenderness and forbearance, knowing that industrious habits are formed with difficulty by all heathen nations. We ought also to remember that these persons have made no common sacrifices in renouncing their connections, their homes, their former situations and means of support, and that it will be very difficult for them to procure employment with heathen masters. In these circumstances, if we do not sympathize with them in their temporal losses for Christ, we shall be guilty of great cruelty.

As we consider it our duty to honour the civil magistrate, and in every state and country, to render him the readiest obedience, whether we be persecuted or protected, it becomes us to instruct our native brethren in the same principles. A sense of gratitude too presses this obligation upon us in a peculiar manner, in return for the liberal protection we have experienced. It is equally our wisdom and our duty also to shew to the civil power, that it has nothing to fear from the progress of Missions, since a real follower of Christ must resist the example of his Great Master, and all the precepts the Bible contains on this subject, before he can become disloyal. Converted heathens, being brought over to the religion of their Christian Governors, if duly instructed, are much more likely to love them, and be united to them, than subjects of a different religion.

To bear the faults of our native brethren, so as to reprove them with tenderness, and set them right in the necessity of a holy conservation, is a very necessary duty. We should remember the gross darkness in which they were so lately involved, having never had any just and adequate ideas of the evil of sin, or its consequences. We should also recollect how backward human nature is in forming spiritual ideas, and entering upon a holy self-denying conversation. We ought not therefore, even after many falls, to give up and cast away a relapsed convert, while he manifests the least inclination to be washed from his filthiness.

In walking before native converts much care and circumspection are absolutely necessary. The falls of Christians in Europe have not such a fatal tendency as they must have in this country, because there the word of God always commands more attention than the conduct of the most exalted christian. But here those around us, in consequence of their little knowledge of the scriptures, must necessarily take our conduct as a specimen of what Christ looks for in his disciples. They know only the Saviour and his doctrine as they shine forth in us.

In conversing with the wives of native converts, and leading them on in the ways of Christ, so that they may be an ornament to the Christian cause, and make known the Gospel to the native women, we hope always to have the assistance of the females who have embarked with us in the mission.

Appendix

We see that in primitive times the apostles were very much assisted in their great work by several pious females. The great value of female help may easily be appreciated, if we consider how much the Asiatic women are shut up from the men, and especially from men of another cast. It behoves us, therefore, to afford to our European sisters all possible assistance in acquiring the language, that they may, in every way which Providence may open to them, become instrumental in promoting the salvation of the millions of native women, who are in a great measure excluded from all opportunities of hearing the word from the mouths of European missionaries. A European sister may do much for the cause in this respect, by promoting the holiness, and stirring up the zeal, of the female native converts.

A real missionary becomes in a sense a father to his people. If he feel all the anxiety and tender solicitude of a father; all that delight in their welfare and company that a father does in the midst of his children, they will feel all that freedom with, and confidence in him which he can desire. He will be wholly unable to lead them on in a regular and happy manner, unless they can be induced to open their minds to him, and unless a sincere and mutual esteem subsists on both sides.

EIGHTHLY. Another part of our work is the forming our native brethren to usefulness, fostering every kind of genius, and cherishing every gift and grace in them. In this respect we can scarcely be too lavish of our attention to their improvement. It is only by means of native preachers that we can hope for the universal spread of the Gospel throughout this immense continent. Europeans are too few, and their subsistence costs too much, for us ever to hope that they can possibly be the instruments of the universal diffusion of the word amongst so many millions of souls, spread over such a large portion of the habitable globe. Their incapability of bearing the intense heat of the climate in perpetual itineracies, the heavy expences of their journies, not to say anything of the prejudices of the natives against the very presence of Europeans, and the great difficulty of becoming fluent in their languages, render it absolute duty to cherish native gifts, and to send forth as many native preachers as possible. If the practice of confining the ministry of the world to a single individual in a church be once established amongst us, we despair of the Gospel's ever

The Serampore Form of Agreement

making much progress in India by our means. Let us therefore use every gift, and continually urge on our native brethren to press upon their countrymen the glorious Gospel of the blessed God.

Still further to strengthen the cause of Christ in this country, and, as far as in our power, to give it a permanent establishment, even when the efforts of Europeans may fail, we think it our duty, as soon as possible, to advise the native brethren who may be formed into separate churches, to choose their pastors and deacons from amongst their own countrymen, that the word may be statedly preached, and the ordinances of Christ administered, in each church, by the native minister, as much as possible, without the interference of the missionary of the district, who will constantly superintend their affairs, give them advice in cases of order and discipline, and correct any errors into which they may fall, and who, joying and beholding their order, and the stedfastness of their faith in Christ, may direct his efforts continually to the planting of new churches in other places, and to the spread of the gospel throughout his district as much as in his power. By this means, the unity of the missionary character will be preserved, all the missionaries will still form one body, each one moveable as the good of the cause may require, the different native churches will also naturally learn to care and provide for their ministers, for their church expences, the raising of places of worship, &c. and the whole administration will assume a native aspect, by which means the inhabitants will more readily identify the cause as belonging to their own nation, and their prejudices at falling into the hands of Europeans will entirely vanish. It may be hoped too, that the pastors of these churches, and the members in general, will feel a new energy in attempting to spread the Gospel, when they shall thus freely enjoy the privileges of the gospel amongst themselves.

Under the divine blessing, if, in the course of a few years, a number of native churches be thus established, from them the word of God may sound out even to the extremities of India, and numbers of preachers being raised up and sent forth, may form a body of native missionaries, inured to the climate, acquainted with the customs, language, modes of speech and reasoning of the inhabitants; able to become perfectly familiar with them, to enter their houses, to live upon their food, to sleep with them, or under a tree; and who may travel from one end of the country to the other almost without expence. These churches will be in no immediate danger of falling into errors or disorders, because the whole of their affairs will be constantly superintended by a European missionary. The advantages of this plan are so evident, that to carry it into complete effect ought to be our continued concern. That we may discharge the important obligations of watching over these infant churches when formed, and of urging them to maintain a steady discipline, to hold forth the clear and cheering light of evangelical truth in this region and shadow of death, and to walk in all respects as those who have been called out of darkness into marvellous light, we should continually go to the Source of all grace and strength; for if, to become the shepherd of one church be a most solemn and weighty charge, what must it be to watch over a number of churches just raised from a state of heathenism, and placed at a distance from each other.

We have thought it our duty not to change the names of native converts, observing from scripture that the apostles did not change those of the first christians turned from heathenism, as the names Epaphroditus, Phebe, Fortunatus, Sylvanus, Apollos, Hermes, Junia, Narcissus, &c. prove. Almost all these names are derived from those of heathen gods. We think the great object which Divine Providence has in view in causing the Gospel to be promulgated in the world, is not the changing of the names, the dress, the food, and the innocent usages of mankind, but to produce a moral and divine change in the hearts and conduct of men. It would not be right to perpetuate the names of heathen gods amongst christians; neither is it necessary or prudent to give a new name to every man after his conversion, as hereby the economy of families, neighbourhoods, &c. would be needlessly disturbed. In other respects, we think it our duty to lead our brethren by example, by mild persuasion, and by opening and illuminating their minds in a gradual way, rather than use authoritative means. By this they learn to see the evil of a custom, and then to despise and forsake it; whereas in cases wherein force is used, though they may leave off that which is wrong while in our presence, yet not having seen the evil of it, they are in danger of using hypocrisy, and of doing that out of our presence which they dare not do in it.

The Serampore Form of Agreement

NINTHLY. It becomes us also to labour with all our might in forwarding translations of the sacred Scriptures in the languages of Hindoostan. The help which God has afforded us already in this work is a loud call to us to "go forward." So far, therefore, as God has qualified us to learn those languages which are necessary, we consider it our bounden duty to apply with unwearied assiduity in acquiring them. We consider the publication of the Divine Word throughout India as an object which we ought never to give up till accomplished, looking to the Fountain of all knowledge and strength, to qualify us for this great work, and to carry us through it to the praise of his Holy Name.

It becomes us to use all assiduity in explaining and distributing the divine word on all occasions, and by every means in our power to excite the attention and the reverence of the natives towards it, as the foundation of eternal truth, and the Message of Salvation to men. It is our duty also to distribute, as extensively as possible, the different religious tracts which are published. Considering how much the general diffusion of the knowledge of Christ depends upon a liberal and constant distribution of the Word, and of these tracts, all over the country, we should keep this continually in mind, and watch all opportunities of putting even single tracts into the hands of those persons with whom we occasionally meet. We should endeavour to ascertain where large assemblies of the natives are to be found, that we may attend upon them, and gladden whole villages at once with the tidings of salvation.

The establishment of native free schools is also an object highly important to the future conquests of the Gospel. Of this very pleasing and interesting part of our missionary labours we should endeavour not to be unmindful. As opportunities are afforded, it becomes us to establish, visit, and encourage these institutions, and to recommend the establishment of them to other Europeans. The progress of divine light is gradual, both as it respects individuals and nations. Whatever therefore tends to increase the body of holy light in these dark regions is "as bread cast upon the waters, to be seen after many days." In many ways the progress of providential events is preparing the Hindoos for casting their idols to the moles and the bats, and for becoming a part of the chosen generation, the royal priesthood, the holy nation. Some parts of missionary labours very

Appendix

properly tend to the present conversion of the heathen, and others to the ushering in the glorious period when "a nation shall be born in a day." Of the latter kind are native free schools.[3]

TENTHLY. That which, as a means, is to fit us for the discharge of these laborious and unutterably important labours, is the being instant in prayer, and the cultivation of personal religion. Let us ever have in remembrance the examples of those who have been most eminent in the work of God. Let us often look at Brainerd, in the woods of America, pouring out his very soul before God for the perishing heathen, without whose salvation nothing could make him happy. Prayer, secret, fervent, believing prayer, lies at the root of all personal godliness. A competent knowledge of the languages current where a missionary lives, a mild and winning temper, and a heart given up to God in closet religion, these, these are the attainments which, more than all knowledge, or all other gifts, will fit us to become the instruments of God in the great work of Human Redemption. Let us then ever be united in prayer at stated seasons, whatever distance may separate us, and let each one of us lay it upon his heart that we will seek to be fervent in spirit, wrestling with God, till he famish these idols, and cause the heathen to experience the blessedness that is in Christ.

FINALLY. Let us give ourselves up unreservedly to this glorious cause. Let us never think that our time, our gifts, our strength, our families, or even the clothes we wear, are our own. Let us sanctify them all to God and his cause. Oh! that he may sanctify us for his work. Let us for ever shut out the idea, of laying up a cowry for ourselves or our children. If we give up the resolution which was formed on the subject of private trade, when we first united at Serampore, the Mission is from that hour a lost cause. A worldly spirit, quarrels, and every evil work, will succeed, the moment it is admitted that each Brother may do something on his own account. Woe to that man who shall ever make the smallest movement toward such a measure. Let us continually watch against a worldly spirit, and cultivate a christian indifference towards every indulgence. Rather let us bear

---

[3] References to Ecclesiastes 11:1, Isaiah 2:20 and 66:8. Fuller changed the last into "a nation shall be born at once."

The Serampore Form of Agreement

hardness as good soldiers of Jesus Christ, and endeavour to learn in every state to be content.

If in this way we are enabled to glorify God with our bodies and spirits which are his—our wants will be his care. No private family ever enjoyed a greater portion of happiness, even in the most prosperous gale of worldly prosperity, than we have done since we resolved to have all things in common, and that no one should pursue business for his own exclusive advantage. If we are enabled to persevere in the same principles, we may hope that multitudes of converted souls will have reason to bless God to all eternity for sending his gospel into this country.

To keep these ideas alive in our minds, we resolve that this agreement shall be read publicly, at every station, at our three annual meetings, viz. on the first Lord's day in January, in May, and October.

[Space for Signatures][4]

Mission-House, Serampore.

---

[4] Fuller's Version has the printed names of nine resident missionaries: William Carey, Joshua Marshman, William Ward, John Chamberlain, Richard Mardon, John Biss, William Moore, Joshua Rowe and Felix Carey.

CONTRIBUTORS

G. Landon Adams: Adjunct Professor in church history at William Carey University, Hattiesburg, Mississippi, and director of the Baptist Student Union. Ph.D. in Church History at the New Orleans Baptist Theological Seminary.

Joshua Bowman: Assistant Professor of Missions and Theology, Cedarville University. Former missionary in Zambia and South Asia; Ph.D. in Missiology from Southeastern Baptist Theological Seminary.

Michael Kumar Chatterjee: Assistant Professor at Union Biblical Seminary, Pune, India. D.Th., History of Christianity, Senate of Serampore College.

Bennie R. Crockett, Jr.: Professor of Religion and Philosophy and Co-director, Center for Study of the Life and Work of William Carey, D.D. (1761–1834), William Carey University, Hattiesburg, Mississippi. Th.D., New Orleans Baptist Theological Seminary; Ph.D., University of Wales.

Pratap Chandra Gine: Rev. Dr. Pratap Chandra Gine, Professor (Emeritus) New Testament, North India Institute of Postgraduate Theological Studies. Served at Eastern Theological College, Jorhat (Assam), at Serampore College (West Bengal), and at the College of Christian Theology (Bangladesh). Ordained minister of Baptist Churches North India. D. Theol., Whitley College, Melbourne.

Johan Kommers: Retired minister of the Protestant Church of the Netherlands with service in the Netherlands, Mozambique and Kenya. Served as a pastor in four congregations in the Netherlands. Master of Theology at the Utrecht University. Ph.D., North-West University, Potchefstroom, South Africa.

Samuel E. Masters: Rector, Seminario Bíblico William Carey, Córdoba, Argentina; Ph.D., The Southern Baptist Theological Seminary.

Peter J. Morden: Principal of Bristol Baptist College, England; Ph.D., Spurgeon's College/University of Wales.

Myron C. Noonkester: Co-director, Center for Study of the Life and Work of William Carey, D. D. (1761–1834), William Carey University, Hattiesburg, Mississippi; Ph.D., University of Chicago.

Matthew Reynolds: Executive Director of Refuge International. Former Area Leader with Pioneers in Asia; Ph.D., The Southern Baptist Theological Seminary.

Johnson Thomaskutty: Professor of New Testament at The United Theological College, Bengaluru, India; Ph.D., Radboud University Nijmegen, Netherland.

Peter de Vries: Social entrepreneur in Kolkata, India, and tour guide in Serampore region. Peter has a special interest in colonial and mission history, and volunteers at the Carey Library and Research Centre (CLRC) to catalogue its holdings. Master of Theology, Laidlaw College, Auckland.

BIBLIOGRAPHY

Primary Sources

a. Manuscripts

Baptist Missionary Society Archives, Angus Library, Regent's Park College, Oxford. *Missionary Journals and Correspondence*, on Microfilm Reels 20-22, 35-45 available at the Southern Baptist Historical Library and Archives, Nashville, TN.

British Library, India Office, *Collection* IOR/F/4/364/9081. Allowance W. Carey April-July 1811.

Center for Study of the Life and Work of William Carey, D. D., 1761-1834, Hattiesburg, MS. *Carey Collection, East India Collection, Ward Collection, Wellesley Collection.*

Carey Center, *Carey Collection 7*. Letter of William Carey to Nathaniel Wallich, April 20, 1824.

Carey Center, *East India Collection* 24. Facsimile copy from The British Library, Add. ms. 39892 f. 61. Warren Hastings, "On the attempt to send missionaries to convert the Hindoos and Mosselmen." (endorsement by Col. S. Toone). Received from Mr. Hastings in 1807.

Carey Center, *East India Collection* 28. "Servants of Bengal." Bound volume of thirteen Company Style paintings, gouache on mica, ca. 1840.

Carey Center, *Ward Collection 2*. Letter of William Ward to W. Hudson, October 8, 1801.

Carey, William. "Carey's Covenant for the Church at Moulton," October 1, 1786. Mss. Moulton Baptist Church.

Carey, William. *Journal*, Mss. Baptist Missionary Society Archives. Deposited in the Angus Library, Regent's Park College, Oxford. Microfilm.

Charlotte Atlee White Rowe's *Journal*, Mss. Yale Divinity School Library, *Special Collections*, New Haven, CT.

Edinburgh University Library, *Special Collections.* La.II.646/70.1 "Letter to William Carey from Nathaniel Wallich (with reply) regarding treatment of patient with calomel." n. d.

Leicester Record Office, collection 24.D.71.II/1. *Church Covenant. March 24, 1793.* Harvey Lane Baptist Church, Leicester.

Potts, E. Daniel. *William Ward: A Biography*, Lismore, NSW 1994. Mss.ftera, CLRC, Serampore.

Serampore Missionaries, *Housekeeping Accounts 1801-1804.* 2 vols. Mss. CLRC, Serampore.

Serampore Missionaries, *Marriage Register*, Vol I. Mss. CLRC, Serampore.

Voigt, Rachel. "Memoir of Hannah Marshman's Earlier Years," n.d., n.p. Typed Mss. CLRC, Serampore.

Ward, William. *Missionary Journal 1799-1811 in 4 Vols.,* transcribed by E. Daniel Potts, Mss. Box IN/16. BMS Archives, Angus Library, Regent's Park College, Oxford.

Wenger, Edward S. "Notes on John Lawson." Mss. "g." CLRC, Serampore.

Wenger, Edward S. "The Rev. Henry Peacock." *Biographical Sketches*, II, 38, Mss. CLRC, Serampore.

Wenger, Edward S. "The Rev. William Moore," *Missionary Biographies*, II, 24. Mss. CLRC, Serampore.

Wenger, Edward S. "The Rev. William Robinson." *Missionary Biographies*, II, 31-35. Mss. CLRC, Serampore.

b. Periodicals

Friend of India (Monthly) Vols. I-XII (1818-1828); (Quarterly) Vols. I-IV (1820-1826). Serampore Mission Press.

Monthly Circular Letters relative to the Mission in India. Vols. I-VIII (1808-1815). Serampore Mission Press. [Changed to:] *Circular Letters* Vols IX-X (1816-1817).

Panoplist and Missionary Magazine. Vol. XI (1815).

Periodical Accounts of the Serampore Mission. Nos. I-XVIII New Series (1820-1826). Nos. XIX-CXIV (1829-1836) 3rd Series. Nos. CXV-CXXII (1837) 4th series. Serampore Mission Press.

Bibliography

Periodical Accounts Relating to the Missions of the Church of the United Brethren, Established among the Heathen. Vol. I. London: BSFG, 1790.

Periodical Accounts Relative to the Baptist Missionary Society. Vols. I–VI (1800–1818). Clipstone: J. Morris. London: Button, Burditt.

The American Baptist Magazine and Missionary Intelligencer. Vol I. New series (1817). Boston: James Loring.

The Annual Report of the Committee of the Baptist Missionary Society. Vols. 1–79 (1819–1896). Bristol: J.G. Fuller, London: J. Haddon. The Mission House.

The Baptist Magazine and Missionary Herald. Vols. 1–37 (1819–1857). London: J. Burditt & W. Button.

The Evangelical Magazine & Missionary Chronicle. Vols. 1–30 (1793–1830). London: T. Chapman, G. Auld, R. Williams, Bensley and Son.

c. *Published Primary Sources (1740–1900)*

[Adam, William]. *Correspondence Relative to the Prospects of Christianity, and the Means of Promoting its Reception in India.* Cambridge: From the University Press—Hilliard and Metcalfe, 1824.

[Anon.], *Sketches of India; or, Observations Descriptive of the Scenery, etc. in Bengal: Written in India in the Years 1811, 12, 13, 14; Together with Notes on the Cape of Good Hope, and St. Helena, Written at those Places, in Feb., March, and April 1815.* London: Black, Parbury, and Allen, 1816.

Anderson, Rufus. *Foreign Missions: their Relations and Claims.* New York: Charles Scribner, and Company, 1869.

Benezet, Anthony. *A Caution to Great Britain and Her Colonies, in a Short Representation of the Calamitous State of the Enslaved Negroes in the British Dominions.* New edn. Philadelphia Printed: London Reprinted and Sold by James Phillips, 1785.

Bengal, Also Fort St George and Bombay Papers, Presented to the House of Commons... Relative to the Mahratta War in 1803. Printed by Order of the House of Commons, 5th and 22nd June, 1804. [London: House of Commons], 1804.

"Biographical Sketch of The Rev. William Carey, D.D., Late Principal of Serampore College, Bengal." *The Congregational Magazine*. Vol. 18. N.S. 121–122 (January 1835):1–10; and (February 1835): 73–83.

Bonar, Andrew R. (ed.), *Incidents of Missionary Enterprise; illustrative of the Progress of Christianity in heathen countries, and of the researches, sufferings, and adventures of Missionaries*. Third edn. Edinburgh: T. Nelson, 1842.

Booth, Abraham. *Glad Tidings to Perishing Sinners: Or, The Genuine Gospel a Complete Warrant for the Ungodly to Believe in Jesus*. London: Printed for the Author; and Sold by W. Button, Paternoster Row; and T. Knott, Lombard Street, 1796.

Brainerd, David. *An Abridgment of Mr. David Brainerd's Journal among the Indians. Or, the Rise and Progress of a Remarkable Work of Grace among a Number of the Indians in the Provinces of New-Jersey and Pennsylvania*. London: For John Oswald, 1748.

"Brief Memoir of Rev. A. B. Lish of Agra" in *The Oriental Baptist*, VI (1852), 363–67.

Brown, John. *A Dictionary of the Holy Bible*. 2nd edn. 2 Vols. Edinburgh: Printed for W. Anderson, 1778.

Brown, M.D., William. *History of the Propagation of Christianity Among the Heathen Since the Reformation*. Vol. 2. 3rd edn. Edinburgh and London: William Blackwood and Sons, 1854.

Brown, M.D., William. *The History of Missions: or, of The Propagation of Christianity Among the Heathen, Since the Reformation*. Vol. 2 First American Edition. Philadelphia: Published by B. Coles, 1816.

Brown, M.D., William. *The History of the Propagation of Christianity Among the Heathen Since the Reformation*. Vol. 2. 2nd edn. Edinburgh: Published by A. Fullarton & Co.; Glasgow: Khull, Blackie, & Co. and Chalmers & Collins; Edinburgh: David Brown and Waugh and Innes; London: W. B. Whittaker; Dublin: R. M. Tims, 1823.

Brown, M.D., William. *The History of the Propagation of Christianity Among The Heathen Since the Reformation*. Vol. 2. First American, from the last London Edition. New York: Printed and Published by T. Low, 1816.

Bibliography

Brown, M.D., William. *The History of the Propagation of Christianity Among the Heathen Since the Reformation*. Vol. 2. London: Printed for Longman, Hurst, Rees, Orme, & Brown, and Edinburgh: David Brown, 1814.

Buchanan, Claudius. *Memoir of the Expediency of an Ecclesiastical Establishment for British India Both as a Means of Perpetuating the Christian Religion among our own Countrymen and as a Foundation for the Ultimate Civilization of the Natives*. London: Cadell and Davies, 1805.

Buchanan, Claudius. *The Works of the Rev. Claudius Buchanan L.L.D.* New York: Whiting & Watson, 1812.

Bulwer-Lytton, Edward. *Richelieu, or the Conspiracy, a Play in Five Acts*. London: Saunders and Otley, 1839.

Bunyan, John. *The Pilgrim's Progress..., Part I, To Which are Added Notes by Mr. William Mason, Recommended by the Rev. Mr. Ryland, of Northampton*. London: Printed for Alex. Hogg, 1784.

Carey, Eustace. *Memoir of William Carey D.D., Late missionary to Bengal, Professor of Oriental Languages in the College of Fort William, Calcutta*. 2nd Edn. London: Jackson & Walford, 1836.

Carey, Eustace. *Supplement to the Vindication of the Calcutta Baptist Missionaries Occasioned by Dr. Carey's "Thirty-two Letters," Dr. Marshman's "Reply to the Rev. J. Dyer" and Mr. John Marshman's "Review."* London: George Wightman, 1831.

Carey, Felix. "The Substance of a Sermon to the Hindoos." In John Rippon, ed. *The Baptist Annual Register for 1801 and 1802*. Vol. II, 840–844. London: Sold by Button and Conder, 1803.

[Carey, Marshman, Ward]. *College for the Instruction of Asiatic Christian and Other Youth, in Eastern Literature and European Science, at Serampore, Bengal*. London: Black, Kingsbury, Parbury and Allen, 1819.

Carey, S. Pearce. "New Light on Dr. Carey," *Baptist Quarterly* 1.7 (1923), 314–321.

Carey, S. Pearce. *William Carey, D.D., Fellow of the Linnaean Society*. London: Hodder and Stoughton, 1923.

Carey, S. Pearce. *William Carey: 'The Father of Modern Missions,'* edited by Peter Masters. London: Wakeman Trust, 1993.

Carey, W. *A Dictionary of the Mahratta Language* (Serampore: s.n., 1810).

Carey, W. *A Grammar of the Bengalee* Language. Serampore: Printed at the Mission Press, 1801.

[Carey, W]. [*Gospel of Matthew in Marathi*], [Serampore: Mission Press], 1805.

[Carey, W]. *The Holy Bible Containing the Old Testament and the New. Translated into the Mahratta [Marathi] Language by the Serampore Missionaries. Vol. V. Containing the New Testament.* Serampore: [Mission Press], 1811.

Carey, William and J. Marshman. *Letters from The Rev. Dr. Carey, Relative to Certain Statements Contained in Three Pamphlets Lately Published by the Rev. John Dyer, Secretary to the Baptist Missionary Society: W. Johns, M.D. and The Rev. E. Carey and W. Yates.* 3rd edn. London: Parbury, Allen, and Co., 1828.

Carey, William and Joshua Marshman. *The Ramayuna of Valmeeki, in the Original Sungskrit. With a Prose Translation, And Explanatory Notes.* Vol. I. Serampore, 1806.

Carey, William et al., *Proposals for a Subscription for Translating the Holy Scriptures into the following Oriental Languages: Shanskrit, Bengalee, Hindoostanee, Persian, Mahratta, Guzerattee, Orissa, Carnata, Telinga, Burmah, Assam, Bootan, Tibet, Malay and Chinese.* Serampore: Mission Press, 1806.

Carey, William H. *Oriental Christian Biography.* 3 vols. Calcutta: Baptist Mission Press, 1850-1852.

Carey, William, Joshua Marshman, William Ward, John Chamberlain, Richard Mardon, John Biss, William Moore, Joshua Rowe, Felix Carey. "Form of Agreement." *Periodical Accounts Relative to the Baptist Missionary Society*, III, No XVI, 198-211. London: Printed by J. W. Morris; Sold by Button and Burditt, 1806.

Carey, William. "A letter from William Carey to Dr. Baldwin," Calcutta, July 23, 1816. *The American Baptist Magazine and Missionary Intelligencer* Vol 1, no. 2. (Boston: James Loring, 1817), 65.

Carey, William. "Remarks on the State of Agriculture, in the District of Dinajpur." *Asiatick Researches*, X (1808), 1-27.

Bibliography

Carey, William. "Speech in the Shanscrit Language" By Mr Carey, Teacher of the Bengalee and Shanscrit Languages Delivered at the Public Disputations, on the 20th day of Sept. 1804" in [Claudius Buchanan] *Primitiae Orientalis: containing the theses in the Oriental languages; pronounced at the public disputations ... by students of the College of Fort William in Bengal with translations*, 94-120. Vol III. Calcutta: College Fort William, 1804.

Carey, William. *An Enquiry into the Obligations of Christians to Use Means for the Conversion of the Heathens. In which the Religious State of the Different Nations of the World, the Success of Former Undertakings, and the Practicability of Further Undertakings, are Considered*. Leicester: Ann Ireland, 1792.

Carey, William. *An Enquiry into the Obligations of Christians, to Use Means for the Conversion of the Heathens: In Which the Religious State of the Different Nations of the World, the Success of Former Undertakings, and the Practicability of Further Undertakings Are Considered*. New facsimile edn. with intro by E. A. Payne. Leicester, London: Ann Ireland; Carey Kingsgate Press, 1792, 1961.

[Carey, William]. "No. IX. Translation of a Speech in the Shanscrit Language, Delivered by the Shanscrit Professor, Acting as Moderator, at the Oriental Disputations on the 20th of September, 1804; Extracted from the Third Volume of the Primitiae Orientales." In *The College of Fort William in Bengal*, 168-178. London: Cadell and Davies, 1805.

[Carey, William]. "From Carey's Unpublished Diary—1794." *The Banner of Truth*, Issue 177 (June 1978): 8-9.

Carter, Terry G. ed. *The Journal and Selected Letters of William Carey*. Macon, GA: Smith & Helwys, 2000.

Church Covenant. March 24, 1793. Harvey Lane Baptist Church. Leicester, The Record Office for Leicestershire, Leicester & Rutland.

Colebrook, H. T. *Hitópadésa, or Salutary Instruction. In the original Sanscrit*. Printed at Serampore, 1804.

College Committee. *First Report of the College, for Asiatic Christian and Other Youth, Instituted at Serampore, August, 1818, under Patronage of the Most Noble the Marquis of Hastings, K.G. &c.* Serampore: n.s., 1819.

Cox Francis A., *History of the Baptist Missionary Society. From 1792 to 1842.* 2 vols. London: T. Ward and Co., and G. & J. Dyer, 1842.

Dealtry, William. *A Letter Addressed to the Rev. Dr. Wordsworth, in Reply to his "Reasons for Declining to Become a Subscriber to the British and Foreign Bible Society.* London: J. Hatchard, 1810.

Denham, W.H. "Memoir of the Late Mrs Marshman," in *Baptist Magazine*, 39 (August 1847), 478–482. London: Houlston and Stoneman, 1847.

Dubois, Abbé J. A. *Description of the Character, Manners, and Customs of the People of India; and of their Institutions, Religious and Civil. Translated from the French Manuscript.* London: Longman, Hurst, Rees, Orme, and Brown, 1817.

Dubois, Abbé J. A. *Letters on the State of Christianity in India; in which the Conversion of the Hindoos is considered as impracticable. To which is added A Vindication of the Hindoos, Male and Female, in answer to a severe attack made upon both by the Reverend ****** London: Longman, Hurst, Orme, Brown, and Green, 1823.

Dubois, Jean-Antoine. *Hindu Manners, Customs, and Ceremonies*, 2nd edn., trans. Henry K. Beauchamp. Oxford: Clarendon Press, 1899.

[Dyer, John], ed. *News from Afar, ... Being a Re-Publication of the Quarterly Papers of the Society from 1822–1832*. London: Baptist Missionary Society, 1832.

Editor, "Announcement Sermon by Rev. Mr. Thomas." *Leicester Herald.* Saturday, March 16, 1793.

Editor, "William Carey, D. D. Poor Law Settlement Order." *Northampton County Magazine*, 4. 1931.

Edwards, Jonathan. "The Justice of God in the Damnation of Sinners." In Sermons and Discourses, 1734–1738 in *The Works of Jonathan Edwards*. Vol. 19. Edited by M. X. Lesser. New Haven: Yale University Press, 2001.

Bibliography

Edwards, Jonathan. *Freedom of the Will*, in *The Works of Jonathan Edwards*, Vol. 1, ed. Paul Ramsey. New Haven: Yale University Press, 1985 [1754].

Edwards, Jonathan. *The Life of David Brainerd*, in *The Works of Jonathan Edwards*, Vol. 7, ed. Norman Pettit. New Haven: Yale University Press, 1985 [1749].

Edwards, Jonathan. *The Life of the Rev. David Brainerd, Missionary to the Indians*. New edn. London: Burton and Smith, and E.W. Morris, 1818.

Edwards, Jonathan. *An Humble Attempt...*, in *The Works of Jonathan Edwards*, ed. Edward Hickman. Vol. 2. Edinburgh: Banner of Truth, 1974 [1834].

Essays by the Students of the College of Fort William in Bengal to which are Added the Theses Pronounced at the Public Disputations in the Oriental Languages on the 6th February, 1802. Calcutta: The Honorable Company's Press, 1802.

Fawcett, John. *Considerations Relative to the Sending of Missionaries to Propagate the Gospel among the Heathens*. Leeds: Printed by Thomas Wright, 1793.

Fawcett, John. *The Sick Man's Employ: or, Views of Death and Eternity Realised, Occasioned by a Violent Fit of the Stone*. New edn. Halifax: Printed by Holden and Dowson, 1800.

Fleming, John [and William Carey]. "A Catalogue of Indian Medicinal Plants and Drugs, with Their Names in the Hindusta'ni and Sanscrit Languages." In *Asiatic Researches* 11, 153-196. London: J. Cuthell et al., 1812.

Form of Agreement, Respecting the Great Principles upon which the Brethren of the Mission at Serampore Think It Their Duty to Act in the Work of Instructing the Heathen. Serampore: Printed at the Brethren's Press, 1805.

Form of Agreement Respecting The Great Principles upon which The Brethren of the Mission at Serampore Think It Their Duty to Act in the Work of Instructing the Heathen. Serampore: Printed at the Brethren's Press, 1805; Calcutta: Reprinted at the Baptist Mission Press, 1874.

Fuller, Andrew Gunton. *The Complete Works of the Rev. Andrew Fuller*. Vol. I. Boston: Gould, Kendall, and Lincoln, 1836.

Fuller, Andrew, *The Complete Works of Rev. Andrew Fuller*. Philadelphia: American Baptist Publication Society, 1845.

Fuller, Andrew. "The Nature and Importance of Love to God." In Andrew Gunton Fuller. *The Complete Works of the Rev. Andrew Fuller with a Memoir of His Life*. London: G. and J. Dyer, 1846.

Fuller, Andrew. *The Life of Andrew Fuller*, ed. C. Ryan Griffith. Berlin / Boston, MA: Walter De Gruyter, 2022 [1816, 1st edn.; 1818, 2nd edn.]

Fuller, Andrew. *Apologetic Works*. Edited by Thomas J. Nettles and Michael Haykin. Vol. 3. Berlin/Boston: Walter de Gruyter, 2021.

Fuller, Andrew. *The Calvinistic and Socinian Systems Examined and Compared as to Their Moral Tendency; in a Series of Letters Addressed to the Friends of Vital and Practical Religion*. Market Harborough: W. Harrod for the Author, 1793.

Fuller, Andrew. *The Gospel Its Own Witness; or, The Holy Nature, and Divine Harmony of the Christian Religion, Contrasted with the Immorality and Absurdity of Deism*. 2nd edn. Clipstone: Printed at the Office of J. W. Morris, 1800.

Fuller, Andrew. The Gospel of Christ Worthy of All Acceptation, Or The Duty of Sinners to Believe in Jesus Christ, With Corrections and Additions; To Which is Added an Appendix, on the Necessity of A Holy Disposition In Order To Believing In Christ (1801). In *The Complete Works of the Rev. Andrew Fuller: With A Memoir of his Life, By Andrew Gunton Fuller*. Vol. 2. Third London Edition. Reprint, Harrisonburg, VA: Sprinkle Publications, 1988.

Fuller, Andrew. *The Gospel Worthy of All Acceptation*. 1st edn. Northampton: Thomas Dicey, 1785.

[Fuller, Andrew]. *Brief Narrative of the Baptist Mission in India*. London: Button and Burditt, 1808.

Ghose, Jogendra Chunder, and Eshan Chunder Bose, eds. *The English Works of Raja Ram Mohun Roy*. Vol. I. Calcutta: Oriental, 1885.

Bibliography

Grant, Charles. *A Poem on the Restoration of Learning in the East; Which Obtained Mr. Buchanan's Prize.* Cambridge: R. Watts at University Press, 1805.

Groves, Harriet. *Memoir of the Late Anthony Norris Groves, containing Extracts from his Letters and Journals.* 2nd edn. London: James Nisbet Co., 1857.

Hall, Robert. *A Sermon Occasioned by the Death of Her Late Royal Highness The Princess Charlotte of Wales, Preached at Harvey-Lane, Leicester, November 16, 1817.* 3rd edn. Leicester: Thomas Combe, 1818.

Hall, Robert. *Help to Zion's Travellers.* Philadelphia, PA: American Baptist Publication Society, 1851.

Henry, Matthew. *Matthew Henry's Commentary on the Whole Bible.* Vol. VI. New York & London: Fleming H. Revell, 1721.

Holmes and Co. *The Bengal Obituary, or a Record to Perpetuate the Memory of Departed Worth, Being a Compilation of Tablets and Monumental Inscriptions from Various parts of the Bengal and Agra Presidencies.* Calcutta: J. Thomas, Baptist Mission Press, 1848.

Holmes, Abel. "Indian Copy of the Hebrew Pentateuch, Discovered by the Rev. Claudius Buchanan, D. D." *American Quarterly Register* 9, no. 1 (August 1836): 59–67.

Hough, James. *A Reply to the Letters of the Abbé Dubois on the State of Christianity in India.* London: L.B. Seeley & Son, 1824.

Hume, David. *An Enquiry Concerning the Principles of Morals.* London: Printed for A. Millar, 1751.

Hume, David. *Essays and Treatises on Several Subjects.* Vol. II *Containing An Enquiry Concerning Human Understanding; A Dissertation on the Passions; An Enquiry concerning the Principles of Morals; and The Natural History of Religion.* New edn. London: Printed for T. Cadell, 1772.

Hume, David. *Essays on Suicide and the Immortality of the Soul.* New edn. Basil: Printed for the Editor of the Collection of English Classics, 1799.

Johnson, Samuel. *A Dictionary of the English Language: In Which the WORDS are deduced from their ORIGINALS, and Illustrated in their Different Significations by EXAMPLES from the best WRITERS.* 2 vols. London: Printed by W. Strahan, 1755, 1765.

Johnson, Samuel. *The Life of the Rev. Isaac Watts, D.D.* London: J. Johnson, and T. Knott, 1791.

Jones, William. *The Works of Sir William Jones. In Six Volumes.* London: Printed for G. G. and J. Robinson, Pater-Noster-Row; and R. H. Evans [Successor to Mr. Edwards], No. 26, Pall Mall, 1799.

Lewis, Charles Bennett. *The Life of John Thomas, Surgeon of the Earl of Oxford East Indiaman, and First Baptist Missionary to Bengal.* London: MacMillan and Co., 1873.

Long, James. "The Banks of the Bhagirathi." *Selections from the Calcutta Review*, Vol II (Aug 1881–Jan 1882): 332–333.

Lumpkin, William L. *Baptist Confessions of Faith.* Second Revised Edition. Revised by Bill J. Leonard. Valley Forge: Judson Press, 2011.

Marsh, Herbert. *A History of the Translations: Which have been Made of the Scriptures, from the Earliest to the Present Age, throughout Europe, Asia, Africa and America. The British and Foreign Bible Society.* London, Cambridge: Rivingtons, Deighton, Nicholson and Barrett, 1812.

Marshman, J. *A Defence of the Deity and Atonement of Jesus Christ, in Reply to Ram-Mohun Roy of Calcutta.* London: Kingsbury, Parbury, and Allen, 1822.

[Marshman, J.], "Bank for Savings applied to India," *Friend of India* (Monthly), II (1819): 73–83.

Marshman, John Clark. *The Life and Times of Carey, Marshman, and Ward: Embracing the History of the Serampore Mission.* 2 Vols. London: Longman, Brown, Green, Longmans, & Roberts, 1859.

Marshman, Joshua. "Hail, precious Book divine!" Hymn <https://hymnary.org/text/hail_precious_book_divine>

Marshman, Joshua. *Letters from the Rev. Dr. Carey Relative to Certain Statements Contained in Three Pamphlets lately published by the Rev. Joh Dyer, Secretary to the BMS, W. Johns, M.D., and the Rev. E. Carey and W. Yates.* London: Parbury, Allen and Co., 1828.

Bibliography

Marshman, Joshua. *Reply to "Missionary Incitement, and Hindoo Demoralization: Including Some Observations on the Political Tendency of the Means Taken to Evangelize Hindoostan." Originally printed in the "Friend of India."* Serampore: Mission Press, 1822.

Marshman, Joshua. *Statement Relative to Serampore, Supplementary to a "Brief Memoir." With Introductory Observations, by John Foster.* London: Parbury, Allen & Co., 1828.

[Marshman, J. and W. Carey]. *Statement Relative to the Administration of the Funds Entrusted to the Serampore Missionaries.* Serampore: s.n., 1820. Signed Pamphlet, CLRC, Serampore.

[Marshman, Joshua] "Letters of the State of Christianity in India." *Friend of India* (Quarterly), X (1824), 187–392.

Martin, Robert Montgomery, ed. *The Despatches, Minutes, and Correspondence of the Marquess Wellesley, K. G. During his Administration in India.* 5 vols. London: John Murray, 1836–1837.

Mason, J. C. S. *The Moravian Church and the Missionary Awakening in England, 1760–1800.* Woodbridge, Suffolk; Rochester, NY: Boydell & Brewer, 2001.

"Memoir of Rev. William Ward: One of the Serampore Missionaries," *American Baptist Magazine*, n.s. V. no 1. (January 1825), 5–12.

Muir, John. *The Inefficiency of the Ganges to Wash Away Sin, with a Statement of the True Atonement.* Calcutta: Baptist Mission Press, 1840.

Murdoch, John. *Catalogue of the Christian Vernacular Literature of India: With Hints on the Management of Indian Tract Societies.* Madras: Caleb Foster, 1870.

Newell, H. *Memoirs of Mrs Harriet Newell, Wife of the Rev. S. Newell, American Missionary to India, Who Died at the Isle of France, Nov 30. 1812, Aged Nineteen Years.* 6th edn. Edinburgh: Ogle, Allardice and Thomson, 1818.

"Notice of New Works in Sanskrit Verse," *Calcutta Christian Observer*, IV (1840), 16–17.

Pearce, Samuel. *Memoirs of the Late Rev. Samuel Pearce, A. M. Minister of the Gospel in Birmingham; With Extracts from Some of His Most Interesting Letters.* Compiled by Andrew Fuller. Clipstone: Printed by J. W. Morris, 1800.

Pearson, Hugh. *Memoirs of the Life and Writings of the Rev. Claudius Buchanan, D.D., Late Vice-Provost of the College of Fort William in Bengal.* Second Edn. 2 vols. Oxford: At the University Press for the Author, 1817.

Powell, Samuel. "Account of Mr. F[ernandez]." *Missionary Magazine* VI (1801): 252–254.

Reports of the British and Foreign Bible Society, with Extracts of Correspondence, &c. Volume the Second, for 1811, 1812, and 1813. London: J. Tilling, 1813.

Robinson, John. "Memoir of the Rev. William Robinson." in *The Missionary Register August 1855*, 329–334. London: Seeley, Jackson, and Halliday, 1855.

Sen, Keshub Chunder. *Jesus Christ: Europe and Asia. Being the Substance of a Lecture ... in the Theatre of the Calcutta Medical College... on Saturday, 5th May, 1866.* London: John Snow & Co., 1866.

[Serampore Missionaries]. *Brief View of the Baptist Missionary Society and Memoir of Translations.* Serampore: Mission Press, 1814.

[Serampore Missionaries]. *Proposals for a Subscription for Translating the Holy Scriptures into the Following Oriental Languages: Shanscrit, Bengalee, Hindoostanee, Persian, Mahratta ... [etc.] and Chinese.* Serampore: Mission Press, 1806.

[Serampore Missionaries]. *Second Appeal on behalf of the Serampore Mission.* Serampore: Mission Press, 1833.

Smith, Adam. *The Theory of Moral Sentiments.* 2nd edn. London: Printed for A. Millar, 1761.

Smith, George. *Short History of Christian Missions, from Abraham and Paul to Carey, Livingstone, and Duff.* Edinburgh: T. & T. Clark, 1884.

Smith, George. *The Life of William Carey, D.D., Shoemaker and Missionary.* London: John Murray, 1885.

Smith, George. *Twelve Pioneer Missionaries.* London: Thomas Nelson and Sons, 1900.

[Southey, Robert]. "Account of the Baptist Missionary Society." *Quarterly Review* I (1809): 193–226.

Bibliography

Spangenberg, A. G. *An Account of the Manner in which the Moravian Church of the Unitas Fratrum, or United Brethren, Preach the Gospel and Carry on their Missions Among the Heathen.* London: H. Trapp, 1788.

Spangenberg, August Gottlieb. *An Exposition of Christian Doctrine, as Taught in the Protestant Church of the United Brethren, or Unitas Fratrum.* London: W. and A. Strahan, 1784.

Statham, John. *Indian Recollections.* London: Samuel Bagster, 1832.

Stennett, Samuel. *Memoirs of the Life of the Rev. William Ward, Late Baptist Missionary in India; Containing a Few of His Early Poetical Productions, and a Monody to his Memory.* London: Printed by J. Haddon, 1825.

Stennett, Samuel. *Memoirs of the Life of the Rev. William Ward.* 2nd edn. London: Simpkin & Marshall, Holdsworth, 1825.

Tennant, William. *Indian Recreations; Consisting Chiefly of Strictures on the Domestic and Rural Economy of the Mahomedans and Hindoos.* 2nd edn. 2 vols. London: Longman, Hurst, Rees, and Orme, 1804.

Tennant, William. *Thoughts on the Effects of the British Government on the State of India: Accompanied with Hints Concerning the Means of Conveying Civil and Religious Instruction to the Natives of that Country.* Edinburgh: Longman, Rees, Hurst, and Orme, 1807.

The First Hindoo Convert: A Memoir of Krishna Pal, a preacher of the Gospel to his countrymen more than twenty years. Philadelphia: American Baptist Publication Society, 1852.

"The First London Confession (1644)." In *Baptist Confessions of Faith*, by William L. Lumpkins, 153–171. Valley Forge, PA: Judson Press, 1969.

"The Second London Confession (1689)." In *Baptist Confessions of Faith*, by William L. Lumpkins, 241–295. Valley Forge, PA: Judson Press, 1969.

The Holy Bible, Containing the Old and New Testaments. Oxford: Printed by T. Wright and W. Gill, Printers to the University, 1769.

The Holy Bible, Conteyning the Old Testament, and the New. London: Robert Barker, 1611.

The People Called Quakers. *The Case of Our Fellow-Creatures, the Oppressed Africans, Respectfully Recommended to the Serious Consideration of the Legislature of Great-Britain.* London: James Phillips, 1784.

The Thirty-Nine Articles of the Church of England. London: Printed for John Rivington, 1758.

Walford, Cornelius. *The Famines of the World: Past and Present.* London: Edward Stanford, 1879.

Ward, William. "Addressed to the Dealers in Human Flesh—On the Loss of Mr. Wilberforce's Bill for the Abolition of the Slave-Trade." *Derby Mercury*, May 12, 1791.

Ward, William. "Letter to [Mr.] Stewart in Calcutta." Serampore, Nov 28, 1806. Angus Library, Regent's Park College, Oxford.

Ward, William. "Moonlight." *Hull Advertiser and Exchange Gazette*, April 23, 1796, 4.

Ward, William. "Necessity of Christianity to India. Population, 150,000,000." Boston, 1821.

Ward, William. "Religious Tracts Anecdotes," *Baptist Magazine*, XIII (1821), 524.

Ward, William. *Account of the Writings, Religion, and Manners of the Hindoos. In Four Volumes.* Serampore: Mission Press, 1811.

Ward, William. *A View of the History, Literature, and Religion of the Hindoos: Including a Minute Description of their Manners and Customs, and Translations from their Principal Works.* 2 vols. 2nd edn. Serampore: Printed at the Mission Press, 1815, 1818.

Ward, William. *A View of the History, Literature, and Mythology of the Hindoos. In Four Volumes.* London: Black, Kingsbury, Parbury and Allen, 1820.

Ward, William. *Brief Memoir of Krishna-Pal. The First Hindoo, in Bengal, who Broke the Chain of the Cast, by Embracing the Gospel.* 2nd Edn. London: John Offor, 1823.

[Ward, William]. *Brief Memoirs of Four Christian Hindoos, Lately Deceased.* Serampore: Mission Press, 1816.

Ward, William. *Farewell Letters to a Few Friends in Britain and America, on Returning to Bengal in 1821.* New York: Bliss & White, 1821.

Bibliography

Ward, William. *History, Literature and Mythology of the Hindoos.* 4 Vols. 3rd edn. Delhi: Low Price Publication, 1990. Reprint. First published 1817–1820.

Ward, William. *Reflections on the Word of God, for Every Day in the Year.* London: W. Simpkin and R. Marshall, 1825.

Ward, William. *The Abolition of the Slave Trade, Peace, and a Temperate Reform Essential to the Salvation of England.* London: Printed for Crosby, 1796.

Ward, William. *The Love of Christ Beareth Us Away. The Design of Death of Christ Explained, a Sermon by William Ward.* London: Black, Kingsbury, Parbury, and Allen, 1820.

Wellesley, Marquis of. *History of the All the Events and Transactions Which Have Taken Place in India: Containing the Negotiations of the British Government, Relative to the Glorious Success of the Late War.* London: John Stockdale, 1805.

Wellesley, Richard Colley. *Notes Relative to the Late Transactions in the Mahratta Empire. Fort William, 15th Dec. 1803.* London: John Stockdale, 1804.

Wilford, F. "Origin and Decline of the Christian Religion in India." *Asiatick Researches*, X (1811), 27–157.

Williams, Charles. *The Missionary Gazetteer: Comprising a Geographical and Statistical Account of the Various Stations of the Church, London, Moravian, Wesleyan, Baptist, and American, Missionary Societies Etc., with Their Progress in Evangelization and Civilization.* London: F. Westley and A.H. Davis, 1828.

Wilson, H. H. *A Glossary of Judicial and Revenue Terms, and of Useful Words Occurring in Official Documents Relating to the Administration of the Government of British India.* London: Wm. H. Allen and Col., 1855.

Winterbotham. William. *The Trial of William Winterbotham, Assistant Preacher at How's Lane Meeting, Plymouth Before the Hon Baron Perryn, and a Special Jury, at Exeter; On the 25th of July, 1793 for Seditious Words Charged to Have Been Uttered in Two Sermons Preached on the 5th. and the 18th. of November, 1792.* Third Edn. London: Printed for William Winterbotham, 1794.

Yates, William. *Memoirs of the Early Life of John Chamberlain, Late Missionary in India. With His Diary of Religious Exercises*. Boston: New England Sabbath School Union, 1831.

Yates, William. *Memoirs of Mr. John Chamberlain, Late Missionary in India*. Calcutta: Printed at the Baptist Mission Press, 1824.

Yates, William. *Memoirs of Mr. John Chamberlain, Late Missionary in India*. Calcutta: Printed at the Baptist Mission Press; London: Re-printed for Wightman and Cramp, 1826.

Yates, William. *Memoirs of Mr. John Chamberlain, Late Missionary in India*. Republished under the Direction of the Committee of the Baptist Missionary Society. With a Preface by F. A. Cox. London: Printed for Francis Westley, and Sold by C. J. Westley, and G. Tyrrell, Dublin, 1825.

Yates, William. *Memoirs of the Early Life of John Chamberlain, Late Missionary in India. With His Diary of Religious Exercises; Abridged from the Calcutta Edition*. Boston: James Loring, Sabbath School Book-Store, 1831.

Secondary Sources

Ali, A. Yusuf. *A Cultural History of India during the British Period*. Bombay: D. B. Taraporevala Sons & Co., 1940, reprinted 1976.

Ali, Muhammad Mohar. *The Bengali Reaction to Christian Missionary Activities 1833–1857*. Chittagong: Mehrub Publications, 1965.

Allen, David L. *The Extent of the Atonement: A Historical and Critical Review*. Nashville, TN: B&H Academic, 2016.

Altman, Michael J. *Heathen, Hindoo, Hindu: American Representations of India, 1721–1893*. Oxford: Oxford University Press, 2017.

Arnold, David. *Science, Technology, and Medicine in Colonial India. The New Cambridge History of India*. Cambridge: Cambridge University Press, 2000.

Baago, Kaj. *Pioneers of Indigenous Christianity*. Madras: Christian Literature Society, 1969.

Bibliography

Baker, Dwight P. "William Carey and the Business Model for Mission." In *Between Past and Future: Evangelical Mission Entering the Twenty-First Century*, ed. Jonathan J. Bonk, 167-202. Pasadena, CA: Evangelical Missiological Society, 2003.

Banerjee, Tapan. *The Mission of Danes from Tranquebar to Serampore*. Chandannagore, Hooghly: Sm. Sabita Banerjee, 2013.

Bauman, Chad M. *Anti-Christian Violence in India*. New York: Cornell University Press, 2020.

Bayly, C. A. *Empire and Information: Intelligence Gathering and Social Communication in India, 1780-1870*. Cambridge: Cambridge University Press, 1996.

Bayly, Susan. *Caste, Society and Politics in India from the Eighteenth Century to the Modern Age*. The New Cambridge History of India, Vol. 4, No. 3. Cambridge: Cambridge University Press, 1999.

Bebbington, David W. *Baptists Through the Centuries: A History of a Global People*. 2nd edn. Waco, TX: Baylor University Press, 2018.

Bebbington, David W. *Evangelicalism in Modern Britain: A History from the 1730s to the 1980s*. Grand Rapids, MI: Baker Book House, 1992.

Bebbington, David W. *The Dominance of Evangelicalism: The Age of Spurgeon and Moody*. Leicester: Inter-Varsity Press, 2005.

Beaver, R. Pierce. "The History of Mission Strategy." In Ralph D. Winter and Steven C. Hawthorne, eds., *Perspectives on the World Christian Movement: A Reader*, 241-252. Third edn. Pasadena, CA: William Carey Library, 1999.

Beck, James R. "Serampore Compact." *Dorothy Carey: The Tragic and Untold Story of Mrs. William Carey*, 199-206. Grand Rapids, MI: Baker Book House, 1992.

Beck, James R. *Dorothy Carey: The Tragic and Untold Story of Mrs. William Carey*. Grand Rapids, MI: Baker Book House, 1992.

Beyreuther, Erich. *Geschichte des Pietismus*. Stuttgart: J. F. Steinkopf Verlag, 1978.

Boyd, Robin H.S. *An Introduction to Indian Christian Theology*. Delhi: ISPCK, 1969, 1975, 2000.

Brackney, William H. *The Baptists*. New York & London: Greenwood, 1988.

Briggs, Asa. *The Age of Improvement, 1783-1867.* 2nd edn. London & New York: Routledge, 2000.

Briggs, John. "She-Preachers, Widows and Other Women: The Feminine Dimension in Baptist Life Since 1600." *Baptist Quarterly* 31, no. 7 (July 1986): 337-352.

Brooke, Jonathan. "'We may have read—but the reality!': Narrating Baptist Missions in Bengal, 1800-1855." Ph.D. diss., University of London, 2005.

Brooker, J. G. "Mission Burial Ground, Serampore." *Bengal Past and Present. Journal of the Calcutta Historical Society* 47. Part 1. Serial no. 93. (January-March 1934): 57-65.

Burrage, Champlin. *The Church Covenant Idea: Its Origin and Its Development.* Philadelphia: American Baptist Publication Society, 1904.

Busi, Suneel Bhanu. "Who are We and What Constitutes Our Identity." In *Religious Identity and Renewal in the Twenty-First Century*, The Lutheran World Federation, 187-207. Leipzig: Evangelische Verlagsanstalt, 2015.

Butler, Iris. *The Eldest Brother: The Marquess Wellesley.* London: Hodder & Stoughton, 1973.

Butler, Phillip. "The Power of Partnership." In Ralph D. Winter and Steven C. Hawthorne, eds., *Perspectives on the World Christian Movement: A Reader*, 753-758. Third edn. Pasadena, CA: William Carey Library, 1999.

Cannadine, David. *The Rise and Fall of Class in Britain.* New York: Columbia University Press, 1999.

Carmichael, Amy. *Gold Cord: The Story of a Fellowship.* London: SPCK, 1932.

Carson, Penelope. *The East India Company and Religion, 1698-1858.* Woodbridge: Boydell Press, 2012.

Chakkuvarackal, T. Johnson. "The Serampore Mission and the Linguistic Renaissance in India," *Bangalore Theological Forum* 35/2 (2003): 123-140.

Chancey, Karen. "The Star in the East: The Controversy over Christian Missions to India, 1805-1813," *The Historian* 60, no. 3 (1998): 507-522.

Bibliography

Char, S. V. Desika. *Hinduism and Islam in India: Caste, Religion and Society from Antiquity to Early Modern Times.* Princeton, NJ: Markus Wiener Publishers, 1993.

Chatterjee, S.K. "Carey and the Linguistic Renaissance in India." In *Carey's Obligation and India's Renaissance,* eds. J. T. K. Daniel and Roger E. Hedlund, 157-175. Serampore: Council of Serampore College, 1993.

Chatterjee, Sunil Kumar. "Ignatius Fernandez." in *William Carey and Serampore,* 2nd edn. Sheoraphuli: S.K. Chatterjee, Laserplus, 2004.

Chatterjee, Sunil Kumar. "William Carey and the Fort William College." In *Carey's Obligation and India's Renaissance.* Eds. J. T. K. Daniel and R. E. Hedlund, 228-237. Serampore: Council of Serampore College, 1993.

Chatterjee, Sunil Kumar. *Hannah Marshman: The First Woman Missionary in India.* Hooghly: Sunil Kumar Chatterjee; Calcutta: S. K. Poddar, People's Little Press, 1987; Sheoraphuli: Laserplus, 2006.

Chatterjee, Sunil Kumar. *William Carey and Serampore.* Third enl. edn. Serampore: The Author, 2008.

Chattopadhyay, Prafulla. "Review of William Ward, History, Literature and Mythology of the Hindoos," *Dharma Deepika,* Vol. 1, no. 2, (1995), 81-82.

Chesterman, A. De M. "The Journals of Brainerd and Carey." *Baptist Quarterly* 19, no. 4 (1961): 147-156.

Chun, Chris. "The Sacrifices of Dorothy Carey and Ann Judson: Two Sides of the Same Coin." In *Expect Great Things, Attempt Great Things: William Carey and Adoniram Judson,* 125-136. Eugene, OR: Wipf and Stock, 2013.

Chute, Anthony L., Nathan A. Finn, and Michael A.G. Haykin, *The Baptist Story: From English Sect to Global Movement.* Nashville, TN: Broadman and Holman, 2015.

Chute, Arthur C. *John Thomas, First Missionary to Bengal, 1757-1801. Introduction by A. J. Gordon.* Halifax, Nova Scotia: Baptist Book and Tract Society, 1893.

Clark, David K. *To Know and Love God: Method for Theology.* Wheaton, IL: Crossway Books, 2003.

Coker, Joe L. "Developing a Theory of Missions in Serampore: The increased Emphasis upon Education as a 'Means for the Conversion of the Heathens'" *Mission Studies* 17/1 (2001): 42-60.

Colley, Linda. *Britons: Forging the Nation 1707-1837*. New Haven, CT: Yale University Press, 1992.

Conroy-Krutz, Emily. *Christian Imperialism: Converting the World in the Early American Republic*. New York: Cornell University Press, 2015.

Coward, Harold. ed. *Hindu-Christian Dialogue: Perspectives and Encounters*. Delhi: Motilal Banarsidass Publishers, 1993.

Cox, Jeffrey. *Imperial Faultlines: Christianity and Colonial Power in India, 1818-1940*. Stanford, CA: Stanford University Press, 2002.

Cox, Jeffrey. *The British Missionary Enterprise since 1700*. New York: Routledge, 2008.

Crow, Paul A. "19th century efforts." In "Christianity," *Encyclopedia Britannica*. June 1, 2022. <https://www.britannica.com/topic/Christianity/19th-century-efforts>.

Dalrymple, William. *The Anarchy: The Relentless Rise of the East India Company*. New York: Bloomsbury, 2019.

Dann, Robert Bernard. *Father of Faith Missions. The Life and Times of Anthony Norris Groves*. Waynesboro, GA, Bletchley, U.K.: Authentic Media, 2004.

Das Gupta, R.K. "William Carey and Bengali Grammar." In *Carey's Obligation and India's Renaissance*, eds. J. T. K. Daniel and Roger E. Hedlund, 187-192. Serampore: Council of Serampore College, 1993.

Das, Sisir Kumar. "Early Bengali Prose: Carey to Vidyasagar." Ph.D. thesis, University of London, 1963.

Das, Sisir Kumar. *Sahibs and Munshis: An Account of the College of Fort William*. New Delhi: Orion Publications, 1978.

Datta, S. K. *The Desire of India*. London: Baptist Missionary Society, 1908.

Davidson, Allan K. *Evangelicals & Attitudes to India 1786-1813: Missionary Publicity and Claudius Buchanan*. Sutton: Courtney Press, 1990.

Davies, Gwyn. *Covenanting with God. The story of personal and church covenants and their lessons for today*. Bryntirion, Bridgend, Mid Glamorgan: Evangelical Library of Wales, 1994.

Bibliography

de Vries, Peter. "William Carey's Advocacy for the Tribal People", in Subhro Sekhar Sircar and Sanjoy Mukherjee, eds., *William Carey: The Multifaceted Genius. A Carey Day 2018 Celebration Committee Publication,* 71-82. Serampore: Council of Serampore College, 2018.

Deweese, Charles W. *Baptist Church Covenants.* Nashville: Broadman Press, 1990.

Delon, M. ed. "Grammar." *Encyclopedia of the Enlightenment,* Vol. 1. London/New York: Routledge, 2001.

Dharmaraj, J. S. "Serampore Missions and Colonial Connections, "*Indian Church History Review* 26, no.1 (1992): 21-35.

Down, Frederick. "Women in the History of Christianity," In *Women Re-Shaping Theology: Introducing Women's Studies in Theological Education in India.* ed. Lalrinawmi Ralte. Delhi: ISPCK, 1998.

Doyle, Sean. "Prophetic Precepts or Divine Preeminence? Rammohan Roy vs. Joshua Marshman on the Significance of Jesus." In *Expect Great Things Attempt Great Things,* edited by Allen Yeh and Chris Chun, 42-59. Eugene, OR: Wipf & Stock, 2013.

Drewery, Mary. *William Carey: Shoemaker and Missionary.* Grand Rapids, MI: Zondervan, 1979.

Dutta, Sutapa. *British Women Missionaries in Bengal, 1793-1861.* London: Anthem Press, 2017.

Edwards, David Lawrence. *Christian England.* 3 Vols. London: William Collins Sons & Co., 1984.

Farrer, Keith. *William Carey: Missionary and Botanist.* Kew, Vic: Carey Baptist Grammar School, 2005.

Ferguson, Donald. "The Settlement of the Danes at Tranquebar and Serampore," *Journal of the Royal Asiatic Society of Great Britain and Ireland* (July 1898): 625-629.

Ferguson, Niall. *Empire: The Rise and Demise of the British World Order and the Lessons for Global Power.* New York: Basic Books, 2003.

Finn, Margot and Kate Smith, eds. *The East India Company at Home, 1757-1857.* London: UCL Press, 2018.

Firth, C.B. *An Introduction to Indian Church History.* Delhi: ISPCK for Senate of Serampore College, 1998.

Fountain, David. "Can the old Church Covenants help us today?" *Sword & Trowel* (December 4, 1985).
Frykenberg, Robert Eric. *Christianity in India: From Beginnings to the Present*. Oxford: Oxford University Press, 2008.
Gardner-Chloros, P. *Code-Switching*. Cambridge: Cambridge University Press, 2009.
George, Annie. "Educational Principles of the Serampore Mission and its Implications for Contemporary Education." In *Serampore Mission: Perspectives in Contexts*, ed. Johnson Thomaskutty, 123–140. New Delhi: ISPCK, 2019.
George, Timothy. *Faithful Witness: The Life and Mission of William Carey*. Birmingham, AL: New Hope, 1991.
Gillette, A. D. ed. *Minutes of the Philadelphia Baptist Association 1707–1807, Being the First One Hundred Years of Its Existence. Tricentennial Edition, 1707 to 2007*. Philadelphia Association Series. Springfield, MO: Particular Baptist Press, 2002.
Gine, Pratap Chandra. "Preface," in *Communication in Theological Education: New Directions*. Edited by Michael Traber. Delhi: ISPCK, 2005.
Giri, K. "William Carey's Approach to the People of Other Faiths, Religious Practices, Caste System, and Conversion." In *Serampore Mission: Perspectives in Contexts*, ed. Johnson Thomaskutty, 123–140. New Delhi: ISPCK, 2019.
Glover, Gareth. *The Two Battles of Copenhagen 1801 and 1807: Britain and Denmark in the Napoleonic Wars*. Barnsley: Pen and Sword, 2018.
Gordon, Stewart. *The Marathas 1600–1818, The New Cambridge History of India*, II, 4 Cambridge: Cambridge University Press, 1993.
Griffiths, Percival. *The British Impact on India*, Routledge Revivals. New York: Routledge, 1952.
Grigg, John A. *The Lives of David Brainerd: the Making of an American Evangelical Icon* Oxford: Oxford University Press, 2009.
Handel, G. F. *The Messiah: An Oratorio*. New York: G. Schirmer, Inc., 1912.
Harrison, Mark. "A Dreadful Scourge: Cholera in early nineteenth-century India," *Modern Asian Studies* 54, no. 2 (March 2020): 502–553.

Bibliography

Haykin, Michael A. G. "The Serampore Form of Agreement (1805)." In *The Missionary Fellowship of William Carey*. In The Long Line of Godly Men Profiles. Edited by Steven J. Lawson, 137-154. Sanford, FL: Reformation Trust, 2018.

Haykin, Michael A. G. and Kenneth J. Stewart. eds. *The Emergence of Evangelicalism: Exploring Historical Continuities*. Leicester: Inter-Varsity Press, 2008.

Hesselgrave, David J. and Edward Rommen. *Contextualization: Meanings, Methods, and Models*. Grand Rapids, MI: Baker Book House, 1989.

Hiebert, Paul G. *"Critical Contextualization,"* Anthropological Reflections on Missiological Issues. Grand Rapids, MI: Baker Books, 1994.

Higginbotham, J. *Men Whom India Has Known: Biographies of Eminent Indian Characters*. Madras: Higginbotham & Co., 1874.

Hilton, Boyd. *The Age of Atonement: The Influence of Evangelicalism on Social and Economic Thought, 1795-1865*. Oxford: Clarendon, 1988.

Hinde, Wendy. *George Canning*. New York: St. Martin's Press, 1973.

Hinkson, Jon. "Missions among Puritans and Pietists." In *The Great Commission: Evangelicals and the History of World Missions*, eds. Martin I. Klauber and Scott M. Manetsch, 23-43. Nashville: B&H Academic, 2008.

Hooper, J. S. M. *Bible Translation in India, Pakistan and Ceylon*. 2nd edn. Revised by W. J. Culshaw. London: Oxford University Press, 1963.

Howells, George. *The Story of Serampore and its College*. Serampore/Cuttack: Orissa Mission Press, 1927.

Hutton, J. E. *A History of the Moravian Church*. London: Moravian Publication Office, 1909.

Hutton, J.E. *A History of Moravian Missions*. London: Moravian Publication Office, 1922.

Hutton, Ronald. *The British Republic 1649-1660*. New York: St. Martin's Press, 2000.

Ivermee, Robert. *Hooghly: The Global History of a River*. London: C. Hurst and Co., 2020.

Jackson, E.M. "Joshua Rowe," in *Dictionary of Evangelical Biography 1730-1860 (DEB)*, ed. Donald M. Lewis, 957. 2 vols. Oxford: Blackwell, 1995.

Jaffe, A. ed. *Stance: Sociolinguistic Perspective.* Oxford: Oxford University Press, 2009.

James, Woba. "The Contribution of the Serampore Missions towards the Ecumenical Movement: A Historical Perspective." In *Serampore Mission: Perspectives in Contexts*, ed. Johnson Thomaskutty, 141-151. New Delhi: ISPCK, 2019.

Johnston, Anna. *Missionary Writing and Empire, 1800-1860.* Cambridge: Cambridge University Press, 2003.

Jones, Kenneth W. *Socio-Religious Reform Movements in British India, The New Cambridge History of British India*, III, 1. Cambridge: Cambridge University Press, 1989.

Jones, Stanly J. "William Carey's Bible Translation Principles: Prospects and Challenges." In *Serampore Mission: Perspectives in Contexts*, ed. Johnson Thomaskutty, 70-93. New Delhi: ISPCK, 2019.

Kidd, Colin. *British Identities Before Nationalism: Ethnicity and Nationhood in the Atlantic World, 1600-1800.* Cambridge: Cambridge University Press, 2000.

Kommers, J. Hans. *Triumphant Love: The Contextual, Creative and Strategic Missionary Work of Amy Beatrice Carmichael in South India.* Eugene, OR: Wipf and Stock, 2020.

Kraemer, Hendrik. *World Cultures and World Religions.* Cambridge: James Clarke Co., 1960.

Lalhmangaiha, Andrew. *Holistic Mission and the Serampore Trio.* The ISPCK Tercentenary Publication. Delhi: Indian Society for Promoting Christian Knowledge, 2010.

Lambrecht, Jan. "First Corinthians," *The International Bible Commentary: An Ecumenical Commentary for the Twenty-First Century*, ed. William R. Farmer. Bangalore: Theological Publications in India, 1998.

Langley, M. H. "The B.M.S. and its Story" in *The Codex*, XXX No 1. (Sept 1942), 4-6.

Latourette, Kenneth Scott. "The Christian Missionary Movement of the Nineteenth and Twentieth Centuries: Some Peculiar and General Characteristics." *The Catholic Historical Review* 23, no. 2 (July 1937): 153-159.

Bibliography

Latourette, Kenneth Scott. *The Great Century: The Americas, Australia, and Africa A.D. 1800-A.D. 1914*, in vol. 5 of *A History of The Expansion of Christianity*. New York: Harper & Brothers, 1943.

Lawrence, Arren Bennet. "Paul, Culture, and Sexual Immorality in 1 Corinthians 5 and 6," *One Gospel, Many Cultures: Doing Theology in Context*. Minneapolis: Fortress Press, 2022.

Liddon, H. P. *Life of Edward Bouverie Pusey*, 4 vols. London: Longmans, Green and Co., 1893.

Majeed, Javed. *Ungoverned Imaginings: James Mill's The History of British India and Orientalism*. Oxford: Clarendon, 1992.

Mangalwadi, Vishal and Ruth. *The Legacy of William Carey: A Model for the Transformation of a Culture*. Wheaton, IL: Crossway Books, 1993/1999.

Mani, Lata. *Contentious Traditions: The Debate on Sati in Colonial India*. Berkeley, CA: University of California Press, 1998.

Manning, Bernard Lord. *The Protestant Dissenting Deputies*, edited by Ormerod Greenwood. Cambridge: Cambridge University Press, 1952.

Marbaniang, Domenic. *Secularism in India: A Historical Analysis*. Itarsi: Domenic Marbaniang, 2005, 2010, 2011.

Marshall, P. J. *Bengal: The British Bridgehead, Eastern India 1740-1828*, The New Cambridge History of India, II, 2. Cambridge: Cambridge University Press, 1987.

Massey, John D., Mike Morris and W. Madison Grace II. *Make Disciples of All Nations: A History of Southern Baptist International Missions*. Grand Rapids, MI: Kregel Academic, 2021.

Masters, Samuel E. "'Will Anyone Say the Lord is not Among Us?' The Serampore Mission and its Covenant." Ph.D. diss., The Southern Baptist Theological Seminary, Louisville, 2020.

Masters, Samuel E. "The Serampore mission and the Moravian connection." *The Journal of Andrew Fuller Studies* 9 (Fall 2024): 56-69.

Mathew, K.V. "Indigenisation: An Old Testament Perspective," *Indian Journal of Theology*, 32/1-2 (1983): 1-8.

Mathew, Prakash Abraham. "The Impact of the Bible through the Protestant Reformation and the Protestant Missionary Movement." In *Serampore Mission: Perspectives in Contexts*, ed. Johnson Thomaskutty, 49–69. New Delhi: ISPCK, 2019.

McClendon, Adam. "The Crucicentrism of Andrew Fuller (1754–1815)." *Churchman* 127, no. 4 (2013): 311–322.

McKim, D.K. *Westminster Dictionary of Theological Terms*. Louisville/London: Westminster John Knox Press, 1996.

McLane, John R. *Land and Local Kingship in Eighteenth-Century Bengal*. Cambridge: Cambridge University Press, 1993.

Mee, Jon. *Romanticism, Enthusiasm, and Regulation: Poetics and the Policing of Culture in the Romantic Period*. Oxford: Oxford University Press, 2003.

Middlebrook, J. B. *William Carey*. London: The Carey Kingsgate Press, 1961.

Midgley, Clare. "Can Women Be Missionaries? Envisioning Female Agency in the Early Nineteenth-Century British Empire." *Journal of British Studies* 45, no. 2 (April 2006): 335-358.

Moessner, Jeanne Stevenson. "The Self-Differentiated Samaritan." In *Images of Pastoral Care: Classic Readings*, ed. Robert C. Dykstra, 62–68. Danvers, MA: Chalice Press, 2005.

Moravians
    <https://www.wmcarey.edu/carey/wmward/Misc%20html/moravian.html>

Morden, Peter J. *The Life and Thought of Andrew Fuller (1754–1815)*. Milton Keynes: Paternoster, 2015.

Morden, Peter J. *Offering Christ to the World*. Milton Keynes: Paternoster, 2003.

Mukhopadhyaya, Indira. "William Carey's Contributions for the Promotion of Sanskritic Studies." In *Carey's Obligation and India's Renaissance*, eds. J. T. K. Daniel and Roger E. Hedlund, 193–201. Serampore: Council of Serampore College, 1993.

Mukhopadhyay, Sakti Sadhan. *Derozio: His Background and Cultural Milieu. A Collection of Sources and Documents*. Kolkata: Kidderpore College, 2008.

Bibliography

Nath Sen, Sailendra. *Anglo-Maratha Relations 1785-1796*. Vol. 2. Bombay: Popular Prakashan, 1974, reprinted 1994.

Neild-Basu, Susan. "The Dubashes of Madras," *Modern Asian Studies* 18, I (1984), 1-31.

Noonkester, M. C. "Mr. Gibbon, Revd. Fuller and the Apocalypse," *Notes and Queries* 237 (1992): 486-489.

O'Connor, Daniel. *The Chaplains of the East India Company, 1601-1858*. London: Bloomsbury, 2012.

Oddie, Geoffrey A. *Imagined Hinduism: British Protestant Missionary Constructions of Hinduism, 1793-1900*. Richmond, Surrey: Curzon, 1979. New Delhi: Sage Publications, 2006.

Oddie, Geoffrey A. *Religious Conversion Movements in South Asia: Continuities and Change, 1800-1900*. Richmond, Surrey: Curzon, 1979.

Ogborn, Miles. *Indian Ink: Script and Print in the Making of the East India Company*. Chicago: University of Chicago Press, 2007.

Ott, Craig and J. D. Payne, eds. *Missionary Methods: Research, Reflections, and Realities*. Pasadena, CA: William Carey Library, 2013.

Oussoren, A. H. "The Bond of the Missionary Brotherhood of Serampore." In *William Carey, Especially His Missionary Principles*, 274-284. Leiden: A. W. Sijthoff's Uitgeversmaatschappij N.V., 1945.

Oussoren, Aalbertinus H. *William Carey Especially His Missionary Principles*. Leiden: Sijthoff, 1945.

Packer, J. I. *The Redemption and Restoration of Man in the Thought of Richard Baxter: A Study in Puritan Theology*. Vancouver, BC: Regent College Publications, 2003.

Patole, James. "The Modern Missionary Movement of the Serampore Trio: A Missiological Perspective." In *Serampore Mission: Perspectives in Contexts*, ed. Johnson Thomaskutty, 232-258. New Delhi: ISPCK, 2019.

Payne, Ernest A. *South-East from Serampore: More Chapters in the Story of the Baptist Missionary Society*. London: The Carey Press, 1945.

Payne, Ernest A., ed. "The Serampore Form of Agreement." *The Baptist Quarterly* 12/5 (1947): 125-138.

Pearn, B.R. "Felix Carey and the English Baptist Mission in Burma." *Journal of the Burma Research Society* xxviii, no. I (1938): 1-91.

Pennington, Brian K. *Was Hinduism Invented? Britons, Indians, and the Colonial Construction of Religion*. Oxford: Oxford University Press, 2005.

Philip, George. "The Centrality of Christ and the Hermeneutical Perspectives of the Serampore Mission." In *Serampore Mission: Perspectives in Contexts*, ed. Johnson Thomaskutty, 164-181. New Delhi: ISPCK, 2019.

Pierson, Arthur Tappan. *The Divine Enterprise of Missions. A Series of Lectures...* New York: The Baker & Taylor Co., 1891.

Plato. *Euthyphro, Apology, Crito, Phaedo, Phaedrus*. With an English Translation by Harold North Fowler. Introduction by W. R. M. Lamb. In The Loeb Classical Library. Cambridge and London: Harvard University Press, 1914.

Porter, Andrew. *Religion versus Empire? British Protestant Missionaries and Overseas Expansion, 1700-1914*. Manchester/New York: Manchester University Press, 2004.

Potts, E. Daniel. *British Baptist Missionaries in India, 1793-1837: The History of Serampore and its Missions*. London: Cambridge University Press, 1967.

Potts, E. Daniel. "The Baptist Missionaries of Serampore and the Government of India, 1792-1813." *Journal of Ecclesiastical History* 15 (1964): 229-246.

Potts, E. Daniel. "William Ward: the making of a Missionary in the 18th Century," *Bicentenary Volume: William Carey's Arrival in India 1793-1993*, 27-34. Serampore: Council of Serampore College, 1993.

Pratt, Zane, David M. Sills and Jeff K. Walters. *Introduction to Global Missions*. Nashville, TN: B&H Publishing, 2014.

Pruthi, R.K. ed. *Brahmo Samaj and Indian Civilization, Culture and Civilization Series*. New Delhi: Discovery Publishing House, 2004.

Qayyum, Muhammad Abdul. *A Critical Study of the Early Bengali Grammars: Halhed to Haughton*. Dhaka: The Asiatic Society of Bangladesh, 1982.

Bibliography

Rao, Potana Venkateswara. "New Wineskins: A Study on Indigenous Christian Missions Theory," *Indian Journal of Research* 3/8 (2014): 169-170.

Ray, N.R. "William Carey—Linguist with a Difference." In *Carey's Obligation and India's Renaissance*, eds. J. T. K. Daniel and Roger E. Hedlund, 153-156. Serampore: Council of Serampore College, 1993.

Reynolds, Matthew M. *The Spirituality of William Ward.* West Lorne, Ontario: H&E Academic, 2023.

Robertson, Bruce C. *Raja Rammohan Ray: The Father of Modern India.* Delhi: Oxford University Press, 1995.

Schattschneider, David A. "William Carey, Modern Missions, and the Moravian Influence." *International Bulletin of Missionary Research* 22, no.1 (1998): 8-12.

Schmidt, Martin. *Pietismus.* Stuttgart/ Köln: Verlag W. Kohlhammer, 1972.

Sengupta, Kanti Prasanna. *The Christian Missionaries in Bengal 1793-1833.* Calcutta: K.L. Mukhopadhyay, 1971.

Seth, Suman. *Difference and Disease: Medicine, Race, and the Eighteenth-Century British Empire.* Edited by Sanjoy Bhattacharya. Cambridge: Cambridge University Press, 2018.

Shenk, Wilbert R. "After Bosch: Toward a Fresh Interpretation of the Church on the World of East Asia in the Twenty-first Century." Paper presented at Union Biblical Seminary, Pune, 21st August 2003. *UBS Journal* 2. 2 (2004): 1-16.

Sivasundaram, Sujit. "'A Christian Benares': Orientalism, Science and the Serampore Mission of Bengal." *The Indian Economic and Social History Review* 44, no. 2 (2007): 111-145.

Smith, A. Christopher. "British Recruits for Serampore, 1800-1825," *The Baptist Review of Theology* 2.2 (Fall 1992): 12-13.

Smith, A. Christopher. "William Ward (1769-1823)." In *The British Particular Baptists, 1638-1910.* ed. Michael A.G. Haykin, 263-264. Vol. 2. Springfield, MO: Particular Baptist Press, 2000.

Smith, A. Christopher. "William Ward, Radical Reform, and Missions in the 1790's." *American Baptist Quarterly* 10 (1991): 218-244.

Smith, A. Christopher. "The Legacy of William Ward and Joshua and Hannah Marshman." *International Bulletin of Mission Research* 23, no. 3 (1999): 120-129.

Smith, A. Christopher. *The Serampore Mission Enterprise: Studies in the Gospel Interface with Indian Contexts.* Bangalore: Centre for Contemporary Christianity, 2006.

Smith, George. *The Life of William Carey D.D.: Shoemaker and Missionary.* London: John Murray, 1885.

Smith, Karen E. "Female Education among Baptists in the Eighteenth Century: Martha (Smith) Trinder (1736-1790) and Henrietta Neale (1752-1802)." *Baptist Quarterly* 48, no. 4 (2007): 168-180.

Stanley, Brian. "Planting Self-Governing Churches: British Baptist Ecclesiology in the Missionary Context." *Baptist Quarterly* 34, no. 8, (1992): 378-389.

Stanley, Brian. *The History of the Baptist Missionary Society, 1792-1992.* Edinburgh: T & T Clark, 1992.

Stetzer, Ed. *Planting Missional Churches.* Nashville, TN: Broadman & Holman, 2006.

Stott, John R. W. "The Bible in World Evangelization." In Ralph D. Winter and Steven C. Hawthorne, eds., *Perspectives on the World Christian Movement: A Reader.* Third edn., 21-26. Pasadena, CA: William Carey Library, 1999.

Sugirtharajah, Sharada. *Imagining Hinduism: A Postcolonial Perspective.* London: Routledge, 2003.

Tamez, Elsa. "Galatians." *The International Bible Commentary: An Ecumenical Commentary for the Twenty-First Century*, ed. William R. Farmer. Bangalore: Theological Publications in India, 1998.

Tavolacci, Laura. "Agriculture as Redemption: Baptist Missionaries, Bengali Elites, and the Agri-Horticultural 'Improvement' of India, 1793-1840." Dissertation, University of California, 2018.

Taylor, Howard. *Hudson Taylor and the China Inland Mission.* London: The China Inland Mission, 1918.

Tennent, Timothy C. *Theology in the Context of World Christianity: How the Global Church Is Influencing the Way We Think about and Discuss Theology.* Grand Rapids, MI: Zondervan, 2007.

Bibliography

Terry, John Mark and Robert L. Gallagher. *Encountering the History of Missions: From the Early Church to Today*. Grand Rapids, MI: Baker Academic, 2017.

"The Bhagavad-Gītā." In *Hindu Scriptures*. Edited with new translation by Dominic Goodall. Berkeley and Los Angeles: University of California, 1996.

Thomaskutty, Johnson and Mathew Chandrankunnel, eds., *Wider Contextualized Biblical Spirituality*. New Delhi: Christian World Imprints, 2021

Thomaskutty, Johnson. "Culture Dynamics in the Johannine Community Context," *One Gospel, Many Cultures: Doing Theology in Context*, ed. Arren Bennet Lawrence, 135-160. Minneapolis: Fortress Press, 2022.

Thomaskutty, Johnson. "Re-reading the Gospel of John in the Light of William Carey's Linguistic Methods." In *Serampore Mission: Perspectives in Contexts*, ed. Johnson Thomaskutty, 94-122. New Delhi: ISPCK, 2019.

Thomaskutty, Johnson. "Wider Ecumenism in John 17:1-26 in the Light of Theological Education in India," *Bangalore Theological Forum* LIV/1 (June 2022): 157-173.

Townsend, Wm. Cameron. "Tribes, Tongues and Translators." In Ralph D. Winter and Steven C. Hawthorne, eds., *Perspectives on the World Christian Movement: A Reader*. Third edn., 309-310. Pasadena, CA: William Carey Library, 1999.

Tupper, H.A. *Two Centuries of the First Baptist Church of South Carolina, 1683-1883*. With Supplement. Baltimore: R. H. Woodward, 1889.

Van den Berg, Johannes. *Constrained by Jesus' Love: An Enquiry into the Motives of the Missionary Awakening in Great Britain in the Period between 1698 and 1815*. Kampen: J. H. Kok, 1956.

Visser, Paul J. *Heart for the Gospel, Heart for the World. The Life and Thought of a Reformed Pioneer Missiologist Johan Herman Bavinck, 1895-1964*. Eugene, OR: Wipf and Stock, 2003.

Vanhoozer, Kevin J., Charles A. Anderson and Michael J. Sleasman, eds. *Everyday Theology: How to Read Cultural Texts and Interpret Trends*. Grand Rapids, MI: Baker Academic, 2007.

Walls, Andrew F. "The Translation Principle in Christian History." In *The Missionary Movement in Christian History: Studies in the Transmission of Faith*, 26–42. Maryknoll, NY: Orbis, 1996.

Walls, Andrew F. *The Missionary Movement in Christian History: Studies in the Transmission of Faith*. Maryknoll, NY: Orbis, 2000.

Wenger, Edward S. *The Story of the Lall Bazar Baptist Church Calcutta: Being the History of Carey's Church from 24th April 1800 to the Present Day*. Calcutta: Edinburgh Press, 1908.

Whelan, Timothy D. ed. *Baptist Autographs in the John Rylands University Library of Manchester, 1741-1845*. Macon, GA: Mercer University Press, 2009.

White, Daniel E. *From Little London to Little Bengal: Religion, Print and Modernity in Early British India, 1793-1835*. Baltimore: Johns Hopkins University Press, 2013.

Williams, C. Peter. "The Church Missionary Society and the Indigenous Church in the Second Half of the Nineteenth Century: The Defense and Destruction of the Venn Ideas." In *Converting Colonialism: Visions and Realities in Mission History, 1706-1914*, ed. Dana L. Robert, 86–111. Grand Rapids, MI: Eerdmans, 2008.

Wintle, Michael. *Eurocentrism: History, Identity, White Man's Burden*. London and New York: Routledge, 2021.

Wolf, William J. "Atonement: Christian Concepts." In *The Encyclopedia of Religion*, edited by Mircea Eliade, I, 495–499. New York & London: Macmillan, 1987.

Wright, Vinita Hampton. "William Ward (1769-1823) Radical, and 'spiritual father'," https://christianhistoryinstitute.org/magazine/article/rest-of-the-serampore-trio

Young, Brian. "'The Lust of Empire and Religious Hate': Christianity, History, and India, 1790-1820." In *History, Religion, and Culture: British Intellectual History, 1750-1950*. Edited by Collini, Stefan, Richard Whatmore, and Brian Young, 91–111. Cambridge: Cambridge University Press, 2000.

Young, Richard Fox. "Church Sanskrit: An Approach of Christian Scholars to Hinduism in the Nineteenth Century," *Wiener Zeitschrift für die Kunde Südasiens*, 23 (1979): 205–231.

Bibliography

Young, Richard Fox. *Resistant Hinduism: Sanscrit Sources on Anti-Christian Apologetics in Early Nineteenth-Century India*. Vienna: Institut für Indologie der Universität Wien, 1981. Leiden: Brill, 1981.

Zhimomi, Kaholi. "Beyond the Serampore Mission Historiography: Redefining Ecumenism from the Context." In *Serampore Mission: Perspectives in Contexts*, ed. Johnson Thomaskutty, 259–281. New Delhi: ISPCK, 2019.

SUBJECT INDEX

A

A. H. Oussoren, 24, 43, 70, 162, 212
accountability, 35, 46
Adivasi, 81
Admiral Nelson, 86
Afghanistan, 98
Age of Atonement, 105, 258
Age of Improvement, 105, 254
Agra, 93, 157, 175, 241, 247
Agricultural Society of India, 62
Ajimere, 175
Akyab, 175
Alexander Burgh Lish, 157
Ali, Muhammad Mohar, 253
Allahabad, 175
Amy Carmichael, 218, 221
Anabaptist communities, 13
Andrew Fuller, 15, 17, 21, 22, 28, 31, 32, 45, 46, 47, 88, 98, 103, 112, 113, 151, 162, 183, 184, 187, 193, 198, 199, 200, 203, 205, 206, 246, 249, 260
Andrew Lalhmangaiha, 182, 183
Andrew Walls, 64, 109
Anglican, 48, 96, 99, 145, 173, 212, 222
Anglicans. *See Anglican*
Anglo-European superiority, 14
Ann Brunsdon, 153
Ann Grant, 153
Anne Chater, 193
Anthony Benezet, 44
apostle Paul, 50, 131, 193, 199, 217

Arminianism, 116
Arracan, 175
atonement, 103, 105, 113, 115, 116, 117, 118, 119, 228

B

Balasore, 175
Bansberia, 175, 216
Baptist Missionary Society, 18, 22, 36, 37, 38, 41, 47, 67, 86, 93, 95, 98, 99, 105, 110, 111, 131, 144, 147, 151, 152, 157, 164, 169, 172, 175, 180, 182, 193, 194, 195, 203, 214, 219, 222, 223, 239, 240, 243, 244, 245, 249, 250, 252, 256, 261, 263
Barrackpore, 146, 172
Bartholomeus Ziegenbalg, 180
Bavinck, 221, 265
Benares, 106, 119, 175, 263
Benevolent Institution, 153, 157
Bengali, 57, 58, 63, 78, 79, 106, 109, 110, 111, 112, 114, 118, 123, 128, 132, 134, 147, 156, 158, 162, 163, 169, 170, 171, 172, 173, 179, 181, 183, 186, 190, 196, 197, 204, 205, 213, 216, 253, 256, 262, 264
Berhampore, 170, 175
bhakti, ix
Bharut, 171
Bhutan, 174, 203, 204
Bhyrub, 128, 129
Bible translation, 56, 62, 63, 77, 95, 98, 109, 110, 181, 205

325

Bible translations. *See Bible Translation*
Birbhum, 170, 223
BMS. *See Baptist Missionary Society*
Bonnet affair, 155
Botany, 158
Boxoo, 48
Brahmin, ix, 99, 168, 169, 213
Brahmins. *See Brahmin*
Brahmo Samaj, 71, 262
Brethren's Press, 22, 36, 37, 41, 42, 103, 246
Brian Stanley, 93, 105, 131, 151, 158, 175, 194, 212, 222
Bristol, 32, 151, 207
British and Foreign Bible Society, 96, 191, 244, 248, 249
Broadmead Church, 151
brother Sutton, 155
Bulwer-Lytton Edward, 242
Bunyan, John, 242
Burma, 152, 153, 174, 175, 205, 262
Bydenaut, 134, 135

C

C. Carapeit Aratoon, 174
Calcutta, 21, 37, 41, 42, 49, 50, 57, 84, 89, 91, 93, 94, 96, 97, 102, 110, 111, 118, 119, 136, 141, 142, 145, 146, 147, 148, 149, 151, 152, 153, 155, 156, 157, 158, 167, 169, 170, 172, 173, 174, 175, 176, 182, 190, 191, 203, 204, 206, 215, 221, 222, 242, 243, 244, 245, 246, 247, 248, 249, 251, 252, 254, 255, 263, 265
Calvinism, 29, 31, 105, 116, 117, 199, 200, 202
Cameron Townsend, 187, 188
Captain Christmas, 91
Caste, ix, 33, 69, 70, 73, 77, 86, 87, 90, 92, 95, 99, 100, 101, 102, 110, 111, 112, 122, 124, 125, 131, 136, 142, 163, 168, 169, 180, 216, 253, 254, 257
Ceylon, 175, 181, 203, 205, 258
Chandernagore, 155, 162, 164
Charak Puja, ix, 165
Charles Wilkins, 101
Charlotte H. White, 158
Charter Act Renewal, 175
China, 211, 220, 264
Chinsurah, 162
Chittagong, 169, 175, 253
Christian village, 142, 143
Christocentric, 197
church discipline, 23, 126, 141, 159, 171
church planting, 28, 31, 32
Churuk. *See Charak Puja*
Claudius Buchanan, 88, 96, 111, 221, 242, 244, 247, 249, 256
College of Fort William, 57, 63, 84, 88, 94, 96, 97, 167, 181, 190, 221, 242, 244, 245, 249, 256
Colombo, 175
Colonialism, 76, 265
communion, 23, 110, 117, 126, 130, 140, 145, 171, 193, 202
Confession of Faith, 48, 105, 116, 140
Contextualization, 56, 61, 258
conversing, 19, 20, 56, 61, 63, 226, 229
Count Zinzendorf, 162, 213, 217
Craig Ott, 213
Creeshnoo, 110, 124, 127, 129, 131, 155
cross-cultural, 54, 55, 64, 66, 94, 101, 106, 152, 168, 181, 193, 195, 209, 224
Crucicentrism, 112, 113, 260
crucified Christ, 15, 112, 120
cruelty to animals, 14, 227
Cultural Exegesis, 54

Index

Cutwa, 42, 95, 135, 170, 171, 174, 175

D

Dacca, 108, 170, 175, 203
Dalit, 81
Danes, 91, 253, 257
Daniel Brunsdon, 21, 93
Danish East India Company, 179
Danish Governor, 125, 148, 180
Das Gupta, R.K., 256
David Brainerd, 106, 107, 108, 195, 202, 220, 241, 245, 257
David Brown, 37, 145, 242
David J. Hesselgrave, 56
debtah, ix, 155
debtahs. *See Debtah*
DEIC. *See Danish East India Company*
deism, 45, 111, 246
Deist, 113
Delhi, 71, 76, 77, 78, 80, 81, 97, 100, 118, 146, 165, 175, 183, 184, 189, 251, 253, 255, 256, 257, 258, 259, 260, 261, 262, 264, 266
Derby Mercury, 40, 251
devotion, 83, 196, 200, 202, 207, 208, 217
Dhaka. *See Dacca*
Diakonia, 221
Dialogue, 80, 255
Dig Darshan, 189
Digah, 158, 175
diglossia, 80
Dinagepore, 171, 175, 203
Dinajpur. *See Dinagepore*
discipleship, 124, 126, 141, 159, 198, 208
disciplined church membership, 14
disinterested benevolence, 15
Dissenters, 83, 86, 88, 96, 113, 118, 144, 145

dissolution of the church, 14
divine love, 15
Dorothy Carey, 43, 87, 152, 223, 253, 255
Dr. Furman, 99
dubashis, 215, 216
Duke of Wellington, 89, 90
Dum Dum, 175
durwan, ix, 123

E

E. Daniel Potts, vii, 20, 21, 25, 38, 57, 84, 88, 115, 152, 155, 163, 180, 182, 183, 187, 196, 216, 240
East India Company, 21, 71, 81, 85, 87, 89, 90, 91, 93, 98, 101, 102, 144, 145, 146, 161, 181, 254, 255, 257, 261
education, 25, 49, 151, 154, 161, 176, 191, 206, 207, 221
Edward S. Wenger, 142, 157, 174, 203, 205, 215
EIC. *See East India Company*
Eleanor Moore, 205
election, 29, 116
Elizabeth Robinson, 193, 203
Elizabeth Sale, 156
Enlightenment, 17, 43, 78, 95, 147, 211, 216, 256
Enquiry, 17, 18, 24, 25, 28, 29, 31, 32, 36, 37, 39, 43, 44, 45, 49, 50, 51, 60, 68, 70, 106, 109, 116, 120, 139, 150, 151, 163, 164, 167, 200, 219, 244, 247, 265
equality, 22, 33, 43, 69, 70, 73, 77, 82, 121, 122, 131, 132, 133, 137, 204
Erasmus, 109
Eric Frykenberg, 215
Ernest Payne, 22, 73
eschatology, 105, 201
Eurasian, 157, 167, 175

evangelism, 28, 32, 69, 70, 72, 75, 82, 88, 90, 95, 96, 98, 101, 102, 124, 166, 171, 176, 191, 215, 221
evangelistic journeys, 162
Ewood Hall, 39, 40, 44

F

Felix Carey, 22, 36, 63, 107, 112, 124, 152, 153, 179, 223, 234, 243, 262
fervor, 96, 124
finance, 214, 219
firanghi, 110
French Revolution, 17, 88
Friend of India, 63, 119, 169, 170, 189, 220, 240, 248
Fuller. *See Andrew Fuller*
Futick, 125, 169
Futika. *See Futick*

G

Ganja, 127
gayatri, ix, 111
Geo. Barlow, 146
George Howells, 207
George III, 83, 84, 87
George Sale, 147
George Whitefield, 29
Goamalty, 114, 115, 174, 175
godliness, 165, 193, 194, 196, 198, 200, 202, 204, 206, 208, 209, 211, 224, 233
Gokol, 124, 125, 126, 127, 128, 129, 130, 132
Gokool. *See Gokol*
gospel, 19, 29, 30, 31, 32, 33, 34, 39, 40, 42, 45, 53, 54, 55, 58, 59, 60, 61, 62, 63, 64, 65, 66, 72, 75, 76, 102, 104, 113, 122, 123, 126, 131, 132, 133, 139, 142, 143, 145, 150, 152, 156, 162, 165, 166, 171, 172, 174, 176, 188, 197, 200, 206, 213, 221, 228, 231, 234
grace, 20, 30, 33, 53, 106, 115, 116, 119, 130, 150, 161, 193, 196, 198, 199, 200, 217, 225, 230, 231
Greenland, 108, 114

H

Halle, 216
Hannah Biss, 205
Hannah Marshman, 94, 150, 151, 153, 154, 156, 158, 203, 207, 208, 215, 240, 255, 263
Hannah More, 151
Harvey Lane Baptist Church, 45, 48, 85, 239, 244
Heathen, 28, 36, 37, 41, 42, 45, 60, 74, 91, 103, 108, 163, 240, 241, 242, 246, 250, 253
Hebrew, 96, 104, 196, 247
Heinrich Plütschau, 68, 180
hemp. *See Ganja*
Henrietta Neale, 151, 263
Henry Venn, 161
Herbert Marsh, 190, 191
Hesselgrave. *See David J. Hesselgrave*
Hilton Boyd, 105
Hindu, ix, 46, 48, 50, 51, 56, 58, 59, 62, 70, 74, 80, 98, 99, 100, 104, 108, 110, 111, 117, 118, 124, 126, 127, 142, 143, 148, 162, 163, 168, 169, 170, 172, 215, 222, 245, 253, 255, 264
Hindu festivals, 162
Hindu pandit, 58
Hindustan, 174, 175
Hindustani. *See Hindustan*
Hooghly, 69, 83, 87, 91, 94, 152, 162, 168, 197, 218, 224, 253, 255, 258
Hospitality, 121, 123
Hudson Taylor, 211, 220, 223, 264

Index

Hull, 25, 40, 72, 187, 188, 189, 251
human responsibility, 30, 105, 199
humility, 22, 137

I

idolatry, 53, 56, 58, 65, 70, 74, 95, 102, 118, 169
Ignatius Fernandez, 174, 215, 254
images, 14, 19, 58, 72, 77, 188, 227
impartial, 20, 126, 129, 228
Imperialism, 76, 255
incarnation, 48, 99, 109, 110, 114, 115, 121
inculturation, 69
indigeneity, 96, 161
Indigenization, 161
infanticide, 69, 165
Isaac Watts, 39, 223, 247
Isle de France, 175

J

J. B. Middlebrook, 182
Jabez Carey, 223
James Chater, 114, 174, 205
James R. Beck, 43, 87, 223
James Williamson, 152, 223
Jan Huss, 91
Jannagar. *See Jannagore*
Java, 175, 203
Jessore, 114, 169, 170, 171, 174, 175
Jesuits, 187
Johann Hinrich Wichern, 221
Johannes Grassman, 180, 216
John Biss, 22, 36, 95, 152, 179, 234, 243
John Bunyan. *See Bunyan, John*
John Chamberlain, 22, 36, 37, 42, 95, 122, 133, 134, 135, 136, 137, 152, 174, 179, 196, 202, 234, 243, 252

John Clark Marshman, 24, 38, 57, 95, 111, 131, 134, 137, 142, 152, 162, 173, 182, 194, 214
John Eliot, 106
John Eve, 199
John Fawcett, 39, 40, 44, 45, 48, 117
John Fernandez, 124
John Fountain, 93, 111, 123, 124, 152
John Lawson, 153, 240
John Mack, 143, 173, 176
John Muir, 119
John Owen, 116
John Peter, 172
John R. Stott, 188
John Ryland Jr, 193, 196, 199
John Sutcliff, 89, 93, 171, 201, 203
John Thomas, 18, 23, 44, 93, 111, 123, 146, 218, 247, 255
John Wesley, 86
Jonathan Edwards, 29, 47, 105, 107, 200, 201, 202, 208, 245
Joshua Marshman, 18, 21, 22, 26, 27, 36, 38, 41, 63, 67, 108, 118, 132, 135, 151, 157, 169, 179, 194, 197, 201, 203, 204, 206, 214, 223, 234, 243, 256
Joshua Rowe, 22, 36, 92, 93, 95, 158, 179, 205, 234, 243, 258
Joymoona, 155
Joymooni. *See joymoona*
justification, 85

K

Kaj Baago, 162
Kangalee, 135
Karl F. Schmidt, 216
Katwa. *See Cutwa*
Keshub Chunder Sen, 58
Keswick Convention, 222
Kettering, 22, 31, 86, 113, 222
Khasi, 157, 158

Kolkata. *See Calcutta, See Calcutta*
Kollador, 128
Koran. *See Qur'an*
Krefting, 146, 148, 149
Krishna. *See Chresnoo*
Krishna Pal, 22, 111, 123, 141, 142, 157, 163, 168, 170, 172, 173, 180, 216, 250
Krishna Prasad, 22, 168, 170
Kron Princesse Maria, 91

L

Lal Bazaar Chapel. *See Lall Bazar*
Lall Bazar, 142, 156, 157, 174, 175, 215, 265
Lancastrian schools, 143
language study, 78, 79
Leicester, 14, 27, 29, 36, 44, 45, 48, 60, 68, 85, 88, 93, 106, 139, 164, 199, 200, 222, 239, 244, 245, 247, 253, 258
Lindeman, Peter, 215
linguistics, 80, 94, 106
Lord Minto, 146, 147, 148
Lord's supper, 142, 197
Lord's Supper, 22, 23, 126, 128, 129, 133
love, xi, 14, 15, 22, 31, 40, 44, 45, 47, 73, 78, 104, 111, 112, 114, 115, 117, 120, 129, 135, 144, 154, 164, 187, 188, 211, 213, 217, 218, 219, 224, 227, 228, 229
Love, 27, 47, 56, 214, 218, 219, 246, 255, 259, 265
Luckphool, 171
Luther, 103, 105, 109, 113, 228
Luther Rice, 152
Lutheran, 68, 71, 254

M

magistrates, 144, 212

Malabar, 84
Malda, 21, 114, 170, 172, 174, 175, 184
Maratha, 84, 85, 87, 261
Marathas. *See Maratha*
Marathi. See Maratha
Mardon, Richard, 22, 36, 93, 95, 114, 115, 174, 179, 234, 243
Marianne Lewis, 156, 222
Marquess Wellesley, 86, 88, 90, 248, 254
Mary Biss, 92
Mary Ward, 153, 154
means, 17, 19, 27, 29, 31, 32, 33, 44, 57, 60, 61, 67, 72, 73, 75, 99, 103, 105, 110, 113, 115, 116, 117, 122, 123, 141, 142, 165, 166, 183, 189, 190, 196, 198, 200, 207, 211, 217, 223, 226, 227, 229, 230, 231, 232, 233
medicine, 56, 93, 219
meekness, 22, 148, 164, 198, 224
Methodism, 86, 103, 228
Michael Haykin, 43, 113, 246
Miss Chaffin, 153
mission stations, 135, 166, 196, 224
Missionary Identity, 35
missions, vii, 15, 18, 28, 29, 30, 33, 35, 39, 55, 56, 64, 65, 66, 67, 69, 73, 74, 75, 81, 90, 94, 96, 144, 146, 150, 156, 174, 179, 180, 186, 214, 215, 221
Mlechas, 165
Mleechas. *See Mlechas*
modern-day missions, 15
moksha, 46, 110
Monghyr, 151, 175
moonshee. See Munshis
Moorad, 171
Moravian, 15, 18, 21, 22, 24, 27, 28, 31, 32, 33, 34, 42, 69, 91, 95, 101, 108, 109, 112, 119, 120, 131, 153,

Index

179, 180, 212, 216, 218, 248, 250, 252, 258, 263
Moulton, 27, 28, 45, 239
Mr. Brock, 222
Mr. Buckingham, 143
Mr. Ellerton, 125, 184
Mr. Lumsden, 146
Mrs. Peacock, 157
Mudnabati. *See Mudnabatty*
Mudnabatty, 108
Muhammad Bakur, 169
Munshis, 97, 256
Muttra, 175
Mysore, 84

N

N. R. Ray, 79
Nagpore, 175
Napoleonic, 87, 88, 92, 257
Nathaniel Brassey Halhed, 101
Nathaniel Forsyth, 174
Nathaniel Wallich, 94, 239
Native Americans, 195
native brethren, 15, 20, 33, 42, 106, 125, 127, 141, 143, 161, 165, 166, 173, 175, 176, 183, 213, 229, 230
native converts, 15, 145, 156, 168, 169, 170, 171, 173, 174, 229, 231
native schools, 154, 191
New Testament discipline, 14
Nicobar Islands, 180
Norris Groves, 223, 247, 256

O

Observations, 95, 157, 169, 241, 248
Olave. *See Bie, Ole*
Ole Bie, 180
Onunda, 168
Orissa, 84, 174, 185, 207, 243, 258
Oussoren. *See A.H. Oussoren*

P

pandit, ix
Particular Baptists, vii, 27, 69, 85, 105, 116, 144, 199, 201, 263
partnerships, 102
Pashtuns, 98
pastors and deacons, 15, 33, 141, 166, 230
patience, 60, 115, 141, 159, 228
Patna, 175, 180, 190
Paul Hiebert, 56
Paulerspury, 223
Pearce Carey. *See Samuel Pearce Carey*
Pearce, Samuel, 46, 144
Persian Pamphlet Affair, 146
Personal Religion, 193
Petruse, 169
Petumber, 130, 171, 182
Philadelphia Baptist Association, 98, 257
Phillip Butler, 186
Pierson, Arthur T., 214, 216, 262
Pietism, 216, 221
Pitamber Singh, 170
Pitt the Younger, 89
Plato, 46, 262
poita, ix, 168
polytheism, 51, 68, 70
poverty, 72, 83, 90, 215, 219
Praeparatio Evangelica, 214
Prafulla Chattopadhyay, 184
Pran Krishnu, 143, 173
prayer, 22, 50, 61, 74, 89, 92, 106, 148, 164, 193, 194, 195, 196, 197, 198, 200, 201, 202, 206, 207, 208, 209, 211, 213, 217, 224, 233
preamble, 20, 28, 29, 30, 31, 103, 199
prejudices, 14, 67, 68, 69, 71, 72, 76, 77, 81, 155, 158, 166, 169, 227, 230, 231
presidency, 147

printing press, 62, 190
Private trade, 219
propitiation, 116
providence, 29, 30, 31, 136, 220
Pudmu Nabhu, 169
purdah, ix, 151
Puritans, vii, 13, 69, 103, 105, 116, 142, 228, 258

Q

Quakers, 44, 64, 72, 222, 227, 250
Qur'an, 147

R

Rabindranath Tagore, 58, 79
Rajmahals, 109
Ram Doolal, 112
Ram Mohan Roy, 69
Ramayana, 148, 183
Ramram Basu, 215
Rangoon, 174, 175
Rasamayi, 125, 130, 131
reading, 19, 20, 31, 47, 51, 59, 61, 78, 79, 80, 81, 100, 107, 108, 114, 119, 156, 196, 226, 264
redemption, 76, 105, 117, 198, 199, 200, 224
Reformation, 37, 42, 43, 78, 80, 91, 95, 99, 109, 113, 228, 241, 242, 258, 260
Reformed, 202, 221, 265
Renaissance, 78, 79, 80, 95, 97, 254, 255, 256, 261, 262
Rev. H. Smylie, 169
Rhoda Mardon, 114
Richard Baxter, 74, 116, 117, 261
Richard Fox Young, 100, 119
Robert Hall, 17, 72, 88
Rolt, James, 142
Rufus Anderson, 161, 219

S

sacrifice, 34, 72, 103, 104, 105, 108, 116, 120, 133, 137, 149, 203, 215, 223, 224, 228
Sally, 157
salvation, 29, 30, 31, 32, 35, 39, 40, 41, 44, 49, 50, 51, 58, 60, 64, 66, 72, 76, 97, 105, 107, 109, 110, 113, 122, 133, 156, 188, 195, 197, 199, 200, 202, 213, 226, 227, 228, 230, 232, 233
Samachar Darpan, 189
Samuel Pearce Carey, 19
Samuel Powell, 23, 51
Sanskrit, 36, 57, 78, 80, 89, 97, 100, 110, 119, 181, 182, 183, 190, 221, 249, 266
Santals, 109
sarkar. See Sirkar
sati, ix, 59, 69, 71, 118, 222
Schmidt. *See Karl F. Schmidt*
Scottish Presbyterians, 13
Scripture, 15, 51, 54, 55, 56, 57, 61, 65, 72, 143, 144, 145, 179, 180, 181, 182, 186, 188, 189, 208
Sebuk Ram, 112
self-denial, 22, 137, 198
Senate of Serampore College, 71, 80, 81, 181, 235, 257
sepoy, ix, 145, 146
Serampore, i, iv, vii, 13, 14, 15, 17, 18, 19, 20, 21, 22, 23, 24, 25, 26, 27, 28, 29, 31, 32, 33, 34, 35, 36, 37, 38, 39, 40, 41, 42, 43, 46, 47, 50, 53, 54, 55, 56, 57, 59, 61, 62, 63, 64, 65, 66, 67, 68, 69, 70, 71, 72, 73, 74, 75, 76, 77, 78, 79, 80, 81, 83, 84, 85, 87, 88, 89, 90, 91, 92, 93, 94, 95, 96, 97, 98, 100, 101, 102, 103, 104, 105, 106, 107, 109, 111, 114, 118, 119, 120, 121, 122, 123, 124, 125, 127, 128, 131,

Index

132, 133, 135, 136, 137, 139, 141, 142, 143, 144, 145, 146, 148, 149, 150, 151, 152, 153, 154, 155, 156, 157, 158, 161, 162, 163, 164, 165, 166, 167, 168, 169, 170, 171, 172, 173, 174, 175, 176, 179, 180, 181, 182, 183, 184, 185, 186, 187, 188, 189, 190, 191, 193, 194, 196, 197, 202, 203, 204, 205, 206, 207, 208, 211, 212, 213, 214, 215, 216, 217, 218, 219, 220, 221, 222, 223, 224, 225, 233, 234, 235, 236, 240, 241, 242, 243, 244, 246, 248, 249, 251, 253, 254, 255, 256, 257, 258, 259, 260, 261, 262, 263, 264, 266

Serampore College, 25, 31, 32, 41, 54, 78, 79, 81, 83, 97, 100, 119, 158, 181, 207, 208, 235, 241, 254, 255, 256, 261, 262

Serampore Mission, vii, 18, 23, 24, 26, 32, 38, 53, 57, 67, 68, 72, 73, 74, 75, 77, 78, 80, 81, 83, 87, 89, 90, 91, 94, 95, 97, 98, 104, 121, 123, 124, 131, 132, 133, 137, 141, 143, 146, 149, 151, 152, 153, 157, 158, 161, 162, 163, 168, 173, 175, 176, 179, 181, 183, 187, 190, 191, 194, 214, 215, 217, 219, 223, 240, 248, 249, 254, 257, 258, 259, 260, 261, 262, 263, 264, 266

Serampore Press, 31, 183, 188, 189, 190

Seringapatam, 84, 89

Sewry, 175

shasters, ix, 173

sins, 14, 19, 72, 112, 116, 119, 127, 155, 227

Sir William Jones, 101, 247

sircar, ix, 129

Sirdhana, 175

Slave Trade, 40, 251

Smith, A. Christopher, 263

smoking, 127, 169

Sociability, 97

social advocacy, 80

soodra, 111, 168

soul, 35, 43, 44, 45, 46, 48, 51, 53, 107, 115, 116, 141, 154, 176, 217, 220, 224, 226, 227, 233

souls, 19, 30, 31, 35, 42, 43, 44, 45, 46, 49, 69, 72, 75, 76, 99, 115, 122, 133, 135, 140, 163, 166, 212, 214, 221, 226, 227, 228, 230, 234

Southey, Robert, 250

sovereignty, 30, 31, 53, 105, 199, 200, 207

Spangenberg, A. G., 250

spiritual warfare, 100

Spirituality, 81, 106, 115, 117, 146, 147, 201, 262, 264

Staffordshire Advertiser, 40

Stennett, Samuel, 40

Sumatra, 175, 203

Sunderbans or Sunderbunds, 143

Sunil Kumar Chaterjee, 94

Surat, 175

Suri. *See Sewry, s*

Sylhet, 157, 158, 170, 172, 175

T

T. B. Macaulay, 96

Tamil Nadu, 68

Tennent, Timothy C., 264

Theodor Fliedner, 221

Theological Education, 81, 165, 189, 256, 257, 264

Theology, 55, 56, 64, 75, 76, 117, 118, 165, 181, 198, 203, 235, 236, 253, 255, 256, 259, 260, 261, 263, 264, 265

Thirty-Nine Articles, 48, 251

Thomas Jefferson, 17

Thomas Paine, 17

Tipoo Sultan, 84

Tranquebar, 68, 91, 168, 179, 180, 216, 253, 257
Transformation, 78, 259
Translation Principle, 109, 110, 111, 119, 265

U

Unitarian, 113, 118
United Theological College, 80, 81, 236
Unna, 122, 127, 129, 130, 131, 132, 155, 164, 170

V

Vellore Mutiny, 90, 97
Vernacular, 171, 249
Vidyalankar, Mrityunjoy, 215

W

W. H. Denham, 208
W. Johns, 27, 38, 176, 243, 248
Warren Hastings, 86, 100, 239
welfare, 19, 44, 139, 155, 173, 230
Wellesley, Marquis of. *See Marquis of Wellesley, See Marquis of Wellesley*
William Brown, 37, 42
William Carey, 14, 17, 19, 21, 22, 24, 25, 27, 28, 29, 33, 34, 36, 37, 38, 39, 41, 42, 43, 44, 45, 47, 48, 49, 57, 58, 60, 62, 63, 67, 68, 69, 70, 71, 74, 75, 77, 78, 79, 81, 83, 84, 87, 88, 89, 90, 92, 94, 96, 97, 106, 107, 108, 109, 110, 121, 123, 124, 132, 136, 139, 141, 143, 145, 146, 150, 152, 154, 158, 162, 163, 164, 167, 168, 171, 172, 175, 179, 180, 181, 182, 185, 186, 188, 189, 190, 192, 194, 196, 197, 198, 200, 202, 203, 206, 207, 211, 212, 213, 215, 216, 218, 219, 221, 223, 234, 235, 236, 239, 241, 242, 243, 244, 245, 250, 253, 254, 255, 256, 257, 258, 259, 260, 261, 262, 263, 264
William Grant, 21, 93, 136, 152
William Moore, 22, 36, 95, 152, 179, 205, 234, 240, 243
William Robinson, 114, 136, 157, 203, 204, 240, 249
William Ward, vii, 15, 18, 20, 21, 22, 24, 25, 36, 37, 38, 40, 41, 46, 50, 59, 67, 69, 70, 72, 73, 81, 87, 89, 90, 93, 94, 97, 98, 103, 104, 106, 108, 110, 111, 115, 117, 121, 122, 123, 130, 132, 142, 146, 147, 151, 152, 155, 161, 163, 170, 172, 179, 182, 183, 184, 186, 187, 188, 189, 190, 191, 192, 194, 198, 212, 215, 224, 234, 239, 240, 243, 249, 250, 255, 262, 263, 265
William Yates, 37, 42, 95, 118, 134, 202
worship, ix, 14, 19, 50, 53, 58, 59, 61, 68, 72, 97, 140, 143, 144, 147, 154, 161, 171, 172, 173, 195, 196, 197, 213, 226, 227, 231
Wycliffe, 109

Z

Zenana missions, 156

The William Ward Project

*The Spirituality of William Ward:
Unsung Hero of the Serapore Trio*
by Matthew Reynolds
(H&E Publishing)

*Redeeming Love Has Been My Theme:
William Ward*
By Samuel E. Masters
(Ettrick Press)